Benefits for
the Workplace of
the Future

Pension Research Council Publications
A list of recent books in the series appears at the back of this volume.

Benefits for the Workplace of the Future

Edited by Olivia S. Mitchell, David S. Blitzstein, Michael Gordon, and Judith F. Mazo

Pension Research Council
The Wharton School of the University of Pennsylvania

PENN

University of Pennsylvania Press

Philadelphia

Copyright © 2003 The Pension Research Council of the Wharton School of the University of Pennsylvania
All rights reserved
Printed in the United States of America on acid-free paper

10 9 8 7 6 5 4 3 2 1

Published by
University of Pennsylvania Press
Philadelphia, Pennsylvania 19104-4011

Library of Congress Cataloging-in-Publication Data

Benefits for the workplace of the future / edited by Olivia S. Mitchell . . . [et al.].
   p. cm.
  Includes bibliographical references and index.
  "Pension Research Council publications"
  ISBN 0-8122-3708-0 (cloth : alk. paper)
  1. Employee fringe benefits—United States. 2. Compensation management—
United States. 3. Labor supply—United States. 4. Pensions—United States.
I. Mitchell, Olivia S. II. Wharton School. Pension Research Council.
HD4928.N62 U62325   2003
331.2′0973—dc21   2002041258

Contents

Preface

Olivia S. Mitchell

In the United States, as in other developed nations, the workforce of the future promises to be quite different from that which we have known in the past. The age distribution has morphed from a pyramid shape, with numerous children on the bottom and few elderly at the top, to a rectangle shape, with about the same number in each age bracket up to age 65. Meanwhile companies have been remaking the workplace over this same period as global markets integrate, requiring ever more skilled labor and more flexible and integrated work teams and redefining what it means to be an employee working at a company.

In this book we explore how these workforce and workplace changes are altering the form and design of employee benefits, and what the future portends. Recent major benefit developments include the 401(k), managed care in the medical field, and the opportunity for less skilled workers to access company stock participation. The greater workplace diversity has been complemented by nontraditional benefits, including child and elder care, flexible medical benefits, employee assistance programs, and investment education. We evaluate these trends and go beyond them, by assessing legal and benefits definitions of the word "employee," along with new ways to design benefit plans. Perspectives from academics, employers, consultants, lawyers, and labor educators offer guideposts for benefits of the future.

Sponsorship for the work leading to this volume was generously provided by the Wharton School, as well as two important University of Pennsylvania institutions, the Boettner Financial Gerontology Center and the Penn Aging Research Center. We are also grateful for support from the Pension and Welfare Benefits Administration of the U.S. Department of Labor. The Pension Research Council benefits from the invaluable efforts of our Senior Partners and Institutional Members and the careful attention of Victoria Jo and Joseph Hirniak. On behalf of the Pension Research Council at the Wharton School, we thank each of these collaborators, along with the editors and contributors who brought this work to fruition.

Introduction: Benefits for the Workplace of the Future

Olivia S. Mitchell

This volume explores how employee benefits of the future will be shaped by market and sociodemographic forces that are both short- and long-term in nature. Over the near term, economic volatility due to the business cycle and economic shocks has depressed employment prospects, compensation, and benefit offerings. Longer-term developments will be led by demographic trends shifting the age, sex, and ethnic/racial mix of the workforce. Other longer-term factors will result from changes in the household and family characteristics of the workforce, which accompany developments in employees' expectations and the reality of new job and labor market attachment patterns. Long-run changes are also being driven by the demand side of the labor market, as employers increasingly respond to innovations in company requirements flowing from the more high-tech, competitive, and in some ways riskier global economy. Finally, the role for government regulation in the benefits marketplace is dynamic: as almost nowhere else, ever-changing legislative and regulatory expectations keep shareholders and employers, employees and unions, and plan professionals such as actuaries and lawyers, always alert.

This complex of factors promises to dramatically restructure both the nature of jobs and workers' employment patterns, with interesting and probably unexpected implications for how firms compensate their employees and provide them with incentives. In this introductory chapter we introduce ideas by reviewing some of the key changes that shaped the U.S. pay and benefits environment over the last century. Next we briefly survey key recent developments. Finally, we summarize the key contributions of this volume and how they illustrate the path forward for benefits for the future workplace.

Compensation and Employment Trends

Around 1900, the U.S. labor force was employed mainly in agricultural and extractive industries. Workers earned relatively little, and most were compensated on the piece-rate system (Cappelli 1999). Few employers offered any sort of noncash benefits and formal insurance markets were virtually nonexistent. In the last century, however, patterns of cash as well as noncash compensation changed dramatically (Table 1).

Employers generally provided benefits aimed mostly at protecting against workplace risk, including disability and premature death. Benefits consisted mainly of insurance, provided as a "one-size-fits-all" or "bundled" offer. Such benefits provided workers with insurance, tax-qualified compensation, access to scale economies and risk pooling, and saving mechanisms. Between the mid-1950s and 1980, retirement plans grew rapidly; these appealed to employers since they functioned as important recruiting and retention tools, along with a means to induce retirement when economically practical.

More recently, however, "unbundled" benefits have become more popular, where firms allow employees to exert substantial flexibility and choice over benefit options. The "à la carte" menu of benefit choices enables many to decide whether they want life insurance and how much; what type of health insurance provider they desire (e.g., HMOs, PPOs, traditional indemnity providers), or perhaps no plan at all, in exchange for cash; whether and how much long-term care insurance to purchase; and so on. Increased choice carries over to the retirement plan environment, where workers can elect whether to participate in a 401(k) or 403(b), how much to contribute, and in what to invest the money.

Long-Term Trends in Benefit Dollars

Today, most are familiar with the "three-legged stool" approach to insurance protection from individual, employer, and governmental sources. Of course that notion did not exist in the United States at the turn of the last century. Rather, workers relied on own or family resources for support in the event of health, economic, and other shocks. Community and religious organizations as well as mutual aid societies sometimes played supportive roles. Labor unions were initially reluctant to engage in providing insurance and other benefits, believing instead that the government should provide such protections (Jacoby this volume, a and b).

As the industrial revolution proceeded, real earnings continued to rise. Workers in the new factory environment began to be exposed to, and require protection against, a wide range of workplace risks. Unions' outlook changed gradually, with these organizations initially moving to offer disability and death coverage, and later setting up retirement systems. Unfortunately during the early days union benefit plan solvency was a continuous concern, and numerous plans became insolvent during the Depression. Subsequently, the tight labor market during World War II spurred benefit enhancements, paired with Supreme Court rulings and federal legislation making benefits a legitimate subject of bargaining. The "golden age" of

TABLE 1. Developments in Compensation Packages over Time

	1890	1925	1950	1975	2000
Health insurance plans		Company MD	Basic medical (e.g., Blue Cross/Blue Shield)	Basic medical plus major medical (commercial carrier) Dental plan Medicare	Choice of health plans (including HMO) Choice of dental, vision, Rx plan Medicare + retiree health insurance
Death and disability plans	Mutual aid associations	Benevolent associations	Fixed-amount life insurance; weekly disability benefit	Life insurance varies with earnings; paid sick leave	Choice of life insurance; personal leave
Retirement plans			Social Security available at age 65 Defined benefit plans	Reduced Social Security benefits at age 62 Defined benefit plans	Full Social Security benefits available at age 67 Defined contribution + 401(k) plans
Earnings	Wages	Wages	Wages	Wage + bonuses	Wages + supplements linked to performance
Time off		Paid holidays	Paid holidays plus vacation	Paid holidays, vacation, personal leave	Consolidated personal leave plan with choice; unpaid family leave

Source: Adapted from BLS (2001): 60–81.

benefit growth occurred after 1950 and continues to the present, during which time benefits have become an increasingly important component of the U.S. compensation package. Today, benefits represent 27 percent of the national compensation package, with large employers devoting even higher percentages to nonwage benefits (see Figures 1, 2, 3).

Today many employers voluntarily provide a rich array of benefits, including paid leave (e.g., vacations, time off), bonuses and supplements, life and health insurance, retirement benefits, and disability insurance. In addition almost one-third of the benefit package is legally mandated, including payments to support the social security system, workers' compensation, and unemployment insurance, among other programs. Figure 4 indicates

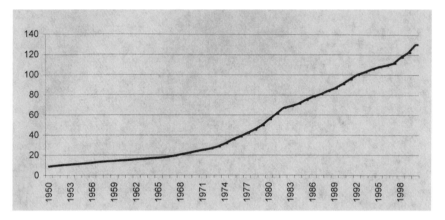

Figure 1. Trend in U.S. manufacturing hourly wage, 1950–2000 (1992 =100). Source: derived from <stats.bls.gov>.

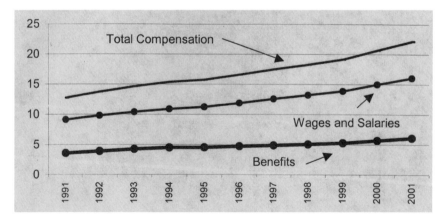

Figure 2. Steady rise in compensation and benefits, 1991–2001. Source: derived from <stats.bls.gov>.

the relative fraction of compensation devoted to each of these broad categories over the last decade.

Recent Changes

Though *real dollars* devoted to employee benefits have continued to rise, there has been little growth in employee *coverage rates* by many voluntarily

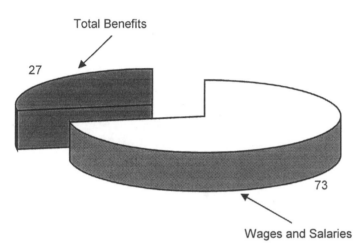

Figure 3. Benefits comprise over a quarter of total compensation. Source: U.S. Department of Labor, Bureau of Labor Statistics (2001).

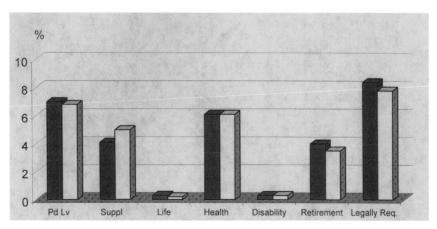

Figure 4. Major benefit components as percentage of total compensation, 1991, 2001. Source: U.S. Department of Labor, Bureau of Labor Statistics (2001).

provided benefits in the United States over the past twenty years. This stasis is in part attributable to changes in employment and in the cost of offering benefits. On the one hand, labor demand has been driven by the need for more skilled workers, but increased marked employment volatility has emerged as companies repeatedly remade themselves to keep up with competition. As a result, job tenure shortened somewhat, particularly for those in managerial, professional/technical, and blue collar jobs (Figure 5). On the other hand, some firms have found that workers are no longer committing to lifetime employment, at times at the expense of company loyalty, as employees grow more attached to careers over employers (Cappelli this volume; Jacoby this volume, a and b). These trends were exacerbated by the rising cost of offering benefits. For instance, a recent study indicated that the administrative costs associated with offering a defined benefit pension plan were more than double the cost of a defined contribution plan, for small firms, and almost 40 percent higher, for larger firms (Mitchell 2000).

Benefits Patterns in the Twentieth Century

During the second half of the twentieth century, employment-based benefits took off in the United States, responding to workers' growing concerns over workplace risk and their concomitant interest in risk management.

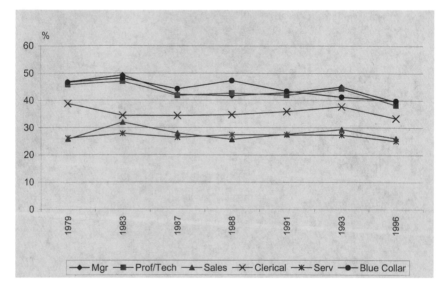

Figure 5. Trends in long-term jobs: employees ages 35–64 with more than ten years tenure by occupation. Source: unpublished data provided by Henry Farber (2001).

Benefits Help Employees and Employers

Benefit growth during the early phase focused on *insurance*, so that the first workplace benefits offered protected against premature death via life insurance and workplace injury via workers' compensation. Risk pooling to cover disability also grew out of this narrow insurance interest.

Not long after, managers began to recognize that key employer-provided benefits could also have spillover effects. These included incentives to attract, retain, and align workers' interests with those of the sponsoring company (Gustman and Mitchell 1992). This alternative perspective offered benefits only to the more long-term loyal employees, a tactic that gave rise to worries over "industrial feudalism" during the 1950s. This approach posited that some benefits prevented long-term workers from leaving their firms, and inferred that this was less than socially optimal. As one example, some saw defined benefit pension plans that lacked vesting provisions as discouraging job change prior to retirement. Subsequent evidence showed that employees with pensions are, in fact, less likely to change jobs than were those lacking such coverage (Even and Macpherson this volume).

Another force driving benefit change during the second half of the twentieth century was employee interest in deferring, reducing, and avoiding taxes. As progressive income taxation became more dominant, benefits became a popular way for higher-paid workers to reduce taxable compensation. For instance, employer expenditures on health insurance premiums are typically pretax, as are contributions up to a limit for disability benefits, retirement plans, and programs such as flexible benefit offerings. Higher earners, in particular, may pay substantially lower lifetime taxes, to the extent they can tax-shelter their compensation in the form of nonwage benefits. This in turn has given rise to all manner of efforts to restrict and limit the tax-qualified status accorded to various benefits, particularly through the nondiscrimination regulations that have proliferated since the passage of the 1974 Employee Retirement Income Security Act (ERISA).

During the first stages of employer-sponsored benefits, they were initially of the "one-size-fits-all" variety. Rather than being linked to specific employees' output levels, as would be true under a piece-rate system, compensation and benefits were tied to jobs rather than the workers in those jobs. This was most evident with the focus of benefits offered to long-term permanent employees; employers typically excluded from coverage all nontraditional employees including part-timers, temporary employees, consultants, contingent workers, and others. This distinction was likely an economically rational one for shareholders, since flexible staff would likely be riskier, and hence more costly to insure, than healthier long-term, better-paid, permanent workers. In addition, firms would likely find it economically sensible to reward long-time workers more generously than short-timers, so as to keep them tied to the firm (Even and Macpherson, this volume). As a result, most benefits provided until about twenty years ago actively cross-subsidized workers in a wide range of ways. For example, health insurance plans were frequently offered on a uniform basis to all, which subsidized the least healthy at the expense of workers in less risky age/sex/family status and pay-level categories.

Over time, however, benefits providers began to change their offerings, moving away from a single package and instead adopting a more flexible approach. This transition was facilitated by regulatory changes permitting firms to set up "cafeteria plans" where employees could tax-defer a portion of their salaries and use this money to purchase additional time off, health coverage, or other benefits. The transition was also spurred by regulatory developments in the health care marketplace, where companies were required to offer a managed care plan if one was available, even if they still had a more costly traditional fee-for-service plan as one of the choices. Increasingly companies permitted employees to elect no health insurance plan at all, in exchange for cash, if they could demonstrate coverage through some other venue.

A similar move toward choice was seen in the pension arena. Today the modal 401(k) participant has a dozen investment options to elect from during the asset accumulation phase. It is also possible to use these 401(k) funds flexibly over the worklife, contributing or not as the worker sees fit, and borrowing from or even cashing out the account while employed (though with tax consequences). This flexibility continues at retirement, with the retiree being permitted to take the entire rollover in cash, rather than being required to annuitize. More surprising is that this increased flexibility has even permeated the defined benefit pension arena, with participants being allowed to cash out the benefit (Mitchell this volume), and in cash balance plans, they can often direct the investments themselves.

Changing Views of the Government's Role in Benefits

Another issue affecting the provision of benefits in the U.S. labor market has to do with popular views of how insurance should be shared between the government and the private sector. As noted above, prior to the Great Depression, a common view was that the "business corporation, rather than government or mutual organizations, should be the primary source of security and stability in modern society" (Jacoby 2001: 43). However the Great Depression undermined beliefs in the ability of the private sector to offer guarantees against risk, and this skepticism found expression in much New Deal legislation. One specific example was the passage of the Social Security act, establishing a prominent and continuing federal role in old-age and survivor insurance (and later, extended to disability benefits as well). This tension between the appropriate roles for the private and public sectors was expressed by Marion Folsom, the head of Eastman Kodak, who played an active role in the establishment of Social Security. His position was that the government should provide only basic minimum protection, rather than covering all needs of the working population (Jacoby 2001). As a result of this tension, company-provided benefits came to be called "fringe" payments, and though they now amount to a substantial component of compensation, they still interact with, and work in concert with, a large social insurance sector.

While there is some reluctance about expanding direct government provision of benefits, the political process has favored imposing a wide variety of legal mandates on company compensation practices. Such mandates may appear to be costless to the government, since no direct budgetary appropriations need to be devoted to direct benefit provision. Thus, for instance, legislators have required companies to offer family leave, workers compensation, and unemployment insurance, though little if any direct government support is offered to sustain the programs. One result of such mandates is that job safety and security may be enhanced. Another is that the mandates raise the cost of employing labor and of doing business, reducing employment and compensation (Mitchell and Mikalauskas 1988).

Another trend has been to permit companies the freedom to decide *whether* they wish to offer a benefit, but then to require that certain mandatory services be included if they offer it. For example, some states require employers with insured health plans to cover chiropractors, mental health practitioners, midwifes, and other types of treatment. As a result, firms are discouraged from offering such plans at all and, if they do, they tend to self-insure rather than risk-pool (Jensen et al. 1995). A related development is the government's increasing effort to control and restrict employment and pay as well as benefits practices. This is most evident in the antidiscrimination arena (e.g., the Equal Employment Act, the Age Discrimination in Employment Act), but policy has also sought to shape the structure of tax-qualified benefits packages (e.g., the Employee Retirement Income Security Act, the Consolidated Omnibus Reconciliation Act, or COBRA). Recently the benefits practice has come into the limelight regarding whether benefit plan participants can litigate over denial of health benefits, and how privacy concerns are managed. Even more salient is the degree of concern over company stock held in retirement and other capital accumulation plans pursuant to the Enron Corp. bankruptcy. Evidently the trend has been toward more, rather than less, government intervention in the benefits arena over the last two decades.

Looking Ahead: Benefit Developments in the Near Term

In the near term and even beyond, the labor market will continue to react to business cycle pressures, volatility in the capital markets, and dislocation associated with being in a heightened state of alert. It is evident that during a recession, some sectors face dislocation (e.g., aviation, tourism), and still others confront financial setbacks that will likely lead to industry downsizing and consolidation (e.g., financial services). Of course some sectors are experiencing both employment and output growth, particularly in the security arena, telecommunications, rail transport, and military-related companies. The events of September 11, 2001 will also continue to shape the path of economic restructuring, with industry retooling and employee as well as customer habits being revisited and revised. As the economy reacts to the perceived need for greater security, it renders some existing capital stock less productive (e.g., airplanes and airports will be used less intensively until security measures are improved). Similarly, current employees may become less productive due to increased security necessitating more time and money devoted to travel, trade, meetings, entertainment, and many other aspects of work and life.

During recessions, downsized and laid off employees tend to lose many of their most valuable employer-provided benefits. Unemployment insurance, while available to most, tends to be relatively short-lived — usually twenty-six weeks in duration. While these benefits could be extended during a prolonged recession, as in the past, many states lack the capability to finance these benefits for the indefinite future. A related concern is joblosers' lack of health insurance coverage. Current U.S. law requires firms to offer extended health insurance coverage to employees losing their jobs for eighteen months, if the former workers elect to pay 102 percent of the average premium. Of course such premiums are expensive for jobless workers that elect to continue the healthcare coverage. They are even more costly to the offering firms, since they must subsidize actual health plan costs over and above the 102 percent charge. How important this benefit proves to be depends on the length of the recession and whether employment picks up soon in sectors offering health care benefits.

Another benefit to become the focus of greater attention going forward is employee pensions (Rappaport, this volume). Stock market volatility tends to erode people's faith in equities as a source of retirement wealth, exacerbated by participants' practice of investing heavily in their own company's stock, now worth a fraction of previous levels. This may generate future demand for safer assets in the pension portfolio, including government bonds, stable value instruments, and deposits. Indeed, when the stock market reopened after the September 2001 terrorist attack, trading volume in 401(k) plans was reported at nine times usual levels (cnn.com 2001). To the extent that laid-off workers still have assets in 401(k) plans, they may also seek to borrow against or redeem the funds, if the recession is prolonged. Defined benefit pension plan sponsors are also at risk since, prior to the recent dive, they held a substantial portion of their pension assets in stocks. In the future they will find that offering these plans will be more costly. In some cases, required additional contributions to keep plans fully funded could even precipitate plan termination and company bankruptcy. This in turn would call on the government's pension insurance entity, the Pension Benefit Guaranty Corporation, to provide the backstop promised in the event of plan insolvency. Ongoing efforts by many firms in the steel industry to offload "legacy" benefits, mainly health care and pensions for retirees, loom large in this picture.

Longer-Term Benefits Trends

Beyond the next few years, U.S. economic growth is predicted to return to long-term levels (see Figure 6). This will likely imply a return to tighter labor markets, exacerbating the skill shortages beginning to be felt at the end of the 1990s. Demographic changes will exacerbate these trends, including the aging of baby boomers, a continued fall in overall labor force participation rates, and declining fertility rates. On the positive side, migration rates have remained relatively high, and skill levels and worker education have risen. These factors should contribute to higher future labor productivity (Riche this volume; Lofgren et al. this volume). Whether the positive influences will be strong enough to permit older workers to retire early, or whether compensation will be driven up so older Americans will continue to be employed, remains to be seen.

One way in which the labor market has changed substantially of late is that new forms of work arrangements have spread over the last two decades, offering alternative views of the nature of work. Houseman (this volume) documents the rise of a nontraditional workforce — including contingent

Average GDP per hour in 1996 Dollars

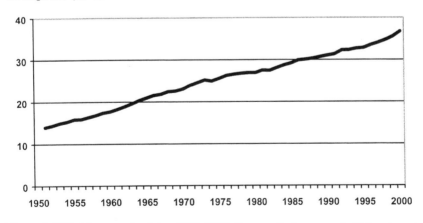

Figure 6. U.S. labor productivity, 1950–2000. Source: Lofgren et al. (this volume).

and temporary workers, part-timers, consultants, and contract employees —
where growth rates in the United States have exceeded those of regular,
full-time employees. Flexible staffing is now a way of life in the American
context, with temporary help agencies now ranking among the largest of
our national corporations (Camden this volume). As this process continues, it will be increasingly important to hold down costs while still providing valuable benefits, particularly those related to productivity. Employers
may seek to defer vesting and delay retirement if labor market shortages
develop more seriously. There will also likely be diminished interest in
"family friendly" benefits, since fewer workers in the future will have young
children living in their households.

Ultimately, the unbundling approach will increase pressure on employers
to provide a widely diversified *menu* of benefit options with fewer cross-
subsidies between employees. Workers will tend to "get what they pay for,"
with pricing being set by the level of benefit provided and the extent of
coverage chosen. Thus, for instance, those who desire to do day-trading in
401(k) accounts may be entitled to do so, but they will have to bear a higher
administrative fee for the privilege, instead of spreading these costs to the
passive indexers. The advent of lower cost benefits administration via global
outsourcing should help mitigate the potential cost increases of the menu
approach (Sabharwal this volume).

A major concern among benefits specialists is that benefits unbundling
may shift risk away from groups better able to bear risk — such as employers and the government — toward individual benefit plan participants, who
are less well equipped to do so. This is a major concern when people have
health and pension plan coverage without adequate information regarding
the risks they shoulder when they elect these plans. One potential response
is that there may be a backlash, with plan participants demanding increased
government intervention in the form of lawsuits, regulatory oversight, and
perhaps even the spread of government pension guarantees.

Some suggest that a substitute for such regulatory overhead might be
found in new private sector institutions that can be devised to facilitate
workplace risk sharing in nontraditional ways. For instance, Kochan (2000)
argues that work "must provide workers and their families security and the
ability to improve their standards of living" while recognizing that there is
a need for "increased interdependence between family, community, and cit-
izenship responsibilities" (2000: 5). His vision suggests that new networks
could "provide the full array of labor market mobility services — networks
of contacts and job opportunities, portable pensions and benefits, education and skill accumulation and life-long learning, and perhaps other personal legal and financial assistance as well" (2000: 11). He proposes that
these new labor market intermediaries could include unions, community
groups, and professional associations, which facilitate mobility and manage
the resulting benefits interdependencies. Interestingly Ghilarducci (this

volume) argues that multiemployer pension plans found in both the private and nonprofit sectors already play this role currently, for an important component of the workforce. In order for this model to spread, relaxing uniform and inflexible benefits standards set by governments and unions would also be required.

A Road Map for the Volume

The future workplace will respond to the need for economic restructuring, inevitable demographic shifts, and consequent changes in the relative role of the government versus the private sector. Similarly, so will benefits and compensation packages, if they are to reflect the stakeholders' objectives as well as constraints imposed by the marketplace. In general, the evidence appears to suggest that the composition and structure of benefits packages will continue to evolve in an "unbundled" direction. Today employers use benefits as recruiting and retention tools, as well as a means to induce optimal turnover. To the extent that benefits become less bundled in the future, this will improve labor market flexibility but will also curtail some of insurance aspects that were appealing about group benefits in the past. Employees wishing to maintain the advantages of tax-qualified compensation and the appeal of automatic saving mechanisms will likely be able to do so. On the other hand, increased career mobility and job volatility mean that benefits will be able to do less in the way of scale economies and risk pooling than in the past.

To illustrate these points, we have grouped the contributions to this volume around three topical sections. The first explores developments in the future workplace and outlines implications for benefit coverage and design. Leading off the discussion is Martha Riche's analysis of "The Demographics of Tomorrow's Workplace," where she argues that employees' longer work lives have redefined how we think about career paths in the future. For instance, she argues that work interruptions and changes of career direction are becoming common for both women and men, giving rise to a "portfolio" of workforce attachments and workplace settings. She also suggests that even jobs traditionally thought of as "bad" (e.g., low pay, little security) might be important for older workers seeking to phase into retirement.

The study by William Even and David Macpherson turns the focus of discussion to health and pension plans, examining how these affect productivity outcomes. They posit that the shift from defined benefit (DB) to defined contribution (DC) plans has predictable effects on worker selection, retention, and retirement. For example, they note that investing DC assets in company stock may enhance productivity by linking pay to company performance, though it also could become increasingly difficult to induce retirement when stock performance is below expectations. They also suggest that health care inflation will induce some companies to move toward a defined contribution health plan format, while others may step back from offering health plans at all.

Marjorie Honig and Irena Dushi continue this theme using empirical analysis to predict how a labor force with increasing shares of women, minorities, and older workers, might behave differently with regard to cash versus non-cash benefits. One surprising finding is that older workers are as interested in saving via their 401(k) accounts, as are younger workers. Less surprising is the finding that older workers seek health insurance more vigorously, particularly if postretirement benefits are offered at group rates. They also see a rising demand for short-term disability insurance but less call for long-term disability coverage. Family-related benefits will change in nature, responding to the needs of workers with fewer children but more elderly parents.

Flexible staffing is likely to influence benefits needs and offerings, and this employment arrangement is becoming increasingly flexible in the U.S. marketplace. In her chapter, Susan Houseman shows that many workers in flexible staffing arrangements are not covered by laws mandating or regulating workplace benefits, which partly explains why employees in these settings are less likely than regular employees to receive benefits such as health insurance and a retirement plan. She also notes that many employers might not specifically move to flexible staffing to limit benefits costs; this is one result of the move toward independent contractors, agency temporaries, on-call workers, and others in flexible arrangements. In reaction, Houseman notes that the IRS and states are making efforts to better enforce existing laws and to crack down on worker misclassification. This helps reduce lost tax revenues and curtails fraud in workers' compensation and unemployment insurance funds.

The final chapter in this section is an examination of trends in company-sponsored retirement plans by Olivia S. Mitchell with Erica Dykes. The only constant in the benefits field seems to be change, and pensions prove no exception. Traditionally, medium and large U.S. firms have been the stalwart providers of employment-linked retirement benefits, but even here, the underlying structure of these plans has not been static. The authors find important changes have taken place in pension financing arrangements, eligibility and benefit formulas, and participant involvement in saving and investment decisions. An ever-evolving legislative environment also influenced pension plan redesign. The authors note that these developments raise questions about the future role of pensions as retirement income vehicles. For example, giving workers access to pension loans and lump sums can undercut productivity enhancement and retirement security objectives.

In the volume's second section, several experts take up broader challenges to benefits and compensation design. First, Anna Rappaport examines how recession and economic volatility influence benefits. She notes that there is much uncertainty as to the severity of any given economic downturn, but this particular market has some unique features: volatile equity markets, lower than expected interest rates, and uncertain product as well as employment conditions. Rappaport predicts that in the short term, plan sponsors will smooth contributions to mitigate the impact on financial statements. Longer term, they will revisit investment strategies and increase communication to plan participants. Cost pressures may induce some plan sponsors to terminate DB plans, while others may maintain the plans but with greater controls over risk. If equity markets remain depressed, firms that offer DC plans will find that both employer and employee assumptions about retirement security are due for reevaluation. Companies that fail to adapt will likely experience greater turnover, as their employees seek better venues in which to accumulate wealth for retirement.

In their chapter, Eric Lofgren, Steven Nyce and Sylvester Schieber turn to the longer time horizon, asking how business conditions will interact with slower labor growth than experienced in the past. They also believe that employers will have to reconsider traditional workforce practices: for instance, firms wishing to attract and keep women workers will have to address issues that have kept substantial numbers of women from participating in the labor market in the past. This means implementing more suitable work-life solutions for working heads of households, such as on-site childcare, flexible work schedules, and eldercare. Similarly, firms hoping to discourage most valuable employees from retiring will have to reevaluate retirement policies and provide greater access to phased retirement. The authors are concerned that labor needs cannot be met simply by hiring new workers, so that firms will instead have to find ways to obtain greater productivity from existing employees. Employers who manage their human assets using effective communication programs, positive work environments, and compensation systems that reward output and accountability, will enhance shareholder value and prosper.

The broader question of how the labor-management relationship is evolving, and what the benefits implications are, is debated by Peter Cappelli and Sanford M. Jacoby. In a special point-counterpoint (reprinted with permission from the *California Management Journal*), Jacoby contends that many, if not most, employees will want relatively paternalistic companies to help them bear and share risk. He also argues that loyalty and commitment will remain key elements of the workplace relationship, particularly in services where supervision and monitoring are often difficult. As a result, benefits that enhance employee stability will be highly valued by both employers and employees in the future. Taking the other side of the debate, Peter Cappelli proposes that the labor market has changed dramatically, virtually eliminating the expectation of long-term job security. This change is partly due to the fact that companies themselves are not very stable (witness the recent Enron and K-Mart bankruptcies) and partly because workers often lack opportunities for advancement. As a result, he sees compensation and development opportunities being mainly driven by outside market forces, rather than by traditional in-house goals and principles. The benefits implications of Cappelli's views are very different, since he believes that employees as well as the firms they work for will seek to make transitions between firms easier. This can be accomplished by enhancing benefit portability, making unemployment insurance more flexible, and assisting workers who face permanent job loss.

Our volume concludes with case and sector studies that provide insights into specific company and sectoral practices. Carl Camden from Kelly Services shows that one-third of his temporary employees are actually long-term workers, and they generate nearly 80 percent of the company's revenue. Many of these employees prefer long-term temporary employment since they prefer the free-agent style. Some of them seek employee benefits, and opportunities are available to obtain these; other workers have very different attitudes toward benefit offerings. The key lesson is that there is much heterogeneity among free-agent workers, so no single benefit solution will likely be satisfactory.

Developments on the international front are provided by Manish Sabharwal from the perspective of a global benefits outsourcing provided. Several years of experience managing U.S. benefits plans from India illustrates how dramatically the benefits business has moved away from the traditional hands-on benefits counselor who sat in the human resources office down the hall.

The volume closes with a study by Teresa Ghilarducci on the possibility of multiemployer models for benefit delivery. In her chapter she admits that many firms and workers lack a lifetime relationship, but she finds an exception to this trend in the multiemployer framework. This structure affords employees in a given sector or industry the opportunity to coalesce market power to obtain scale economies for pensions and health care plans. In this case, she believes that jointly managed plans do well to enhance coverage while improving portability and income security.

The author thanks the Pension Research Council for research support and Henry Farber for providing unpublished data. Opinions are solely those of the author.

References

Camden, Carl. This volume. "Benefits for the Free-Agent Workforce."
Cappelli, Peter. 2000. "Market-Mediated Employment: The Historical Context." In *The New Relationship: Human Capital in the American Corporation*, ed. Margaret Blair and Thomas A. Kochan. Washington, D.C.: Brookings Institution Press. 66–101.
Cappelli, Peter. 1999. *The New Deal at Work: Managing the Market-Driven Workforce*. Boston: Harvard Business School Press.
———. This volume. "Career Jobs Are Dead."

Choi, James J., David Laibson, and Andrew Metrick. 2000. "Does the Internet Increase Trading? Evidence from Investor Behavior in 401(k) Plans." NBER Working Paper W7878. September.

cnn.com. 2001. "401(k) Activity Hits Record." <cnnfn.cnn.com/2001/09/18/pensions/ q_retire_401k>

Even, William E. and David A. Macpherson. This volume. "Benefits and Productivity."

Farber, Henry S. 2001. Unpublished data provided to the author.

Farber, Henry S. and Helen Levy. 2000. "Recent Trends in Employer-Sponsored Health Insurance Coverage: Are Bad Jobs Getting Worse?" *Journal of Health Economics* 19, 2: 93–119.

Ghilarducci, Theresa. This volume. "Delinking Benefits from a Single Employer: Alternative Multi-Employer Models."

Gustman, Alan L. and Olivia S. Mitchell. 1992. "Pensions and the U.S. Labor Market." In *Pensions and the Economy: Sources, Uses, and Limitations of Data*, ed. Zvi Bodie and Alicia H. Munnell. Pension Research Council. Philadelphia: University of Pennsylvania Press. 39–87.

Honig, Marjorie and Irena Dushi. This volume. "How Demographic Change Will Drive Benefits Design."

Houseman, Susan N. This volume. "The Benefits Implications of Recent Trends in Flexible Staffing Arrangements."

Jacoby, Sanford M. 2001. "Risk and the Labor Market: Societal Past as Economic Prologue." In *Sourcebook of Labor Markets: Evolving Structures and Processes*, ed. Ivar Berg and Arne Kalleberg. New York: Plenum Press.

———. This volume (a). "Are Career Jobs Headed for Extinction?"

———. This volume (b). "Reply: Premature Reports of Demise."

Jensen, Gail, Kevin D. Cotter, and Michael A. Morrisey. 1995. "State Insurance Regulation and an Employer's Decision to Self Insure." *Journal of Risk and Insurance* 62: 185–213.

Kochan, Thomas A. 2000. "Building a New Social Contract at Work: A Call to Action." Presidential Address to the 52nd Annual Meeting of the Industrial Relations Research Association. Institute for Work and Employment Research, Sloan School of Management, Massachusetts Institute of Technology. Task Force Working Paper.

Lofgren, Eric P., Steven Nyce, and Sylvester J. Scheiber. This volume. "Designing Total Reward Programs for Tight Labor Markets."

Mitchell, Olivia S. 2000. "Developments in Pensions." In *Handbook of Insurance*, ed. Georges Dionne. Boston: Kluwer Academic. 873–99.

Mitchell, Olivia S. with Erica L. Dykes. This volume. "New Trends in Pension Benefit and Retirement Provisions."

Mitchell, Olivia S. and Angela Mikalauskas. 1988. "The Impact of Government Regulation on the Labor Market." In *Mandating Benefits*, ed. Dallas L. Salisbury. Washington, D.C.: EBRI.

Rappaport, Anna M. This volume. "Implications of the Difficult Economy for Retirement Plans."

Riche, Martha Farnsworth. This volume. "The Demographics of Tomorrow's Workplace."

Sabharwal, Manish. This volume. "Developments in Global Benefits Administration."

U.S. Department of Labor. 2001. *Report on the American Workforce*. Washington, D.C: U.S. DOL.

Part I
The Future Workplace and Implications for Benefit Coverage and Design

Chapter 1
The Demographics of Tomorrow's Workplace

Martha Farnsworth Riche

Nearly two decades ago, the Hudson Institute announced an important demographic shift in America's workforce (Johnston 1987). Combining projected population growth with demographic-specific projections of the labor force, that study reported that the workforce of the future would include many more women and members of racial and ethnic minorities than ever before. This finding, summarized in *Workforce 2000*, caught employers' attention, and it produced intensive efforts to help increasingly diverse workers and managers work well together.

An equally challenging workforce transformation will take place in the next two decades. In addition to the continuing trend toward greater gender and racial/ethnic diversity, two less well-known demographic trends will further diversify the workplace. Specifically, there will be more diversity in workers' ages, and more diversity with regard to workers' household/family characteristics. Both changes will require increased attention to what workers need and want in the way of benefits, as well as to how compensation packages are designed to attract, retain, and manage the workforce of the future.

In this chapter we describe and assess demographic trends expected to shape the nation's workforce during the first two decades of the twenty-first century. The analysis relies on projections of the working-age population, which, in turn, rely on trends in fundamental demographic processes including particularly births, deaths, immigration, and household composition. Consequently we forecast the size and makeup of the nation's future potential workforce rather than making projections of labor force participation by groups. Since tastes and traditions affect labor force participation as well as economic developments in somewhat unpredictable ways, labor force projections generally assume a continuation of current work patterns and are limited to the near term.[1] By contrast, our goal is to draw attention to demographic changes that may shape the labor force as a whole in the future.

Dimensions of the Future Workforce

Simple population growth will continue to increase the size of the U.S. workforce over the next several decades. The U.S. population grew by nearly 35 million people between 1990 and 2000, and the outlook for the twenty-first century is for more growth. If current trends in natural growth (the excess of births over deaths) and net migration continue, the U.S. population is expected to more than double by 2100.[2]

We consider next the working-age population, a group is traditionally defined as including people ages 16–64 based on legal age thresholds used to define the "economically active" population. Over the next two decades, this age group is projected to grow by about 14 percent. Virtually all of this growth will be in minority populations, as they are currently defined, since these groups tend to have higher fertility rates than the majority population, and to account for a major share of new immigrants.

One problem with the traditional definition of the "economically active" population is that these age thresholds do not accurately track work patterns now, and they may do worse in the future. At the entry end of the labor market, labor force participation has declined slightly for the young (ages 16 to 24). This is because young Americans are increasingly likely to continue their schooling, as compared to the past. Although the majority of young students, both full and part time, combine schooling with work today, research suggests that work has become more casual for people in this age group. Consequently, permanent attachment to the labor force does not occur until about age 25, even for people who do not pursue higher education (Oppenheimer, Kalmjn, and Lim 1997).

At the exit end of the labor market, participation rates for people age 55+ are also changing. A post–WWII long-term decline has been reversed of late, particularly for men ages 55–64 (Fullerton 1999). Surveys also indicate that many younger people expect to work beyond age 65. Meanwhile, there are indications that people in the later working ages can increasingly combine work with retirement income; thus retirement may also become less well defined in the future. Changes in the salience of work at particular life stages are explored in more depth below. For now, they serve to warn against using simple population growth trends to draw specific conclusions about the size of the future workforce.

The Composition of the Working-Age Population

The demographic changes reshaping the U.S. work force in the twenty-first century are first and foremost age-driven, representing deep demographic change in the nation's age structure. These changes are rooted in the reality of a longer, healthier life expectancy allied with Americans' continuing preference for a two-child family. The U.S. today anticipates having a population with roughly equal numbers of people in every age group except the oldest for the first time in history. For most historical periods, a nation's age structure resembled a pyramid, with a wide base representing the large share of babies born, a narrowing midsection indicating that many died in early childhood and less often later, and a narrow apex since only a few survived to old age. In that world, half the population consisted of children, and many of those died before they had children of their own. The few elderly, along with the children, were cared for by the people in the middle (see Figure 1).

The U.S. age picture for 1970 depicted in Figure 1 represents this traditional population pyramid, slightly "cinched" at the middle by the Depression babies, and then widened by the baby boom. The picture for 2020, by contrast, is more of a population "pillar," because each age group is projected to be roughly the same size (except the oldest ones). Contrary to popular perception, the share of middle-aged and older people is not increasing because young adults are having fewer children. Indeed, for more than a decade, U.S. fertility has steadily reflected Americans' long-standing preference for two children, and more babies have been born each year than the year before. But with fewer people dying before reaching old age, the bars toward the top are becoming wider.

As a result, the size of each ten-year age cohort is expected to become more similar by 2020 (see Table 1). In 2000, the seven youngest cohorts that encompass the working-age population ranged in size from 20.1 million to 42.3 million. This numerical difference will be nearly erased by 2020, assuming the continuation of current birth, death, and migration patterns. In contrast, aside from the distorting effects of the baby boom (and subsequent

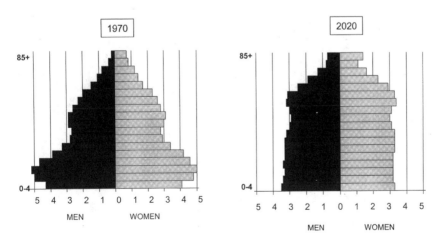

Figure 1. From pyramids to pillars (percent of population). Source: U.S. Bureau of the Census (1975, 2000c).

"baby bust"), ten-year age groups were roughly the same size until age 40 twenty years ago; after age 40, they were much smaller. So the increase in the working-age population is largely among people in later middle-age, as more Americans survive to older ages.

Other things equal, the shift in population patterns would be expected to generate a similar shift in labor force patterns, with future growth concentrated among workers ages 45 and older. Specifically, if current trends continue, the largest growth will be among workers ages 55–64. By 2010 the median age of the labor force is expected to approach age 41, surpassing its previous record age set in 1962. At the same time, the youth labor force will be larger than it has been since the 1970s.

This suggests two kinds of issues facing employers. First, companies will need to assess what they want from older workers, and what it will take to produce this outcome, whether it be training, benefits, or incentives to leave or change rungs on the occupational ladder. Second, companies must assess what kind of changes in pay and benefits as well as jobs that they need to make to manage a mix of older and younger workers successfully.

Household Differences

These population shifts are also changing the household profile of the working-age population, as household structures tend differ across young, middle-aged, and older adults.[3] Perhaps the most important impact on benefits is the changing ratio between households with and without children, a shift contributing to rising women's labor force participation in particular.

Longer life expectancies are compressing child-rearing into less than half the working life: Americans now average only 35 percent of the years between ages 20 and 70 in parenting, although there are considerable differences by gender and by race (King 1999).[4] Today fewer of the nation's households have children living with them, with predictable effects on labor force participation rates as well as on benefit packages.

TABLE 1. U.S. Population in 2000 and Projections to 2020 (millions)

Age group	2000	2020
under 10	38.9	43.5
10 to 19	39.9	42.7
20 to 29	36	42.9
30 to 39	41.7	41.9
40 to 49	42.3	37.4
50 to 59	30.5	40.5
60 to 69	20.1	38.1
70 to 79	16.1	23.3
80 +	9.2	12.4

Source: U.S. Bureau of the Census (2000c).

The shift toward relatively equal sized age groups is making households more diverse, as well as proportionately larger in number. When most of today's employers and managers grew up, the modal family arrangement was a married couple with one or more children.[5] By contrast today, due to longer life expectancies and fewer children, there are more married couples without children. Put simply, couples today have more years together after their children have reached age 18. The 2000 Census found that the traditional family represented barely 35 percent of all family households, and less than one quarter of all households. Meanwhile, married couples without children had become the nation's most common living unit. Single-parent households (more than four in five headed by a woman) were also more common, growing from 4 percent of family households in 1950 to over 13 percent in 2000.

Households that do not contain a family (i.e., persons related by blood or marriage) are also becoming more prevalent. Single-person households are now the nation's second most numerous household type, accounting for more than a quarter percent of all households. This is not surprising, considering that people ages 65+ represent the largest share of single-person households. However, single-person households are common in every age group — one in ten Americans ages 25 to 44, the most common ages for marriage, lives alone.

These trends imply that employers must begin to rethink how employment and benefits packages reward individuals versus workers in households, as well as how they interact with workers' transitions between the two sets. Young persons starting families are in a very different economic and

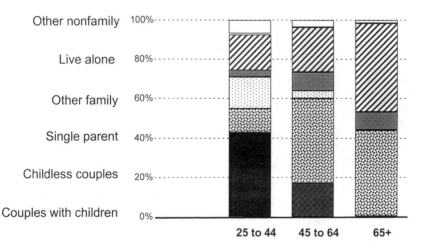

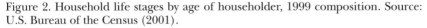

Figure 2. Household life stages by age of householder, 1999 composition. Source: U.S. Bureau of the Census (2001).

social milieu than are older workers whose children have left home. Today's current focus on work and family issues will of course continue to be valuable, but in the future, employers will also need to focus on rewarding and motivating the majority of the working-age population not involved in raising children.

Racial and Ethnic Differences

The nation's minority populations have grown rapidly in recent decades, making an understanding of their employment wants and needs more than a gesture of sensitivity or an accommodation to civil rights laws. In addition to relatively high fertility rates, particularly among Hispanics, the minority population has grown via massive immigration experienced since the 1970s.

Most immigrants come to the United States in search of better employment opportunities, and thus the are often young adults; as a result, they account for a substantial share of workforce growth. This is particularly true for Asians and Hispanics. In addition, these populations are also extremely diverse, ranging from highly educated computer professionals from South Asia to poorly educated day laborers from Central America.

Nationwide, non-Hispanic whites currently account for 72 percent of the working-age population; the minority population is becoming both more

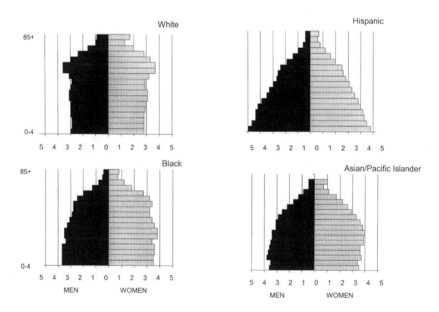

Figure 3. Projected distribution of minority population by age, 2020. Source: U.S. Bureau of the Census (2001).

diverse and more numerous. The 2000 Census found that Hispanics (who can be of any race) slightly outnumber non-Hispanic blacks. However, both groups each account for more than 12 percent of the population, and Asian and Pacific Islanders account for nearly 4 percent. Although the number of American Indians (including Alaska Natives) nearly tripled over the century, they account for less than 1 percent of all Americans.

If recent trends continue, non-Hispanic whites will account for about 63 percent of the working-age population in 2020, Hispanics for 17 percent, non-Hispanic blacks for 13 percent, Asian and Pacific Islanders for 6 percent, and American Indians for 1 percent.[6] This represents major shifts in diversity within segments of the working-age population. First, minorities are younger than the majority population. The non-Hispanic white population had a median age of 38.1 in 1999, nearly a dozen years older than the Hispanic population (26.5). American Indians (28.3) were almost as young as Hispanics, while the median ages of the African-American population (30.3) and the Asian and Pacific Islander population (32.0) were not much higher.[7] Younger populations tend to contain more families with children; fewer than half of non-Hispanic white family households now have children in them, compared to over half of minority family households (see Table 2). As a result of all these trends, the "old-style" workforce — younger adults raising families — is increasingly minority, while the "new-style" workforce — older adults without children at home — is disproportionately white.

Changes in the proportion of husband-wife families, especially among households with children, also have profound labor force implications. About 80 percent of white and Asian-Pacific Islander families are husband-wife families, compared with fewer than 50 percent of black families and 70 percent of Hispanic families. In contrast, 54 percent of black family households are female-headed, two-thirds with children. Nearly a third of Hispanic family households are female-headed, again two-thirds with children. Households with two parents have the possibility of two incomes; households with just one parent have only one person who must also fill the role of caretaker.

Simultaneous changes in the nation's age structure and its racial and ethnic composition will continue to modify the nation's household composition. Overall, families with children in them will become a smaller share of the nation's households — they will barely outnumber the growing share of households that consist of people living alone, if current trends continue. However, these trends are very different for minority groups, all of which will have significantly more families with children (see Table 3).

Blacks will be most likely to confront work and family challenges, inasmuch as almost 20 percent of black households will consist of single-parent families in the future, if current trends continue, while only 14 percent will live in "traditional" families. Blacks will also have proportionately more single-person households than whites, suggesting strong interest in benefits

TABLE 2. Households by Type and Race/Hispanic Origin: 1999 and 2020 (projected) (percent distribution)

	Total		White		Black		Asian/other		Hispanic*	
	1999	2020	1999	2020	1999	2020	1999	2020	1999	2020
Married couples, no children under 18	29	32	31	35	16	18	25	31	19	24
Single persons	26	27	25	27	29	31	20	20	15	16
Married couples, children under 18	24	20	25	21	16	14	33	29	36	32
Single parent families	9	8	8	6	22	19	8	6	16	14
Other families	7	8	6	6	14	15	9	9	10	11
Other nonfamilies	6	5	6	5	4	4	6	5	5	4

Source: Riche (2001a), U.S. Census Bureau (2000a).
Percentages may not equal 100 because of rounding.
* Hispanics may be of any race and are included in each racial group as appropriate; their households are projected independent of the projections by race.

TABLE 3. Households by Type and Race/Hispanic Origin, 2020 (households (percent distribution))

	All races		White		Black		Asian and other races		Hispanic*	
All households	128,806	(100.0%)	103,165	(100.0%)	18,116	(100.0%)	7,525	(100.0%)	16,959	(100.0%)
Married couples, no children under 18	41,141	(31.9%)	35,649	(34.6%)	3,197	(17.6%)	2,295	(30.5%)	3,997	(23.6%)
Single person	35,204	(27.3%)	28,098	(27.2%)	5,580	(30.8%)	1,526	(20.3%)	2,773	(16.4%)
Married couples, children under 18	26,130	(20.3%)	21,412	(20.8%)	2,531	(14.0%)	2,187	(29.1%)	5,354	(31.6%)
Single parent families	10,182	(7.9%)	6,380	(6.2%)	3,364	(18.6%)	440	(5.8%)	2,317	(13.7%)
Other families	9,977	(7.7%)	6,538	(6.3%)	2744	(15.1%)	695	(9.2%)	1788	(10.5%)
Other nonfamilies	6,172	(4.8%)	5,088	(4.9%)	700	(3.9%)	383	(5.1%)	730	(4.3%)

Source: Riche (2001a).
Hispanic household projection is independent of the projections by race.
* Hispanics may be of any race.

geared to individuals, particularly if they must pay for care they receive. In contrast, Hispanics may be more interested in family-oriented benefits. In any case, all groups will have higher concentrations of single-person households in the future.

Work and the Life-Course

Looking backward, during the latter half of the twentieth century, Americans tended to enter the labor market some time between ages 16–21, and some men took time out for military service. Women still devoted considerable nonmarket time to raising children and, if they remained married, might not return to the labor force at all. In any case, retirement took place in the late 50s and early 60s. Throughout the work life, seniority and experience entitled workers to expect higher pay and often higher status.

Looking ahead, demographic and economic trends are creating new life patterns for working-age Americans, particularly longer periods of education when young, and longer healthy life expectancies among the old. These patterns influence workers' needs and preferences for work, pay, and benefits, which in turn will have potent implications for employers. The traditional pattern is fragmenting along several dimensions, roughly correlated with age.

Young Adults

Although age 18 still denotes the age of maturity in the United States, legally and statistically, the reality is that economic maturity is increasingly delayed for young adults. Relatively few Americans under the age of 25 have completed schooling, become economically independent, acquired a residence, and formed a family. Instead, this life stage has become one offering young adults a diversity of activities undertaken in no particular order (Rindfuss 1991). In the past, high school graduates divided into two groups: a minority who went to college, and a majority who went directly to jobs or home-making. Looking ahead, it will be increasingly common for most high school graduates to continue their education in a variety of educational settings and often in combination with other activities. The patterns are already clear: in 1999, nearly two out of three high school graduates enrolled in college the following fall, up from one in two in 1978 (National Center for Education Statistics 1999; U.S. Bureau of Labor Statistics 2000b). Nearly 90 percent of part-time students ages 16 to 24 were also in the workforce in 1999, as were 56 percent of full-time students (U.S. Bureau of Labor Statistics 2000a).

In sum, more young adults are continuing their education, fewer young adults are going straight to full-time work, more young adults are combining school and work, and some are doing none of the above. It is taking longer, for young men at least, to make the transition from high school to stable employment. One research team found that it took seven years before 40 percent of black male high school dropouts found full-time year-round work, while 70 percent of black male college graduates worked full-time year-round within a year of graduation (Oppenheimer, Kalmjn, and Lim 1997).

Spending more time in school and taking longer to become attached to the workforce has caused many young adults to delay leaving their parents' home for independent living (Goldscheider, Thornton, and Young-DeMarco 1993; Goldscheider and Goldscheider 1993). In 1999, some 60 percent of the civilian population aged 18–24 was living with parents or other relatives (66 percent of males, 56 percent of females). About half of the remainder (19 percent) was married or a single parent (13 percent of males, 25 percent of females), while the rest were living alone or sharing with someone else.[8] Coincident with this lack of tight labor market attachment are peripatetic mobility patterns among this age group. Young adults are the most geographically mobile, with 12.5 percent of the civilian population aged 18–24 moving across county lines between 1998 and 1999, as compared to about half that rate for all age groups (U.S. Census Bureau 2000d). It appears that this life phase has become a post-adolescent stage when many young people transition gradually into adult life by engaging in variety of activities, in a variety of places, simultaneously or consecutively, and in no particular order.

Peak Working Ages

Peak labor force participation in the United States occurs between ages 25 and 54 (Fullerton 1999). From a labor force and benefits perspective, however, it is probably best to divide this peak working period into two stages of roughly equal duration. During the first, usually younger, stage, people have family responsibilities and many (usually women), subordinate market work to home work. During the second phase, people tend to have fewer family responsibilities and work can become a primary focus. Demographic change in America is increasing the number of workers in stage 2, and making them roughly equal to the number of workers in stage 1.

Stage 2 is particularly relevant for women workers. Given the compression of parenting into the earlier part of the peak working age, women reach stage 2 with their child-care responsibilities largely behind them. Already more than half of the women in the U.S. workforce have no children at home; about one-quarter have school-age children, and only one-sixth have a preschool child (U.S. Bureau of Labor Statistics 2001). It is interesting, in this light, that popular discussions of women's labor force choices, working conditions, and benefits tend to focus on the "work/family conflict," reflecting the presumption that traditional gender roles continue throughout life. But what we have demonstrated is that employers might more usefully distinguish between workers (of both sexes) in stage 1 versus those in stage 2. During the first stage, workers are simultaneously paying off educational and mortgage debt, starting new careers, and having children — during what are likely to be their lowest earnings years. During the second stage, when earnings tend to be higher, people generally have fewer childrearing and housing costs, and instead begin to focus on saving for retirement. In addition some care for elderly parents, though lengthening life expectancy is tending to postpone this concern to later life. Employers who understand these influences will be in a better position to satisfy these new needs, rather than being unaware of them.

Older Adults

The concept of retirement in the United States was invented during the twentieth century. Whereas most people worked until a few years before death at the beginning of the century, fewer than one in six men ages 65 and older, and fewer than one in ten women, was in the labor force by 2000 (U.S. Bureau of Labor Statistics 2001). Now most people retire before age 65, though retirement is also becoming a process rather than a clearly delineated event (Treas 1995).

One reason for this trend is that life expectancies have been rising rather dramatically over time. Currently, Americans tend to live 18 years after attaining age 65, up from about 12 years in 1900; life expectancy after age 65 is projected to increase even more in the twenty-first century (National Center for Health Statistics 2001). In addition, the aging of the baby boom will speed the growth of the older population over the next few decades. Both developments imply that "senior citizens" will account for 16.5 percent of the U.S. population by 2020, and the percentage will grow over the remainder of the century.

Since mortality improvement at older ages is a relatively recent phenomenon, occurring mostly after 1960, many today still contemplate old age using out-of-date stereotypes. But research now indicates that *healthy* life expectancy is rising just as quickly as *total* life expectancy, so that each new generation attaining old age is actually less "old" than its predecessor (Manton, Corder, and Stallard 1997). A new standard of energy and vitality in the population seems to have pushed old age well into the 70s and beyond, partly due to better education about health and partly due to medical advances.

Given the large growth in the older population and its improving health status, policymakers may seek to extend the work life, rather than providing income support for early retirees. Changes in Social Security and other government programs may be a catalyst, but already workers and their employers are making adjustments. For example, the shift from defined benefit to defined contribution pensions has changed incentives for early retirement. On the other hand, extending the work life to older ages will require abandoning the assumption that people can spend an entire work life in a single occupation, or that career ladders can be climbed in only one direction. Echoing young adults, healthy older adults seem to be living a life stage increasingly characterized by diversity, combining regular, intermittent, and self-employment, with school, travel, and leisure pursuits, in no particular order.

In sum, during their working ages, Americans pass through several stages that determine what they contribute in the workplace and what they want from their work lives. Also having roughly equal numbers of people at all working ages will mean that the labor force will include people at each of these life stages. This spells the need for a greater range of working conditions and benefits than ever before.

Changes in Job Context

Ongoing changes in economic organization and operations are also tugging the nation's labor force into new ways of working. Underlying many of these changes is the continuing shift of the nation's employment into the service sector. Technology continues to improve productivity in the traditional manufacturing industries, where output growth has outpaced employment. Meanwhile, services are expected to account for three of every four U.S. jobs by 2010 (Thomson 1999). Some of this growth in services is attributable to the same demographic changes reshaping the population — for instance, the growth in health services reflects a longer-lived population reliant on continued advances in diagnosis, treatment, and care. Yet many others are rooted in productivity-enhancing industries such as computers and communications. These are important growth industries in themselves, and the way they reshape business is also enhancing productivity in business services, management and public relations, research and testing, personnel services, and renting and leasing.

From a workforce perspective, some of the industrial restructuring involves outsourcing jobs that were previously performed in-house, moving them to new specialized companies. To some extent, then, such outsourcing is eliminating rungs from the career ladder, as positions that were formerly filled through on-the-job exposure and training now develop career ladders of their own outside traditional large employers. This shift challenges some companies to supervise and carefully manage the employees they "own" versus those they "rent." This challenge is rendered even more interesting by different employment spells for different skills and tasks, including the growing use of temporary employees (see Camden this volume; Houseman this volume). These employees work for a set period on a contractual or fee basis, thus adding a new set of diversity issues — tenure, training, status, pay, mobility, and the like — to the demographic diversity palette.

Occupational Shifts

Changes in the structure of occupations are also ahead. The twenty occupations predicted to grow most rapidly in the future are mainly in computing and health care, where they will offer relatively high wages and require a relatively educated workforce. Nevertheless these represent less than 20 percent of the overall growth in employment projected by the Bureau of Labor Statistics for this decade. By contrast, the thirty occupations accounting for nearly half the projected job growth pay lower-than-average wages, and require no more than on-the-job training. Put another way, 70 percent of the fastest growing occupations generally require post-secondary education or training, compared to only a third of the occupations with the largest numerical growth.[9]

From a socioeconomic perspective, these trends might imply a twenty-first century version of the two-tier or hollowed-out workforce, with growth in high-paying occupations requiring human capital investment, and growth in low-paying occupations without such requirements. The Bureau of Labor Statistics notes that occupations requiring an associate's degree or higher, which accounted for 25 percent of all jobs in 1998, will account for 40 percent of the job growth by 2010. Meanwhile, jobs requiring just a high school education and short-term on-the-job training will account for 57 percent. As a result, these trends suggest a continuation of today's skill mix, expressed in terms of educational attainment. It is interesting, nonetheless, that both groups of growing occupations concentrate in the area of personal, human, and business services, where people tend to work with people. Meanwhile, technological and other well-known changes are reducing the demand for numerous occupations where people work with "things." A natural consequence of the trend is that there will be a broad need for more training and standards relating to interpersonal skills.

It should also be recalled that focusing on changes in occupational demand misses the largest labor force pattern, where new employees will simply replace older ones in occupations where demand remains steady. These occupations may be found in every sector, but they are most concentrated in traditional manufacturing and agricultural-related occupations. In many cases, "older" is a literal description of people who have completed their work life and moved into a new life stage. In many other cases, particularly in low-paying service occupations like food preparation, "older" simply means "previous," as young workers move on to other fields. So-called "poor" jobs may never be appealing to many during their peak working years, but they could become attractive to people transitioning into or out of the working life.

The longer work lives produced by demographic trends suggest that workforce planners need to sharpen their understanding of career paths, including interruptions, reversals, and changes of direction for both women and men in their industries as well as the economy as a whole. Similarly, the rise of contract, temporary work is broadening the portfolio of workforce attachments as well as workforce settings. It is probably time to acknowledge the new work-life models, instead of remaining wedded to old concepts. Certainly the fact that many employees undergo lengthy transitions into and out of peak working years suggests that even "poor" jobs can play a role for workers at different stages in their lives.

Mobility and Migration

Trends in cross-national mobility are difficult to predict, since they are a function of political as well as economic and demographic influences. The Census Bureau has recently moved to project the impact of international migration on the U.S. population based on current trends instead of continuing past tradition of assuming a constant value.[10] These trends include population growth rates in the sending countries, since job-seeking is normally the driver of migration for young adults who make up the bulk of migrants. Estimates suggest that the United States should expect increasing numbers of immigrants from high-growth countries in South Asia, Sub-Saharan Africa, and the Middle East between now and 2020. At the same time, the Bureau expects a slowing in family reunification patterns from Mexico, and a slowing of refugees from the Balkans. Overall, falling fertility rates in the Western Hemisphere should be expected to slow Hispanic immigration, while high rates in other regions should increase the inflow of Black and Asian populations.

Several changes should be expected in the makeup of the U.S. workforce between now and 2020 (though changes in public policy can obviously turn around migration projections). First, over a million immigrants are expected to arrive each year, mostly of working age and seeking employment. Second, immigrants will be increasingly Black and Asian, and they will come from cultures that are generally very different from the dominant U.S. culture. Finally, immigrants can be expected to concentrate at the two extremes of the educational scale: highly educated and barely educated.

Traditionally immigrants have concentrated geographically as they locate with countrymen who came here before them. Over the last two decades, most immigrants to the United States have concentrated in a few states, mostly on the East or West Coasts. Subsequently, competition for jobs and housing in coastal states led unskilled U.S.-born workers to migrate to places in the country's interior, particularly non-Hispanic whites and blacks (Frey 1993). Another factor is the effect of industrial restructuring on unskilled and semiskilled blue-collar jobs that may have prompted less educated workers to move in search of new opportunities (Wright, Ellis, and Reibel 1997). In any case, managing racial and ethnic diversity in the workplace will be an even greater challenge across different parts of the country, as the immigration flow continues.

Continuing globalization will also expand how managers handle work, pay, and benefits. For instance, the flow of foreign-born workers who return home to seek new work or to retire, can be expected to increase. This is true to the extent that improved communications and transportation technology allow foreign-born workers to maintain ties to their homeland while they are here. Also there are simply more foreign-born people in the U.S. working-age population today, as a result of high emigration patterns in the past (U.S. Bureau of the Census 2001). Such patterns pose a challenge for handling issues such as long-term pension vesting, retiree health benefits, and deferred compensation.

Globalization is also prompting more U.S. companies to move operations overseas. Economic integration is increasing, just as unprecedented numbers of young people in developing countries are swelling the world's labor force. In the past, massive migration of working-age people resolved regional imbalances between labor supply and labor demand. In the future, migration will still be a partial solution, but the numbers of job-needy workers are far larger than industrialized nations are willing to absorb. Instead, globalization permits employers to export jobs, thus creating a new global division of labor (Riche 2001b). Benefits managers in such multinational enterprises are having to redesign benefits within a broader, global perspective, and they must confront the challenge of a wider array of workers and worker needs and preferences.

Pay and Benefits Implications

Many misinterpreted the earlier landmark study, *Workforce 2000*, as suggesting that women and minorities would become a majority of the future workforce, rather than simply a majority of *net entrants*. In the present context, we hasten to point out that the U.S. labor force will continue to grow over the next two decades, even as net inflows are changing. During this period the U.S. workforce will become older, more evenly divided among men and women, and more racially and ethnically diverse, both across and within groups. And it will become less engaged with simultaneously raising families, while more concerned with meeting individual interests. Consequently, employers will need to consider a broader range of worker need when shaping pay, benefits packages, and working conditions.

Implications for Age-Related Benefits and Pay

As work lives lengthen, they may feature more interruptions than in the past, and undoubtedly they will involve more movement between employers, occupations, and industries. As a result, benefit portability will become an increasingly important issue. Managing turnover to maximize organizational effectiveness will also challenge human resource managers. As an example, low employee turnover has recently been linked to declining corporate performance (*New York Times* 2000). Benefits may become as much a tool for managing worker departures as for managing recruiting and retention.

On-the-job education and training is also likely to be perceived as a career-building benefit, as life-long learning becomes a necessity in a fast-changing employment environment. Employer reluctance to invest in training that might give a competitor a short-term boost may become less salient from a work-life perspective. Echoing the medieval apprentice system, employees might find it useful to trade pay now for skill investments that promise future higher pay. Employers who provide valuable credentials could also offer skills-acquisition in lieu of pay.

An adaptable employer in the future might make a virtue of accommodating interrupted and intermittent labor force participation, abetting career and job changes. For instance, young adults have long gained experience and information about the world of work from seemingly "dead-end" jobs, while earning money to pay for higher education. Similarly, mid- and late-career adults sometimes outgrow the careers they prepared for while lacking methods to build new ones. Internships and mentoring techniques could be used to attract new employees, just as employers currently profit from outsourcing to temporary employees whom later they may convert to permanent hires.

The changing workforce will also require employers and employees to rethink careers. Traditionally, career mobility has been seen as a steady upward progression, with retirement at the top. This was a useful premise when organizations had pyramidical career structures, and there were fewer workers at successively older ages. In the future, lateral and downward mobility will be needed to accommodate a long-lived workforce with roughly equal numbers at all ages. If status issues can be handled with care, flexible career ladders may better accommodate workers' changing health and physical needs, as well as their family and financial needs, in the future.

Geographic mobility normally diminishes at older working ages, but new tools may also help employers turn geographic flexibility into a benefit over the work life. For instance, employees can work from remote locations, at home, or out of a satellite office to save time and money commuting to headquarters. Geodemographic search tools may be used by employers seeking pockets of untapped skills among retirees, or the underemployed who are not willing to leave their communities. In some cases employers may even establish plants where people prefer to live.

The key principle in this reformulation of pay, benefits, and working conditions is that managers must understand where a given job can fit into workers' life stages, and then design pay and benefits appropriately. For example, part-time fast-food jobs traditionally appealed to teenagers still in school; when a dearth of baby bust teenagers developed, McDonald's turned to semiretired workers who valued the flexible scheduling and human contact. The U.S. military is currently having trouble recruiting and keeping young adults, particularly when they start having families. As a result, the armed services seeking skilled people are now considering mature recruits interested in travel and saving for retirement.

Implications for Household-Related Benefits and Pay

Increasing diversity of workers' family and living arrangements also has implications for pay, benefits, and working conditions of the future. Perhaps the most important is due to the compression of family obligations into stage 1 of the work life, as it is squeezing working parents for time and for money, whether they are single or wed. Employers seek ways to ease that squeeze by providing daycare and sometimes allowing parents to bring new babies to work. They also provide benefits that address the financial squeeze as in the federal government's move to allow agencies to repay college loans for recruits with highly needed technical, professional, and administrative skills.[11]

A challenge in this area is that companies must be even-handed vis-à-vis benefits for workers not currently raising children. In addition to empty-nest couples and singles, this includes workers living in subfamilies (families living with another family member) and cohabiting. Cohabiting, in particular, will continue to be common as the share of workers raising children declines. Longer life spans also raise issues of generational care needs within families, and employers should be aware that most care, whether in the form of time or money, goes from older to younger family members. In any case, employers must avoid favoring one family "arrangement" over another, if only because workers can transition rapidly between these.

Helping workers manage their time can be a substantial benefit for people committed to families, as well as for those with other preoccupations. Alternative work schedules can be a boon; so too can time-saving help from employers via managing administrative chores for health plans. Ford Motor Company offers an interesting example of adaptive benefits over the life course, establishing centers for social services ranging from child care for working parents, to book clubs for retirees. The firm's union sought improved childcare and services for school-age children, to which the firm added benefits including time- and trouble-saving features for older workers like tax planning and travel assistance.

Longer work lives are also heightening women's role in the workforce, as the primary growth in labor force participation is among women at an age with few or no traditional family obligations. Employers can probably expect a surge in work intensity and interest from midlife women employees. Focusing benefits on the individual worker, rather than the worker's family, may become more effective in the future, given the fact that women and men may face different timing issues over the life course. The key idea is to give workers a broader array of choices, and employers who analyze the needs of people in their labor market will be better equipped to target benefits and pay for effective recruiting, retention, and turnover.

Other Diversity Issues

In the U.S. context, "diversity" implies acknowledging and managing racial and ethnic differences in the workplace. In the future, these issues will continue to be salient, and ongoing racial and ethnic changes will surely reinforce the need for "diversity management." Possibly, however, over the next twenty years the dwindling (in relative terms) majority may become more accustomed to accommodating a wider array of people, and an increasingly multiracial population might blur racial and ethnic distinctions. Nevertheless, labor markets vary enormously in their geographical, racial, and ethnic makeup, so employers might be called on to manage this variation by, for instance, counseling key employees to become more sensitive to diversity issues. At the same time, there is a greater need for employees with good interpersonal skills, as the growth occupations tend to be those that deal with people. This means paying attention to managing diversity among customers, such as knowing when to have sales people sensitive to customer needs. Geographic concentration in demographic characteristics will always require tailoring policies and practices to the appropriate labor market, whether in terms of race/ethnicity, age structure, or worker's living arrangements.

Conclusion

Challenging workforce transformations await the employer of the future. Greater gender and racial/ethnic diversity will be paired with more diversity in workers' ages, and more diversity with regard to workers' household/family characteristics. These changes will powerfully shape what workers need and want in the way of benefits, and what companies offer to attract, retain, and manage the workforce of the future.

Notes

1. The United States Bureau of Labor Statistics (BLS) produces short-term projections of the labor force at regular intervals. A recent projection appeared in 1999 and extends to 2008 (Fullerton 1999). See also <www.bls.gov> for further information.

2. All the population (but not household) projections in this chapter come from the middle series produced by the United States Census Bureau for 1999–2100, and released on January 13, 2000 at <www.census.gov/population/www/projections/natsum.html>. Household projections are the responsibility of the author and are

based on the Census Bureau's population projections (Riche 2001a). These projections extend farther into the future than official household projections. Like labor force participation, household projections are subject to unpredictable variation in tastes and traditions and should thus be viewed as purely illustrative of the direction taken by current trends.

3. A household consists of all people who occupy a housing unit. A house, an apartment or other group of rooms, or a single room is regarded as a housing unit when it is occupied or intended for occupancy as separate living quarters; that is, when the occupants do not live and eat with any other persons in the structure and there is direct access from the outside or through a common hall. There are two major categories of households, "family" and "nonfamily." A family household includes the related family members and all the unrelated people, if any, such as lodgers, foster children, wards, or employees who share the housing units. A nonfamily household can be a person living alone in a housing unit, or a group of unrelated people sharing a housing unit such as partners or roomers. The count of households excludes group quarters.

4. Women spend slightly more of their lives parenting, men slightly less, as women tend to retain custody of their children after divorce. However, given remarriage rates, men spend about twice as much time as women as custodial than biological parents, as well as mixed (biological and custodial) parents. Overall, white men spend an estimated 93 percent of the time white women do in parenting; African-American men spend an estimated 83 percent of African-American women's time.

5. For statistical purposes, the official definition of children is "under age 18, living in the home."

6. Since Hispanic is an ethnic not a racial identification, it is possible that a shift in identification patterns could reshape these Census Bureau projections. The Census Bureau reports that most Hispanics indicate they are white when they are required to elect a race on a survey. Currently government policy allows people to specify more than one race, generating more than sixty combinations. It is not yet clear how population projections will account for this broader array of self-definitions.

7. For these and other demographic facts not specifically referenced, see Riche (2000).

8. Data are from the March 1999 Current Population Survey, tabulated for the author.

9. Several occupations are contained in both groups, mostly in computing, health care, and social services (Braddock 1999).

10. The Census Bureau does not have a dynamic model, as no unifying theory of future change exists. Instead it is based "on a large amount of underlying current detail, coupled with some consideration of factors that could influence its change in the future" (U.S. Bureau of the Census 2000b).

11. Effective 2001, federal agencies are authorized to repay federally insured student loans when necessary to recruit or retain highly qualified professional, administrative, or technical people.

References

Braddock, Douglas. 1999. "Occupational Employment Projections to 2008." *Monthly Labor Review* 122, 11: 51–77.

Camden, Carl T. This volume. "Benefits for the Free-Agent Workforce."

Frey, William H. 1993. "Interstate Migration and Immigration for Whites and

Minorities, 1985-90: The Emergence of Multi-Ethnic States." Population Studies Center Research Report 93-297. Ann Arbor: University of Michigan.

Fullerton, Howard N., Jr. 1999. "Labor Force Projections to 2008: Steady Growth and Changing Composition." *Monthly Labor Review* 122, 11: 19–32.

Goldscheider, Frances K. and Calvin Goldscheider. 1993. *Leaving and Returning Home in Twentieth Century America.* Population Bulletin 48, 4. Washington, D.C.: Population Reference Bureau.

Goldscheider, Frances K., Arland Thornton, and Linda Young-DeMarco. 1993. "A Portrait of the Nest-Leaving Process in Early Adulthood." *Demography* 30, 4: 683–99.

Houseman, Susan N. This volume. "The Benefits Implications of Recent Trends in Flexible Staffing Arrangements."

Johnston, William B. 1987. *Workforce 2000: Work and Workers for the Twenty-First Century.* Indianapolis: Hudson Institute.

King, Rosalind Berkowitz. 1999. "Time Spent in Parenthood Status Among Adults in the United States." *Demography* 36, 3: 377–85.

Manton, Kenneth G., Larry Corder, and Eric Stallard. 1997. "Chronic Disability Trends in Elderly United States Populations, 1982-1994." *Proceedings of the National Academy of Sciences* 94: 2593–98.

National Center for Education Statistics. 2000. *Digest of Education Statistics, 1998.* Table 183. <nces.ed.gov>.

National Center for Health Statistics. 2001. "United States Life Tables." *National Vital Statistics Report* 48, 8. February.

Oppenheimer, Valerie Kincade, Matthijs Kalmjn, and Nelson Li. 1997. "Men's Career Development and Marriage Timing During a Period of Rising Inequality," *Demography* 34, 3: 311–30.

Riche, Martha Farnsworth. 2000. *America's Diversity and Growth: Signposts for the Twenty-First Century.* Population Bulletin 55, 2. Washington, D.C.: Population Reference Bureau.

———. 2001a. "The Implications of Changing U.S. Demographics for U.S. Cities." Washington, D.C.: Brookings Institution, Center on Urban and Metropolitan Policy. <www.brookings.edu/es/urban/urban.htm>.

———. 2001b. "Global Demographic Trends: Implications for an Inclusive Workplace." Paper presented at a Conference on International Cross-Cultural Perspectives on Workforce Diversity: The Inclusive Workplace, Bellagio, Italy, July 23–26.

Rindfuss, Ronald R. 1991. "The Young Adult Years: Diversity, Structural Change, and Fertility." *Demography* 28, 4: 493–512.

Thomson, Allison. 1999. "Industry Output and Employment Projections to 2008." *Monthly Labor Review* 122, 11: 33–50.

Treas, Judith. 1995. *Older Americans in the 1990s and Beyond.* Population Bulletin 50, 2. Washington, D.C.: Population Reference Bureau.

U.S. Bureau of Labor Statistics. 2000a. "Labor Force Status of Persons 16 to 24 Years Old by School Enrollment, Educational Attainment, Sex, Race, and Hispanic Origin, October 1999."

———. 2000b. "College Enrollment and Work Activity of 1999 High School Graduates." <www.bls.gov>.

———. 2001. "Employment Status of the Civilian Noninstitutional Population by Age, Sex, and Race." <www.bls.gov >.

U.S. Bureau of the Census. 1975. *Historic Statistics of the United States, Colonial Times to 1970, Bicentennial Edition, Part 2.* Series A 119–34. Washington, D.C.

———. 2000a. Current Population Survey, March 1999. Tabulation for the author.

————. 2000b. "Methodology and Assumptions for the Population Projections of the United States: 1999 to 2100." Population Division Working Paper 38, issued January 13.

————. 2000c. "Projections of the Total Resident Population: Middle Series, 1999 to 2100." NP-T3.

————. 2000d. "Table 1. General Mobility, by Region, Sex, and Age." Internet release date July 12. <www.census.gov/>.

Wright, R. A., M. Ellis, and M. Reibel. 1997. "The Linkage Between Immigration and Internal Migration in Large Metropolitan Areas in the United States." *Economic Geography* 73, 2: 234–54.

Chapter 2
Benefits and Productivity

William E. Even and
David A. Macpherson

Private sector employees now receive over one-quarter of their entire compensation in the form of employee benefits, and in large firms the fraction is even higher. The generosity and structure of these benefit programs influences workers' productivity in numerous ways. One reason is that workers are heterogeneous in terms of their willingness to trade wages for benefits. As a result, any given firm's benefit package will attract and retain a nonrandom group of workers. Another reason is that employee benefits can alter lifetime earnings profiles. As a consequence, they can be used to alter employee retention rates and vary worker incentives for retirement.

This chapter discusses how two of the most prominent employer-provided benefits — pensions and health insurance plans — influence productivity. In particular we investigate how pension plan design and the availability of employee or retiree health insurance influence workforce selection, retention, retirement behavior, and worker effort. Drawing from available evidence, we examine trends in these benefits, and explore how they might alter future workplace patterns.

Changes in Pension Structure and Design

In the North American labor market, employers offer several different types of pension plans. Defined benefit (DB) plans generally promise a life annuity at retirement, the amount of which usually depends on earnings, years of service, and some generosity rate. For example, a DB plan could provide a benefit equal to 1 percent of final average salary per year of service, where final average salary is computed using the worker's three highest years of earnings. DB plans have minimum service and/or age requirements for the immediate receipt of benefits on departure for the firm. For example, a plan might require that the worker be either sixty-five years of age or have at least thirty years of service. If a worker does not satisfy the age and service requirements for full benefits, the plan may allow the worker to collect reduced benefits for an early retirement (see Mitchell this volume).

In a defined contribution (DC) plan, the employee usually contributes a percentage of salary into a pension plan, and the employer may provide a match. The pension assets may be managed by a pension fund manager, or may be self-directed by the employee. On vesting, the plan participant earns a legal right to the plan balance. In the subset of plans known as 401(k) pensions, participants may elect how much of their salary they want to contribute to the pension. Relative to traditional DC plans, 401(k)s have the advantage of giving employee the ability to contribute pretax dollars to the plan.

In recent years a newer form of pension has been devised in the United States, known as a cash balance plan, sometimes referred to as a "hybrid." This has both DB and DC features, since the employee is credited with a fixed percentage of pay annually and guaranteed a rate of return on the account balance. The cash balance plan is similar to a DC plan since a participant's return is generally linked to a market-based prevailing interest rate (such as the Treasury bond rate). On the other hand, all employee contributions are pooled into a single investment account, and employees have a claim on the fund equal to prior contributions plus investment returns promised by the plan. As a result, the plan has a DB-like feature: at any given point in time, the plan could be over- or underfunded.

The Changing Composition of Pension Offerings

In the last two decades, DB plans have become much less popular in the United States, while DC plans, particularly the 401(k) plan, are increasingly common (Mitchell this volume; EBRI 2001). Several explanations for this shift have been offered, including higher administrative costs in DB plans; employment shifts across industries and from large to small firms; a decline in unionism; the rise of 401(k) plans; workers' interests in having more portable pensions; and firms' interests in having pensions encourage later retirement.

Several analysts have investigated whether employment shifts can account for the long-term shift in the United States from DB to DC plans (Gustman and Steinmeier 1992; Clark, McDermed, and Trawick 1993; Kruse 1995; and Ippolito 1995). The preponderance of the evidence is suggests that about half of the shift can be accounted for by economic restructuring — that is, by industrial shifts in employment, the decline in unionism, and the movement from large to small firms. It also appears that most of the shift during the 1980s was not the result of DC plans being formed to replace terminated DB plans. Rather, most new DC plans emerged at firms that did not previously offer a pension plan. During the 1990s, however, it appears that terminated DB plans were replaced by 401(k) and other DC plans (Papke 1999).

One reason that 401(k) plans took off was that clarifying regulations were issued by the Treasury Department in 1981 permitting their growth. Over the last twenty years, they continued to grow because they allow employees to contribute pretax dollars. Moreover, evidence now suggests that 401(k) plans have better-targeted selection and retention effects than other pension types (Ippolito 1997), a point we return to below.

The conversion of traditional DB plans to cash balance plans has attracted a good deal of media and legislative attention in recent years. The cash balance plan was first created by Bank of America in 1985 (Clark and Schieber 2000). Initially, only a few companies copied this new type of pension, but by 1997, 6 percent of workers covered by DB plans in the private sector were in cash balance plans (Ippolito 2001). While this is a relatively small fraction of all covered workers, it was nearly double the coverage rate for cash balance plans found two years earlier. Since cash balance plans are virtually identical to DC plans, some of the explanations for the growth of DC plans can be used to explain why a firm would want to convert to a cash balance plan (i.e., increased portability and encouraging later retirement). An important question is why a firm would convert its DB plan to a cash balance plan instead of starting a new DC plan. One explanation is that terminating a DB plan and replacing it with a DC plan could have tax consequences that could be avoided by conversion to a cash balance plan (Ippolito 2001). Legislation passed in 1986 imposed a 10 percent excise tax on a reversion of assets from an overfunded DB plan, a tax rate increased to 15 percent in 1988, and to 50 percent in 1990. If a firm has an overfunded DB plan and wanted to switch to a DC plan, it would now have to pay the 50 percent reversion tax when it terminated the DB plan. On the other hand, if it simply converted to a cash balance plan, there would be no reversion of excess assets, yet now the firm has essentially established a DC plan and avoided the reversion tax.

Effects of Changing Pension Design on Selection and Retention

We illustrate how the switch from DB to DC plans affects various dimensions of productivity; the time path of wealth accrual in the two plans types may be compared. In a DB plan, the pension value at a particular age can be computed as the present value of the life annuity that the worker would receive if she terminated employment with the firm at that age. In a DC plan, the value of the pension at a particular age is simply the account balance determined by prior contributions plus accumulated interest. Given specific assumptions regarding plan parameters, these values can be computed explicitly. Following the U.S. Department of Labor (1999) data for medium and large establishments, we note that 95 percent of DB plans offer an early retirement option, with an average early retirement reduction factor of 4.9 percent per year. The most popular normal and early retirement ages are 65 and 55, respectively, and the average generosity rate is 1.5 percent per year of service. We use these parameters for our benchmark DB plan. In addition, the benchmark worker is assumed to begin employment with the firm at age 35 at a starting salary of $30,000. Both the nominal interest and wage growth rates are assumed to equal 6 percent. Under these assumptions, the contribution rate required in a DC plan to create an identical amount of wealth at normal retirement age is 14.6 percent.

Pension wealth is plotted for this hypothetical worker between ages 50 and 75 in our benchmark DB and DC plans in Figure 1. Since the contribution rate of the DC plan is chosen to generate the same level of pension wealth in the DB plan at age 65, the DB and DC wealth lines intersect at age 65. For a departure at any age other than 65, DB wealth is lower than DC wealth. This emphasizes the fact that, relative to DC plans, DB plans penalize early or late retirements.

An alternative way of comparing the incentives in DB and DC plans is to examine the rate at which pension wealth accumulates over time. We define pension accrual as the increase in pension wealth from one year to the next, subtracting out interest that is earned on the prior year's balance. Then the pension accrual rate is computed by dividing pension accrual by the worker's salary in that year. Figure 2 compares the pension accrual rates in our benchmark DB and DC plans. The accrual pattern in the DC plan is flat, as it equals the contribution rate assumed fixed over the worker's career. By contrast, in the DB plan, the accrual rate starts out low, rises until the normal retirement age, and then drops after the normal retirement age. In this particular comparison, the accrual rate in the DB plan is less than that in the DC before age 55 and after age 65. After age 55 and before age 65, the DB has the higher accrual rate.

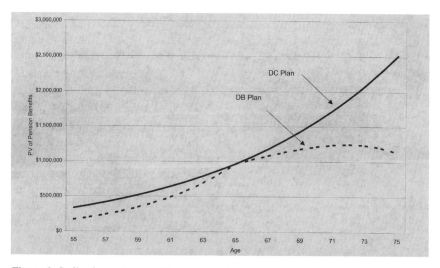

Figure 1. Stylized pension wealth patterns, defined benefit and defined contribution plans. Source: author's calculations.

If the worker leaves at any age other than age 65, he has less pension wealth accumulated in a DB than a DC plan. The difference between DB and DC wealth at a particular age has thus been referred to as a "capital loss" in the literature (Gustman and Steinmeier 1995). Early retirement provisions can reduce the capital loss for early retirees. The capital loss for the DB plan, with and without an early retirement provision, is illustrated in Figure 3. Here the DB plan capital loss rises from zero at age 35, to its peak at slightly over 1.5 times salary at age 51. Between age 51 age 65, the capital loss drops to zero. After age 65, the capital loss begins to rise again.

Because the DB and DC plans generate such different wealth accumulation profiles, they have the potential to affect workforce productivity in several ways. Specifically, relative to the DC plan (or a cash balance plan), the DB backloads pay and thus penalizes workers that leave prior to retirement. This has selection, retention, and direct productivity effects (Gustman, Mitchell, and Steinmeier 1994). The selection effects of a pension refer to the effect of the pension on the type of workers that are drawn to the firm. Retention effects refer to the impact of the pension on the chance that the worker quits.

Compared to a DC plan, a backloaded DB plan will be more attractive to workers who expect to stay with the firm for a long period of time. For example, women with below-average quit rates tend to work at firms with pension plans (Even and Macpherson 1990). Also firms with a pension (particularly a DB plan) are more attractive to workers with low discount rates, compared to firms without any pension.[1] The fact that pensions may attract low discounters suggests that they can attract workers who have

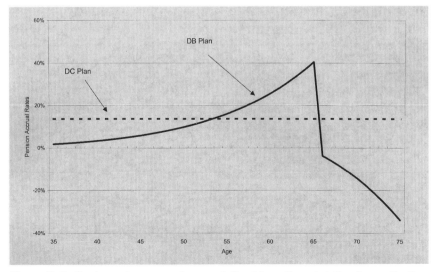

Figure 2. Stylized pension accrual rates, defined benefit and defined contribution plans. Source: authors' calculations.

a greater chance of being promoted, receive higher job performance ratings, and are less likely to call in sick (Ippolito 1997).

Though theory suggests that DB plans do more to retain employees than DC plans, this has proven difficult to show empirically. Thus in practice, workers with DB and DC plans have virtually identical turnover (Gustman and Steinmeier 1995; Even and Macpherson 1996). One explanation is that firms offering pensions might pay above-market or so-called "efficiency wages," so the high wages might dominate the backloading effect of DB plans. An alternative explanation for the DC effect on mobility might be that DC plans attract low discounters and low discounters are less likely to quit. The fact that new employees who do not participate in their company's 401(k) plan are more likely to quit supports this view (Kusko, Poterba, and Wilcox 1994; Ippolito 1997; Even and Macpherson 2001). This is consistent with Ippolito's (1997) theoretical model, which indicates that firms offering DB plans do a better job of stopping high discounters from accepting employment at the firm. Firms with DC plans do a better job of encouraging high discounters who are hired, to eventually quit.

Compared to traditional DC plans, a 401(k) pension has the potential to create yet distinct selection and retention effects. For example, in a traditional DC plan the employer contributes a fixed percentage of pay into the plan, whereas in a 401(k) plan the employee chooses how much to contribute and the employer provides a matching contribution. The 401(k) plan will be more successful at encouraging high discounters (less productive) workers to leave the firm since they will not value employer matching contributions. As a consequence, even though the firm may not be aware of

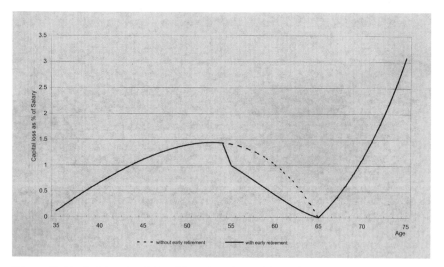

Figure 3. Capital loss in defined benefit plans with and without early retirement incentive feature. Source: authors' calculations.

which workers are actually high discounters, it is able to pay them less and encourage them to leave.

In addition to selection and retention effects, the switch to DC plans can also affect worker productivity by influencing monitoring costs and worker effort. For instance Lazear (1979) proposes that backloaded pay may be used to conserve on monitoring costs, arguing that workers shirk less when they are subject to a pension capital loss if they are dismissed. The evidence does support this view, in that DB plans appear to enhance productivity by 5 to 8 percentage points more than DC plans (Dorsey, Cornwell, and Macpherson 1998).

DC plans can also have other effects, potentially enhancing productivity by using company stock to tie worker compensation to firm profitability. There are numerous ways to make company stock part of the DC plan (Wiatrowski 2000). Employee stock ownership plans (ESOPs) are the most obvious mechanism, but employers also do this in other ways by providing matching contributions in 401(k) plans that take the form of company stock. Alternatively, a company can give employees the option to choose how their pension funds are invested and make company stock one of the choices. Yet another possibility is to include a stock purchase plan that allows employees to purchase company stock at a discount, or to provide a stock option plan, in either a qualified or nonqualified vehicle.

Two areas of research shed light on the extent to which employee stock ownership can enhance productivity: ESOP and executive compensation studies. In studies comparing ESOP with non-ESOP firms, most research reports finding the ESOP firms averaging 6.2 percent higher productivity (Blasi, Conti, and Kruse 1996). However, there is some evidence that such productivity effects are relatively small for larger companies, potentially reflecting free-rider problems. There is also a substantial body of research studying executive compensation in the United States, where much of the deferred compensation takes the form of company stock or stock options. The CEOs of the largest 500 industrial companies received approximately 35 percent of their compensation in the form of stock options in 1996; this was nearly 10 percentage points higher than observed four years previously (Murphy 2000). Several studies report positive effects of executive stocks or stock options on company performance, indicating that companies offering long-term incentive plans exhibited greater increases in return on equity than those without these plans (Leonard 1990; Murphy 1999; Abowd and Kaplan 1999).

While executives have long received compensation that is linked to company performance, the growth in DC plans now extends contingent compensation down to more levels of employees. Recent research indicates that if workers have company stock as an investment option in their 401(k) plan, approximately one-third of the assets were held in the form of company stock (VanDerhei, Holden, and Quick 2000). If the employer controlled the investment choice of at least part of the participant balances, slightly over one-half of the assets were held in company stock. In addition, stock option plans are now offered to rank-and-file employees, presenting yet another means of linking pay to company performance.

Nonmanagerial/nonprofessional employees are relatively unlikely to have stock option plans — available in only about 10 percent of publicly traded companies — but nearly one-half of the plans existing in 1998 were either expanded or added since 1996 (Lebow et al. 1999). These plans not only tie compensation to firm performance, but they also defer compensation by restricting the exercise date on the option to some point in the future. Of course a concern about linking pay and performance is that holding pension assets in employer stock reduces portfolio diversification and may subject employees to increased investment risk. In addition, if employees are heavily invested in company stock, companies may find it difficult to shed workers when profitability is low.

Effects of Changing Pension Design on Retirement Outcomes

Another way pensions can influence workforce patterns is via their retirement incentives. As the DC-covered worker approaches retirement, his pension accrual rate tends to be constant; by contrast in a DB plan, the accrual rate varies depending on the plan's early and normal retirement age provisions. Relative to a DC plan, a DB plan creates incentives to retire somewhere between the early and normal retirement age. The observed national switch to DC plans may therefore make it more difficult for firms to forecast labor force retirement patterns. Another issue is that of late, firms offering DB plans appear to have adjusted benefit formulas to reduce retirement incentives, relative to DC plans. For example, the fraction of percentage of DC-covered employees having a cost-of-living increase over the past five years dropped from 41 percent in 1985, to 4 percent in 1995 (U.S. Department of Labor various years). This decline might reflect the slowdown of inflation, but reduced cost-of-living adjustments do encourage workers to retire later.

Among DC plans, the growth of 401(k) plans might also influence retirement age patterns. One reason is that, relative to traditional DC plans, low-income workers save less in 401(k) plans, whereas middle and high income workers tend to be saving about the same (Even and Macpherson 1998). In addition, having 401(k) plans increased the variance of pension assets across workers, largely because of higher variance in contribution rates.[2] The greater variation in retirement asset accumulation will probably produce greater variation in retirement ages.[3]

Another important change in pension design is the effect of rate of return risk on the accumulation of pension assets. With DB plans, the rate of growth in pension assets is driven by variations in wage growth. In DC plans, variations in the rate of return on pension assets are important. In 401(k) plans, workers are frequently given control over the asset allocation of their pension accounts. Holden and VanDerhei (2001) estimate that three-quarters of 401(k) assets are held, directly or indirectly, in equity securities. Since workers in DC and 401(k) plans are exposed to greater rate of return risk, retirement behavior may become more sensitive to the performance of equity markets. Thus if equity markets perform poorly, the resulting wealth loss could prompt workers to defer retirement. Moreover, if workers have invested heavily in their employers' stock, their retirement wealth becomes closely tied to the firm's performance. When the firm is faced with declining demand and profits, stock prices drop and workers are less able to retire. This makes it more difficult for firms to shed workers through voluntary retirements when profits are falling (Rappaport this volume).

Changes in Employee Health Insurance Offerings

The percentage of U.S. workers with employer-provided health coverage has fallen in the last two decades, from 83 percent in 1980, to 71 percent in 2000. Additionally, workers with employer-provided health insurance are paying a larger share of the premium: covered workers who must pay some fraction of the premium rose from 56 percent in 1980, to 74 percent in 2000 (authors' tabulations of March Current Population Surveys). Additional evidence on employees of medium and large firms indicates that those having to pay part of the cost of single coverage rose from 36 percent to 69 percent between 1985 and 1997, and the percentage contributing toward the cost of family coverage rose from 56 to 80 percent over the same period (U.S. Department of Labor various years).

Undoubtedly, rapidly escalating health insurance costs are part of the explanation for declining health insurance coverage rates and increased employee contributions toward coverage. These changes in health insurance benefits will have selection and retention effects that could have both positive and negative effects on firm profits. Of course, employer-provided health insurance is likely to be most attractive to workers with health problems, risk averse workers, and workers with low discount rates. As yet, however, there is no empirical evidence demonstrating how the selection effects of employer-provided health insurance coverage might work, in terms of discount rates or risk aversion.

By contrast, there is a long literature establishing the fact that firms offering health insurance tend to draw less healthy workers (Cutler and Zeckhauser 2000). One interesting feature of employer-provided health insurance is that, like DB pensions, it provides a means to backload pay. If firms require all workers to contribute an identical dollar amount for health insurance (either implicitly or explicitly), they effectively reward older workers with a more valuable benefit. For example, data from three private insurance carriers reveals that the typical health insurance premium is 3.5

to 4.0 times higher for a 60-year-old than for a 30-year-old, and the annual cost of the plans is between $2,100 and $3,500 higher for the 60-year-old (<www.ehealthinsurance.com>). Health insurance coverage also rewards men and women differentially: at young ages, private insurance markets charge higher rates for women. At older ages, the reverse is true. Differential usage and differential premium charges also reward married and single people differentially: many employers charge employees less than the marginal cost of family coverage and thus favor married workers, particularly those with large families. If all employees contributed the same dollar amount for coverage, offering health insurance would select and retain older workers, workers with families, and workers without coverage from a spouse. Retention of unhealthy workers will be exacerbated by the fact that many insurance plans do not cover preexisting conditions, resulting in what has been called "job lock" in the literature. One study found that employer-provided health insurance cuts voluntary turnover by 25 percent (Madrian 1994).[4]

As the cost of health insurance has risen over time, these selection and retention effects will become more pronounced. Increased heterogeneity in the workforce, along the lines outlined by Riche (this volume), may also amplify the effects. For example, as the fraction of workers with spouses that also have coverage increases, workers will place less value on employer-provided subsidies for family care, and the firm will have greater difficulty in attracting and retaining such employees. If firms find these selection and retention effects of health insurance undesirable, they can dampen the effects by charging extra for family and/or individual coverage, which may explain the trend toward larger percentages of employees having to pay for health insurance costs, as noted above.

A new model recently arrived on the health insurance scene is the "defined contribution" health insurance plan as distinct from the traditional "DB" approach to health plans (EBRI 2000). In the old model, employers elected a health insurance plan and assumed the risk regarding premium fluctuations. In a DC health insurance model, the employer typically promises to contribute a fixed dollar amount toward the health plan, and the employee must pay for any cost in excess of the employer contribution. Employees are usually offered a menu of health insurance options to choose among. The DC health insurance plan can be designed so that the employer reduces the variance in its contribution for health insurance across employees. This, in turn, makes it less likely that the health insurance plan generates undesirable selection or retention effects.

Changes in Retiree Health Insurance Offerings

U.S. companies have also moved away from offering retiree health insurance coverage over time, as indicated in Table 1. Here we report the fraction of full-time private sector workers with health insurance coverage, where the health insurance was also offered to retirees. In 1988, 45 (37) percent of workers were in plans that provided benefits to retirees under age 65 (Medicare eligible); this had fallen to 35 (34) percent by 1997. In addition, the percentage of employees having to pay part of the cost of retiree health insurance has also grown over time. Among workers with health insurance coverage for retirees under age 65, the share of workers with retiree health coverage completely paid for by the employer fell from 53 to 29 percent between 1988 and 1997. The corresponding figures for coverage for Medicare eligible retirees are 54 percent and 32 percent.

A number of empirical studies have examined whether retiree health insurance influences retirement patterns, and the majority concludes there is a powerful effect. For instance Karoly and Rogowski (1994) find that men aged 55–62 with retiree health insurance coverage are 8 percentage points more likely to retire early over a two-year period, a change equal to 50 percent of the baseline probability. Other studies also find that older workers with retiree health coverage are more likely to retire early.[5] To the extent that retiree health insurance coverage is falling over time, this will reduce companies' ability to induce early retirement. This may be exacerbated to the extent that the Medicare program experiences financial shortfalls in years to come.

TABLE 1. Trends in Employee Participation in Company-Sponsored Medical Plans, by Provision for Coverage After Retirement

	Participation rates (%)					
	1988	1989	1991	1993	1995	1997
Under Age 65 With employer-paid retiree health insurance coverage	45	41	43	44	36	35
Retiree contribution	21	21	23	27	25	22
Employer pays all	24	18	16	13	9	10
Not determinable	<1	1	4	4	4	3
Age 65 and over With employer-paid retiree health insurance coverage	37	36	41	41	32	34
Retiree contribution	16	18	20	23	22	20
Employer pays all	20	17	17	14	6	11
Not determinable	<1	1	4	4	4	3

Source: U.S. Department of Labor (various years). Includes full-time employees in medium and large private establishments.

Conclusions

We have reviewed the theoretical and empirical literature on the impact of pensions and health insurance on assorted dimensions of employee productivity. As pensions continue to shift from DB to DC plans, we believe this will have predictable effects on selection, retention, and retirement patterns. First, since the DC is a more portable pension, employee retention rates could fall. Second, DC plans present employees with a different type of retirement income risk and may attract a different type of worker than a DB plan. Third, linking retirement to capital market performance will make retirement patterns more volatile, as they respond to stock market returns. Last, including company stock in DC portfolios can improve productivity by linking pay to company performance, but it also might make it more difficult to induce retirement during slow economic periods.

Changes in health insurance offerings will also have productivity effects. As health care inflation rises, due partly to population aging, this will continue to spur employers' interest in "defined contribution" health plans as distinct from the traditional defined benefit offerings. Some firms may pull back from offering health plans at all, since doing so attracts certain types of workers that may be problematic, the more heterogeneous the workforce becomes. Additional research on how benefit plans influence worker productivity would be most fruitful. For example, relatively little is known about the selection and retention effects of particular aspects of 401(k) design, including matching rates, use of company stock, investment education, and the like. It would also be interesting to better understand how the shift from DB to DC plans will affect future retirement patterns. Finally, if employers are less likely to offer, and pay for, active and retired worker health insurance, it will be important to investigate alternative models for coverage in the future.

Notes

1. Curme and Even (1995) show that, controlling for other personal characteristics, the probability of coverage by a DB plan is 14 percentage points lower for workers who are borrowing-constrained than for those who are not. The effect of borrowing constraints on DC coverage is not statistically significant.

2. For an analysis of the adequacy of retirement savings for the typical household near retirement age, see Moore and Mitchell (2000).

3. Moreover, following the logic of Ippolito (1997), the high discounters (bad workers) will accumulate the least in their 401(k) plans and will be the least able to afford retirement at an early age. Offsetting this, however, is the fact that high discounters may be willing to retire with a lower pension balance since they place a lower value on their standard of living in the late years of life.

4. Gruber and Madrian (1994) imply that the "job-lock" associated with health insurance has been reduced by the 1985 Consolidated Omnibus Budget Reconciliation Act (COBRA). Prior to this act, more than twenty states had passed continuation of

coverage laws legislation mandating employers to provide departing workers the opportunity to purchased continued coverage for a limited period of time.

5. Blau and Gilleskie (1997) find that retiree health insurance increases the job exit rate by 26 percent to 80 percent of the baseline probability and Rogowski and Karoly (2000) report that the upper-bound effect of retiree health insurance on exit rates is 68 percent of the baseline probability. Using earlier data, Gustman and Steinmeier (1994) find a smaller impact of retiree health insurance; however, Rogowski and Karoly (2000) suggest that their study underestimates the effect of retiree health insurance due to measurement error in their eligibility for retiree health measure.

References

Abowd, John M. and David S. Kaplan. 1999. "Executive Compensation: Six Questions That Need Answering." NBER Working Paper 7124. May.

Blasi, Joseph, Michael Conte, and Douglas Kruse. 1996. "Employee Stock Ownership and Corporate Performance Among Public Companies." *Industrial and Labor Relations Review* 50, 1 (October): 60–79.

Blau, David M. and Donna B. Gilleskie. 1997. "Retiree Health Insurance and the Labor Force Behavior of Older Men in the 1990's." NBER Working Paper 5948.

Clark, Robert L., Ann A. McDermed, and Michelle White Trawick. 1993. "Firm Choice of Type of Pension Plan: Trends and Determinants." In *The Future of Pensions in the United States*, ed. Ray Schmitt. Pension Research Council. Philadelphia: University of Pennsylvania Press. 115–25.

Clark, Robert L. and Sylvester J. Schieber. 2000. "An Empirical Analysis of the Transition to Hybrid Pension Plans in the United States." Paper presented at Conference on Public Policies and Private Pensions, Brookings Institution, Washington, D.C., September.

Cutler, David M. and Richard Zeckhauser. 2000. "The Anatomy of Health Insurance." In *Handbook of Health Economics*, vol. 1a, ed. Anthony J. Culyer and Joseph P. Newhouse. Amsterdam: Elsevier. 563–643.

Curme, Michael A. and William E. Even. 1995. "Pension Coverage and Borrowing Constraints," *Journal of Human Resources* 30, 4 (Fall): 701–12.

Dorsey, Stuart, Christopher Mark Cornwell, and David A. Macpherson. 1998. *Pensions and Productivity*. Kalamazoo, Mich.: W.E. Upjohn Institute for Employment Research.

Employee Benefit Research Institute (EBRI). 1997. *EBRI Databook on Employee Benefits*. 4th ed. Washington, D.C.: Employee Benefit Research Institute.

———. 2000. *EBRI Heath Benefits Databook*. Washington, D.C.: Employee Benefit Research Institute.

———. 2001. "EBRI Research Highlights: Retirement and Health Data." *EBRI Issue Brief* 229. January.

Even, William E. and David A. Macpherson. 1990. "The Gender Gap in Pensions and Wages." *Review of Economics and Statistics* 72, 2 (May): 259–65.

———. 1996. "Employer Size and Labor Turnover: The Role of Pensions." *Industrial and Labor Relations Review* 49, 4 (July): 707–28.

———. 1998. *The Impact of Rising 401(k) Pension Coverage on Future Pension Income*. Report to Pension and Welfare Benefits Administration, U.S. Department of Labor, Washington, D.C. May.

———. 2001. "Determinants and Effects of Employer Matching Contributions in 401(k) Plans." Working Paper. Miami University Department of Economics, Oxford, Ohio.

Farber, Henry S. 2000. "Mobility and Stability: The Dynamics of Job Change in Labor Markets." In *Handbook of Labor Economics*, vol. 3, ed. Orley Ashenfelter and David Card, Amsterdam: Elsevier Science, North-Holland. 2439–83.

Fullerton, Howard N., Jr. 1999. "Labor Force Projections to 2008: Steady Growth and Changing Composition." *Monthly Labor Review* 122, 11 (November): 19–32.

Gruber, Jonathan and Brigitte C. Madrian. 1994. "Health Insurance and Job Mobility: The Effects of Public Policy on Job-Lock." *Industrial and Labor Relations Review* 48, 1 (October): 86–102.

Gustman, Alan L. and Thomas L. Steinmeier. 1992. "The Stampede Toward DC Pension Plans: Fact or Fiction?" *Industrial Relations* 31, 2 (Spring): 361–69.

———. 1994. "Employer Provided Health Insurance and Retirement Behavior." *Industrial and Labor Relations Review* 48, 1 (October): 124–40.

———. 1995. *Pension Incentives and Job Mobility.* Kalamazoo, Mich.: W.E. Upjohn Institute for Employment Research.

Gustman, Alan L., Olivia S. Mitchell, and Thomas L. Steinmeier. 1994. "The Role of Pensions in the Labor Market: A Survey of the Literature." *Industrial and Labor Relations Review* 47, 3 (April): 417–38.

Holden, Sarah and Jack L. VanDerhei. 2001. "401(k) Plan Asset Allocation, Account Balances, and Loan Activity in 1999." *EBRI Issue Brief.* February.

Ippolito, Richard A. 1995. "Towards Explaining the Growth of DC Plans." *Industrial Relations* 34, 1 (January): 1–20.

———. 1997. *Pension Plans and Employee Performance.* Chicago: University of Chicago Press.

———. 2001. "Issues Surrounding Cash Balance Plans." Working Paper. George Mason University School of Law, Washington, D.C.

Karoly, Lynn and Jeannette Rogowski. 1994. "The Effect of Access to Post-Retirement Health Insurance on the Decision to Retire Early." *Industrial and Labor Relations Review* 48, 1 (October): 103–23.

Kruse, Douglas. 1995. "Pension Substitution in the 1980s: Why the Shift Toward DC?" *Industrial Relations* 34, 2 (April): 218–41.

Kusko, Andrea, James M. Poterba, and David Wilcox. 1994. "Employee Decisions with Respect to 401(k) Plans: Evidence from Individual Level Data." NBER Working Paper 4635. February.

Lazear, Edward P. 1979. "Why Is There Mandatory Retirement?" *Journal of Political Economy* 87, 6 (December): 1261–84.

Lebow, David, Louise Sheiner, Larry Slifman, and Martha Starr-McCluer. 1999. "Recent Trends in Compensation Practices." Working Paper. Washington, D.C.: Board of Governors of the Federal Reserve System. July.

Leonard, Jonathan S. 1990. "Executive Pay and Firm Performance." *Industrial and Labor Relations Review* 43, 3 (February): 13–29.

Madrian, Brigitte C. 1994. "Employment-Based Health Insurance and Job Mobility: Is There Evidence of Job-Lock?" *Quarterly Journal of Economics* 109, 1 (February): 27–54.

Mitchell, Olivia S. with Erica L. Dykes. This volume. "New Trends in Pension Benefit and Retirement Provisions."

Moore, James F. and Olivia S. Mitchell. 2000. "Projected Retirement Wealth and Saving Adequacy." In *Forecasting Retirement Needs and Retirement Wealth*, ed. Olivia S. Mitchell, P. Brett Hammond, and Anna M. Rappaport. Pension Research Council. Philadelphia: University of Pennsylvania Press. 68–94.

Murphy, Kevin J. 2000. "Executive Compensation." In *Handbook of Labor Economics*, vol. 3, ed. Orley Ashenfelter and David Card. Amsterdam: Elsevier Science, North-Holland. 2485–2563.

Papke, Leslie. 1999. "Are 401(k) Plans Replacing Other Employer-Provided Pensions? Evidence from Panel Data." *Journal of Human Resources* 34, 2 (Spring): 346–68.

Rappaport, Anna M. This volume. "Implications of a Difficult Economy for Company-Sponsored Retirement Plans."

Riche, Martha Farnsworth. This volume. "The Demographics of Tomorrow's Workplace."

Rogowski, Jeannette and Lynn Karoly. 2000. "Health Insurance and Retirement Behavior: Evidence from the Health and Retirement Survey." *Journal of Health Economics* 19, 4 (July): 529–39.

U.S. Department of Labor. 1989, 1990. *Employee Benefits in Medium and Large Firms, 1988 and 1989.* Bureau of Labor Statistics Bulletin. Washington, D.C.: U.S. Government Printing Office.

———. 1993, 1995, 1998, 1999. *Employee Benefits in Medium and Large Private Establishments (various years).* Bureau of Labor Statistics Bulletin. Washington, D.C.: U.S. Government Printing Office.

———. 1999. *Employee Benefits in Medium and Large Private Establishments 1997.* Bureau of Labor Statistics Bulletin. Washington, D.C.: U.S. Government Printing Office.

VanDerhei, Jack, Sarah Holden, and Carol Quick. 2000. "401(k) Plan Asset Allocation, Account Balances, and Loan Activity in 1998." *EBRI Issue Brief 218.* February.

Wiatrowski, William J. 2000. "Putting Stock in Benefits: How Prevalent Is It?" *Compensation and Working Conditions* 5, 3 (Fall): 2–7.

Chapter 3
How Demographic Change
Will Drive Benefits Design

Marjorie Honig and Irena Dushi

This is a time of profound change in the American labor force. The work-force is older than ever before. Growing awareness of increased life expectancy is focusing attention on the financial demands of longer lifetimes and may induce delayed retirement. This financial motivation is reinforced by the rising age of eligibility for full Social Security benefits, pension conversions to age-neutral wealth accrual profiles, and increasingly, employer cutbacks in retiree health insurance benefits (see Lofgren, Nyce, and Schieber this volume). Women comprise an increasing share of the labor force at all ages, drawing greater attention to their need to balance family and work responsibilities. Finally, the racial and ethnic composition of the population is changing, altering the mix of cultural attitudes toward family and work (Riche this volume).

This chapter examines how the aging of the labor force and its changing composition will influence the future demand for employer-sponsored benefits. We investigate the age, sex, racial, and ethnic patterns of demand for employer-sponsored 401(k) plans, health and disability insurance, and family-oriented benefits, and evaluate their implications for the desired mix of benefits in the future. We focus here on benefits that tend to be discretionary for the employee; that is, we exclude benefits such as pensions and paid vacations that, if offered, are provided to all covered employees at a workplace (Mitchell this volume). We also focus our analysis on benefits that impose an explicit cost to the employee in terms of contributions, deferred compensation, or foregone alternative benefits. This is so that we can separately identify demand for these benefits from the demand for other characteristics of the job, to the extent possible.

Employer-Sponsored Saving: 401(k) Plans

Plans such as 401(k)s in the private sector (and 403(b) plans in the public and nonprofit sectors) are voluntary individual savings accounts, to which employers and employees may contribute. These are a form of defined contribution plan and permit tax deferral of employee contributions.[1] Taxable income is reduced by employee contributions up to a limit of $11,000 in 2002 (gradually increasing to $15,000 by 2006), and the allowable total of employee and employer contributions will rise from 50 percent of the employee's salary in 2002 to 100 percent in 2011 and thereafter.[2] Investment returns are tax-free and withdrawals are taxed as income. Withdrawals prior to age 59½ incur a 10 percent tax penalty if they are not rolled over into another qualified account. Employers who contribute into these accounts may make either a fixed contribution, or they can match part or all of employee contributions.

To determine how an aging labor force might alter the demand for employer-provided savings mechanisms such as 401(k) plans, we ask whether age per se appears to influence the decision to participate in such plans, after controlling for other economic and demographic factors that might influence these decisions. An economic life cycle model of saving behavior would predict that workers borrow against future earnings early in their work lives, to finance family formation and the purchase of homes. During middle age, they start to consume less than they earn, permitting them to pay off debts and begin accumulating assets. These assets accrue interest, to be reclaimed and consumed later, when workers' abilities or tastes for work are diminished. Tax considerations also play a role, since the value of tax-deferred saving rises with income. For this reason older persons may continue to save even beyond retirement. A desire to leave a bequest, along with increased longevity, may also extend the saving period among older persons.

In the United States, 401(k) plans are discretionary for employees in the sense that decisions regarding participation and current contributions are not directly tied to the employment decision (unlike automatic enrollment in defined benefit and non-401[k] defined contribution plans). To analyze how age influences the demand for 401(k) plans, we undertake statistical analysis of pension participation by age. Specifically, we ask whether employees offered plans are enrolled (have a nonzero balance), and, conditional on having an account, whether they expect to contribute to accounts during the year. Since employees may enroll in plans at any time, and those with previously established plans can opt to cash out account balances (usually with a penalty) or decide not to make further contributions to an account, their participation at any given age reflects current interest in this form of saving.

We analyze the employee decision to participate in a 401(k) plan as a function of plan features, firm characteristics, and characteristics of the individual reflecting his or her life cycle stage, liquidity position, and time preference. In addition to age, we include a number of demographic characteristics expected to influence the saving decision including sex, race, ethnicity, marital status, and education. We are particularly interested in whether the decision to participate in a 401(k) differs by sex because of the increasing proportion of women in the older labor force. Measures of income and wealth (earnings, spouse earnings if married, and home ownership) are included because higher income is likely to be associated with lower liquidity constraints and with larger benefits from tax deferral of income.

Further factors influencing plan participation include an indicator of whether the employer contributes to employee accounts in the form of a fixed contribution or a match to employee contributions. Plans with employer contributions increase the initial return on employee savings and thus provide an incentive to employees to participate. Because many workers offered a 401(k) plan in our data responded that they do not know if their employer contributes to accounts, we control for employee knowledge of employer contributions.[3] We also include a variable indicating whether a worker is covered by a defined benefit or non-401(k) defined contribution retirement plan. The predicted effect of these pensions is theoretically ambiguous. They may indicate stronger preferences for saving, in which case their availability would have a positive influence on enrollment in 401(k) plans, or they may allow retirement saving goals to be attained in the absence of additional saving through a 401(k) plan.[4]

This analysis examines 2,532 male and 2,070 female full-time workers aged 16–64 employed in firms offering 401(k) plans, drawn from the 1993 Employee Benefits Supplement to the April Current Population Survey (CPS).[5] Men and women are examined separately, because of our interest in examining the implications of the increasing share of women in the labor force, and because saving decisions at each age may differ by gender and marital status may affect such decisions differentially by gender.

401(k) Participation Results

Figure 1 depicts influences on the probability of participation in a 401(k) plan for full-time male and female workers offered plans by their employers. Age, race, and ethnicity are examined, as well as marital status and the employment status of spouses of married workers. Bars indicate the difference in the likelihood of participation of a particular group, ages 16–24, for example, relative to a reference age group (ages 35–44), calculated as a percentage of the mean participation rate.[6] An asterisk above or below the bar indicates that this difference is statistically significant at the 5 percent level or higher.

This figure indicates that older male employees are equally likely to participate in a 401(k) plan as are middle-aged workers (ages 35–44, the base group), after holding constant other demographic characteristics and a number of economic factors predicted to affect saving in a tax-deferred employer-sponsored plan. By contrast, middle-aged female employees ages 45–54 (55–64) are 13 (30) percent more likely to enroll in a 401(k) plan relative to the base age group. This suggests that life cycle motivations to save differ by sex, perhaps due to differential concerns about financing longer lifetimes, by the enhanced benefits of tax-deferral among higher-wage workers, by diverse bequest motives, or by the length of time spent in the labor force. The results also show that younger workers save less, as predicted by the life cycle model. Males ages 16–24 are 27 percent, and females 28 percent, less likely to have a positive balance in a 401(k) plan.

The likelihood of participation in 401(k) plans does not vary significantly by race: non-Hispanic black employees and those of other races (primarily Asian) enroll at the same rates as non-Hispanic white employees. Men of Hispanic origin, however, are significantly less likely (19 percent) to enroll relative to their non-Hispanic counterparts.

Married women with nonworking spouses are 24 percent less likely to participate in a 401(k) plan than are single women, but women with working spouses are no more likely to participate than single women.[7] Neither marriage nor the working status of a spouse influences the participation decisions of men, however. No other influences on this decision, including control variables not shown in Figure 1, are statistically different between men and women.[8]

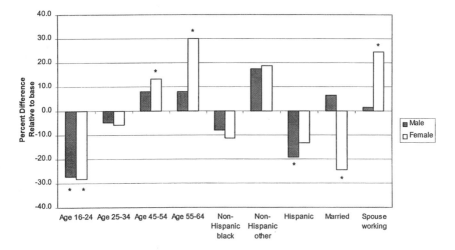

Figure 1. 401(k) plan participation by age, race/ethnicity, and sex: percent difference, full-time workers offered plans. Source: authors' calculations. Percent change represents marginal effect on 401(k) participation relative to the sample mean. * denotes significance at 5 percent level or higher.

401(k) Contribution Results

Holding a current balance in a 401(k) account may reflect a previous saving decision that, because of employee inertia, remains in place. In this case, a more contemporaneous measure of employee saving in 401(k) plans may therefore be provided by examining whether employees are currently contributing to their accounts. Figure 2 shows how groups differ relative to a reference group in their probability of making a contribution during the current year. The groups examined are employees with positive account balances by age, race, ethnicity, and by whether the employer provides matching contributions, the effect of which differs significantly by sex.[9]

Here age plays no special role for men or women: younger and older employees are no less or more likely to make a contribution to an existing 401(k) account than are their age 35–44 counterparts. Non-Hispanic black men and women are, however, 27 and 23 percent, respectively, less likely to contribute to their accounts than their non-Hispanic white counterparts. Also, Hispanic women are 33 percent less likely to contribute than non-Hispanic women. Interestingly, among Hispanics, men are less likely to have a 401(k) account (Figure 1) and women with accounts are less likely to contribute to them, relative to non-Hispanics. Having an employer who matches

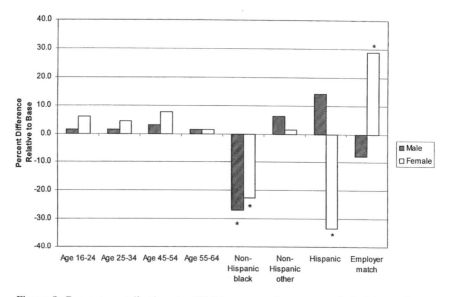

Figure 2. Current contributions to 401(k) accounts by age, race/ethnicity, and sex: percent difference, full-time workers with accounts. Source: authors' calculations. Percent change represents marginal effect on 401(k) participation relative to the sample mean. * denotes significance at 5 percent level or higher.

contributions increases the probability that women contribute by 29 percent, but has no effect on whether men contribute.[10]

Results for 401(k) Participation and Contributions for Employees in New Jobs

To provide another measure of decision making regarding 401(k) plans, we next examine the participation and contribution decisions of full-time workers with less than five years of tenure on their jobs. Among older workers, new jobs may represent "bridge" jobs after retirement from long-term career jobs, which are increasing in importance as older workers extend their working lives, or they may reflect the impact of unanticipated job changing resulting from the increased incidence of downsizing among older workers in recent years (Siegel et al. 2001). On leaving an employer, a worker must make an explicit decision to cash out a 401(k) account or to roll it over into a new 401(k) account with the new employer, if this option is available, or into an IRA. Thus, the decision to participate in 401(k) plans in new jobs offering the option reflects current or recent demand for this savings vehicle.

To evaluate this, Figure 3 shows differences in the probability of participation in a 401(k) plan just for employees with fewer than five years employment in jobs offering plans.[11] Age and race/ethnicity patterns differ from those in Figure 1: men ages 16–24 on new jobs are no less likely to

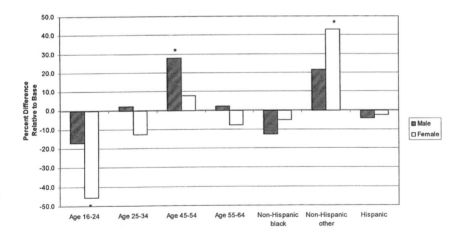

Figure 3. 401(k) plan participation by age, race/ethnicity, and sex: percent difference, full-time workers with tenure less than five years offered plans. Source: authors' calculations. Percent change represents marginal effect on 401(k) participation relative to the sample mean. * denotes significance at 5 percent level or higher.

participate in 401(k) plans than their counterparts of ages 35–44; however, older men (45–54) are 28 percent more likely to participate than middle-aged employees. For women the opposite pattern operates: young women (16–24) are 46 percent less likely to enroll, but older women are no more likely to enroll than middle-aged women.

Non-Hispanic women of "other" races in new jobs are 43 percent more likely to participate than their non-Hispanic white counterparts, whereas there is no significant difference between these two racial groups in Figure 1. Hispanic men at all tenure levels (Figure 1) were less likely to participate than non-Hispanic men; in new jobs, however, there are no differences in participation between these two groups.[12] There are no observed age differences in the likelihood of contributing to existing 401(k) accounts in new jobs among either women or men, and only one racial difference: Non-Hispanic black women are 46 percent less likely to contribute than non-Hispanic white women.[13] We thus do not provide a corresponding figure for contributions into accounts on new jobs.

In summary, these age patterns suggest that workers in their 50s and 60s are at least as likely to hold balances in 401(k) plans as workers in their late 30s and early 40s, other things equal. Furthermore, women ages 45–64 and new male hires ages 45–54 are more likely to participate in 401(k) plans. On these grounds, we infer that demand for such plans will remain strong, as the representation of older workers in the labor force increases. Moreover these patterns suggest that a rising share of women in an aging labor force will also add to demand for this form of saving. This is because 401(k) participation rates are higher among women ages 45–64 compared to middle-aged women, than are the rates of older men relative to middle-age men. Our findings also suggest that an increasing proportion of workers of Hispanic origin in the labor force may increase participation in 401(k) plans.

Employer-Sponsored Health Insurance

It is likely that the future demand for job-based health insurance will also rise, for several reasons. Health care needs increase with age, boosting demand for coverage and shifting demand toward medical services most pertinent to older workers' health problems. However, the costs of providing employer-sponsored insurance may also grow: older workers are likely to require more expensive medical services per health care incident than will younger employees, and they may also have a higher incidence of medical care interventions. Health insurance will become more costly as employers pass on increased health insurance costs rather than reduce other employee benefits or wages. Price increases can be reflected directly through increases in employee contributions, co-payments, and deductibles, or indirectly through reductions in covered services and frequency of services.

Price increases would be expected to reduce the demand for health insurance by some older workers (after controlling for health needs), and since employers cannot offer differential health packages to younger and older employees (Reno and Eichener 2000), this will likely curtail younger workers' demand as well.

An increasing share of women among younger full-time workers might be expected to expand demand for employer-provided health insurance toward those related to reproductive services, and away from services directed toward younger men. The extent of this shift, and the consequent burst in employer costs, will depend on the relative expenses of these services and the net increase in demand for insurance. The latter will vary depending on the extent to which demand for these services by women is already being met by coverage under husbands' insurance, and the extent to which increased labor market activity by women further reduces the number of children per household. The effect on demand for medical services, and thus employers' insurance costs, arising from the increased proportion of women in the older labor force, depends on whether older women require fewer or more medical services than older men, or less or more expensive services, and the extent to which these services are currently covered under family coverage.

Finally, the extent to which the changing racial and ethnic composition of the population changes the demand for employer-based health insurance depends on the differential health needs of the populations concerned and their relative attitudes toward risk. Wide disparities in health status and insurance coverage have been found across racial and ethnic groups. Among adults ages 18–64, Hispanics and blacks are more likely than whites to be in fair or poor health and less likely to be in excellent health (Weigers and Drilea 1996). Furthermore, lack of insurance is far more common among Hispanics (35 percent) than among either blacks (25 percent) or whites (15 percent). Racial and ethnic minorities, particularly Hispanics, are both more likely to lack access to job-based coverage and to turn it down when it is available (Cooper and Schone 1997).[14]

Only 39 percent of full-time workers in the private sector offered health insurance are offered coverage for themselves fully paid by their employers; only 22 percent are offered family coverage fully paid by their employers (McDonnell and Fronstin 1999). Thus, participation in an employer-sponsored insurance plan is a discretionary decision involving costs to the majority of workers that must be weighed against competing claims on the household budget. We posit that the demand for job-related health insurance is a function of current and projected individual and family health needs, the relative price of employer-sponsored insurance, and individual and family preferences regarding risk. In the absence of a direct measure of workers' health status, we posit that health needs are negatively correlated with education, income, and wealth, and positively correlated with age. Since lower income and wealth may be associated with greater liquidity constraints that may inhibit households from purchasing insurance, however, we are unable to predict a priori the effect of income and wealth, measured here by family earnings and home ownership, on the demand for health insurance. Family health needs are measured by the presence of a spouse and/or minor children. The relative price of own-employer insurance is a function of its price, and the prices of medical services purchased directly in the market, quality-equivalent individual insurance purchased in the market, and, for married workers, coverage under a spouse's plan. Lacking good data on such prices, we include coverage under another health insurance plan and, for married workers, coverage under a spouse's plan. We also control for whether the employer offers workers the opportunity to obtain coverage at a group rate after retirement. We include sex, race, and ethnicity to reflect individual and cultural differences in risk preferences.

To assess the impact of age and labor force diversity on the probability of participation in an employer-sponsored health insurance plan, we use a sample of 11,441 full-time workers in the 1993 Employee Benefits Supplement to the April CPS who reported that they were offered and eligible to participate in a plan offered by their employer.[15] This sample is split by sex and marital status because the health needs of men and women may differ over the life cycle and family coverage may be available through spouses' plans.[16] Because information on whether the employer offers retiree insurance is provided only for workers aged 45 and above, we interact a dummy variable for the availability of retiree insurance with the age categories of 45–54 and 55–64. This interaction term indicates the additional effect of retiree insurance coverage on the probability of participating in an employer's health insurance plan.[17] The effect of the age variable alone indicates the probability of participation, relative to the omitted age group, for workers not offered this option.

Figure 4 shows how the probability of participating in an employer's health insurance plan varies by age, race, and ethnicity for married full-time male and female workers offered and eligible for coverage, vis-à-vis a baseline group. Three additional influences on the participation decision — the availability of retiree insurance, education, and the presence of children — are also included because their effects differ by sex.[18] Participation rates are very high for both groups: .94 for men and .82 for women (see Appendix Table 4). Figure 4 indicates that there are statistically important age differences in the likelihood of enrolling in an employer's health insurance plan, although the magnitudes of these variations are not large. Among younger employees, married women ages 16–24 are 9 percent less likely, and men ages 25–34 are 3 percent less likely, to enroll than employees ages 35–44, the reference group.

The availability of retiree health insurance is a strong influence on the demand for health insurance among older workers. Among employees in firms not offering retiree insurance, men ages 45–54 are more likely (by 5 percent) to enroll than men ages 35–44, whereas there is no difference among women between these two age groups (this difference by sex is statistically significant). By contrast, both women and men ages 45–64 in firms offering retiree insurance are more likely to participate, by six to 14 percent more.[19]

There are also significant racial differences in participation in employer health insurance. Non-Hispanic black men and women are more likely to participate (by 4 and 6 percent, respectively) than non-Hispanic white employees. Non-Hispanic men of other races are also more likely to enroll (6 percent more).[20] Interestingly, a high school diploma or above increases enrollment in health insurance by men (from 5 to 8 percent depending on level of education), but not by women. The presence of children decreases participation by women by four percent, but does not affect the decisions of men.[21] Participation in employer-sponsored health insurance among single employees does not exhibit the strong age and racial differences observed for married employees and we therefore do not include a figure with results for this group. The only important age-related effect is higher participation (by 6 percent) by men ages 45–54 who are offered retiree health insurance (Appendix Table 3, cols. 3 and 4).[22]

What are the implications of these findings for a changing labor force? The most striking result is that older workers' demand for health plans that include the option of retiree insurance is very strong. Enrollment rates of older married employees in these plans are significantly higher than in plans not including this option, and thus likely to increase as the labor force ages. Delayed retirement may attenuate this change, but on net, it is likely

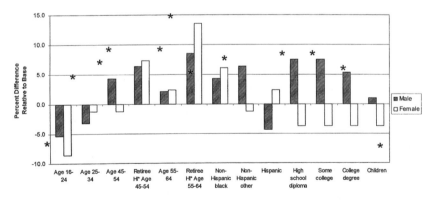

Figure 4. Probability of participation in health insurance plan by age, race/ethnicity, and sex: percent difference, full-time married workers offered and eligible for coverage. Source: authors' calculations. Percent change represents marginal effect on health insurance.

that an older workforce will exert increased pressure on employers to provide retiree insurance. Employer provision of retiree insurance has declined over time in response to its higher cost, however.[23] Thus a reversal of the trend of the past decade will undoubtedly involve shifting more of the costs to retirees, constricting some of the expected increase in demand.

Participation in plans with provision for retiree insurance is strikingly high among older married men and women. If the insurance policy does not include this option, demand is weaker among women than men, however. Thus, the effect of an increasing share of women in an older labor force may be to reduce demand for employer-sponsored health insurance overall. By contrast, more non-Hispanic non-white employees would be expected to increase demand for health insurance benefits.

Employer-Sponsored Disability Insurance

An aging labor force may also influence the demand for job-based disability insurance, which provides partial wage replacement in the case of temporary or permanent inability to work.[24] For one, older workers are more likely to be disabled, boosting demand for this type of insurance. The price of this insurance would be anticipated to rise if more claimants comprise a larger share of an employer's workforce. This increase in price, whether direct or through benefit reductions, would be likely to decrease demand by younger workers. The cost of short-term disability insurance is usually paid by employers. However, disability insurance is often included as one of the competing options in a firm's cafeteria health plan so selection of this type of benefit may preclude the selection of an alternative benefit. Employers providing long-term disability coverage often offer a base wage replacement rate (40 percent is common) at no or low cost to the employee but provide higher replacement rates with pro-rated employee contributions.

To examine the empirical link between demand for job-related disability insurance and workforce mix, we again turn to the 1993 Employee Benefits Supplement of the April CPS. These data do not report workers' health or disability status so we again must posit that good health and the absence of disability are positively correlated with income, education, and wealth (measured here by family earnings and home ownership), and negatively correlated with age. We include sex, race, and ethnicity variables to reflect individual and cultural differences in disability status and risk preferences.

As above, we examine only full-time workers offered and eligible for employer-provided health insurance, and who knew whether their employers provided short-term/long-term disability insurance.[25] Unfortunately, survey respondents were not asked whether they were offered this form of insurance. Rather, they were asked only if they would receive benefits if they became disabled, that is, whether they opted for this type of insurance when offered. Because we are unable to identify all employees offered disability coverage, we use as our sample employees offered *health* insurance on the assumption that this group is most likely among full-time workers to have been offered short- and long-term disability insurance.[26] Our findings therefore provide only rough estimates of differences in take-up rates by age, sex, race, and ethnicity.[27]

Figure 5 depicts patterns in the decision to elect short-term disability insurance among full-time employees by age, race and ethnicity, and two additional factors whose effects differ by sex — earnings and health insurance coverage.[28] There is only one significant age difference and the magnitude is small: men ages 45–54 are 4 percent more likely to elect coverage for short-term disability than employees ages 35–44, the reference group. There are also racial and ethnic differences, although once again the magnitudes are small. Non-Hispanic black men and women are 6 and 5 percent, respectively, more likely to elect coverage than non-Hispanic white employees. Non-Hispanic women of other races, however, are 8 percent less likely to opt for this coverage.

Among both men and women, earnings have small, but statistically important effects on participation in short-term disability insurance. Interestingly, the direction of the effect differs and this difference is statistically significant. A 10 percent increase in weekly earnings is associated with a lower likelihood of enrolling among men, but a higher likelihood among women (resulting in changes of about 1 percent in participation). Participating in the employer's health plan, treated as jointly determined with

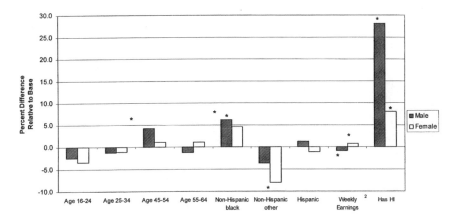

Figure 5. Short-term disability insurance participation by age, race/ethnicity, and sex: percent difference, full-time workers offered health insurance. Source: authors' calculations. Percent change represents marginal effect on short-term disability insurance participation relative to the sample mean. Weekly earnings indicates change resulting from 10 percent increase in monthly earnings. * denotes significance at 5 percent level or higher.

disability insurance to account for unobserved risk aversion, is associated with higher enrollment rates for both men and women, but the magnitude of the effect is significantly larger for men than for women (an increase of 28 percent among men compared to 8 percent for women). [29]

Age differences are more striking for participation in long-term disability insurance than for short-term insurance (Figure 6).[30] The youngest women (ages 16–24) are 23 percent more likely to enroll in coverage for long-term disability compared to middle-aged women, and women ages 25–34 are 8 percent more likely. Enrollment for disability coverage among women during their reproductive years is not unexpected, although it is somewhat surprising that this pattern is not reflected in short-term disability coverage as well. Older men (ages 55–64), by contrast, are 13 percent less likely to opt for long-term disability coverage. The latter finding suggests that older men may have met saving goals so that the loss of earnings does not jeopardize retirement living standards to the extent that it may for middle-aged employees.[31]

There are also strong differences by race and ethnicity in participation in long-term disability insurance, and the pattern varies from that observed in Figure 5 for short-term disability. Non-Hispanic black men are 10 percent more likely to opt for long-term disability coverage than non-Hispanic white men, but non-Hispanic men of other races are 21 percent less likely

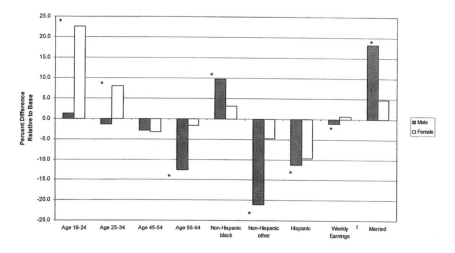

Figure 6. Long-term disability insurance participation by age, race/ethnicity, and sex: percent difference, full-time workers offered health insurance. Source: authors' calculations. Percent change represents marginal effect on short-term disability insurance participation relative to the sample mean. Weekly earnings indicates change resulting from 10 percent increase in monthly earnings. * denotes significance at 5 percent level or higher.

to elect coverage. Hispanic men are 11 percent less likely to enroll than their non-Hispanic counterparts. By contrast, there are no differences by either race or ethnicity among women.

The effects of earnings on participation are identical to those observed for short-term disability. Ten percent higher earnings are associated with a decline in the likelihood of participation among men but an increase among women. Both effects are small, about a 1 percent change in participation, but the difference between men and women is significant. The effect of being married also differs by sex: marriage increases the likelihood that men will opt for this coverage by 18 percent but does not influence enrollment rates among women.[32]

These findings suggest that the increasing participation of women of childbearing age in full-time jobs is likely to increase demand for long-term disability insurance, but that an aging labor force is likely to offset this change. The relatively higher demand among older men for temporary earnings replacement would be expected to increase participation in short-term disability insurance, as those of ages 45–54 are going to comprise a higher proportion of the labor force of the future.

Employer-Sponsored Family Benefits

Over the last two decades, employee compensation packages have become considerably more complex, due in large part to the addition of a number of family-oriented benefits — family leave, flexible work schedules, unpaid time off, and child and elder care assistance. Interest in these benefits has grown because there are more married women in the labor force and because increases in the divorce rate and in childbearing outside marriage have increased the number of single parents in the labor market. These trends have set the stage for a national debate on how to balance the competing interests of work and family. Polls indicate that the public believes it is important for employers to provide more "family-friendly policies."[33] Family benefits are appearing at the bargaining table between employers and unions; the newest products of collective bargaining include round-the-clock childcare, health and wellness programs, and access to continuing education. The evidence presented below suggests that companies are offering more extensive work/life policies and programs to help workers balance work and family responsibilities. Anecdotal evidence indicates that firms are also turning to alternative forms of compensation such as allowing parents to bring infants to work and providing childcare, recreation programs for teenagers, and book clubs for retirees (Belluck 2000; Greenhouse 2000).

Although the development of family-related policies has focused primarily on childcare, eldercare assistance has been on the agenda for at least a decade. The proportion of the elderly requiring help with daily activities increased from 35 percent in 1984 to nearly 43 percent ten years later (Tracey 2000). Middle-aged and older workers are thus more likely to face greater demands on their time from elderly parents and relatives, and interest in work arrangements such as flexible scheduling and assistance with arranging elder care is likely to increase in the future.[34]

In this section, we examine trends over time in the proportion of employees offered family-related benefits. We use published data for 1989–97 from the Employee Benefits Surveys (EBS) in Medium and Large Firms of the Bureau of Labor Statistics. We also use published data for 1995 and 2000 from the Family and Medical Leave Act (FMLA) Establishment Surveys and the related Employee Surveys commissioned by the Department of Labor.[35]

Changes over time in the proportion of full-time employees in medium and large firms offered various types of family benefits are shown in Table 1. The proportions of full-time workers offered family benefits such as childcare, adoption assistance, and long-term care insurance increased slightly over time, but eldercare assistance increased substantially between 1989 and 1993, the only years for which data are available. Flexible benefits plans and reimbursement accounts allow employees to pay for expenses such as childcare, eldercare, and medical care deductibles not covered by other plans on a salary reduction basis.[36] The proportions of employees offered these plans increased from 13 percent in 1988 to 54 percent in 1995, but then decreased to 45 percent in 1997. Coverage for medical benefits such as well-baby care and immunization increased substantially from 31 and 29 percent, respectively, in 1988, to 66 and 52 percent in 1997. This evidence suggests that in recent years an increasing proportion of employees in medium and large firms have been offered family-related benefits.

While there was little change between 1988 and 1997 in the percentage of employees offered *paid* time off, the proportion offered *unpaid* leave increased considerably during this period. The proportion of employees offered unpaid maternity leave increased from 33 to 60 percent, and the proportion offered unpaid paternity leave increased from 16 to 53 percent. Following the introduction of FMLA in 1993, which requires employers to provide unpaid leave but does not address the issue of paid leave, the proportion of full-time employees offered unpaid family leave (both maternity and paternity leave) increased from 84 percent in 1995 to 93 percent in 1998.[37]

The FMLA Establishment Surveys of 1995 and 2000 provide information on the proportion of firms offering family-related benefits. While only 11 percent of establishments are covered by the FMLA, they represent 58 percent of all employees (Cantor et al. 2001). Among firms covered by the FMLA, 84 percent offered all five types of benefits mandated by FMLA in 2000, whereas only 34 percent of noncovered establishments offered these benefits. The gap, moreover, had narrowed since 1995, when 88 percent of covered establishments offered benefits, compared to 21 percent of noncovered establishments. It appears that uncovered establishments were increasingly providing family benefits in order to compete with covered establishments in a tight labor market. However, the majority of uncovered establishments do not provide all benefits mandated by the FMLA, and many grant family and medical leave "depending on the circumstances," and not always to all employees all of the time (Cantor et al. 2001).

We now turn to the FMLA Employee Surveys of 1995 and 2000 to examine the characteristics of employees exercising family benefit leave options provided under FMLA. The proportion of workers taking leave remained fairly constant (about 16 percent) between 1995 and 2000 (Table 2). In

TABLE 1. Family Benefits: Percentage of Full-Time Employees Offered Coverage

	1988	1989	1991	1993	1995	1997
Medical benefits						
Well-baby care	31	34	36	48	60	66
Immunization and innoculation	29	28	30	37	47	52
Family benefits						
Child care	4	5	8	7	8	10
Adoption	5	5	8	7	11	10
Elderly care	na	3	9	31	na	na
Long-term care insurance	na	3	4	6	6	7
Flexible benefit plans and/or reimbursment accounts	13	24	37	53	54	45
Employee assistance programs	43	49	56	62	58	61
Family time-off benefits						
Paid						
Personal leave	24	22	21	21	22	20
Maternity leave	2	3	2	3	na	na
Paternity leave	1	1	1	1	na	na
Family leave	na	na	na	na	2	2
Unpaid						
Maternity leave	33	37	37	60	na	na
Paternity leave	16	18	26	53	na	na
Family leave[1]	na	na	na	na	84	93

Source: Author's tabulations from EBS in Medium and Large Firms, U.S. BLS (selected years).
* After passage of the FMLA in 1993, maternity and paternity leave are included in the broader category of family leave. Family leave includes paid and unpaid leave for maternity, adoption, care of a newborn child, and family illness. Also included is short-term leave, which is paid time off from work for reasons such as childrens' medical appointments and parent-teacher conferences.
na = not available.

both years, the most common reasons for the longest leave were the employee's own health, care for a newborn or newly adopted child, and care for an ill parent. Between 1995 and 2000, the incidence of leave-taking for own health decreased from 61 to 47 percent. At the same time, the incidence of leave-taking to care for an ill parent increased from 8 to 11 percent, and for an ill spouse, from 4 to 6 percent. Leave-takers in both years were more likely to be female and middle-aged (35–49). Over the five-year period, the proportion of leave-takers ages 50–64 increased by one-third (from 15 to 20 percent).

We might have expected that, with the introduction of FMLA in 1993, the proportion of employees taking leave would have increased more than indicated in Table 2. There are many reasons, however, why employees may be reluctant to take up this option — concerns shown in the bottom panel of Table 2. More than half of all employees reported that they worried about not having enough money to pay bills, and about one-quarter worried either that their job might be lost or that a leave would hurt advancement.[38]

TABLE 2. Employees Taking Leaves from Work: Reason for Leave by Demographic Characteristics

Leave-takers as percentage of employees	1995	2000
Reason for taking the longest leave	16	17
Own health*	61	47
Maternity-disability*	5	8
Care for a newborn, newly adopted, or placed foster child	14	18
Care for ill child	9	10
Care for ill spouse*	4	6
Care for ill parent*	8	11
Demographic characteristics		
Sex		
Male	44	42
Female	56	58
Age		
18–24	11	10
25–34	30	28
35–49	41	40
50–64*	15	20
65+	3	2
Concerns about leave		
Job might be lost		27
Leave might hurt job advancement		26
Seniority would be lost		13
Not having enough money for bills		54
Other reasons		13

Source: Derived from Cantor et al. (2001).
* Denotes significant change between 1995 and 2000 surveys.

We now examine the distribution of reasons for leave by age and sex in 1995 and 2000 (Table 3). For both men and women, the largest change over this period is the shift from leave-taking for one's own health reasons to leave-taking for family concerns. In 2000, both men and women were more likely to take leave to care for an elderly parent and men were more likely to take leave to care for a newborn or older child than in 1995. Men and women of all ages, and particularly employees age 35 and older, were much more likely to take a leave in 2000 to care for parents than five years previously. We expect this trend to continue as the baby boom generation ages and experiences increased care-giving demands from parents. Younger leave-takers (ages 18–34) were more likely to take maternity disability leave and to care for a newborn, adopted, or foster child.

Respondents in the 2000 FMLA Survey of Employees were asked whether their employers provided benefits other than those covered under FMLA. A high proportion (45 percent) reported that they were offered flextime; 43 percent reported they were offered employee assistance; and 25 percent reported they were offered job sharing (Figure 7). These proportions match quite closely the proportions of employees rating the respective benefits as important (the largest discrepancy is unmet demand for flextime) and suggest that employers are responding to the needs of their workforces.

In summary, the evidence confirms that family-oriented benefits have become an important part of the employee compensation package. Increasingly, firms are providing benefits that accommodate the work-and-family pressures felt by an increasing share of employees. As the workforce ages and

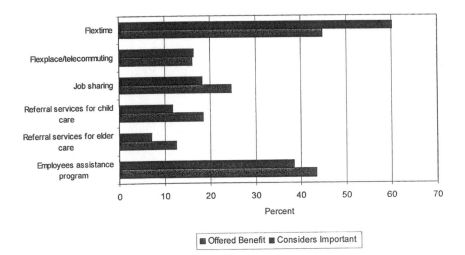

Figure 7. Employees offered benefits not covered under Family and Medical Leave Act and perceiving benefits as important. Source: Cantor et al. (2001).

Page 76 Marjorie Honig and Irena Dushi

TABLE 3. Leave-Takers by Reason for the Longest Unpaid Leave, by Age and Gender (percent)

Year	Own health		Maternity-disability		Care for newborn, adopted, or foster child		Care for children		Care for spouse		Care for parents	
	1995	2000	1995	2000	1995	2000	1995	2000	1995	2000	1995	2000
Sex												
Male	67	52	—	—	15	22	7	9	6	7	6	10
Female	57	44	8	13	14	15	10	10	2	5	9	12
Age												
18–24	59	49	10	24	18	19	8	—	—	—	—	—
25–34	43	29	9	13	28	39	12	9	3	3	5	7
35–49	67	49	2	4	9	10	8	16	4	6	11	16
50+	83	66	—	—	—	—	—	4	7	11	6	13

Source: Derived from Cantor et al. (2001).

the share of women continues to increase, we expect that family benefits will become an even larger part of employee compensation. An enhanced benefit package, however, is likely to come at a cost to the employee in terms of lower wage growth. As a result, wage compensation can be expected to comprise a smaller share of total compensation (Gruber 1998).

Conclusions

An aging labor force, with increasing shares of women and minorities, is likely to change the mix of nonwage compensation offered by employers and desired by employees. There is little evidence that older workers have any lesser interest in saving through 401(k) plans than workers in their 30s. Indeed, older women at all tenure levels are more likely to maintain 401(k) accounts, as are older men in new jobs. The frequency of contributions into these accounts, moreover, does not diminish with age. Not surprisingly, demand for health insurance is greater among older employees, especially if it includes the option of coverage after retirement at group rates. We predict that demand for short-term disability insurance will increase, but demand for long-term disability will decrease, because earnings replacement for older workers is more critical in the short run than over an extended period that may approach, or exceed, the expected remaining work life.

Finally, we foresee an increased demand for a wide range of family-related benefits due to the increasing family-and-work needs of women with children and of middle-aged and older workers of both genders with elderly parents. Changes in the provision of these benefits in the last few decades suggest that employers appear to be responding to these needs and that the compensation package for future workers may be more benefits intensive than its current configuration.

APPENDIX TABLE 1. Probability of Participation and Contribution in 401(k) Plan: Full-Time Workers Offered Plans (robust standard errors in parentheses)

	All tenure levels				Tenure less than five years			
	Participation		Contribution		Participation		Contribution	
	Male	Female	Male	Female	Male	Female	Male	Female
	(1)	(2)	(3)	(4)	(5)	(6)	(7)	(8)
Age 16–24	-.17** (.06)	-.15** (.06)	.01 (.07)	.04 (.07)	-.08 (.07)	-.18** (.06)	-.11 (.10)	.01 (.10)
Age 25–34	-.03 (.03)	-.03 (.03)	.01 (.03)	.03 (.04)	.01 (.05)	-.04 (.05)	.04 (.06)	.07 (.07)
Age 45–54	.05 (.03)	.07* (.03)	.02 (.03)	.05 (.04)	.13* (.07)	.03 (.06)	-.02 (.08)	.06 (.08)
Age 55–64	.05 (.04)	.16** (.05)	.01 (.04)	.01 (.05)	.01 (.11)	-.03 (.12)	.04 (.11)	.01 (.15)
Non–Hispanic black	-.05 (.05)	-.06 (.04)	-.17** (.06)	-.15** (.06)	-.06 (.08)	-.02 (.07)	-.09 (.10)	-.29** (.11)
Non–Hispanic other	.11 (.06)	.10 (.06)	.04 (.06)	.01 (.07)	.10 (.10)	.17* (.09)	-.01 (.11)	-.08 (.12)
Hispanic	-.12* (.06)	-.07 (.06)	.09 (.06)	-.22** (.08)	-.07 (.08)	-.02 (.08)	.14 (.11)	-.13 (.12)
High school diploma	.05 (.05)	.07 (.07)	.07 (.06)	.09 (.10)	-.02 (.09)	.03 (.12)	.11 (.12)	.23 (.16)
Some college	.08 (.05)	.07 (.07)	.07 (.06)	.08 (.10)	-.06 (.09)	.06 (.12)	.10 (.12)	.20 (.16)
College degree	.14** (.05)	.06 (.07)	.14* (.06)	.08 (.10)	-.05 (.10)	.02 (.13)	.16 (.13)	.17 (.19)

Weekly earnings/1000	.22**	.33**	.03	.08	.35**	.29**	.02	.11
	(.04)	(.06)	(.04)	(.06)	(.07)	(.09)	(.07)	(.11)
Married	.03	-.13**	-.06	-.06	.13*	-.07	-.16*	-.01
	(.04)	(.05)	(.04)	(.06)	(.06)	(.08)	(.07)	(.12)
Spouse working	.02	.13**	.08**	.03	-.08	.10	.15**	-.01
	(.03)	(.05)	(.03)	(.06)	(.05)	(.08)	(.06)	(.12)
Home ownership	.04	.11**	.03	.05	-.02	.10*	.03	-.03
	(.03)	(.03)	(.03)	(.04)	(.04)	(.04)	(.06)	(.06)
His DB or DC pension[1]	.03	.06*	.04	.10**	.08	.09	.05	.13
	(.02)	(.03)	(.02)	(.03)	(.06)	(.06)	(.07)	(.08)
Employer match[2]	.12**	.15**	-.05	.19**	-.06	-.02	.05	.20*
	(.04)	(.04)	(.04)	(.05)	(.07)	(.07)	(.08)	(.10)
Mean of dependent variables	0.63	0.53	0.63	0.66	0.47	0.40	0.61	0.64
N observed	2532	2070	1582	1098	903	870	430	360
Pseudo R²	.08	.08	.02	.04	.08	.07	.04	.04

Source: Author's calculations using Employee Benefits Supplement to the 1993 April CPS.
The dependent variable equals 1 if the individual participates/contributes to a 401(k) plan. Probit estimates indicate marginal probability effects calculate at the sample means. They measure the marginal effect of a one unit change in a continuous variable on the probability of participation/contribution, and the average difference of the predicted probability of a dummy variable being 0 and 1. Adjusted CPS adult supplement weights are used. Omitted age, racial, and educational categories are age 35–44, non-Hispanic white, and less than high school diploma, respectively. * and ** denote significance at the 5 percent and 1 percent levels, respectively.
[1] Variable treated as endogenous.

APPENDIX TABLE 2. Sample Means for 401(k) Plan Participation and Contribution Equations: Full-Time Workers Offered Plans (percent)

	All tenure levels				Tenure less than five years			
	Participation		Contribution		Participation		Contribution	
	Male	Female	Male	Female	Male	Female	Male	Female
	(1)	(2)	(3)	(4)	(5)	(6)	(7)	(8)
Age 16–24	6.6	7.8	3.2	4.4	15.7	16.4	8.8	9.7
Age 25–34	28.1	28.9	25.3	25.6	42.1	41.1	41.9	40.8
Age 35–44	32	30.4	33.1	31	27.1	25.0	29.5	28.9
Age 45–54	23.2	24	26.8	27.7	10.9	14.3	14.9	16.9
Age 55–64	10.1	8.8	11.5	11.3	4.1	3.1	4.9	3.6
Non-Hispanic white	85.7	81.5	87.3	83.6	83.1	80.7	84.2	82.2
Non-Hispanic black	5.9	9.2	5.1	7.7	7.5	8.3	6.5	6.7
Non-Hispanic other	3.3	4.2	3.9	4.6	3.6	4.6	5.1	5.6
Hispanic	4.3	4.3	3.3	3.4	5.2	5.9	3.9	5.3
High school drop out	5.8	3.3	4.6	2.4	6.1	4.0	4.9	2.5
High school diploma	27.4	30.6	25.2	29.6	26.4	26.8	25.3	24.7
Some college	28.2	31.0	26.5	29.7	28.9	32.9	24.2	31.4
College degree	38.6	35.0	43.7	38.3	38.6	36.3	45.6	41.4
Weekly earnings ($)	730	527	802	585	616	459	719	512
(standard deviation)	(373)	(273)	(385)	(296)	(352)	(249)	(385)	(284)
Married	73.3	58.2	77.6	60.2	62.3	55.5	69.3	59.7
Spouse working (married)	67.8	87.1	67.3	88.2	68.9	88.6	66.1	90.7
Home ownership	76.2	71.8	81.0	78.2	59.1	57.6	63.7	64.7
Has DB or DC pension	54.3	52.4	58.8	59.4	32.8	33.1	43.9	43.3
Employer match	28.9	25.1	34.7	32.2	28.5	24.3	38.1	34.4
Mean of dependent variable	0.63	0.53	0.63	0.66	0.47	0.40	0.61	0.64
N observed	2532	2070	1582	1098	903	870	430	360

Source: See Appendix Table 1.

APPENDIX TABLE 3. Probability of Participation in Employer-Sponsored Health and Disability Insurance: Full-Time Workers Offered and Eligible for Coverage (robust standard errors in parentheses)

	Health insurance				Short-term disability		Long-term disability	
	Married		Single					
	Male	Female	Male	Female	Male	Female	Male	Female
	(1)	(2)	(3)	(4)	(5)	(6)	(7)	(8)
Age 16–24	-.05 (.04)	-.07* (.03)	.01 (.04)	.02 (.03)	-.02 (.03)	-.03 (.03)	.01 (.04)	.14** (.03)
Age 25–34	-.03* (.01)	-.01 (.01)	.02 (.03)	.01 (.02)	-.01 (.01)	-.01 (.02)	-.01 (.02)	.05* (.02)
Age 45–54	.04* (.01)	-.01 (.02)	.01 (.04)	.01 (.03)	.03* (.01)	.01 (.02)	-.02 (.02)	-.02 (.02)
Age 55–64	.02 (.02)	.02 (.02)	.06 (.04)	.05 (.02)	-.01 (.02)	.01 (.02)	-.09** (.03)	-.01 (.03)
Non-Hispanic black	.04* (.02)	.05** (.01)	.04 (.02)	.01 (.02)	.05** (.02)	.04* (.02)	.07* (.03)	.02 (.03)
Non-Hispanic other	.06** (.021)	-.01 (.03)	.03 (.03)	.04 (.02)	-.03 (.03)	-.07* (.04)	-.15** (.05)	-.03 (.05)
Hispanic	-.04 (.02)	.02 (.02)	-.04 (.05)	.02 (.02)	.01 (.02)	-.01 (.03)	-.08 (.04)	-.06 (.04)
Retiree HI* Ages 45–54	.06** (.02)	.06** (.01)	.06* (.01)	—[1]	—	—	—	—
Retiree HI* Ages 55–64	.08** (.01)	.11** (.01)	—	.04 (.03)	—	—	—	—
Has spouse HI²	-.13** (.03)	-.14** (.01)	—	—	—	—	—	—
Has other HI²	-.10** (.02)	-.05** (.02)	-.15** (.04)	-.15** (.04)	—	—	—	—
High school diploma	.07** (.02)	-.03 (.03)	-.03 (.04)	.02 (.02)	.08** (.02)	.09** (.02)	.08* (.03)	.08* (.04)
Some college	.07** (.02)	-.03 (.03)	-.03 (.04)	.04 (.02)	.13** (.01)	.13** (.02)	.10** (.03)	.11** (.04)

APPENDIX TABLE 3 (continued)

	Health insurance				Short-term disability		Long-term disability	
	Married		Single					
	Male	Female	Male	Female	Male	Female	Male	Female
	(1)	(2)	(3)	(4)	(5)	(6)	(7)	(8)
College degree	.05*	-.03	-.03	.02	.20**	.16**	.20**	.12**
	(.02)	(.03)	(.05)	(.02)	(.01)	(.02)	(.03)	(.04)
Weekly earnings/1000	.09**	.09**	.07	.26**	-.10**	.14*	-.11**	.10
	(.02)	(.03)	(.05)	(.07)	(.03)	(.05)	(.04)	(.06)
Children	.01	-.03**	-.02	-.02	—	—	—	—
	(.01)	(.01)	(.02)	(.02)				
Married	—	—	—	—	.09**	.03	.13**	.03
					(.02)	(.03)	(.03)	(.03)
Spouse working	.08*	.09**	—	—	.01	.02	.01	.06
	(.05)	(.03)			(.01)	(.02)	(.02)	(.03)
Home ownership	.01	-.02*	.05*	.03	.02	.04*	.03	.04
	(.01)	(.01)	(.02)	(.02)	(.01)	(.02)	(.02)	(.02)
Has HI²	—	—	—	—	.23**	.07**	.40**	.31**
					(.02)	(.02)	(.03)	(.03)
Mean of dependent variable	0.94	0.82	0.93	0.94	0.82	0.87	0.71	0.62
N observed	5664	3733	790	1254	6241	4902	5483	4182
Pseudo R²	.10	.09	.14	.15	.10	.07	.09	.06

Source: Authors' calculation using Employee Benefits Supplement to the 1993 April CPS. The dependent variable equals 1 if the individual participates in the plan. Probit estimates indicate marginal probability effects calculated at the sample means. They measure the marginal effect of a one unit change in a continuous variable on the probability to enroll in a plan, and the average difference of the predicted probability of a dummy variable being 0 and 1. Adjusted CPS adult supplement weights are used. Omitted age, racial, and educational categories are ages 35–44, non-Hispanic white, and less than high school diploma respectively.
* and ** denote significance at the 5 percent and 1 percent levels respectively.
[1] Insufficient variation to estimate the marginal effect.
[2] Variable treated as endogenous.

APPENDIX TABLE 4. Sample Means in Employer-Sponsored Health and Disability Insurance Equatios(%): Full-Time Workers Offered and Eligible for Coverage

	Health insurance				Short-term disability		Long-term disability	
	Married		Single					
	Male	Female	Male	Female	Male	Female	Male	Female
	(1)	(2)	(3)	(4)	(5)	(6)	(7)	(8)
Age 16–24	2.7	4.7	30.5	15.5	4.6	5.2	4.5	4.6
Age 25–34	26.8	29.9	35.4	31.5	27.9	29.8	27.0	29.0
Age 35–44	34.1	33.7	21.9	32.2	33.2	33.7	33.7	34
Age 45–54	24.6	23.7	10.8	13.2	23.3	23.2	23.6	24.1
Age 55–64	11.8	8.1	1.4	7.6	10.9	8	11.2	8.3
Non-Hispanic white	85.7	83.8	75.9	67.3	85.0	79.9	85.8	80.2
Non-Hispanic black	4.9	6.6	11.8	20.9	5.7	10.3	5.1	10.3
Non-Hispanic other	3.4	3.8	4.6	4.5	3.4	3.9	3.3	3.8
Hispanic	5.0	4.7	6.8	6.2	4.9	4.9	4.7	4.7
Retiree HI* Age 45–54	11.1	8.1	4.2	—	—	—	—	—
Retiree HI* Age 55–64	5.8	3.1	—	3.1	—	—	—	—
Has Spouse HI	13.6	35.7	—	—	—	—	—	—
Has Other HI	5.9	5.1	10.8	8.4	—	—	—	—
High school drop out	8.3	5.5	9.2	7.0	8.2	5.8	7.9	5.5
High school diploma	32.0	35.8	43.7	41.6	33.3	37.1	32.7	37.2
Some college	27.0	28.3	28.7	32.5	27.4	29.0	27.4	29.1
College degree	32.7	30.4	18.4	18.9	31.1	28.1	32.0	28.2
Weekly earnings ($)	714	489	482	422	694	479	709	486
(standard deviation)	(377)	(261)	(291)	(226)	(375)	(256)	(380)	(259)
Children	60.5	51.5	31.3	52.1	—	—	—	—
Married	—	—	—	—	88.8	74.2	89.2	74.6
Spouse working (married only)	68.5	86.4	—	—	68.6	86.6	68.6	86.6
Home ownership	82.3	81.9	73.0	60.1	81.5	77.1	82.2	77.9
Has HI	—	—	—	—	91.6	81.9	91.4	81.6
Mean of dependent variable	0.94	0.82	0.93	0.94	0.82	0.87	0.71	0.62
N observed	5664	3733	790	1254	6241	4902	5483	4182

Source: See Appendix Table 3.

Notes

1. We thus refer to 401(k) plans and non-401(k) defined contribution plans.

2. At the time the data used in this study were collected (1993), the limit on employee contributions was $10,500 and the total of employee and employer contributions could not exceed the lesser of $35,000 or 25 percent of the employee's salary. These limits were in effect through 2001 and were raised in the Economic Growth and Tax Relief Reconciliation Act of May 2001, effective 2002.

3. Some 40 percent of men and 46 percent of women among full-time workers do not know if their employer contributes to their retirement account. Our empirical analysis uses a two-stage procedure to first estimate the probability of an employer match as a function of individual, firm, and industry characteristics, controlling for knowledge of the match, and second we include the predicted value of the match in both participation and contribution equations.

4. We exclude tenure on the current job because there is no theoretical basis for including tenure in a savings function. Several analysts have found longer tenure, when included as an exogenous variable, associated with a higher probability of participating in a 401(k) plan (Andrews 1992; Even and Macpherson 1995; Munnell et al. 2000). Even and Macpherson (1999), however, found tenure insignificant when treated endogenously. Our preliminary analysis confirmed their findings so we omit it as a regressor in our analysis.

5. The 1993 supplement is the last of three CPS supplements (earlier surveys were in 1983 and 1988) providing detailed information on a number of employer-sponsored benefits. Currently there are no plans to continue this series. The samples from the 1993 supplement used in this analysis exclude part-time employees and the self-employed as well as workers for whom critical data are missing. We exclude part-time employees because the saving functions of the youngest and oldest workers in particular, whose decisions are of special interest in this study and who have relatively high rates of part-time employment, may differ depending on whether they are in part-time or full-time jobs. Overall, offer and participation rates are higher for full-time employees (39 and 68 percent, respectively) than for part-timers (14 and 41 percent, respectively).

6. Estimated mean participation rates are 0.63 for men and 0.53 for women (Appendix Table 2; this table also includes mean values of explanatory variables). These results are based on profit estimations of the probability of participation in 401(k) plans that control for education, earnings, home ownership, pension coverage, and whether the employer contributes to the 401(k) plan. Marginal probability estimates appear in Appendix Table 1, cols. 1 and 2. Reported marginal probabilities and differences by sex are based on an interaction model using a pooled sample.

7. Because we include a variable for whether an employee's spouse is working, the bar in Figure 1 for being married represents the effect of being married on 401(k) participation for employees with a nonworking spouse. The bar representing a working spouse shows the additional effect of having a working spouse. The effect on participation of being married and having a working spouse is measured by the sum of the two effects.

8. A number of other factors were found to significantly influence the participation decisions but these effects did not differ between men and women (see Appendix Table 1). A 10 percent increase in earnings increases the probability of participation by 3 percent among both men and women. Among men, having a college degree increases the probability of participation by 22 percent relative to participation among high school dropouts. Homeownership increases participation by women by 21 percent. Being covered by a defined benefit or non-401(k) defined contribution pension, treated as jointly determined with participation to remove

unobserved tastes for saving, increases participation by women by 11 percent. The presence of an employer matching contribution, also treated as an endogenous influence, increases the probability of participation among men and women by 19 and 28 percent, respectively.

9. Specifically, survey respondents are asked whether they intend to make a contribution in the current year. Marginal probability estimates appear in Appendix Table 1 (cols. 3 and 4). Among employees with 401(k) accounts, the estimated mean probability of intending to contribute is 0.63 for men and 0.66 for women (Appendix Table 2). About 25 percent of account holders reported that they did not know if their employers matched their contributions.

10. Two other factors influence contribution decisions but do not differ significantly between men and women. As in the case of the participation decision, a college degree increases (by 22 percent) the likelihood that men will contribute to their accounts and having a pension increases (by 15 percent) the likelihood that women will contribute.

11. Marginal probability estimates appear in Appendix Table 1, cols. 5 and 6. The estimated mean probability of participation in new jobs is 0.47 for men and 0.40 for women (Appendix Table 2).

12. One other important influence on participation in 401(k) plans differs between all jobs and new jobs (see Appendix Table 1, cols. 5 and 6). For men and women at all tenure levels, an employer match is a powerful incentive to participate, but not for employees in new jobs. Other influences on participation are similar between the two groups of jobs. Among women, being a homeowner and having a pension plan increase the probability of participating in a 401(k) plan in both cases. Higher weekly earnings also increase participation in both cases for men and women alike.

13. Small cell sizes may contribute to the lack of significant contribution effects among workers in new jobs. Marginal probability estimates appear in Appendix Table 1, cols. 7 and 8. Contribution rates are significantly lower (by 26 percent) for men with nonworking spouses, and 31 percent higher for women whose employers match their contributions. Among employees in new jobs who have a 401(k) account, 61 percent of men and 64 percent of women expect to contribute in the current year (Appendix Table 2).

14. Based on data from the 1987 National Medical Expenditure Survey and the 1996 Medical Expenditure Panel Survey (MEPS), the authors find that the rate of access to job-based insurance for Hispanic workers fell from 71 percent in 1987 to 67 percent in 1996, although it remained stable for other groups. Take-up rates declined from 1987 to 1996 for all racial/ethnic groups, and take-up rates of Hispanic workers were significantly lower than those of white workers in both years.

15. As above, we exclude part-time employees, the self-employed, and those for whom critical data are missing.

16. The four subsamples consist of 5,664 married men, 3,733 married women, 790 single men, and 1,254 single women.

17. Workers in the omitted category, ages 35–44, may be in firms offering retiree insurance. To the extent that their decision to participate in their firm's health plan is influenced by this option (which we believe unlikely), the marginal effects for age 45+ represent lower-bound estimates of the effect of the availability of retiree insurance.

18. The results shown in Figure 4 are based on profit estimations of the probability of participation in employer-sponsored health insurance, and control for coverage under spousal and other types of insurance, weekly earnings, homeownership, and employment status of spouse. Marginal probability estimates appear in Appendix Table 3 (cols. 1 and 2).

19. The bars above variables "Age 45–54" and "Age 55–64" indicate the probability of enrolling (relative to ages 35–44) of employees in firms not offering retiree insurance, while the interaction terms, "Retiree HI *Age 45–54" and "Retiree HI *Age 55-64," indicate the probability of participation by employees offered retiree health insurance (relative to ages 35–44).

20. This is not the case for women of other races, and the difference by sex is significant.

21. Several other control variables are significant but their effects do not differ by sex. Coverage under spouses' insurance reduces participation among men by 14 percent and among women by 17 percent; coverage under other insurance decreases participation by 11 by men and by six percent by women. (Both variables are treated as jointly determined with the decision to participate in one's own employer plan.) A 10 percent increase in weekly earnings increases participation by both men and women, although the magnitudes of the effects are small (about 1 percent). Having an employed spouse increases the likelihood of participation among men by 9 percent and among women by 11 percent. Homeownership decreases participation among women by 2 percent.

22. A number of other factors are important for the participation decision, however. Coverage under other insurance significantly reduces participation by both men and women by 16 percent. Ten percent higher earnings increase enrollment by women by 1 percent, and homeownership increases participation by men by 5 percent. The estimated mean probability of participation is .93 for single men and .94 for single women (Appendix Table 4).

23. In medium- and large-size private firms, the proportion of full-time employees participating in employer medical plans who were provided with the option of retiree health insurance fell from 45 percent in 1988 to 35 percent in 1997 for retirement below age 65, and from 37 to 34 percent for retirement at ages 65 and above (McDonnell and Fronstin 1999).

24. In medium and large establishments, 53 percent of full-time workers were covered by short-term disability and 42 percent by long-term disability insurance in 1995; among small establishments, comparable percentages were 29 and 22.

25. The samples used here consist of 6,451/5,660 male and 5,118/4,352 female full-time workers.

26. Among firms offering health insurance, 71 percent offered short-term disability insurance and 49 percent offered long-term disability insurance (Gruber 1998).

27. These estimates are biased if, within the sample of workers in firms offering health insurance, workers of a particular age would be more or less likely to match themselves with firms that also offer disability insurance.

28. Marginal probability estimates appear in Appendix Table 3 (cols. 5 and 6). The estimated mean probability of participation is 0.82 for men and 0.87 for women.

29. Also notable is the finding that education plays an important role in the decision to opt for short-term disability insurance, one of the rare instances in this study in which education influences the choice of employer-sponsored benefits. Among men, a high school diploma and above increases participation by 10 to 24 percent (depending on level of education) compared to participation among high school dropouts; among women, participation increases by 10 to 18 percent. Being married is associated with a higher likelihood of participation among men (by 11 percent), whereas homeownership increases participation by 5 percent among women.

30. Marginal probability estimates appear in Appendix Table 3, cols. 7 and 8. The estimated mean participation rate is 0.71 for men and 0.62 for women.

31. Because of the limitations of the data, it is also possible that workers in this age group, while eligible for health insurance, are less likely to be employed in firms that offer long-term disability insurance.

32. Participation in the employer's health plan, controlling for unobserved preferences for insurance, is associated with higher participation among both men and women, in contrast to participation in short-term disability coverage (by 56 and 50 percent, respectively). Like enrollment in short-term disability insurance, higher education significantly increases the probability of participation among both men (from 11 to 28 percent) and women (13 to 19 percent).

33. See, for example, *Family Matters: A National Survey of Women and Men,* conducted for the National Partnership For Women and Families, February 1998 (<www.nationalpartnership.org/survey/survey.htm>).

34. Johnson and Lo Sasso (2000) find that among adult children with surviving parents, 26 percent of women and 15 percent of men aged 53–63 reported that they spent at least one hundred hours caring for or helping parents during the previous twelve months. Women engaged in eldercare were found to have reduced hours of paid work by 43 percent on average and men by 28 percent.

35. The EBS data are at the firm level and employee characteristics are not available. The Establishment Surveys allow us to examine firm response to employee demand, while the Employees Surveys provide information on changes over a five-year period in the utilization of family benefits by the demographic characteristics of employees.

36. A flexible benefits plan, often called a cafeteria plan, allows participants to elect a combination of various taxable and tax-deferred forms of compensation, including cash, health insurance, 401(k) plan contributions, life insurance, child care, and additional vacation days. A flexible spending (reimbursement) account allows employees to set money aside on a pretax basis for qualified unreimbursed medical or dependent care expenses. These accounts may exist either within a full flexible benefit plan or separately as a stand-alone plan. They can be funded by salary-reduction arrangements, employer contributions, or both. Employees must determine how much they wish to contribute to the spending account in advance and they forfeit unused funds at the end of the year.

37. The 1993 Family and Medical Leave Act enables working families to take leave to meet essential caregiving responsibilities without the risk of losing their jobs or imposing undue burdens on employers. The FMLA obligates employers with more than 50 employees to provide 12 weeks of unpaid leave each year to employees for five reasons: own health; maternity leave; care for a new born, newly adopted, or placed foster child; care for spouse; or care for elderly parents. Leave provided under FMLA is job-protected, and requires covered employers to continue to maintain group health insurance benefits for eligible employees on FMLA leave. Prior to 1993, the United States had no national family and medical leave legislation, although the Pregnancy Discrimination Act of 1979 did require firms that offered temporary disability programs to cover pregnancy like any other disability. Some employees had access to leave through union contracts, employer policies, or state statutes, but coverage provided under these provisions was rarely as comprehensive as coverage under the FMLA. Many employees had no family or medical leave coverage prior to the FMLA.

38. Among those who indicated that they needed leave but did not take it, 78 percent said they could not afford to take leave. Many feared that either their job might have been lost (32 percent) or advancement would have been hurt (43 percent). In addition, 21 percent of leave-needers reported that their leave request was denied by their employer (Cantor et al. 2001).

References

Andrews, Emily. 1992. "The Growth and Distribution of 401(k) plans." In *Trends in Pensions 1992*, ed. John A. Turner and Daniel J. Beller. Washington, D.C.: U.S. Government Printing Office. 149–76.

Belluck, Pam. 2000. "A Bit of Burping Is Allowed, If It Keeps Parents on the Job: Employers Are Welcoming Babies." *New York Times*, November 22.

Cantor, David, Jane Waldfogel, Jeffrey Kerwin, Mareena McKinley Wright, Kerry Levin, John Rauch, Tracey Hagerty, and Martha Stapleton Kudela. 2001. *Balancing the Needs of Families and Employers: Family and Medical Leave Surveys*. Report submitted to U.S. Department of Labor. Rockville, Md.: Westat.

Cooper P. F. and B. S. Schone. 1997. "More Offers, Fewer Takers for Employment-Based Health Insurance: 1987 and 1996." *Health Affairs* 16, 6: 142–49. AHCPR Pub. 98-R008.

Even, William E. and David A. Macpherson. 1995. *Educational Attainment and Trends in Pension Coverage*. Report to U.S. Department of Labor Pension and Welfare Benefits Administration.

———. 1999. "Employee Participation in 401(k) Plans." Mimeo. Miami University of Ohio.

Greenhouse, Steven. 2000. "Ford to Offer Social Services for Workers and Retirees." *New York Times*, November 22.

Gruber, Jonathan. 1998. "Health Insurance and the Labor Market." Working Paper 6762. Cambridge, Mass.: National Bureau of Economic Research.

Ippolito, Richard A. 1997. *Pension Plans and Employee Performance*. Chicago: University of Chicago Press.

Johnson, Richard W. and Anthony T. Lo Sasso. 2000. *Parental Care at Midlife: Balancing Work and Family Responsibilities near Retirement*. Retirement Project Brief Series 9. Washington, D.C.: Urban Institute. March.

Lofgren, Eric P., Steven A. Nyce, and Sylvester J. Schieber. This volume. "Designing Total Reward Programs for Tight Labor Markets."

McDonnell, Ken and Paul Fronstin. 1999. *EBRI Health Benefits Databook*. Washington, D.C.: EBRI-ERF.

Mitchell, Olivia S. This volume. "New Trends in Pension Benefit and Retirement Provisions."

Munnell, Alicia H., Annika Sundén, and Catherine Taylor. 2000. "What Determines 401(k) Participation and Contributions?" Working Paper 2000-12. Center for Retirement Research at Boston College, Chestnut Hill, Mass.

Reno, Virginia and June Eichener. 2000. "Ensuring Health and Income Security for an Aging Workforce." *Health and Income Security for an Aging Workforce*. Report 1. Washington, D.C.: National Academy of Social Insurance. December

Riche, Martha Farnsworth. This volume. "The Demographics of Tomorrow's Workplace."

Siegel, Michele, Charlotte Muller, and Marjorie Honig. 2001. "The Incidence of Job Loss: The Shift from Younger to Older Workers: 1981–1998." Working Paper 2001-1. New York: International Longevity Center-USA.

Tracey, Elizabeth. 2000. "Costs of Care for Elderly Growing." *Reuters Health Information*, November 14.

U.S. Bureau of Labor Statistics. 1999. *Employee Benefits in Medium and Large Private Establishments, 1997*. Washington, D.C.: U.S. Government Printing Office.

Weigers, Margaret E. and Susan K. Drilea. 1999. *Health Status and Limitations: A Comparison of Hispanics, Blacks, and Whites, 1996*. MEPS Research Findings 10. AHRQ Pub. 00-0001. Rockville, Md.: Agency for Health Care Policy and Research.

Chapter 4
The Benefits Implications of Recent Trends in Flexible Staffing Arrangements

Susan N. Houseman

The U.S. labor market has seen important growth in temporary and contract employment of late. Best-documented is rise in temporary agency employment, which grew 265 percent between 1990 and 2000, and accounted for about 10 percent of net employment growth over the decade. Although time series data on other types of temporary and contract employment arrangements do not exist, employer surveys suggest that employment in other flexible staffing arrangements has grown as well (Houseman and Polivka 2000).

This chapter considers the benefits implications of the growth in flexible staffing arrangements. Traditionally, benefits offered at the employers' discretion have primarily targeted regular, full-time workers. Similarly, laws mandating benefits, like workers' compensation or family and medical leave, and laws regulating benefits, like pensions and health insurance, are designed with the full-time, regular employee in mind. The growth in various flexible staffing arrangements raises concerns about whether workers in temporary and contract arrangements are adequately covered by key benefits and regulations governing them. It also raises concerns that employers' desire to control benefits costs has stimulated some of the growth in these arrangements.

I begin by providing some background on flexible staffing arrangements: the definition of various types of temporary and contract positions in government statistics, available evidence on trends in these arrangements, and the characteristics of workers in these arrangements. Next, I examine several key questions related to benefits: How does the incidence of benefits vary between those in flexible staffing and regular arrangements? How do regulations governing benefits cover workers in various flexible staffing arrangements? And, is savings on benefits costs an important motivation for employers to use certain flexible staffing arrangements? A brief discussion of policy issues concludes.

Understanding Terminology

Our focus is on workers in a variety of so-called flexible staffing arrangements: agency temporaries, leased employees, contract company workers, independent contractors, direct-hire temporaries, and on-call workers. In the first four categories of employment, workers usually are not regarded as legal employees of the establishment for whom they are performing work.[1] "Agency temporaries" work for a staffing agency that places them with a client company. The agency temporary generally works at the client's worksite, and typically, though not always, the assignment is for a short period of time (less than a year). The work the agency temporary performs usually is directed by the client, though temporary help agencies increasingly are sending a supervisor to monitor their workers at the clients' site (Peck and Theodore 1998). In the case of "employee leasing," a company leases all or a portion of its workforce on a fairly permanent basis from a leasing company or professional employment organization (PEO). The workers are on the payroll of a PEO, but their work is typically directed by the client company. Often temporary help agencies also lease workers. "Contract company workers" work for a company that contracts out their services to a client company. In the definition used by the Bureau of Labor Statistics (BLS) and in the data reported below, contract company workers also perform their work at the client's worksite and usually work for just one client at a time. Typically, their work is supervised by the contract company, not by the client.

The distinction between agency temporary, leased employee, and contract company worker is often blurred. For instance, widely cited statistics on employment in the temporary help industry from the Bureau of Labor Statistics establishment survey, the Current Employment Statistics (CES), actually cover help supply services, which incorporates many leased employees. Many other government statistics on workers in flexible staffing arrangements come from supplements to the February Current Population Survey (CPS) on Contingent and Alternative Work Arrangements, which have been conducted biannually since 1995. In these supplements, workers were simply asked to identify themselves as employed or paid by a "temporary help agency," by a "leasing company," or by a "company that contracts out your services," and the meaning of these terms was left to the interpretation of the respondent.[2] The lack of a single definition of leasing companies and leased workers was cited in a recent Department of Labor report (KRA Corporation 1996).

Legally, "independent contractors" are self-employed. The only statistics on the number of independent contractors come from the CPS Supplements on Contingent and Alternative Work Arrangements. In that survey, workers who stated that they worked as independent contractors, independent consultants, or freelance workers were classified as independent contractors.[3] In the BLS data, independent contractors may or may not perform their services at the client's worksite.

In contrast to the other flexible staffing arrangements, "direct-hire temporaries" and "on-call workers" are employees of the company where they work. Direct-hire temporaries are hired for a limited period of time, for instance for seasonal work or for a special project. On-call workers may be hired for an indefinite duration, but they do not have regularly scheduled hours. Instead they are called in to work on an as-needed basis, often to fill in for an absent employee or to help with an increased workload. Substitute teachers and many hospital employees are on-call workers.

The Extent of Flexible Staffing Arrangements

Table 1 presents the distribution of the workforce by staffing arrangement, according to data from the February 1999 CPS. To avoid double counting, the employment categories are mutually exclusive. One possibility for overlap across categories occurs with direct-hire temporaries, since some on-call workers, wage and salary independent contractor workers, and contract company workers are hired on a short-term basis. The percentage of workers in these categories who are also direct-hire temporaries is indicated in Table 1. The category "other direct-hire temporaries" refers to those short-term hires not classified in another flexible staffing arrangement. Including the on-call, independent contract, and contract company workers who are also direct-hire temporaries, direct-hire temporaries account for over 3 percent of the workforce.[4] In addition, a small number work on an on-call basis for a contract company and in the table, are classified as on-call workers.[5]

TABLE 1. Distribution of Employment by Work Arrangement

Employment arrangement	Percent of workforce	Percent direct-hire temporaries	Percent working part-time
Agency temporaries	1	na	23
On-call or day laborers	2	33	53
Independent contractors	6	1	27
Contract company workers	0.5	17	11
Other direct-hire temporaries	3	100	52
Other self-employed	5	na	22
Regular employees	83	na	17

Source: Author's tabulations from the February 1999 CPS Supplement on Contingent and Alternative Work Arrangements.
na = not applicable.

Independent contractors comprise the largest category of flexible staffing arrangements. In fact, over half of all the self-employed call themselves independent contractors, independent consultants, or freelancers. Collectively, agency temporaries, on-call workers, independent contractors, contract company workers, and direct-hire temporaries comprise about 12 percent of the workforce.

It is noteworthy that agency temporaries account for only 1 percent of total employment in the CPS Supplement, whereas they account for about 2 percent of employment in the CES. Data from the National Association of Temporary Staffing Services suggests employment in temporary services is slightly less than that reported in the CES, but is much higher than that reported in the CPS. It is generally presumed that the CPS understates employment in temporary help agencies.[6]

Those in flexible staffing arrangements are more likely to work part time than workers in regular wage and salary positions. This is particularly true for on-call workers, day laborers and other direct-hire temporaries. Somewhat surprisingly, agency temporaries are only somewhat more likely to be employed part time than are regular employees.

Data on the number of workers hired by employee leasing companies are not currently available. In the February 1995 CPS Supplement, respondents were asked if they were paid by an employee leasing agency. A very small percentage (0.3 percent) responded in the affirmative. Subsequent field tests by the BLS showed considerable confusion among respondents over that question, so it was omitted from subsequent surveys.

Trends in Flexible Staffing

Very little is known about trends in most flexible staffing arrangements in the United States; agency temporary employment is the only flexible staffing category for which a relatively long time series exists. As noted above, the CES provides information on employment in the help supply services industry, which is comprised primarily of temporary help agencies. According to this source, employment in the temporary help industry grew dramatically in the last two decades. From 1982 (the first year for which data on this industry are available) to 2000, the share of nonfarm payroll employment in help supply services grew from 0.5 percent to 2.6 percent. Statistics for on-call, independent contractor, contract company, and direct-hire temporary workers were first collected in the February 1995 Supplement to the CPS. Between 1995 and 1999, the percentage of employment in these categories was stable, but this four-year time period is too short to determine any trend, particularly because the economy was in rapid expansion.[7]

In the absence of employment data on specific flexible staffing arrangements, some researchers have looked at the growth in business services employment (e.g., Abraham 1990). In addition to including agency temporaries within help supply services, the business services sector is thought to include many employed as contract company workers. Figure 1 depicts indexes of employment in help supply services, business services, and the aggregate non-farm payroll sector over the 1982–2000 period. Help supply services grew more rapidly than aggregate business services, which grew more rapidly than aggregate employment over the period. Within the business services sector, help supply services was the fastest growing component. However, each component of the business services sector also increased faster than aggregate employment over the period.

Evidence from employer surveys also points to growth in various flexible staffing arrangements. For instance, in a Conference Board (1995) survey of members, 34 percent of companies reported sizable growth in their use of direct-hire temporaries in the preceding five years and 24 percent expected sizable growth in the coming five years. Thirty-one percent reported sizable growth in their use of independent contractors and 28 percent expected sizable growth in their use of independent contractors in the next five years. Data from BLS Industry Wage Surveys in 1986 and 1987 show growth in contracting out of services in manufacturing industries between 1979 and 1986–87 (Abraham and Taylor 1996). In a survey of members of the Bureau of National Affairs, a larger percentage of employers reported an increase than a decrease in their use of direct-hire temporaries, on-call workers, administrative or business support contracts, and production subcontracting relative to regular workers between 1980 and 1985 (Abraham 1990). In a nationally representative survey of employers conducted in 1996, a much

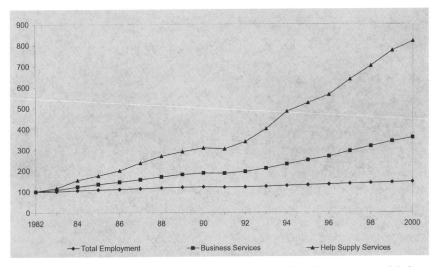

Figure 1. Employment index (1982 = 100). Source: U.S. Department of Labor, Bureau of Labor Statistics.

larger percentage of employers had contracted out work previously done in-house than had brought work back in-house since 1990. Moreover, two-thirds of respondents to this survey predicted that organizations in their industry would increase their use of flexible staffing arrangements in the coming five years (Houseman 1997, 2001). Thus, it is reasonable to assume that there has been recent growth in other types of flexible staffing arrangements besides temporary help, though the extent of the growth is not well known.

Characteristics of Workers in Flexible Staffing Arrangements

The distribution of worker characteristics varies considerably across staffing arrangements (see Table 2). Agency temporaries, on-call workers, and direct-hire temporaries are disproportionately female and young. A disproportionate number of agency temporaries are black or Hispanic, while a large percentage of on-call workers are high-school dropouts. In contrast, independent contractors and contract company workers are disproportionately male, older, more educated, and in the case of independent contractors, white.

The occupational and industrial distribution of employment by work arrangement is shown in Table 3. It is not surprising that many agency temporaries work in administrative support occupations, but many others work as operators and in the manufacturing sector. On-call workers, independent contractors, and direct-hire temporaries are heavily represented in the construction and services industries. A large share of contract company workers is found in services and precision production occupations. Over one quarter of direct-hire temporaries are in professional occupations and over half are in services industries.

The government is a major employer of workers in several flexible staffing arrangements. Over 20 percent of on-call, day, and contract company workers and over 30 percent of direct-hire temporaries work for federal, state, or local government (see Table 4).[8]

Benefits Among Workers in Flexible Staffing Arrangements

Because of the diversity in average worker, industry, and occupational characteristics across staffing arrangements, one cannot generalize about the quality of jobs in flexible staffing arrangements. For instance, compared to regular employees, agency temporaries, on-call and day laborers, and other direct-hire temporaries tend to earn lower wages, whereas contract company and independent contractors earn similar or higher wages.[9] The same patterns are evident with respect to job stability: the jobs of agency temporaries, on-call and day laborers, and other direct-hire temporaries are less stable

TABLE 2. Characteristics of Workers by Working Arrangement (percent distribution)

	Agency temporaries	On-call or day laborers	Independent contractors	Contract company workers	Other direct-hire temporaries	Other self-employed	Regular employees
Gender							
Male	42	50	66	71	48	63	52
Female	58	50	34	29	52	37	48
Age							
16–19	6	10	1	5	16	0	5
20–24	21	11	3	10	23	3	10
25–34	29	23	18	32	23	14	24
34–44	19	24	30	28	17	28	28
45–54	15	15	26	17	11	26	21
55–64	7	10	15	7	6	20	9
65+	3	8	7	2	4	9	2
Race/ethnicity							
White	61	72	85	75	69	84	74
Black	21	12	6	11	10	4	12
Hispanic	14	13	6	6	13	6	11
Other	5	3	4	8	9	6	4
Education							
< High school	16	20	8	7	16	8	12
High school	32	30	30	23	19	31	32
Some college	36	28	28	33	33	26	29
College +	17	22	34	37	32	35	27

Source: Author's tabulations from February 1999 CPS Supplement on Contingent and Alternative Work Arrangements.

TABLE 3. Occupational and Industry Distribution of Employment by Work Arrangement (%)

	Agency temporaries	On-call or day laborers	Independent contractors	Contract company workers	Other direct-hire temporaries	Other self-employed	Regular employees
Occupation							
Executive, administrative	4	5	21	11	7	25	14
Professional	7	22	19	30	31	12	15
Technical	4	4	1	7	3	1	4
Sales	2	5	17	2	7	21	12
Administrative support	36	9	3	4	20	5	15
Services	8	24	9	18	14	11	14
Precision production	9	11	19	15	6	7	11
Operators	19	2	2	1	3	1	6
Transportation occupations	2	8	4	3	2	2	4
Laborers	8	7	1	6	4	1	4
Farming and forestry	1	3	4	3	4	14	1
Industry							
Agriculture	0	3	5	0	4	15	1
Mining and construction	3	12	20	7	6	7	5
Manufacturing	34	5	5	21	6	6	18
Transportation, communication, utilities	10	9	6	16	3	4	8
Trade	12	16	14	5	14	26	22
Finance, insurance, and real estate	10	3	9	10	3	6	7
Services	32	50	42	27	60	36	34
Public administration	1	3	0	14	5	0	5

Source: Author's tabulations from February 1999 CPS Supplement on Contingent and Alternative Work Arrangements.

TABLE 4. Distribution of Employment Between the Private and Government
Sectors, by Work Arrangement (%)

	Private			Government			
	Total	Profit	Non-profit	Total	Federal	State	Local
Agency temporaries	98	97	1	2	0.5	0.5	1
On-call or day laborers	77	71	6	23	2	5	16
Contract company workers	96	93	3	4	2	1	2
Other direct-hire temporaries	69	58	11	31	4	14	13
Regular employees	84	78	6	16	3	4	9

Source: Author's tabulations from February 1999 CPS on Contingent and Alternative Work
Arrangements.
Figures may not sum to totals because of rounding.

than those of regular workers in the sense that they are more likely to lead
to a job switch or unemployment, whereas the jobs of contract company
workers and independent contractors have similar or even more stability
compared to those of regular workers (Houseman and Polivka 2000).

The one issue that cuts across workers in all flexible staffing arrangements is benefits: Workers in flexible staffing arrangements are far less
likely to have benefits such as health insurance or a retirement plan than
are regular workers. Table 5 shows the incidence of health insurance and
retirement benefits by work arrangement. Because many employees who are
eligible to participate in an employer-provided health insurance or retirement plan decline to do so, it is interesting to look not only at the percentage of workers who receive these benefits from their employer, but also at
the percentage that are eligible to receive them. Among wage and salary
employees (a category that includes agency temporaries, on-call workers,
contract-company workers, direct-hire temporaries, and regular workers)
those in flexible staffing arrangements are much less likely than regular
workers to participate in and be eligible to participate in a health insurance
and retirement benefit plan.

The incidence of these benefits is particularly low among agency temporaries. Whereas 64 percent of regular workers receive health insurance
through their employer and 76 percent are eligible to participate in an employer health insurance plan, just 9 percent of agency temporaries receive
health insurance through their employers and only 28 percent are eligible
to participate in an employer health insurance plan. Only 7 percent of
agency temporaries participate in an employer retirement plan and only
12 percent are eligible to do so, compared to 58 percent and 63 percent
of regular employees who participate or are eligible to participate, respectively, in an employer retirement plan.

TABLE 5. Incidence of Health Insurance and Retirement Plan, by Work Arrangement (percent)

	Health Insurance			Retirement Plan		
	Health insurance	Health insurance through employer	Eligible for health insurance from employer	Covered by employer pension plan or has tax deferred retirement account	Participates in employer pension plan	Eligible to participate in employer pension plan
Agency temporaries	43	9	28	20	7	12
On-call or day laborers	69	21	30	38	25	29
Independent contractors	76	na	na	43	na	na
Contract company workers	84	60	76	55	42	46
Other direct-hire temporaries	75	26	35	27	18	22
Other self-employed	83	na	na	47	na	na
Regular employees	86	64	76	65	58	63
Part-time	88	17	32	33	21	26
Full-time	76	73	84	70	64	69

Source: Author's tabulations from February 1999 Supplement on Contingent and Alternative Work Arrangements.

One might be less concerned about the absence of benefits if workers in flexible staffing arrangements had health insurance available from other sources or saved for retirement through a tax-deferred retirement account. However, agency temporaries, on-call workers, independent contractors, and direct-hire temporaries are much less likely to have health insurance coverage from any source as compared to regular employees. Over half of agency temporaries have no health insurance from any source. Similarly, workers in all types of flexible staffing arrangements are much less likely than regular employees to have some type of retirement plan. Statistical analysis shows that workers in all flexible staffing arrangements are significantly less likely to be eligible to participate in an employer-sponsored health insurance or pension plan or to have health insurance from any source, even after controlling for worker and job characteristics (Houseman 1997). These findings are consistent with evidence from an employer survey showing that while employers typically offer benefits like paid vacations and holidays, paid sick leave, health insurance and a retirement plan to their full-time regular employees, they rarely offer these benefits to employees who are on-call workers or temporaries (Houseman 2001).

Flexible Staffing Arrangements by Benefits Regulations

Various federal and state laws mandate that employers provide specified employees with certain benefits, including workers' compensation, unemployment insurance, and family and medical leave. If the employer chooses to offer employees benefits like a retirement or health insurance plan, federal laws also regulate the provision of these benefits. For instance, if an employer chooses to offer a retirement plan to employees, the benefit plan must meet certain conditions specified in the Employee Retirement Income and Security Act (ERISA) and the IRS tax code in order to receive favorable tax treatment. One purpose of these requirements is to ensure that the beneficiaries of such in-kind, tax-deferred income are not primarily highly compensated employees. Specifically, under ERISA a tax-qualified pension plan must cover at least 70 percent of all non–highly compensated employees who worked one thousand hours or more over the last twelve months. Provisions in the IRS tax code stipulate that self-insured health insurance plans not discriminate in favor of highly compensated individuals as well (Collins 1999; Miller 2000).

These laws mandating or regulating benefits were written with the traditional employee — a full-time, permanent worker — in mind. The large and growing number in flexible staffing arrangements, however, has sparked concern that existing law is inadequate to protect these workers. A related concern is that, although businesses have many legitimate reasons for using alternative arrangements, legal loopholes provide an added incentive to use these arrangements in order to avoid or reduce benefits costs.

Several factors affect whether and how workers in flexible arrangements are covered by benefits regulations. The first is whether the worker is an employee or an independent contractor. Laws governing benefits pertain only to employees, and independent contractors, who are self-employed, are not covered. If the worker is an employee, another issue is who is the statutory employer for the purposes of the benefits regulation. This issues arises in the context of temporary agency workers, contract company workers, and leased employees, who are paid by one employer but perform work for another. Finally, benefit laws typically include hours or earnings thresholds and thus exclude many temporary and part-time workers from coverage.

Who Is an Employee? Determining Independent Contractor Status

Independent contractors, by definition, are self-employed and because they are not employees, independent contractors are not covered by employment, labor, and related tax laws. Employers may be tempted to reclassify employees as independent contractors in order to avoid taxes, benefits, and other liability. Whether or not a worker is covered by a particular employment, labor, or tax law hinges on the definition of an employee. Yet, statutes usually fail to clearly define the term "employee," and no single standard to distinguish between employee and independent contractor has emerged.

For example, the IRS uses the so-called "20-factor test," in which it assesses the degree of control the company exercises over the way the work is performed by an independent contractor. If the company exercises too much control, the worker is deemed to be an employee. The IRS "20-factor, right-to-control" test is used to assess an employers' tax liability. A similar test is used in most states to determine status under workers' compensation laws.

The so-called "economic realities test" or a hybrid of the right-to-control and economic realities test often is used by courts to determine independent contractor status in other circumstances. In essence, the economic realities test makes it harder to classify a worker as an independent contractor, because, in addition to considering the degree of control the employer exercises, it takes into account the degree to which a worker is economically dependent on the business. The economic realities test is used to determine employee status under the Family and Medical Leave Act (entitling workers to unpaid leave under certain circumstances), the Fair Labor Standards Act (establishing a minimum wage), and the Worker Adjustment and Retraining Act (providing for advance notice in event of plant closings and mass layoffs). Additionally, it is often applied by courts in determining independent contractor status in civil rights cases under Title VII of the Civil Rights Act, the Age Discrimination in Employment Act, and the Americans with Disabilities Act. States use a variety of other tests to determine independent contractor status for unemployment insurance purposes.[10] This plethora of tests defining independent contractor status applied across federal and state laws makes it possible for a worker to be classified as an independent contractor under one law, but as an employee under another.

Who Is the Employer? Determining Joint-Employer Status

Besides failing to define who are "employees," most statutes also fail to spell out who the employer is. There is potential ambiguity on this issue when businesses use temporary agency, leased, or contract workers. Although the primary employer is generally the temporary help, leasing, or contract company, the client may be regarded as a "joint employer" under some laws.

Perhaps by virtue of the fact that it is a recent statute, the Family and Medical Leave Act is one of the few laws to explicitly address possible joint-employer relationships. When a leasing or temporary help agency is the primary employer, a client company may be required to place the individual in the same or comparable position upon his or her return from FMLA leave. Additionally, leased and temporary workers will count as employees of the client company for the purposes of determining employment levels for FMLA. Thus, although the FMLA only covers employers with fifty or more employees, a small employer may have to provide FMLA benefits to all workers if the number of regular plus temporary and leased employees is fifty or more (Pivec and Massen 1996).

Congress tried to clear up the ambiguity — and stem abuses — regarding benefits provision to leased employees in 1982. Businesses allegedly were "firing" their non–highly compensated staff and leasing them back through leasing agencies to avoid providing benefits to these employees. Under section 414(n) in the Tax Equity and Fiscal Responsibility Act of 1982, leased and temporary help workers must be counted by the client firm as employees for the purposes of qualifying retirement plans and certain other fringe benefits (such as life insurance and cafeteria plans) if the workers have provided these services "on a substantially full-time basis for at least a year" and the client primarily controls or directs the work of the leased or temporary employees. The rule does not apply to health insurance plans (Klein 1996).

Several states have passed legislation clarifying joint-employer liability in workers' compensation cases. New York State has actually ruled that the client is the common law employer of leased employees and is primarily responsible for providing workers' compensation benefits. However, most states have not clarified joint-employer status in workers' compensation cases, leaving the courts to resolve these issues where there is some dispute. Court rulings on the issue, in turn, have been inconsistent (Bowker 1997). Similarly, no guidelines have been drawn up clarifying joint employer status under OSHA or other health and safety regulations.

Exclusions from Benefits Regulations

Even if a worker is clearly classified as an employee of a particular organization, that worker still may be exempted from coverage by various benefits laws with which its employer must otherwise comply. For instance, under ERISA, a tax-qualified pension plan is required to only cover 70 percent of all non–highly compensated employees who worked 1000 hours or more in the preceding 12 months. Thus, many on-call, temporary, and part-time workers may be excluded from employer-provided pension plans. Similarly, although regulations governing self-insured health insurance plans generally require that organizations offering such insurance offer it to all non–highly compensated employees, temporary and part-time workers are exempted (Collins 1999; Miller 2000). The Family and Medical Leave Act of 1993 — which requires employers to provide employees with up to 12 weeks of job-protected, unpaid leave during any 12-month period to care for a new born or adopted child, recuperate from a serious health condition, or care for an immediate family member who has a serious health condition — covers only employees who have worked for that employer at least 1200 hours during the 12 months immediately preceding the date the leave commences (Klein 1996).

Unemployment insurance programs vary from state to state, but all specify that an employee work a minimum number of weeks and/or earn a certain minimum amount within a base period to qualify for unemployment insurance. The purpose of these requirements is to prevent those with insufficient attachment to the workforce from receiving benefits. As with ERISA and FMLA, however, these requirements effectively preclude many in temporary and part-time positions from being covered.

Even when temporary workers fulfill the minimum earnings and work time requirements to qualify for unemployment compensation, they may be disqualified on other grounds. For instance, if workers separate from a temporary job with a predetermined expiration date, they might be disqualified from receiving unemployment insurance on the grounds that they voluntarily accepted a job with an ending date, and so the unemployment might be deemed voluntary. Several states have passed laws precluding disqualification for this reason. Workers employed through a temporary help agency also can be disqualified from receiving unemployment benefits if they fail to report to the temporary help agency for a new assignment after their last assignment ends. From the employers' perspective, temporary agencies do not want to raise their unemployment insurance tax rates, which are experience-rated, by covering workers whom they could place in other assignments. From the workers' perspective, agency temporaries may need time off with unemployment insurance coverage to look for permanent employment and not covering these workers may relegate them to a cycle of short-term, dead-end jobs. Ambiguity also exists as to whether an agency temporary who quits in the middle of an assignment for "good cause," such as hazardous working conditions, must accept another offer of employment through the same temporary help agency (National Employment Law Project 1997).

A related issue is whether temporary agency workers can refuse an assignment without jeopardizing their unemployment benefits. This issue is particularly pertinent when state employment agencies refer unemployment insurance recipients to temporary services. In the absence of state requirements, federal law stipulates that if an assignment offers "wages or other conditions of employment [that] are substantially less favorable than those prevailing for similar work in the locality, or are such as tend to depress wages or working conditions," the assignment is unsuitable. However, specific factors vary from state to state and may be decided on a case-by-case basis (National Employment Law Project 1997).

Employers' Use of Flexible Staffing Arrangements to Reduce Benefits Costs

From the above discussion, workers in all flexible staffing arrangements are much less likely than regular full-time workers to receive health and pension benefits from their employers, even after controlling for worker and job characteristics. In addition, benefits regulations often do not apply to those in flexible staffing arrangements. This raises the question of whether and to what extent employers use various flexible staffing arrangements in order to circumvent regulations and reduce benefits costs.

Here it is important to distinguish between two situations. One is that employers may make illegal use of flexible staffing arrangements, in part, to avoid benefits regulations. The other is that because flexible staffing arrangements are associated with fewer regulations and hence lower benefits costs, employers make more legal use of these arrangements than they would in the absence of the regulations.

With respect to the former, recent high-profile cases such as those involving Microsoft and Time Warner have highlighted the problem in which companies misclassify employees as independent contractors or temporary workers and thereby save on pension, health insurance, and other benefits costs. It is widely believed that the fraudulent use of contract and temporary workers is largely motivated by workers' compensation costs. Each state requires that employers purchase workers' compensation insurance, which provides benefits to employees in the event of an occupational injury, but independent contractors, being self-employed, are not covered by these laws. One problem, particularly prevalent in the construction industry, is that companies reportedly will require workers to be "independent contractors" to avoid workers' compensation costs. When these workers become injured, they are reclassified as employees and file for workers compensation (Montana Legislative Council 1994).

Another issue in workers' compensation is that workers sometimes are misclassified, particularly by temporary help and leasing agencies, which usually are responsible for purchasing workers' compensation insurance for temporary or leased employees. The insurance rate depends partly on the occupation in which the worker is classified, and some agencies allegedly misclassify workers in order to obtain lower rates. Although several states have taken steps to crack down on misclassification by leasing companies, little has been done to eliminate such practices by temporary help agencies (Klein 1996).

A related problem is that typically workers' compensation rates are based on experience rating of the leasing or temporary help agency. Allegedly, some leasing or temporary help agencies hire a minimal number of people for some period of time to establish a low rate and then move large numbers of leased or temporary employees into this operation. When the rate increases, they close this "company" and move the employees into another such operation. Some have recommended that the workers' compensation rate be tied to the client company in response to this practice.[11]

As with workers' compensation, it is believed that some businesses avoid paying unemployment insurance (UI) or pay rates that are too low by misclassifying workers as independent contractors or by establishing low experience rates in shell companies before transferring leased or temporary agency employees to their payrolls (De Silva et al. 2000). One study found substantial evidence of UI rate manipulation among leasing companies (KRA Corporation 1996).

In most cases, employers' use of flexible staffing arrangements is perfectly legal, and evidence from employer surveys shows that savings on benefits costs is one of several reasons employers use these arrangements.[12] For instance, in a survey of 21 large companies, 38 percent using direct-hire temporaries, 19 percent using agency temporaries, and 29 percent using independent contractors did so, in part, to reduce health care costs (Christensen 1995). In a large nationally representative employer survey, 16 percent of businesses cited avoiding fringe benefits costs as a very important reason they used agency temporaries or contract company workers and another 22 percent said this factor was moderately important (Kalleberg, Reynolds, and Marsden 1999). Although less than 12 percent of employers in another nationally representative survey of employers stated they used various flexible staffing arrangements to save on wage and benefits costs, surveyed employers indicated that they often saved on labor costs, especially benefits costs, by using these arrangements. Moreover, survey evidence suggests that employers who offer more generous benefits to their regular, full-time employees are more likely to use workers in various flexible staffing arrangements (Houseman 2001; Mangum, Mayall, and Nelson 1985).

Of course, firms do not necessarily save on labor costs by using flexible staffing arrangements, even if the wages and benefits of these workers are less than those of regular employees. Detailed cost-benefit analyses on the use of "contingent" workers in several firms showed in some cases the higher costs associated with turnover, training, and lower productivity of contingent workers outweighed the savings from lower wage and benefit costs (Nollen and Axel 1996). Thus, although firms may be motivated to use flexible staffing arrangements in order to save on wage and benefit costs, firms sometimes incur higher overall labor costs by using these arrangements.

Conclusions

Three key points emerge from the above discussion. First, workers in flexible staffing arrangements are less likely than regular employees to be covered by laws mandating or regulating workplace benefits. Second, workers in such arrangements are less likely than regular employees to receive benefits such as health insurance and a retirement plan, through their employer or from any source. Finally, although reducing benefits costs is not the only reason employers use independent contractors, agency temporaries, on-call workers, and others in flexible arrangements, it is an important factor motivating many employers to use them, and the level of and growth in these arrangements would almost certainly be lower in the absence of this incentive.

This situation has provoked a number of policy responses and proposals for change. Most significant has been stepped-up enforcement of existing laws by the IRS and states to crack down on misclassification of workers as independent contractors and to stem the loss of tax revenues and workers' compensation and unemployment insurance fraud. States have also sought to cut down on fraud particularly in the area of workers' compensation associated with some temporary agency operations.

Others have proposed making a uniform set of rules to determine who is an employee and who is the employer, thereby greatly simplifying the system and reducing unintentional misclassification of workers as independent contractors and confusion over employer responsibilities to workers. The Commission on the Future of Worker-Management Relations (1996) specifically recommended that a standardized test to determine independent contractor status be based on the more restrictive concept of economic realities. Besides simplifying the law, this would make it more difficult for employers to legally classify workers as independent contractors than tests currently used for many purposes. Similarly, with temporary help agencies, contract companies, and other joint-employer situations, the commission recommended that the employer legally responsible for the worker be determined based on the economic realities of the relationship, and not simply on notions of control. Doing so, it asserted, "would remove the incentives that now exist for firms to use variations in corporate form to avoid responsibility for the people who do their work" (36).

Others have proposed more sweeping changes to the laws that would force employers to provide equal or prorated benefits to many more workers in flexible staffing arrangements (Callaghan and Hartmann 1991; duRivage 1992; National Employment Law Project 1997, 1999). Although this approach has gained little backing in the United States, laws regulating the use of flexible staffing arrangements and requiring employers to provide equal social protections to workers in these arrangements are common in Europe (Schoemann and Schoemann 2000).

In closing, it should be pointed out that better enforcement of existing laws and the enactment of laws to require equal treatment of workers in the provision of benefits would not necessarily increase benefits receipt and improve welfare among workers. Increases in benefits costs associated with these actions, if unmatched by reductions in wages, could lead to lower employment levels. In addition, faced with the prospect of having to extend health insurance, pension, and other voluntary benefits to more workers, employers instead could cut back on the benefits they choose to offer.

Notes

1. A discussion of legal issues related to who is the employer and who is the employee under various employment and labor laws is provided below.

2. In fact, due to confusion over terminology, the question on employee leasing was dropped from the 1997 and 1999 CPS Supplements. Contrast the way information is collected on these flexible staffing arrangements with the way information is collected on part-time workers. Instead of being asked if they work part-time, workers are asked if they usually work fewer than thirty-five hours per week. Based on this response, they are classified as part time or full time.

3. In these surveys about 12 percent of those who call themselves independent contractors also say they are employees, not self-employed. Legally, however, independent contractors must be self-employed.

4. Although the CPS does not include a specific question classifying individuals as direct-hire temporaries, I constructed this category from questions in the 1999 February Supplement. Specifically, individuals were classified as direct-hire temporaries if they indicated that their job was temporary or they could not stay in their job as long as they wished for any of the following reasons: they were working only until a specific project was completed, they were temporarily replacing another worker, they were hired for a fixed period of time, their job was seasonal, or they expected to work for less than a year because their job was temporary.

5. The classification scheme used in this table follows that used in Houseman and Polivka (2000).

6. Some of the difference in the CPS and CES figures on temporary agency employment stems from differences in the type of data collected in the two surveys. Specifically, the CES counts jobs in the temporary help services industry, while the CPS counts workers whose main jobs are in this industry. Consequently, individuals registered with more than one temporary agency would show up once in the CPS, but would show up more than once in the CES, if they worked two or more jobs for two or more temporary help agencies during the survey week. Also, multiple job holders with secondary jobs in the temporary help industry would not be counted

in the CPS as agency temporaries, whereas those workers' secondary jobs would be counted in the CES. Another possible explanation for the differences is that, in spite of questions in the CPS designed to avoid this problem, some respondents may still view the client to whom they are assigned as their employer and thus fail to report that they are paid by a temporary help service. The widespread confusion over who is their employer is evidenced by the fact that among those identified as agency temporaries in the CPS, over half at first incorrectly named their client, rather than the temporary help agency, as their employer. Finally, many establishments classified as temporary help agencies in the CES may also provide contract company workers or leased employees (Polivka 1996).

7. Future CPS Supplements on Contingent and Alternative Work Arrangements will provide valuable evidence on trends in these work arrangements.

8. In Table 3, the industry public administration captures some, but not all of public sector employees. Many public sector employees work in the services sector, for example, for public hospitals and public schools.

9. See Houseman (1999) for a summary of evidence on wages of workers in various flexible staffing arrangements compared to wages of workers in regular jobs.

10. Joerg (1996, chapters 3 and 7) contains a detailed discussion of the IRS 20-factor test, the economic realities test, and various other tests.

11. See KRA Corporation (1996), Clark (1997), and Montana Legislative Council (1994) for a discussion of these issues.

12. Other particularly important reasons include accommodating fluctuations in staffing needs, screening workers for regular positions, and accessing special skills. I provide a more complete discussion of evidence pertaining to why employers use various flexible staffing arrangements in Houseman (1999, 2001).

References

Abraham, Katharine G. 1990. "Restructuring the Employment Relationship: The Growth of Market-Mediated Work Arrangements." In *New Developments in the Labor Market: Toward a New Institutional Paradigm*, ed. Katharine G. Abraham and Robert McKersie. Cambridge, Mass.: MIT Press. 85–120.

Abraham, Katharine G. and Susan K. Taylor. 1996. "Firms' Use of Outside Contracts: Theory and Evidence." *Journal of Labor Economics* 14, 3: 394–424.

Bowker, Lindsay Newland. 1997. "Employee Leasing: Liability in Limbo?" *Risk Management* 44, 6: 37–47.

Callaghan, Polly and Heidi Hartmann. 1991. *Contingent Work: A Chart Book on Part-Time and Temporary Employment*. Washington, D.C.: Economic Policy Institute.

Christensen, Kathleen. 1995. *Contingent Work Arrangements in Family-Sensitive Corporations*. Boston: Center on Work and Family, Boston University.

Clark, Charles S. 1997. "Contingent Work Force." *CQ Researcher* 7, 40.

Collins, Michael J. 1999. "A Primer on the Self-Insured Health Plan Nondiscrimination Rules." *Journal of Pension Planning and Compliance* 25, 2: 1–15.

Commission on the Future of Worker-Management Relations. 1996. *Report and Recommendations of the Commission on the Future of Worker-Management Relations*. Issued January 9, 1995. Report DLR, No. 6, Special Supplement. Washington, D.C.: Bureau of National Affairs.

Conference Board. 1995. "Contingent Employment." *HR Executive Review*. New York: Conference Board.

De Silva, Lalith, Adrian Millett, Dominic Rotondi, and William Sullivan, with Elizabeth Fischer and Mark Sillings. 2000. "Independent Contractors: Prevalence and

Implications for Unemployment Insurance Programs." Office of Workforce Security Occasional Paper 2000-05, U.S. Department of Labor, Employment and Training Administration. Washington, D.C.: Office of Workforce Security.

DuRivage, Virginia L. 1992. "New Policies for the Part-Time and Contingent Workforce." In *New Policies for the Part-Time and Contingent Workforce*, ed. Virginia L. DuRivage. New York: M. E. Sharpe.

Houseman, Susan N. 1997. "Temporary, Part-Time, and Contract Employment: A Report on the W.E. Upjohn Institute's Employer Survey on Flexible Staffing Arrangements." Report prepared for the U.S. Department of Labor, Office of the Assistant Secretary for Policy.

———. 1999. "Flexible Staffing Arrangements: A Report on Temporary Help, On-Call, Direct-Hire Temporary, Leased, Contract Company, and Independent Contractor Employment in the United States." Report prepared for the Office of the Assistant Secretary for Policy, U.S. Department of Labor, contract no. 4030UQQF-99-2531-11354-000-00.

———. "Why Employers Use Flexible Staffing Arrangements: Evidence from an Establishment Survey." *Industrial and Labor Relations Review* 55, 1 (October): 149–70.

Houseman, Susan N. and Anne E. Polivka. 2000. "The Implications of Flexible Staffing Arrangements for Job Stability." In *On the Job: Is Long-Term Employment a Thing of the Past?* ed. David Newmark. New York: Russell Sage Foundation.

Joerg, Nancy E. 1996. *Welcome to the World of Independent Contractors and Other Contingent Workers*. Chicago: CCH Incorporated.

Kalleberg, Arne L., Jeremy Reynolds, and Peter V. Marsden. 1999. "Externalizing Employment: Flexible Staffing Arrangements in U.S. Organizations." Unpublished paper, University of North Carolina at Chapel Hill.

Klein, Jeffrey S. 1996. "Weighing the Legal Considerations." In *Managing Contingent Workers: How to Reap the Benefits and Reduce the Risks*, ed. Stanley D. Nollen and Helen A. Axel. New York: American Management Association. 183–208.

KRA Corporation. 1996. *Employee Leasing: Implications for State Unemployment Insurance Programs*. Final Report, submitted to Unemployment Insurance Service, U.S. Department of Labor, contract no. K-4280-3-00-80-30.

Mangum, Garth, Donald Mayall, and Kristen Nelson. 1985. "The Temporary Help Industry: A Response to the Dual Internal Labor Market." *Industrial and Labor Relations Review* 38, 4: 599–611.

Miller, Walter W. 2000. "Self-Insured Medical Plans: Cost Savings for Employers, But Design Must Consider Nondiscrimination Standards." *Journal of Taxation of Employee Benefits* 7, 5: 218–23.

Montana Legislative Council. 1994. "Workers' Compensation Emerging Issues: Independent Contractors, Contractor Licensing, and Employee Leasing: A Report to the Governor and 54th Legislature."

National Employment Law Project. 1997. *Mending the Unemployment Compensation Safety Net for Contingent Workers*. New York: National Employment Law Project.

———. 1999. *Workplace Equality for "Nonstandard" Workers: A Survey of Model State Legislation*. New York: National Employment Law Project.

Nollen, Stanley D. and Helen A. Axel, eds. 1996. *Managing Contingent Workers: How to Reap the Benefits and Reduce the Risks*. New York: American Management Association.

Peck, Jamie and Nikolas Theodore. 1998. "The Business of Contingent Work: Growth and Restructuring in Chicago's Temporary Employment History." *Work, Employment, and Society* 12, 4: 655–74.

Pivec, Mary E. and Nina Massen. 1996. "FMLA's Reach Extends to Contingent Work Force." *National Law Journal* 18, 6: C12–C13.

Polivka, Anne E. 1996. "Contingent and Alternative Work Arrangements, Defined." *Monthly Labor Review* 119, 10: 3–9.

Schoemann, Isabelle and Klaus Schoemann. 2000. "In Search of a New Framework for Flexibility — (Re)Regulation of Non-Standard Employment Relationships in the EU." Paper presented at the Conference on Nonstandard Work Arrangements in Japan, Europe, and the United States, August 25–26, Kalamazoo, Michigan.

Chapter 5
New Trends in Pension Benefit and Retirement Provisions

Olivia S. Mitchell with Erica L. Dykes

The past twenty years witnessed a rather striking transformation in the world's pension environment. Population aging and workforce changes in virtually all developed countries have sparked new forms of retirement provision. This pressure, combined with global financial market integration, has altered how people think about, and save for, retirement. As a case in point, many countries in the Western Hemisphere have moved away from a defined benefit (DB) pension model toward defined contribution (DC) plans, where participants' assets are accumulated and invested in capital markets. This has been a strong trend in Latin America, and similar changes have emerged in the United Kingdom, Germany, and most recently, Japan. The U.S. pension environment has changed as well, with workers increasingly interested in retirement accumulation accounts and moving into defined contribution pensions in response to the robust stock market performance at the end of the twentieth century. In the United States, as elsewhere, rising life expectancies and longer periods of labor market attachment have also enhanced the appeal of pensions for groups that previously lacked coverage years ago, such as among women.[1] Employers here, as elsewhere, are increasingly willing and even eager to provide new forms of pensions, responding to changes in the industrial and occupational mix of employment, and to an interest in using pensions to induce particular worker behaviors.[2] The pension arena has also been shaped by U.S. regulatory developments including legislation liberalizing tax treatment of pension funding levels, contribution amounts, and benefit payouts (McGill et al. 1996). In sum, the last two decades have been favorable to a dynamic pension environment in the United States, just as in the rest of the world.

Nevertheless, the historical legacy in the U.S. pension arena has been the defined benefit model, and as such, this plan type remains important to millions of workers and their employers. Nevertheless, companies that provided DB plans did not stand still: these sponsors too altered many aspects of plan design over time, changing eligibility rules, benefit offerings, and payout requirements over time. In this chapter we highlight some of the key developments in the U.S. pension environment over the last two decades. We trace plan evolution by evaluating Employee Benefits Survey (EBS) information on pensions offered to full-time workers employed in medium-size and large establishments. These surveys, fielded by the U.S. Bureau of Labor Statistics (BLS), are summarized in individual-year tabulations that we have compiled into time series tables on private sector pension plan characteristics in the United States.[3] After describing key retirement plan features, we report on time trends in retirement provisions and benefit formulas in U.S. defined benefit and defined contribution plans. We conclude with a discussion of implications for the American workplace going forward.

Overview of Pension Design and Pension Features

In the United States, employer-sponsored pensions are traditionally classified into defined contribution and defined benefit plans.[4] The worker covered by a DB pension receives a promise of an eventual retirement benefit that depends on a specified formula. Here the retiree payment is typically a function of the covered worker's age, pay, and/or service levels. In most cases the benefit is paid as a life annuity. By contrast, the employee with a defined contribution pension tends to have choice as to whether to participate in the plan, and if so, how much to contribute to his retirement saving account. In addition, the plan sponsor often adds to the participating employee's account by means of a match over employee contributions. Pension contributions are then invested in the capital market, and generally the DC participant has choice over investment options into which his own (and sometimes his employer's) funds are deposited. Usually, the contributions and earnings on the investments must be preserved for retirement, but sometimes an active worker may access his funds for hardship or some other purpose, often via a loan. On leaving the firm, the departing worker may receive his accrual in the form of a lump sum (though receipt of the lump sum may trigger a tax penalty unless he is at least age 59 and a half). Alternatively the departing worker may take his pension benefits in the form of a periodic amount or buy a life annuity. The value of the plan accrual at any given date depends on the amounts contributed and investment returns over the entire worklife.

Sponsors of both types of pension plans have ample choice regarding a range of eligibility, contribution, vesting, benefit, withdrawal, and retirement provisions and formulas. In addition, plans may embody different provisions regarding post-retirement benefit increases and special payouts (e.g., disability or lump sum cashouts), along with other features. In this investigation we determine how pension plans of medium-size and large establishments in the private sector have changed over the last two decades, to determine which trends might point the way for pensions of the future.

Understanding how pension provisions and benefit entitlements have changed over the last two decades is important since these provisions powerfully affect the nature of the pension promise, and in turn they influence worker and firm behavior (cf. Even and Macpherson this volume; Gustman and Mitchell 1992; Gustman et al. 1995). For instance, a pension-covered employee allowed to take a loan or a lump-sum cashout from his plan after a short vesting period gains access to his pension saving early in the work life, a practice that some worry contributes to inadequate old-age protection. An employee prohibited from taking a loan or cashing out his pension when young lacks early access to his accrued pension, so he may end up with a better-funded retirement period than his counterpart. On the other hand, some plan sponsors argue that inability to access the funds early in life might discourage participation. These and other structural features of pensions also influence worker turnover patterns. That is, vesting and benefit formulas can deter mobility for younger employees, and they can also induce workers to remain on the job longer if the plan offers substantial rewards for continued work (cf. Fields and Mitchell 1984). Other times, as in the case of defined contribution pensions, retirement benefits may depend on amounts contributed and how the worker chose to invest his pension assets. It has been shown that investment decisions depend to a large degree on how successful employers are in communicating benefit plan attributes to employees (Mitchell and Schieber 1998).

Before turning to a more detailed discussion of pension trends evident in the EBS over time, it is useful to briefly review key pension terminology and how pension provisions work.

Plan Participation and Vesting

Workers covered by a private pension are often not permitted to join their pension plan immediately; rather, many plans limit participation to workers who remain at the firm more than one year, and sometimes also limit coverage to those over the age of 21. The Employee Retirement Income Security Act (ERISA) of 1974, as amended, mandated that pension plan participation requirements cannot be more stringent that this (plans may be more generous). What is meant by "plan participation" matters, of course, since some pensions begin to count years of service for benefit purposes from the date that the worker becomes a plan participant. "Vesting" in a pension plan is important since it refers to the juncture at which the worker gains a legal claim to an eventual benefit from a pension plan in which he is a participant. Many establishments do not offer new workers an immediate claim on a retirement benefit; rather, workers will earn claim only when they meet employment criteria specified in the plan's vesting formula. One criterion often used is a minimum number of years of service; in 1974, ERISA spelled out several permitted vesting schedules including the most common "10-year cliff vesting rule," requiring workers to vest at 10 years of service. Subsequently vesting standards were eased under the Tax Reform Act of 1986, with most plans now using a "5-year rule" for cliff vesting.

Retirement Eligibility Requirements

Most U.S. pension plans require that a covered employee must complete a requisite number of years of service and/or attain a specified age, in order to be entitled to receive a pension plan payout. Thus, for example, a worker may be eligible for early retirement at age 55 with ten years of service, while normal retirement might be defined as leaving at age 65 with at least ten years of service. Such plan-based age and service requirements are most prevalent in DB plans, but they can also be found in DC pensions. When they exist, the rules establish conditions under which the worker can claim plan benefits. Eligibility requirements play a particularly crucial role in DB plans, since here age and service influence not only access to benefits, but also the level of benefits payable. For instance, an early retiree might receive a lower annual benefit amount than the one payable at the plan's normal retirement age. A higher benefit at the plan's normal retirement age recognizes the fact that at a later age, a worker has more years of service, possibly a higher pay level, and fewer years of life remaining over which to draw a benefit. In addition, DB plans frequently structure their benefit formulas so as to subsidize early retirement (cf. Fields and Mitchell 1984). Hence retirement requirements are important insofar as they establish when a worker may begin to receive subsidized early payouts.

For many years, U.S. plan sponsors were permitted to use their pension formulas to induce older workers to leave their jobs, mainly by limiting pension accruals after a specific age (Mitchell and Luzadis 1998). In 1986, however, in an effort to reduce the extent of age discrimination, the Omnibus Reconciliation Act required private pensions to continue accruing benefits after the normal retirement age; this ruling took effect for plans in 1988. (Collectively bargained plans were permitted to come into compliance somewhat later.) As a consequence, retirement eligibility rules for private sector pension plans have become more liberal over time, somewhat increasing benefit incentives to remain employed at older ages.

Retirement Contribution and Benefit Provisions

DB and DC plans use a wide range of definitions to determine contribution and benefits. In the DB case, participants' payouts at retirement generally are formula driven. Some benefit formulas provide for flat monthly dollar benefit entitlements per year of service, while others base benefits on employee pay, age, and/or service at retirement. When DB formulas depend on earnings, the employer generally specifies what percentage of earnings will be paid per year of service. A related issue is that earnings-based plans differ in terms of which definition of earnings they consider relevant. For instance, straight-time pay alone may be considered, or a plan may add overtime, shift pay, and/or commissions into the formula. In addition, pay-based plans differ in terms of the period of time over which earnings are computed. In a career earnings plan, pay during the entire period of employment is considered; conversely, a terminal earnings plan focuses on compensation just prior to retirement. Even terminal earnings benefit formulas generally include more than the final year's pay in the formula; it is not uncommon to use the worker's highest or last five years as the basis for a final average pay figure.

In other cases, corporate DB formulas may be "integrated" with social security rules, using two general patterns.[5] "Offset" formulas typically reduce a pension benefit payment by some fraction of the worker's primary social security amount, while an "excess" plan will apply lower pension benefit accruals to earnings below the Social Security taxable wage base (or some similar threshold) and higher benefit accumulations to earnings above this amount. Terminal earnings plans tend to use the offset approach when they are integrated, while career earnings plans tend to use the excess method. Integration is less common in plans using flat dollar amounts.

Defined benefit pension plans have various other benefit rules applying to retirement benefits under special conditions. For instance benefit "reduction factors" are important in determining the rate at which payouts may be reduced for workers retiring prior to the normal retirement age. If such reduction factors are not "big enough," they can actually encourage rather than discourage early retirement. In other cases, workers can gain access to pension accruals for special reasons, including for early receipt of vested benefits and for disability. Such access has raised policy concerns since permitting employees to cash out their vested accrued benefits may reduce eventual retirement accumulations (Fernandez 1992). Disability pensions are another way in which workers can receive benefits prior to becoming qualified for a regular pension, and hence these too play a role in workers' economic security benefits.

The institutional structure of defined contribution plans is just as varied as among their DB counterparts, but along somewhat different dimensions. Many different types of DC plans exist, categorized by the BLS into plans it called "retirement" plans, versus those deemed "capital accumulation" plans. The former were distinguished by prohibiting withdrawal of accruals prior to retirement, whereas the latter afforded easier access to accumulated assets. Over time, however, this distinction has become clear, so that the BLS notes that today "most defined contribution plans can be used to provide retirement income or to accumulate financial assets" (BLS 1989:

107). In addition, many of these plans allow lump-sum cashouts rather than a benefit annuity. Several new types of DC plans have also arrived on the scene, sometimes distinguished according to the source of their finances, or by how their assets are held. Examples include savings and thrift plans, profit-sharing programs, money purchase pension plans, employee stock ownership/stock bonus plans, and 401(k) plans. "Savings and thrift" plans are those where workers contribute a percentage of their pay and employers generally offer some amount of matching contribution (perhaps up to a maximum). The tax treatment of employee contributions depends on both individual plan structure and overall tax code limitations on the amount of compensation that can be tax deferred. Savings and thrift plans often permit workers to borrow from or make taxable withdrawals from their plans in special circumstances (e.g., educational or medical expenses). "Profit sharing" plans offering deferred income tend to link employer contribution levels to company profits, and then allocate the employer contribution levels to company profits, and then allocate to employer contribution based on workers' pay or other formulas. Early withdrawals or loans are rather less common here than in other plans. In "money purchase" plans, employer contributions are fixed as a fraction of earnings, whereas in "stock ownership and stock bonus" plans the employer contributions are usually in the form of company stock. And from the late 1980s on, 401(k) pensions have grown quite rapidly.

Changes in Pension Plans over Time

The U.S. Department of Labor's Bureau of Labor Statistics fielded an Employee Benefits Survey and has published tabulated data from these surveys in various years between 1980 and 1997. We follow the Labor Department's approach in what follows, first discussing DB plan features, and then turning to DC plans.[6]

Defined Benefit Plans

Three important characteristics of defined benefit pension plans worth emphasizing are participation, eligibility, and vesting rules; withdrawal and benefit formulas; and other special provisions. We take up each in turn.

Participation, eligibility and vesting. DB pensions in the United States provide specific criteria that covered employees must meet, before becoming full-fledged pension participants. Such requirements are justified by the employer's need to reduce administrative costs that would otherwise be incurred for young workers who are most likely to change jobs. Participation requirements are also thought to curtail turnover by offering workers an incentive to remain with the company (Gustman and Mitchell 1992). Under ERISA, full-time employees age 25 or older must be granted participant status after completing one year of service. Participation rules were subsequently amended by the 1984 Retirement Equity Act (REA), which for most plans lowered the participation requirement to age 21 as of mid-1986.

Trend data on plan participation requirements appear in Figure 1 and Table 1, which show that DB plans have continued to reward minimum service. Thus in 1981, 59 percent of DB participants had minimum age and/or service requirements and the fraction grew to 68 percent in 1997. About half of the DB participants had only a single year of service for participation, with the other half covered by the "age 21/service 1" rule; virtually no DB plan had an "age-only" criterion. Both are consistent with the REA. Prior to 1988, firms could hire older workers without incurring large pension obligations, and as of 1981, some 60 percent of covered workers were in plans of this type. The 1986 Omnibus Reconciliation Act (OBRA) outlawed this practice, and it likely had a large effect on DB plans that had previously imposed a maximum age for participation (a cap on service years is still permitted).

When a worker becomes a DB plan participant, he must typically satisfy a plan service requirement before gaining a legal vested right to his accrued benefit. Economists have argued that these requirements deter worker turnover, imposing a pension loss if a worker changes employers (cf. Even and Macpherson this volume; Ippolito 1986). Pension law curtailed the extent of this loss, first in 1974 when ERISA legislated permissible vesting formulas including a "10-year cliff" rule requiring an employee to be 100 percent vested after ten years of service. Subsequently, the 1986 Tax Reform Act (TRA) further lowered vesting rules, requiring a single-employer plan to convert to a five-year schedule if using cliff vesting (or seven years if graded vesting was in place); the five-year approach was adopted by most

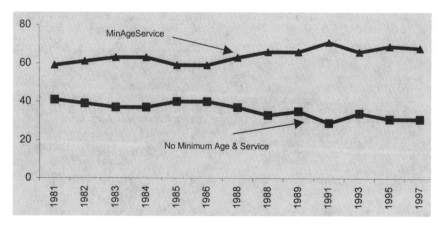

Figure 1. U.S. defined benefit plans continue to reward minimum service. Source: U.S. Department of Labor, Bureau of Labor Statistics, various years.

plans by 1989. The potent impact of these rule changes is revealed in Figure 2, which indicates that the fraction of DB plan participants with cliff vesting hovered around 89 percent during the 1980s, began to rise in the 1990s, and ended at 96 percent. At the same time, the modal number of years until vesting fell between 1988 and 1989, consistent with the declining legal threshold. Overall, vesting requirements in DB plans have definitely eased, as compared to the early 1980s.

Contributions. Most private sector DB plan participants are not required to contribute to their pension plans out of their own salary or earnings: only 3 to 5 percent of DB participants are required to make employee contributions. This differs markedly from public pension plan participants, where most employees contribute directly (Mitchell and Hustead 2000).

TABLE 1. Age and Length of Service Requirements for Pension Participation: Defined Benefit Pension Plans, 1981–97

Type of requirements	Percent of full-time participants				
	1981	*1985*	*1991*	*1995*	*1997*
No minimum age and/or service requirements					
	41	40	29	31	31
With minimum age and/or service requirements					
	59	59	71	69	68
Service only	20	23	26	27	28
≤1 year	na	21	26	25	27
Age only	4	3	4	3	1
Age and service	35	32	39	36	36
Age 25 and 1 year*	na	na	na	na	na
Age 21 and 1 year*	na	13	36	34	34
With maximum age limitation**	58	61	na	na	na

Source: Mitchell (1992); U.S. Department of Labor, Bureau of Labor Statistics, "Employee Benefits in Medium and Large Firms, 1981–1997," and unpublished data from the BLS for 1988† figures.
na means data not available; — means < 0.5 percent.
Data exclude supplemental pension plans. Column sums may not equal totals because of rounding.
† In 1988 the BLS changed its sampling frame to include smaller firms and more industries than before. As a result, the EBS tabulations for 1998 and after are not precisely comparable with earlier figures though a comparison tabulation using both methodologies indicates results are close.
* The Employee Retirement Income Security Act (ERISA) of 1974 required that pension plans allow full-time employees age 25+ with at least one year of service to participate. The Retirement Equity Act of 1984 required that nearly all plans allow participation to full-time employees age 21+ with at least one year of service by June 1986. The 1986 data surveyed plans prior to the law change.
** ERISA permitted plans to impose a maximum age for participation within 5 years of the plan's normal retirement date. The Omnibus Reconciliation Act of 1986 eliminated such maximums for plan years beginning in January 1988, with slightly later dates for collectively bargained plans.

Withdrawal and benefit formulas. Next we focus on changes in conditions under which plan participants may access their pension accruals, and here too there has been much change. DB plans in the United States typically have required benefits to be paid as annuities, and plans usually set a minimum age and/or service years threshold that must be satisfied for the worker to retire and receive payments. Important trends in this area appear in Table 2, where we see that early retirement was and has remained the norm in the DB environment, with over 95 percent of covered employees having access to it since 1980. But there have also been important changes in the early retirement scene. For instance, a criterion based on age or service alone has declined, whereas having the "right" mix of age plus service is growing. Nevertheless, these trends are not uniform: in the late 1980s there was a peak in the fraction of workers permitted to leave at age 55 with ten years of service, but this practice appeared to fall in favor during the 1990s. Conversely, it has became easier to retire with only five years of service at age 55, and the fraction of DB plan participants in this group rose from 3 percent to 20 percent between 1980 and 1997. It is interesting that relatively few participants are in plans where they must satisfy an additive age plus service requirement (5 percent in 1980, and 8 percent in 1997).

Turning to "normal" retirement requirements, most DB plans require workers to meet certain age requirements and/or age plus service requirements to receive full, unreduced, benefits, as shown in Table 3. Just under half of all participants were subject to normal retirement eligibility rules that depended on age alone in 1980, with that fraction remaining fairly stable over the entire period. Where age does serves as the criterion for normal retirement, the most common threshold has been age 65 (which is consistent

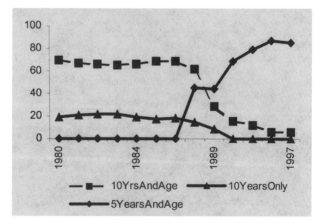

Figure 2. Vesting getting easier in U.S. defined benefit plans. Source: U.S. Department of Labor, Bureau of Labor Statistics, various years.

with the traditional "normal" Social Security retirement age in the past). Very few DB participants may retire on service alone: only 11 percent could receive normal retirement benefits by virtue of service alone in 1980 (with thirty years of service as the typical cutoff) and by 1997, the figure was down to 5 percent of participants. Requirements involving both age plus service are more common, and the data indicate a growing propensity of DB plans to provide normal retirement at age 62 with some minimum years of service. In 1981, 17 percent of the participants were able to retire at 62 with full benefits and by 1997 this fraction had risen to 21 percent. In other words there is some trend toward permitting workers to retire before age 65 and receive full (unreduced) benefits. These patterns are in line with findings from other studies indicating that some DB plans have encouraged earlier retirement over time (Luzadis and Mitchell 1991; Mitchell and Luzadis 1988). Whether this pattern will persist into the tight labor markets projected for the next twenty years (Lofgren et al. this volume) remains to be seen.

Benefit formulas in the DB plan environment appear in Table 4, where it is notable that the simple "flat dollar" formula per year of service approach is falling steadily (from 30 percent of participants in 1980 to 23 percent in 1997). The decline in flat dollar plans may be the result of falling unionization rates in the U.S. workforce, since these plans were traditionally

TABLE 2. Minimum Age and Service Requirements for Early Retirement: Defined Benefit Pension Plans, 1980–97

Type of requirement	Percentage of full-time participants					
	1980	1981	1985	1991	1995	1997
Plans permitting early retirement*	98	98	97	98	96	95
Service requirements alone	10	5	4	7	na	8
30 years required	9	5	4	6	na	8
Age requirements alone	9	10	9	6	na	3
Age 55	8	9	9	5	na	3
Age and service requirements						
Age 55 and 5 years	3	4	3	17	na	20
Age 55 and 10 years	na	36	43	32	na	30
Age 55 and 15 years	na	11	8	10	na	9
Age 60 and 10 years	na	4	4	4	1	2
Age 62 and 10 years	na	—	—	2	—	1
Age plus service sum	5	9	10	6	4	8
Sum ≤ 80	na	na	5	2	3	6
Sum ≥ 85	3	6	4	1	—	1
Plans not permitting early retirement	2	2	3	2	4	5

Source: See Table 1.
* Early retirement is defined as the point when a worker can retire and immediately receive accrued benefits based on service and earnings; benefits are reduced for years prior to the normal age.

TABLE 3. Minimum Age and Service Requirements for Normal Retirement: Defined Benefit Pension Plans, 1980–97*

Type of requirement	Percent of full-time participants					
	1980	1981	1985	1991	1995	1997
Service requirements alone	11	14	14	8	6	5
30 years required	11	14	14	7	5	4
Age requirements alone	45	46	37	39	48	41
Age 60	2	2	4	2	1	3
Age 62	4	4	4	6	3	3
Age 65	39	39	29	30	36	29
Age and service requirements	37	33	39	46	48	46
Age 55 and 30 years	na	2	2	1	3	—
Age 60 and 30 years	na	2	3	2	2	2
Age 62 and 10 years	na	8	11	7	9	11
Age 62 and 15–20 years	na	**2	4	4	7	3
Age 62 and 30 years	na	2	2	—	2	1
Age 65 and 5 years	2	1	1	10	9	15
Age 65 and 10 years	na	3	2	4	2	3
Age plus service sum	6	7	10	6	9	8

Source: See Table 1.
* At normal retirement a participant can retire and receive unreduced benefits immediately.
** Data available for 15 years' service only instead of 15–20.

TABLE 4. Benefit Formulas in Defined Benefit Pension Plans, 1980–97

Formula based on	Percent of full-time participants					
	1980	1981	1985	1991	1995	1997
Dollar amount*	30	32	29	23	23	23
Earnings	68	66	70	70	69	67
Terminal earnings	53	50	57	56	58	56
Career earnings	15	16	13	14	11	11

Source: See Table 1.
* Dollar amount refers to a flat monthly amount per year of service.

associated with collective bargaining agreements. Today, most DB plans base benefits on workers' earnings, with ⅔ of all participants having this link to benefits. Also interesting is the fact that terminal rather than career earnings are so prominent for DB benefit formulas, with only 11 to 15 percent of DB participants having benefits computed using career earnings. Most plans used five years' pay, with five consecutive years being the most common approach. Using terminal earnings links retirement benefits to individual performance at the end of the work life and is probably better protected from inflation, as compared to career average plans. It is also of interest to recognize DB plans have increasingly tied benefits to workers' straight-time or base pay, rising from 44 percent in 1988 to 62 percent by 1995 (Figure 3). DB plans have also cut reliance on extra compensation, being increasingly unlikely to credit benefits based on shift differentials, bonuses, and commissions. This may signal a reduction in the incentive-based portion of pensions, or may indicate a cut in benefit value for older workers.

Another change in the DB environment is the changes in the extent to which benefits paid are integrated with Social Security. Table 5 indicates that 45 percent of DB plan participants had their benefits integrated with Social Security in 1980; the integration fraction crept up for a time, but then fell back to 49 percent by 1997. At the same time, there have been major changes in the way Social Security integration is handled. Specifically, between 1980 and 1997, the fraction of workers with benefits offset by Social Security payments fell from 30 percent to 13 percent; what grew

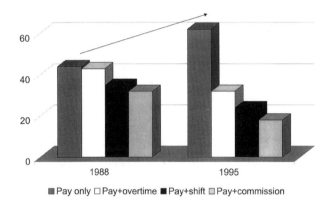

■ Pay only □ Pay+overtime ■ Pay+shift □ Pay+commission

Figure 3. U.S. defined benefit plans move to base pay in formula, less other compensation. Source: U.S. Department of Labor, Bureau of Labor Statistics, various years.

TABLE 5. Integration of Benefit Payments with Social Security: Defined Benefit Pension Plans, 1980–97

Type of formula	Percent of full-time participants					
	1980	1981	1985	1991	1995	1997
Without integrated formula	55	57	39	46	49	51
With integrated formula	45	43	61	54	51	49
Benefit offset by SS payment*	30	33	40	19	14	13
Excess formula**	16	10	27	36	37	36

Source: See Table 1.
* Pension benefit calculated is reduced by a portion of primary Social Security payment.
** Pension formula applies lower benefit ratio to earnings subject to Social Security taxes below a specified dollar threshold.

instead was the prevalence of plans with "excess formulas." In such a case the DB formula might provide 1 percent of pay up to the Social Security earnings threshold per year of service, for example, with some higher fraction (such as 1.5 percent) for pay above this level. So while there is no overall change in the extent of Social Security integration reported, the *type* of integration used has changed substantially.[7] It is of interest to recognize that these changes in pension integration practices coincide with large Social Security payroll tax increases; though a causal relationship cannot be proven here, the correlation is striking.

For those who retire early, DB payments are often reduced to recognize that early retirees will receive these payouts over a longer period of time. Table 6 summarizes trends in DB plan early retirement reduction factors, and the evidence indicates that that early retirement subsidies have been the norm over the entire period. This may be concluded because the typical early retirement reduction factor is less than 6 percent per year, and a 6 percent factor is generally deemed as that which represents actuarial neutrality (McGill et al. 1996).[8] Reduction factors also apply to vested workers who leave their employers, and the data (not shown) indicate that vested terminated workers also tend to face benefit reductions of 6 percent or less. Finally, 90 percent of DB plans permit vested terminated workers to take their benefits prior to normal retirement, but only about half face the same reduction as applied to early retirees.

Because DB benefit formulas are difficult to interpret, the BLS for a time presented a very useful set of tabulations for "hypothetical" workers' benefits on reaching normal retirement age, using six standardized pay levels and three seniority profiles. Plan information was used to compute "replacement rates," defined as the ratio of the DB retirement plan benefits to the worker's final year of earnings; see Table 7. Unfortunately these computations were no longer published after 1993; for the available period, however,

TABLE 6. Reduction Factors for Early Retirement: Defined Benefit Pension Plans, 1982–97

Type of formula	Percent of full-time participants				
	1982	*1985*	*1991*	*1995*	*1997*
Early retirement reduction factor where applied					
Uniform percentage* per year	46	49	47	40	43
6.0% or more	24	17	19	19	21
Percent varies with					
Age	30	49	49	57	57
Service	3	2	3	3	4

Source: See Table 1.
* Uniform percentage early retirement factors may approximate actuarial reductions.

they suggest that DB plan replacement rates rose with service for a given pay level and generally rose for a given service/earnings combination until 1991. After that time, there was a substantial fall in computed replacement rates. Why this might be has not yet been explained in the literature.

A final aspect of DB payout design is highlighted in Figure 4, which describes changes in employer willingness to permit retiring workers to take their benefits as a lump sum instead of a life annuity. Lump sums were extremely rare in traditional DB plans but the trend is sharply upward: in 1991, only 14 percent of participants could take any lump sum, but six years later, almost one-quarter (23 percent) of DB participants could do so. Of those with access to a lump sum, the majority was generally permitted to take the entire amount in a lump sum. This trend underscores other evidence indicating a decline in retirement income annuitization in the United States (Brown et al. 2001).

TABLE 7. Average Pension Replacement Rates for Specified Illustrative Workers: Defined Benefit Pension Plans, 1984–93

	*Retirement annuity as percentage of final earnings**				
Illustrative worker with	*1984*	*1985*	*1989*	*1991*	*1993*
10 years of service and final annual earnings of					
$ 20,000	9.9	9.8	10.9	na	na
30,000	9.7	9.5	9.9	na	na
45,000	—	—	—	10.8	6.4
55,000	—	—	—	10.8	6.3
65,000	—	—	—	10.8	6.3
20 years of service and final annual earnings of					
$ 20,000	18.8	19.1	21.1	na	na
30,000	18.5	18.6	19.8	na	na
45,000	—	—	—	20.9	13.5
55,000	—	—	—	20.8	13.3
65,000	—	—	—	20.1	13.3
30 years of service and final annual earnings of					
$ 20,000	27.4	28.3	31.3	na	na
30,000	26.5	27.3	29.4	na	na
45,000	—	—	—	30.2	21.5
55,000	—	—	—	29.0	21.0
65,000	—	—	—	29.1	21.0

Source: See Table 1.
* The maximum private pension was calculated using the earnings and service shown, not reduced for early retirement or joint-and-survivor annuities. Replacement rates refer to the ratio of the retirement pension to the final year's earnings.

Special provisions in DB plans. In the private sector, few pensions are protected against inflation by formal indexation; as a rule, private pension benefits are usually delivered as fixed nominal annuities. This is not a major concern for many older workers and retirees during low-inflation periods, but even a modest 3 percent inflation rate can cut the real value of the benefit in half in only twenty-four years. Despite this, the evidence reveals that DB pension benefits are only rarely tied to an explicit cost of living index (COLA). In 1995, for instance, only 7 percent of EBS participants had a COLA, and only 3 percent had an automatic escalator. Frequently benefits are not increased at all post-retirement, as can be seen by the fact that only 4 percent of the participants had plans with discretionary benefit increases in 1995. This is extraordinary given the generally strong equity market performance seen by many plans during the 1980s and 1990s, but it attests to the low inflation rates experienced over the period.

In addition to these other benefit provisions, private pensions often impose a ceiling on benefit amounts payable to retirees. The prevalence of this phenomenon has been declining: in 1984, for instance, 42 percent of the participants faced a benefit maximum; by 1997, only 33 percent were capped. In plans that did limit benefits, they tended to do so by capping the number of years of service that may be counted for benefit purposes. In 1997, for instance, 31 percent of the DB participants faced a maximum limit on service years. The modal choice for a maximum has generally been between thirty and thirty-nine years of service since 1984.

In addition to early and normal retirement, most DB plan participants — three-quarters, on average — also had the promise of special disability payouts (Figure 5). The prevalence of disability pensions has declined over time, however, down to 75 percent by 1997, from a high of 90 percent

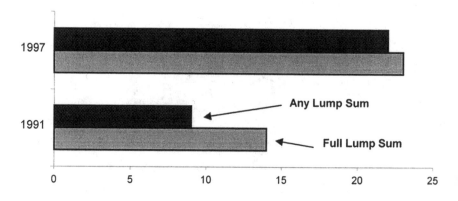

Figure 4. More defined benefit plans permit lump sum withdrawals. Source: U.S. Department of Labor, Bureau of Labor Statistics, various years.

during the late 1980s. It is not clear why this drop occurred, though it might be due to the rising cost of private disability insurance over the period. In addition, many DB plans tightened employee access to disability benefits by requiring that employees wait a longer time to qualify for long-term disability benefits: in 1997 only 46 percent of the workers were eligible for immediate disability benefits, down from a high of 70 percent in 1980. Other aspects of the disability insurance plans were also tightened, with disabled employees becoming less likely to received credit service until the establishment's retirement date, and less likely to receive unreduced normal benefits.

Defined Contribution Plans

The growth spurt experienced in DC pension plans over time occurred in parallel with changes in coverage and vesting patterns, contributions and withdrawals, and special features of 401(k) plans.

Plan types, coverage, and vesting. There appears to have been a strong downward trend in coverage by retirement and capital accumulation plans during the 1980s, but this is partly a result of the fact that what this set of plans referred to has varied over time. While EBS tabulations include money purchase and profit sharing plans, saving and thrift plans, we focus here on cash and deferred salary reduction plans including 401(k)s.[9] "Coverage" here is defined as being employed in an establishment offering a pension plan; some workers may not be actual participants if they had not yet vested or had elected not to contribute to the plan and there was no minimum employer contribution. In any event, the BLS data suggest that the percentage of full-time employees lacking pension coverage rose from 8 percent to 21 percent from 1985 to 1991 and coverage declines were largest in the DB, money purchase, and profit-sharing plan categories. By contrast, there was

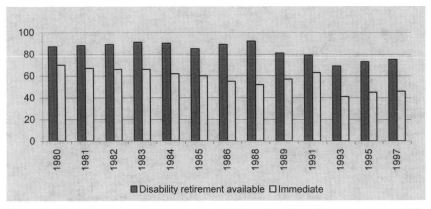

Figure 5. Disability retirement provisions in U.S. defined benefit plans. Source: U.S. Department of Labor, Bureau of Labor Statistics, various years.

rapid growth in coverage by savings/thrift plans where worker coverage jumped from only 18 percent in 1985 to more than one-third in 1995. This trend reinforces conclusions from other data sources indicating that the U.S. workforce boosted DC plan participation, but DB plan coverage fell over time (Piacentini and Cerino 2000; Turner and Beller 1999).

Requirements for participation and vesting in DC plans tend to be relatively minimal, with as many as one-quarter of 401(k) plan participants allowed immediate participation. And even when a participation criterion is in place, it is generally no more than service of up to a year. Vesting patterns for 401(k) plans indicate that one-third of the participants can vest immediately on joining the plan, in sharp contrast to DB plans where virtually no employees have full and immediate vesting. For those lacking immediate DC plan vesting, participants were evenly split between cliff vesting (after five years) and graduated vesting (with two-thirds vesting at five years or later). The trend to shorter cliff vesting is in part a result of the 1986 Tax Reform Act requiring most plans using cliff vesting to convert to a five-year schedule as of 1989.

Contribution and pre-retirement access patterns. In DC plans it is more common to have both employee and employer contributions, as compared to DB plans, where employer-only contributions are the norm in the private sector, as noted above. Data on employee contributions in 401(k) plans are provided in Table 8, and they indicate that most employee contributions are a function of workers' earnings — almost 90 percent in 1997. Employer contributions for DC plans reported by the EBS were generally of the matching variety, with the modal match being 6 percent of pay (Figure 6).

One area of interest has to do with whether employees may access their accounts prior to retirement. It has been argued that DC plans tend to permit loans from employee accounts, and outright withdrawal is often allowed in the event of hardship.[10] These conclusions hold for 401(k) plans, where over half of plan participants could obtain funds from their plans via a loan in 1997, up from 43 percent in 1993 (Figure 7). Furthermore, the modal participant in such plans could obtain a loan for any reason, not just for hardship, and those permitted freer access increased from 39 percent to 45 percent. Therefore employee access definitely became easier in 401(k) plans over time.

TABLE 8. Employee Contributions in 401(k) Plans, 1997

	1997
Plans using fraction of earnings	87
10%	9
10–15%	53
16–19%	18
Other	8

Source: See Table 1.

Investment choices. One feature contributing to the widespread popularity of DC pension plans over the last two decades is the fact that they typically offer employees some degree of control over their pension investments. The EBS data indicate that different provisions typically apply to employee versus employer contributions. Thus some 87 percent of employees with 401(k) plans could elect among investment choices for their own contributions and 65 percent could elect investment options for employer contributions. It also appears that the modal number of investment choices available for both employee and employer contributions has risen over time (see Figure 8).

Pension payout trends. Distribution of pension assets at retirement may take various forms. In general, lump-sum payouts are prevalent in the DC environment and almost all participants have such access. Of more concern to those focused on the adequacy of retirement income is the fact that a minority of participants with DC plans has access to an annuity, and this

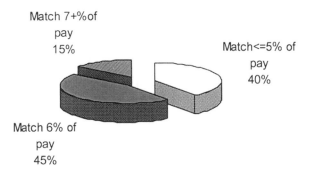

Figure 6. Employer match as percent of pay in 401(k) plans. Source: U.S. Department of Labor, Bureau of Labor Statistics, various years.

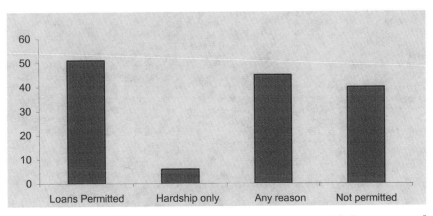

Figure 7. Access to 401(k) accumulations a concern. Source: U.S. Department of Labor, Bureau of Labor Statistics, various years.

percentage has fallen over time: In 1993, 34 percent of 401(k) plan participants could take their funds as a life annuity, and by 1997 this option was available to only 27 percent. As a result, workers retiring from a DC plan are less likely to have available to them the traditional annuity payout option that once was identified as a key element needed to protect retirees against longevity risk.[11]

Conclusions

Medium-size and large firms in the United States have traditionally been the most reliable providers of employment-linked retirement benefits (Sass 1997). Nevertheless, the evidence provided here shows that in these firms, the pension environment has been far from static. Most plan features and design elements examined have changed over time, sometimes in dramatic ways. Changes were seen in pension financing arrangements, eligibility and benefit formulas, and the extent to which plan participants can allocate and access their retirement plan accumulations both before and after retirement. Because the EBS surveys used here evaluated pensions only in medium and large establishments, and because some of the tabulations are not provided in a consistent fashion over time, the time series evidence is to some extent imperfect. Nevertheless, the information affords a uniquely valuable insight into U.S. private sector pension plan changes over the last two decades: the clear message is that *change is the only constant* in the U.S. pension environment.

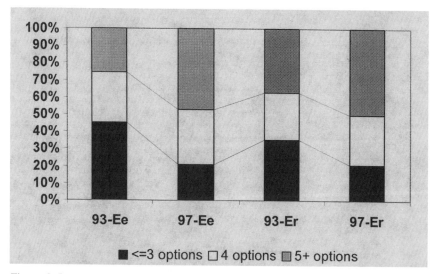

Figure 8. Investment choices in 401(k) plans for employee (Ee) and employer (Er) contributions, 1993 and 1997. Source: U.S. Department of Labor, Bureau of Labor Statistics, various years.

Some lessons regarding the DB pension environment include the fact that few DB participants contribute to their own pensions directly from their salaries in the private sector, a phenomenon that differs markedly from public sector pensions. Another finding is that DB plan sponsors have increasingly provided workers with access to early retirement, along with readier access to normal retirement. Pension benefit formulas have also moved toward final rather than career earnings, and benefit integration with social security has changed, particularly regarding the type of integration required. Pension replacement rates appear to have fallen over time, benefit ceilings are firmly in place, and disability benefit provisions have become more stringent. Other key findings for DB plans include the following:

- DB participation rules have become more stringent, while vesting rules have eased.
- DB benefit formulas increasingly link benefits to straight-time and terminal pay, rather than to incentive-based pay. After retirement, these private sector DB plans do not typically index benefits to inflation.
- Normal retirement ages have fallen in the DB environment, with participants gaining access to unreduced benefits earlier than age 65. Early retirement is also typically subsidized at actuarially favorable rates.
- It is increasingly possible for retirees to take their DB pension benefit as a lump sum, suggesting reduced protection against longevity risk.

While few U.S. firms are starting DB plans from afresh these days, the DC environment is clearly an area of substantial growth. Here, employee contributions as a function of earnings are the norm. Commonly too, employers match these contributions at a modal rate of 6 percent of pay; but employer matching appears to be falling over time. Other changes in DC plan characteristics include the following:

- DC plan participants are increasingly able to elect where to invest their own and their employer's contributions. Over time, participants have gained access to diversified stock and bond funds, but fewer are permitted to invest in own-employer stock, common stock funds, and guaranteed insurance contracts.
- DC participants may access their DC accounts via loans prior to retirement; and after retirement, fewer participants can access a life annuity as a payout option. This too implies reduced protection against longevity risk.

These developments in the pension environment raise questions about the future role of pensions as retirement income vehicles. For example, many pension systems have low hurdles for employee vesting and participation, making it easier for mobile workers to gain benefit rights. Yet giving employees access to loans and lump sums, and permitting plan participants to take lump sums, may undercut productivity enhancement and retirement security objectives. Allowing earlier retirement may be preferred by some workers and their employers, but this trend goes against other efforts to extend the work life as population aging continues. Also the ever-changing legislative environment has also driven changes in pension plan redesign. In the past, policymakers have sometimes provided contradictory signals to plan sponsors and employees as to the appropriate role of pensions. As an example, plan development has sometimes been spurred by tax concessions and permitting large Social Security offsets. However, at other times, regulatory policy has curtailed plan saving and permitted the leakage of pension accumulations through loans and cashouts.

Researchers examining pension design to date have not always recognized the dynamic nature of the pension environment. Our evidence indicates that future pension growth will be concentrated in the DC arena, with increasing participant control being exerted over all aspects of the plans — including contributions, investment mix, and payouts. They will grow more flexible as accumulation plans, allowing portability and earlier access, but they will probably offer disability and other ancillary benefits. As the labor market ages and pension plans are asked to play new roles in retirement security, they will continue to change. In the United States, at least, private pensions have not been cast in stone. Rather, the pension institution responds to external stimuli including labor market pressures, to internal corporate requirements, and to legislative change as well as financial market developments.

Notes

Support for this research was provided by the Pension and Welfare Benefits Administration of the U.S. Department of Labor. Useful comments were provided by Daniel Beller, Phyllis Fernandez, David McCarthy, and Jack Vanderhei. Opinions and conclusions are solely those of the author.

1. For a discussion on the role of pensions in women's retirement income see Levine et. al. (2000, 2001).

2. For a discussion of these and other effects see Even and McPherson (this volume), Gustman et al. (1995), Ippolito (1986), and Mitchell (2001).

3. Trends in public pension characteristics are discussed in Mitchell and Hustead (2000).

4. The discussion in this section builds on Mitchell (1992). Cash balance plans are sometimes seen as a third type of plan, in that they combine elements of both DB and DC pensions. However, these are DB plans under U.S. law, because the plan sponsor guarantees the promised rate of return on participant assets, and are not tabulated separately in available EBS survey reports (Clark and Schieber 2001; Rappaport et al. 1998).

5. For a more complete discussion of integration with Social Security see McGill et al. (1996).

6. In analyzing these trends, the reader should note that over time some pension definitions were altered by the BLS: changes were driven by regulatory reform, market conditions, and external developments (such as the boom in the U.S. stock market during the 1990s). Thus since the mid-1980s the survey tracked profit sharing and savings/thrift plans, and more recently it added 401(k) information. In addition, some series collected in the 1980s were not continued over the entire period, and new series were added for the first time in the early 1990s. The BLS also did not use identical table formats across all years, it phased out some tabulations and changed definitions over time. Finally, in some cases tabulations cannot be compared because they use a different base over which the prevalence of a certain feature is computed. For instance, it is not possible to derive a time series on the percentage of workers with multiple plans of particular types, since the base over which these numbers were calculated changed in the early 1990s. Here we provide as much data as possible, recognizing that the changes render some of these tabulations time-inconsistent; greater consistency in data collection and reporting would be beneficial for the future.

7. Changes in pension integration practices over this period are probably also due to the Tax Reform Act of 1986 that limited the permissible difference between contributions paid and benefits received by low-paid versus highly-paid employees (see McGill et al. 1996).

8. Early retirement may also be subsidized in other plans using factors that vary with age and service, but this cannot be determined from available tabulations.

9. A further issue is that "retirement" plans are defined in the EBS as plans where employer contributions are required to remain in the participant's account until retirement, death, disability, termination, hardship, or attainment of age 59½. By contrast "capital accumulation" plans are defined to be those where a participant may withdraw the money under other circumstances.

10. Exactly what constitutes a hardship according to plan sponsors is somewhat imprecise. The BLS indicates that possible reasons include purchase or repair of primary residence, illness or death in the family, education of an immediate family member, or sudden uninsured loss.

11. In some cases, a DC plan retiree can roll a lump sum into an individual retirement account and then purchase an individual life annuity. That retiree would, however, loose access to the group risk pool and would be forced to pay for adverse selection costs as well as possibly higher loadings in the individual retail market (Mitchell et al. 1999).

References

Brown, Jeffrey R., Olivia S. Mitchell, James M. Poterba, and Mark J. Warshawsky. 2001. *The Role of Annuity Markets in Financing Retirement.* Cambridge, Mass.: MIT Press.

Clark, Robert L. and Sylvester J. Schieber. 2001. "Taking the Subsidy Out of Early Retirement: Converting to Hybrid Pensions." In *Innovations in Managing the Financial Risks of Retirement,* ed. Olivia S. Mitchell, Zvi Bodie, P. Brett Hammond, and Stephen P. Zeldes. Pension Research Council. Philadelphia: University of Pennsylvania Press.

Even, William E. and David A. Macpherson. This volume. "Benefits and Productivity."

Fernandez, Phyllis. 1992. "Pre-Retirement Lump Sum Distributions." In *Trends in Pensions 1992,* ed. John A. Turner and Daniel J. Beller. Washington, D.C.: U.S. Department of Labor, PWBA.

Fields, Gary S. and Olivia S. Mitchell. 1984. *Retirement, Pensions, and Social Security.* Cambridge, Mass.: MIT Press.

Gustman, Alan L. and Olivia S. Mitchell. 1992. "Pensions and the U.S. Labor Market." In *Pensions and the Economy: Sources, Uses, and Limitations of Data,* ed. Zvi Bodie and Alicia H. Munnell. Pension Research Council. Philadelphia: University of Pennsylvania Press. 39–87.

Gustman, Alan L., Olivia S. Mitchell, Andrew A. Samwick, and Thomas L. Steinmeier. 1999. "Pension and Social Security Wealth in the Health and Retirement Study." In *Wealth, Work, and Health: Innovations in Survey Measurement in the Social Sciences,* ed. Robert Willis. Ann Arbor: University of Michigan Press. 150–208.

Gustman, Alan L., Olivia S. Mitchell, and Thomas Steinmeier. 1994. "The Role of Pensions in the Labor Market." *Industrial and Labor Relations Review* 47, 3: 417–38.

———. 1995. "Retirement Measures in the Health and Retirement Survey." *Journal of Human Resources* 30 Supplement): S57–S83.

Ippolito, Richard A. 1986. *Pensions, Economics, and Public Policy.* Homewood, Ill.: Dow Jones-Irwin.

Levine, Phillip, Olivia S. Mitchell, and James F. Moore. 2000. "Women on the Verge of Retirement: Predictors of Retiree Well-Being." In *Forecasting Retirement Needs and Retirement Wealth,* ed. Olivia S. Mitchell, P. Brett Hammond, and Anna M. Rappaport. Pension Research Council. Philadelphia: University of Pennsylvania Press. 167–207.

Levine, Phillip B., Olivia S. Mitchell, and John W. Phillips. 2001. "Worklife Determinants of Retirement Income Differentials Between Men and Women." In *Innovations in Retirement Financing,* ed. Olivia S. Mitchell, Zvi Bodie, P. Brett Hammond, and Stephen Zeldes. Pension Research Council. Philadelphia: University of Pennsylvania Press.

Lofgren, Eric P., Steven A. Nyce, and Sylvester J. Schieber. This volume. "Designing Total Reward Programs for Tight Labor Markets."

Lumsdaine, Robin and Olivia S. Mitchell. 2000. "New Developments in the Economics of Retirement." In *Handbook of Labor Economics,* vol. 3, ed. Orley Ashenfelter and David Card. New York: North-Holland. 3261–3308.

Luzadis, Rebecca and Olivia S. Mitchell. 1991. "Explaining Pension Dynamics." *Journal of Human Resources* 26 (Fall): 679–703.

McGill, Dan M., John J. Haley, Gordon P. Goodfellow, and Sylvester J. Schieber. 1996. *Fundamentals of Private Pensions.* 7th ed. Philadelphia: University of Pennsylvania Press.

Mitchell, Olivia S. 1992. "Trends in Pension Benefit Formulas and Retirement Provisions." In *Trends in Pensions 1992,* ed. John A. Turner and Daniel J. Beller. Washington, D.C.: U.S. Department of Labor, PWBA. 177–216.

———. 2001. "Developments in Pensions." In *Handbook of Insurance,* ed. Georges Dionne. New York: Kluwer Academic. 873–99.

Mitchell, Olivia S. and Edwin C. Hustead, eds. 2000. *Pensions in the Public Sector.* Pension Research Council. Philadelphia: University of Pennsylvania Press.

Mitchell, Olivia S. and Rebecca Luzadis. 1998. "Changes in Pension Incentives Through Time." *Industrial and Labor Relations Review* 42 (October): 100–108.

Mitchell, Olivia S., David McCarthy, Stanley C. Wisniewski, and Paul W. Zorn. 2000. "Developments in State and Local Pension Plans." In *Pensions in the Public Sector,* ed. Olivia S. Mitchell and Edwin C. Hustead. Pension Research Council. Philadelphia: University of Pennsylvania Press.

Mitchell, Olivia S., James M. Poterba, Mark J. Warshawsky, and Jeffrey R. Brown. 1999. "New Evidence on the Money's Worth of Individual Annuities." *American Economic Review* (December): 1299–1318.

Mitchell, Olivia S. and Sylvester J. Schieber, eds. 1998. *Living with Defined Contribution Pensions.* Pension Research Council. Philadelphia: University of Pennsylvania Press.

Piacentini, Joseph S. and Timothy J. Cerino. 2000. *EBRI Databook on Employee Benefits.* Washington D.C.: EBRI.

Rappaport, Anna M., Michael L. Young, Christopher A. Levell, and Brad A. Blalock. 1998. "Cash Balance Pension Plans." In *Living with Defined Contribution Pensions,* ed. Olivia S. Mitchell and Sylvester J. Schieber. Pension Research Council. Philadelphia: University of Pennsylvania Press. 29–45.

Sass, Steven A. 1997. *The Promise of Private Pensions.* Cambridge, Mass.: Harvard University Press.

Turner, John A. and Daniel J. Beller, eds. 1999. *Trends in Pensions 1988.* Washington, D.C.: U.S. Department of Labor, PWBA.

U.S. Department of Labor, Bureau of Labor Statistics (BLS). Various years. *Employee Benefits in Medium and Large Private Establishments.* U.S. Department of Labor Bulletin. Washington, D.C.: U.S. Government Printing Office.

Part II
Emerging Challenges to Benefits and Compensation Design

Chapter 6
Implications of the Difficult Economy for Company-Sponsored Retirement Plans

Anna M. Rappaport

After two decades of economic growth in the United States, a combination of forces has propelled the economy and benefit plan sponsors into a new and less prosperous environment. Equity markets, particularly NASDAQ stocks, have fallen dramatically, and some stocks are down 80 percent or more from their recent highs (Value Line Investment Survey 2001). High technology, once an engine of growth, has fallen out of favor. An electric power crisis gripped California and people speculate about similar problems for other parts of the country. Utility companies, long seen as a safe investment, now seem to have an uncertain future. Many financial service and insurance firms have released disappointing earnings.

How have pensions responded to this negative economic news? In theory, pensions are long-term arrangements, so pension investing should reflect the long-term prognosis for the economy. In the United States, pensions are provided by both defined benefit (DB) and defined contribution (DC) plans, with sponsors making investment decisions in the DB case, and employees making many more decisions in DC case. In both types of plans, investment decisions should be made with a view to the long term during which funds will be accumulated, as well as the lengthy period during which funds will be drawn down.

In practice, of course, pension plans have always operated in an environment of economic turmoil and change. Nevertheless, in our view, recent economic developments will likely have a greater impact on pension plans than did earlier shifts in economic conditions. This is partly because of the growth of DC plans, which implies that more of the pension assets are employee-controlled. Though some participants take the long view, others find this difficult to do, especially if they are nearing retirement. In addition, many people were unprepared for the reemergence of the business cycle, since the period of economic growth leading up to 2001 was so very long.

The economic uncertainty also coincides with another benefits trend, namely, the growing importance of employee stock ownership. The National Center for Employee Ownership recently reported that 13 percent of employer stock is now owned by employees through various employee benefit programs and broad-based stock option programs (NCEO 2001). Firms that stressed employee ownership in the past may now be forced to revisit retirement benefit design, in view of the stock market's erratic performance.

The prevalence of company stock in retirement plans and other compensation means that employees have become concerned not just about market performance, but also about the performance of their own company's stock. Table 1 illustrates the performance of broad market indexes for one and five years ending first quarter, 2001, as compared to well and poorly performing Dow index individual stocks. The impact of the economy on individual plans depends on the plan's specific investments and, of course, on participants' investment elections. Those heavily concentrated in a single company stock are likely to be more exposed to market fluctuations, than are more broadly diversified plans holding the market basket.

When stock is available as a DC plan investment, the amount people elect to hold in company stock depends on whether there is employer-directed investment in that stock. Table 2 confirms that plans having employer-directed investments tend to be more heavily concentrated in equities overall, than are other DC plans. Furthermore, DC participants tend to invest 20 percent of their account balances in company stock when investment in employer stock is voluntary. But when an employer directs some of the balance to company stock, 48 percent of the total balance (including 29 percent of the participant-directed balance) tends to be invested in company stock (Holden and VanDerhei 2001).

TABLE 1. Performance of Stock Market Indexes Compared to Individual

	1-year change (ending 3/31/01)		5-year change (ending 3/31/01)
S&P 500	−23%		+80%
NASDAQ	−60%		+67%
Dow winners			
Phillip Morris	+126%	Wal-Mart	+339%
Boeing	+47%	Microsoft	+324%
Dow losers			
AT&T	−62%	AT&T	−48%
Intel	−60%	Kodak	−44%

Source: Wall Street Journal, 2001 <www.wsj.com>.

Another theme influencing the corporate environment is the "war for talent." Over 90 percent of multinational employers indicated that this is a priority in the human resources field (Mercer 1999). The recruiting and attraction problems that companies face vary with the business cycle as well as the product life cycle, implying a need for specific skills. More recently, companies have been faced with having to simultaneously layoff and hire for growth areas, at the same. Looking at the long term, there will be significant skill shortages as the baby boomers retire with a smaller cohort replacing them (see Lofgren et al. this volume; Riche this volume). Even though equity prices have declined, employment has thus far remained relatively robust; business is still faced with key skill shortages. Figure 1 illustrates U.S. unemployment patterns in the last thirty years, indicating that it remains below historical levels.

In the twenty-first century, demographics will increasingly interact with economics. Slowly, the definition of retirement is changing, as people build

TABLE 2: Impact of Company Stock on Asset Allocation by Age (1999)

Age cohort	Equity funds	Company stock	Balanced funds	Bond funds	Money funds	GICs[a]
Plans with employer-directed and participant-directed balances						
Total balances (employer-directed and participant-directed)						
20s	36.6%	48.1%	5.5%	0.6%	3.4%	5.4%
30s	32.1	52.4	5.3	0.7	2.2	7.0
40s	30.2	50.9	5.6	1.1	3.3	8.4
50s	29.8	46.4	6.4	1.5	4.5	11.2
60s	28.8	36.1	7.2	2.9	8.7	15.9
All	30.2	47.6	6.0	1.4	4.2	10.2
Participant-directed balances only						
20s	47.2	34.8	7.0	0.8	3.9	6.1
30s	46.6	33.3	7.5	1.0	2.8	8.6
40s	44.2	30.9	7.9	1.6	4.5	10.4
50s	41.0	28.8	8.2	2.1	6.0	13.4
60s	35.6	22.6	8.7	3.6	10.6	18.5
All	42.1	29.3	8.1	2.0	5.6	12.5
Plans with company stock investment option but no employer-directed contributions						
Total balances						
20s	58.6	17.7	8.3	1.7	6.2	4.4
30s	56.5	19.5	8.6	1.9	5.1	5.9
40s	51.1	20.9	9.2	2.3	5.5	8.6
50s	45.9	20.4	10.4	3.1	6.2	12.1
60s	38.2	18.7	11.3	4.1	8.4	17.6
All	48.7	20.2	9.7	2.7	6.1	10.4

Source: Derived from Holden and VanDerhei (2001).
Minor investment options are not shown; therefore row percentages will not add to 100 percent. Employer-directed balances are invested in the plan sponsor's company stock.
[a] Guaranteed investment contracts.

phased retirement programs and move into new careers. Baby boomers are crossing the age-55 threshold, the age at which retirement has been permitted in many corporate pension plans. Some organizations have even earlier retirement ages, as in public utilities and health care. What is changing is that workers with liberal early retirement benefits are increasingly leaving their long-term employers, and then they are moving into "bridge" jobs, or jobs in new organizations that can be part time or in a new area.

Concerns Regarding Retirement Plan Financing

Poor capital market performance has a negative effect on retirement plans, though how this plays out depends on the relative movement of equity markets and interest rates. Sometimes changes in these items offset each other, and in other cases, they compound each other. Indeed, if pension expense is large compared to the earnings of the company, a change in pension expense results in a material change in earnings per share.

Issues Pertinent to Defined Benefit Plan Finances

A plan sponsor offering a DB plan must spread long-term plan costs over employees' working lifetimes, based on actuarial methods and assumptions. The one-year cost of a pension plan is specified as the value of benefits earned (or attributed to) the current year, adjusted by a portion of the difference between plan assets and liabilities. If plan assets exceed liabilities, pension law and accounting standards consider the plan to be overfunded; if liabilities exceed assets, there is an unfunded liability.[1] For DB plan valuation, pension expense must be computed as the amount charged for the plan and reported in the organization's profit and loss statement; this value

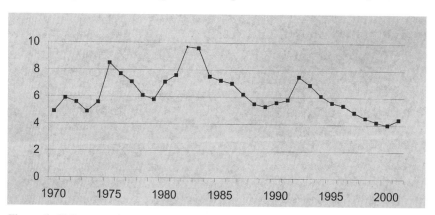

Figure 1. U.S. unemployment rates over time. Source: U.S. Department of Labor, Bureau of Labor Statistics (2000). Unemployment rate in 2001 an average of first 7 months.

is determined subject to the requirements of the accounting profession. Pension contributions refer to the cash contributed to the plan, and amounts are determined by U.S. pension law.

Table 3 compares the key characteristics of these alternative pension cost calculations, which differ because they serve different underlying goals. For

TABLE 3. Characteristics of Pension Expense and Pension Contributions

	Pension expense (amount charge to profit and loss)	Pension contributions (cash contributed to pension fund)
Applicable rules	Securities and Exchange requirements and financial rules (Statement of Financial Standards Number 87)	Federal law, the Internal Code defined a minimum contribution and a maximum limit
Goals	Proper matching of revenue and expense and comparability of results between companies	For the minimum, security of plan participants and for the limitation of what can be invested tax deferred fund
Choice of methods for calculation	Very limited	More flexibility
Method prescribed for measurement of assets	Market value, with some permitted	Market value, with some permitted
Discount rate used in calculating liabilities	Must be based on current market and adjusted annually if rates change	Based on long-term expected
Special problems with calculation	Changes in discount rates create significant volatility; can be a problem when asset values and discount rates drop at the same time	In some cases, contributions are volatile. There are discontinuities the spreading of surplus and liability. If there is a surplus and liability. If there is a surplus, no contribution is allowed. If the unfunded liabilities exceed limits, extra contributions are needed
Added costs for plans	None	Additional PBGC premiums are required
If assets exceed liabilities	The excess (or surplus) is used to offset pension cost and gradually recognized as income in the profit loss statement	No contribution is permitted

Source: William M. Mercer, Inc., unpublished.

accounting rules, one goal is to match revenue and expense, since the allocation of costs over time is critical. A second objective is to support comparability of financial results across organizations. For pension funding law, the intent is to ensure that adequate funds are set aside to meet obligations to participants, and also to ensure that funds on which investment income tax is deferred are not excessive. These two sets of rules sometimes come into conflict, making it difficult for the nonspecialist to interpret the differences.

When interest rates fall and equity returns disappoint, this has a particularly painful impact on DB plans. The 2000 market decline produced substantial increases in both pension expense and pension contributions for some organizations, due to declines in assets and increases in liabilities. Some firms also had very large pension liabilities compared to their shareholder equity and other measures of organization size.

An illustration of how pension costs can be affected appears in Table 4. Here the cost can be considered to be the value of benefits earned in the current period, since assets fully cover benefits earned in the past. However, if asset values fall by 25 percent and the value of liabilities rises by 10 percent, the plan's financial position changes dramatically. A 50 basis-point drop in the discount rate boosts plan liabilities by about 10 percent. To show how this unfavorable climate can produce major changes in the sponsoring company's financial position, note that Company A's cost is the

TABLE 4. Illustration of Pension Plan Financial Position Under Different Scenarios

	Company A— established company	Company B— mature company: retirees outnumber active employees
Scenario 1: illustration of pension plan financial position: Value of benefits earned, liabilities and assets for two companies		
Value of benefits earned in current year	$10,000,000	$10,000,000
Liability for benefits Earned to date	$60,000,000	$150,000,000
Assets	$60,000,000	$150,000,000
Scenario 2: illustration of pension plan financial position changes due to adverse change in economic situation: Discount rate up ½%, assets down 25%		
Value of benefits earned in current year—lower	$11,000,000	$11,000,000
Liability for benefits earned to date	$66,000,000	$165,000,000
Assets	$45,000,000	$112,500,000
Unfunded amount to be spread into future costs	$21,000,000	$52,500,000

Source: Author's calculations.

$11M benefit value plus amortization of $21M. Company B must amortize $52.5M. The situation would be even more dramatic had assets exceeded liabilities prior to the change; the firm would have gone from making no contribution to having to make a substantial contribution. Such changes in pension expenses and contributions can be moderated somewhat by using smoothing techniques, but these can only work to some extent.

An indication of the financial health of DB plans prior to the market downturn is available from data collected by the Pension Benefit Guaranty Corporation (PBGC 1999). At the outset of 1997, underfunded DB plans held assets reported at $353B and liabilities of $401B, for a total underfunding of $48B. By contrast, overfunded plans held assets of $1,014B and liabilities of $790B for a total overfunding level of $223B. What this meant is that many plan sponsors entered the downturn with very well funded plans; indeed some had not made cash contributions for several years.

In practice, market fluctuations affect each pension plan's asset mix, funding level, and investment policy differently. While the precise picture for DB plans going forward is not fully known yet, some have called 2000 "the worst year in pension history" (Ryan 2001). This is based on expected returns on pension assets assuming a representative portfolio of 5 percent cash, 30 percent bonds, 60 percent S&P 500 equities, and 5 percent international equities. This asset mix produced an asset return of 2.5 percent for 2000, which combined with an anticipated increase in pension liabilities of 26 percent. The result for this representative DB plan was a negative change in funding by 28.5 percent. By contrast, the worse previous year for DB plans was 1995, when the funding position fell by 12.5 percent (Ryan 2001).[2] Clearly, an unfavorable economic environment will likely increase both pension expense and funding requirements for many firms. To the extent that a plan sponsor bases its funding and expense calculations on smoothed asset values, the impact may be smaller; for others, it will be of greater concern.

Issues Specific to Defined Contribution Pensions

The 1990s saw rapid growth in retirement system assets, resulting from mainly from DC plan growth. When markets fell (see Figure 2), this was to some extent offset by new cash flowing into retirement account mutual funds (Investment Company Institute 2001). In other words, DC plan finances rose even in unfavorable equity market periods, due to the continued interest of participants in equity markets.

While smoothing can take place in DB plans, investment variability directly affects individual account balances in DC plans. Such changes do not directly impact the plan sponsor, but poor investment results can harm morale and may even cause employees to delay retirement (Even and Macpherson, this volume). When employees are dissatisfied with benefits, this can also increase turnover. Some DC plans are organized as employee stock ownership plans, and in other cases, the employer match in a 401(k) plan may be entirely in company stock. It is also the case that employee contributions are sometimes automatically invested in company stock, though in many instances stock may be one of several investment options. Table 5 shows that plans offering company stock tend to have participants allocate somewhat more of their assets in equity, on average, than plans not permitting company stock.

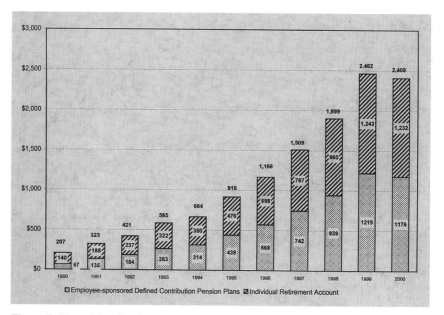

Figure 2. Mutual fund retirement assets, 1990–2000 ($ billions). Source: Investment Company Institute. Components may not add to totals because of rounding.

TABLE 5. Average Asset Allocation by Investment Options (1999)

Plans	Equity funds	Company stock	Balanced funds	Bond funds	Money funds	GICs[a]
			(percentage of account balances)			
All plans	53.4	19.1	6.7	4.6	4	10.5
Plans without company stock or GICs	71.1	na	9.7	9.0	7.7	na
Plans with GICs[a]	62.3	na	10.6	3.7	3.9	16.8
Plans with company stock	44.5	36.3	3.9	6.7	5.5	na
Plans with company stock and GICs[a]	47.9	23.9	5.5	1.8	1.6	18.7

Source: Derived from Holden and VanDerhei (2001).
[a] Guaranteed investment contracts.

One measure of the success of a DC plan is the plan's ability to deliver enough money to ensure that participants can afford to retire. Yet many plan sponsors do not focus on this outcome, preferring instead to offer participants the opportunity to save more and diversity investment portfolios. Typically, employers do not investigate actual account balances and savings rates, nor do they project them to retirement. Larger employers typically offer a combination of DB and DC plans, and while they may predict expected DB benefits, they are less likely to look at projected savings in DC plans. It is not uncommon for companies to presume that benefits will be adequate, if employees contribute the maximum they are eligible to receive their company match. Midsized employers in particular tend not to study these issues in much depth.

Going forward, however, the focus may become one of greater attention to retirement. In this case, plan sponsors will be required to ask whether employees are saving enough money for retirement, whether the available investment options provide an adequate range of choice, and whether employees appear to make reasonable asset allocation decisions. The implications of investment variability may become very different as well. For companies that offer both a DB and DC plan, it may be easier to manage expectations than for those that offer only DCs. In the DC-only case, employers might elect to redesign their basic plans, the investment options offered, and/or the participant education program (Wray 2001).

In considering these issues, it is important to remember that nearly all DC accumulations tend to be paid out as lump sums, and an increasing number of DB plans offer lump sums as well (Mitchell this volume). In contrast to the life annuity payout form, lump sums expose retirees to a wide range of risks including the possibility of outliving assets, investment losses, unexpected medical costs, cost of care due to frailty, loss of a spouse, and loss of functionality (Rappaport 2000).

How Market Volatility Affects Older Workers

People reaching retirement in the United States today have widely different levels of wealth, as well as different resources and levels of income. For instance, the poorest two quintiles of the elderly received more than 80 percent of income from Social Security, and had a net worth excluding home equity of under $21,000 (in 1996; Friedland 1999). Poor equity markets would therefore have little effect on this group. On the other hand, this group is also the most likely to need employment in later life, due to economic reasons. If fewer jobs are available, or if pay is lower, this group will be hardest hit. At the top end of the economic spectrum are older persons having substantial wealth. These people have considerable financial investments, some of which are equities, and hence they will be directly affected by poor market performance. For this group, some of the impact of a decline in investment values will also be felt via reductions in estates or bequests, rather than through cuts in living standards during retirement. While many in this group will have adequate resources for a comfortable retirement, they may still feel vulnerable to economic volatility.

In the middle of the distribution of well-being are older persons who depend on diverse income sources and have middling financial assets. Some have DB pension plans, and for them, market fluctuations such as those experienced in the recent past will likely have only a modest effect. In contrast, retirees having only a DC plan may be hurt when the market sinks. Those holding a riskier portfolio, which loses value, may need to postpone retirement or return to work, and/or cut living standards.

Table 2 reported DC plan asset allocations for those plans that included company stock as an investment option. In Table 6 we depict average asset allocation by age for plans with and without company stock. For employees in their 60s, 44 percent of 401(k) account balances are invested in equity funds, 16 percent in company stock and 7 percent in balanced funds (Holden and VanDerhei 2001). If we assume balanced funds are half stock, this accounts for a total 63 percent of plan assets in equities for employees in their 60s; across participants of all ages, the proportion in equities is 76 percent. To the extent that DC plans represent a significant component of retirement assets, equity returns are a major concern.

Retiree Health Issues

Somewhat distinct issues arise when calculating retiree health plan costs. One reason is that most such plans are operated on a pay-as-you-go basis; that is, annual cash contributions are set to cover each year's benefit payouts. For purposes of the profit and loss statement, these benefit plans are treated like pensions, and as such, they are subject to special accounting rules. These rules require that the sponsoring company calculate a balance sheet liability representing the discounted present value of benefits for retirees, as well as for active employees based on service to date. While equity markets do not directly influence the costs of such pay-as-you-go plans, the concern is that health care costs have risen quite rapidly recently. Figure 3 shows total medical cost trends over the period 1990–2000. Per capita retiree health care costs increased in 1999 by 10.7 percent for retirees not yet eligible for Medicare, and 17 percent for retirees who were Medicare eligible (Mercer 2001). Prescription drug costs are a major factor in the costs for the Medicare eligible retirees.

In companies where both pension and retiree health costs are rising simultaneously, management will be forced to reassess options for bringing these retiree health costs under control. These include boosting retiree contributions for retiree health insurance, tightening plan eligibility, and modifying benefits so as to reduce costs. They might also involve rearranging

TABLE 6. Average Asset Allocation in 401(k) Plans for Age (1999)

Age cohort	Equity funds	Balanced funds	Bond funds	Money funds	GICs[a]	Company stock	Other stable value funds	Other	Unknown	Total
				(percentage of account balances)						
20s	63.4%	7.3%	3.8%	3.9%	3.8%	16.4%	0.3%	0.7%	0.4%	100.0%
30s	60.6	6.7	3.6	3.4	4.9	19.5	0.3	0.7	0.3	100.0
40s	55.9	6.7	3.9	3.8	7.9	20.4	0.4	0.8	0.3	100.0
50s	51.7	6.7	4.7	4.0	11.6	19.4	0.9	0.8	0.4	100.0
60s	44.2	6.7	6.8	4.9	19.2	15.6	1.7	0.7	0.3	100.0
All	53.4	6.7	4.6	4.0	10.5	19.1	0.7	0.8	0.3	100.0

Source: Derived from Holden and VanDerhei (2001).
[a] Guaranteed investment contracts.

the pension package to shift some benefit costs to employees, so as to increase workers' incentives to save for retirement.

Conclusions

There is considerable uncertainty as to how long and how deep this economic downturn will be. Retirement plan sponsors, employees, and retirees are coping with a combination of difficult equity markets, lower interest rates, and uncertain job market conditions. Under such circumstances, plan sponsors may respond by using permitted smoothing methods to reduce the impact on their financial statements, and by careful selection of actuarial assumptions within acceptable parameters. In the short to medium term, investment strategies will also be reviewed, although not necessarily changed. DC plan sponsors are being called on to increase communication to plan participants about market conditions, helping them put market movements in historical perspective. Increased oversight of fund choices may also be expected.

Long-term responses will likely be more varied. Cost pressures can force or encourage some plan sponsors to terminate DB plans, continuing a long-term trend in the United States. Other employers will review plan design, seeking a greater degree of risk management. This is consistent with the overall trend in retirement plans during the last decade that has transferred risk from employers to employees. Employers have terminated or frozen traditional DB pension plans, replaced them with cash balance plans, 401(k) pensions, and other DC arrangements. New firms offer no retirement benefits, or DC plans alone. Companies have increasingly relied

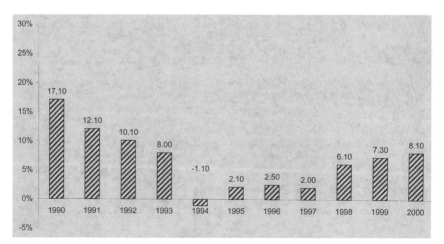

Figure 3. Trends in medical care costs over time. Source: Merck Incorporated (2000).

on their own stock as a savings and retirement vehicle, and employer subsidies for retiree medical benefits have been reduced or eliminated.

For the most part, employees have accepted this trend toward risk transfer. One reason is likely the buoyant equity market over the last two decades. Many people may believe that their retirement savings accounts (and other assets) were a sufficient cushion against such risks. But if equity markets stay depressed, employer and employee assumptions about retirement security are due for a fundamental reevaluation. This will first occur at companies that traditionally have emphasized stock purchase through ESOPs, broad-based stock option plans, and by using stock to match employees' 401(k) contributions. It will be sharpest when firms experience a sharp and prolonged downturn in the value of that stock. Of course, many of these companies also suffer from other problems (including survival), so that retirement plan issues may be postponed. Should these firms then be acquired, the new owner must address such issues. If they are not acquired, they often lack financial resources sufficient to make any substantive improvements in benefit offerings. Such companies may experience greater turnover, as their employees seek better venues in which to accumulate wealth for retirement.

For other companies, however, the problems will be less obvious and will not seem to require such immediate action. But a long-term recession will nevertheless challenge many peoples' fundamental assumptions. Plan sponsors have assumed double-digit investment returns will continue. Likewise, many employees and retirees anticipate that the high returns of the last two decades will persist. If expectations are not met, plan sponsors may need to modify their retirement programs, and baby boomers will either have to retire later, consume less, or both. Some retirees not currently working may have to return to work, as resources dwindle.

Business cycles have long been part of the pension planning environment. Yet severe downturns challenge thinking, if people and organizations have forgotten that such downturns can and do occur. In the past, DB plan sponsors generally took into account business cycle patterns when they managed pension plans; such views are less prevalent today. In a DC environment, the impact of equity market shocks is directly absorbed by participants. As the environment increasingly moves to one where participants bear risk, it is important that they learn to plan better for economic shocks.

Notes

1. Different methods can be used to value both assets and liabilities, so that a plan might have an unfunded liability according to one calculation but a surplus in another; see McGill et al. (1996).

2. The impact of assumptions is also greater today than when ERISA was enacted in 1974. Federal rule changes have imposed stricter limits on plan funding, restricting well-funded plans from making deductible contributions, and poorly funded

plans must now make extra contributions to catch up faster. Even the definition of funding has changed, so that market fluctuations can now have a more dramatic impact on plan funding. Some firms are also holding higher equity allocations in their pension plans and hence will be more vulnerable to changes in equity prices.

References

Even, William E. and David A. Macpherson. This volume. "Benefits and Productivity."
Friedland, Robert B. 1999. *Demography Is Not Destiny.* Washington, D.C.: National Academy on Aging Society.
Holden, Sarah and Jack L. VanDerhei. 2001. "401(k) Plan Asset Allocation, Account Balances, and Loan Activity in 2000." EBRI Issue Brief 239. Washington, D.C.: Employee Benefit Research Institute.
Investment Company Institute (ICI). 2001. *Mutual Funds and the Retirement Market in 2000.* Investment Company Institute Research in Brief 10, 2. Washington, D.C.: Investment Company Institute.
Lofgren, Eric P., Steven A. Nyce, and Sylvester J. Schieber. This volume. "Designing Total Reward Programs for Tight Labor Markets."
McGill, Dan M., Kyle N. Brown, John J. Haley, and Sylvester J. Schieber. 1996. *Fundamentals of Private Pensions.* 7th ed. Philadelphia: University of Pennsylvania Press.
Mercer, Incorporated. 1999. *Managing Multinational Retirement Programs.* Survey Report. New York: William M. Mercer.
————. 2000. *The Mercer/Foster Higgins National Survey of Employer Sponsored Health Plans.* New York: William M. Mercer.
Mitchell, Olivia S. with Erica L. Dykes. This volume. "New Trends in Pension Benefit and Retirement Provisions."
National Center for Employee Ownership (NCEO). 2001. "ESOPs, Stock Options, and 401(k) Plans Now Control 12.8% of Corporate Equity." NCEO Library <www.nceo.org>.
Pension Benefit Guaranty Corporation (PBGC). 1999. *Pension Insurance Data Book.* Washington, D.C.: Pension Benefit Guaranty Corporation.
Rappaport, Anna M. 2000. *Retirement Needs: The Perspective of the Individual.* Retirement Needs Framework Monograph. Schaumburg, Ill.: Society of Actuaries.
Riche, Martha Fransworth. This volume. "The Demographics of Tomorrow's Workplace."
Ryan, Ronald J. 2000. *2000: Worst Year in Pension History.* New York: <www.ryanlabs.com>.
U.S. Department of Labor, Bureau of Labor Statistics (BLS). 2000. "Employment Situation." <www.bls.gov>.
Value Line Investment Survey. 2001. *Selection and Opinion.* New York: Value Line Publishing: 4317. April 13.
Wall Street Journal. 2001. <www.wsj.com>. Historical Information. New York: Dow Jones & Company.
Wray, David. 2001. *Current Trends in Profit Sharing and 401(k) Plans.* Chicago: Profit Sharing Council.

Chapter 7
Designing Total Reward Programs for Tight Labor Markets

Eric P. Lofgren, Steven A. Nyce, and Sylvester J. Schieber

Over the last several years, U.S. employers have had to scramble for workers of all sorts in unprecedented ways. After experiencing personnel shortfalls during the late 1990s, the Navy has pursued new recruiting approaches: in 2001, for instance, it sent almost every Harvard undergraduate an e-mail invitation to apply to become a commissioned officer in the U.S. Navy (Gizzle 2001). The furniture store, Ikea, also has sought new ways to attract job applicants, by posting want ads on the walls of restrooms (*Seattle Post-Intelligencer* 2000). A recent article in *HR Magazine* (Tyler 2001) told of recruiting of a mechanical engineer from Detroit to San Francisco. With two job offers in hand, he took the one that included an "employer-assisted housing" program. Manufacturing jobs continue to decline in the U.S. economy, but there are still many employers that need workers.

Some people believe that the recent economic slowdown, starting in 2000, may dampen employers' efforts to find creative new ways of recruiting staff. The reality is, that despite news of layoffs, unemployment rates in the United States remain low by historical standards. Even with the collapse of many dot.com firms, there are still technology jobs going unfilled. For example People3 Inc., a Gartner company that analyzes trends in information technology, predicts that demand for IT workers will outpace supply by at least 20 percent over the next four years. Dot.com workers thrown out of jobs at high-technology firms are often able to find technology jobs in more traditional firms, as the latter adopt their own e-business innovations (Goodridge 2001).

The U.S. economy has clearly been the most vibrant of all the major countries over the last decade. Now the question is whether that vibrancy can be maintained in the face of changing labor markets. In this chapter we suggest that tight labor markets of the last decade have generated a variety of unique approaches to finding, attracting, and retaining workers.

Furthermore, we argue these will persist over most of the coming decade, and we conclude that employers of the future may even confront greater challenges in staffing than they have in the past.

Economic Output and the Supply of and Demand for Labor

Economists have developed macroeconomic models to investigate the linkages between economic production levels and the supply of workers who generate it. In such models, three key factors contribute to production: human capital, physical capital, and technology. Workers and their inherent work-related capabilities comprise the human capital that can be used in the productive processes of an economy. Physical capital refers to the plants and equipment, as well as hardware and software, available for workers to use in the production of goods and services. Technology comprises the level of knowledge and know-how that is embedded in production processes.

One premise of such models is that more physical capital makes workers more productive, up to a point. For example, one worker with one air gun might drive as many nails in a day as three workers with regular hammers. In this simple example, one carpenter with an air gun can substitute for three carpenters with regular hammers. But substitution of capital for labor cannot go on forever: workers simply cannot fully utilize more tools without limit.

Economic models also posit that technology evolves over time and can enhance productivity of physical capital, human capital, or both. It can also change the way in which capital and labor can be substituted for each other. There are two important aspects to technology improvement in the U.S. economy. First, it evolves because of research and development activities, but once discovered, new inventions can generally be widely adapted (unless the creators limit distribution to other enterprises through patent or other law). In general though, discovery does not automatically translate into enhanced worker productivity; instead it must be adapted to become effective. Second, technology is adapted at uneven rates across economic sectors, so its overall effect on productivity is also uneven across sectors and over time.

The final central premise of economic production models is that human capital can be expanded along two dimensions if necessary. First, the number of workers can be increased or the hours worked by employees can be increased. Such an increase in labor supply is generally anticipated to lead to increased production. Second, any given pool of workers can also acquire new skills that make them more productive. Over time in the United States, the supply of human capital has grown and worker characteristics have changed in ways that have enhanced average productivity levels.

One way to measure the amount of human capital employed focuses on the number of workers employed. This is a crude measure since it does not account for the variability in work hours, nor does it take account of employees' different characteristics. Nevertheless, it does provide a rough estimate of how worker productivity has changed in recent decades. Figure 1 illustrates the growth in the U.S. workforce since 1946, along with the increase in the inflation-adjusted gross domestic product (GDP) that these workers produced. Annual observations are given relative to the baselines for labor supply and output in 1946, so the results can be thought of as an indexed level of activity against those bases.

The data show that that U.S. civilian employment levels rose by 2.4 times between 1946 and 2000, and real gross domestic product rose 6.2 times. In other words, workers now produce about two-and-a-half times as much output as their forebears did in 1946. Part of this productivity increase is attributable to enhanced skills of modern workers as compared to those in 1946. But a substantial additional portion is due to these workers having more capital to work with, and to new technology making them more productive. The result of this growth in productivity over time is that the average U.S. standard of living today is far higher than in 1946. Inflation-adjusted GDP per capita rose about 3.2 times over the period,[1] with an annualized growth rate in per capita GDP over the last half of the twentieth century of an annualized decadal growth of between 1.73 and 2.87 percent.[2]

Whether this pattern of steadily rising output per capita will persist into the future is a key question. To some extent, it is a "chicken and egg" issue, since rising demand for goods and services is what pulls an economy

Index levels of GDP ($1996) and workers in the U.S. economy

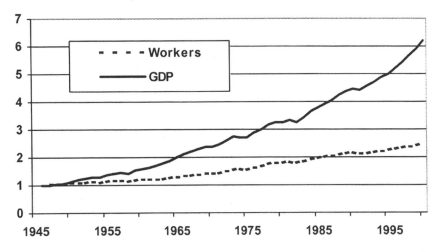

Figure 1. Civilian employment and real gross domestic production in the United States for selected years relative to 1946 baseline levels. Source: U.S. Department of Commerce (2000, 2001), Council of Economic Advisors (2001).

forward. During periods of high demand, economic growth tends to be high as producers organize their activities to meet consumers' appetites. Low unemployment, overtime, and other vestiges of a high-performance economy generally characterize such periods, and they combine to make workers earn relatively high pay that further stimulates the demand for goods and services. During booms, worker productivity increases, whereas labor productivity improvements slow or even fall during economic slowdowns. In recessions, surplus capacity develops as employers cut production; initially they may be reluctant to lay off surplus labor due to substantial investments in their know-how and experience. Since it may be cheaper to carry surplus labor than to have to find, hire, and train new workers when economic growth resumes, labor productivity improvements tend to slow or stall during such periods.

Many groups seek to forecast future economic activity; Table 1 reports projections of GDP growth developed by the Congressional Budget Office (CBO), the Clinton administration, and an average of approximately fifty private-sector forecasts known as the "Blue Chip" series. The evidence indicates that there is a relatively narrow band around forecasters' economic growth projections over the coming decade. These economic projections are consistent with the historical experience of ever-improving U.S. standards of living (measured by increasing income). Using the CBO projections for real GDP growth from 2001 through 2010, we estimate that GDP in 2010 (in $1996) will be about $12.5 trillion, or over one-third larger than in 2000. Using Census Bureau projection of the population for 2010, we estimate that per capita output in 2010 will be approximately $41,850 (in $1996). This implies an annual GDP per capita growth rate of 2.14 percent over this decade, a rate of improvement consistent with historical patterns.[3]

TABLE 1. Change in Projections of Average Annual Growth of Real GDP, 1997–2001

Date projection published[a]	Projection period	CBO	Blue chip	Clinton administration
2001	2001–2010	3.0	3.3	3.1
2000[b]	2000–2009	2.8	2.7	2.8
1999[b]	1999–2008	2.3	2.4	2.3
1998	1998–2007	2.2	2.3	2.3
1997	1997–2006	2.1	2.3	2.3

Source: CBO (2001).
[a] Congressional Budget Office (CBO) and Clinton administration projections were published in January and completed in November or December of the previous year. Blue Chip, an average of over fifty private-sector forecasts, publishes long-term projections twice a year, in March and October; the projections shown here are those published in October of the previous year.
[b] About 0.3 percentage points of the change between these projections stemmed from a benchmark revision to gross domestic product during 1999 that, for the first time, included software in GDP.

There are only two ways that an economy can increase the supply of goods and services available to its population at rates in excess of population growth: to import more, or to produce more. Unless the U.S. economy is permitted to substantially increase its trade deficit (other nations must be are willing to provide the capital to do so), our ability to improve the standards of living in the United States are to a substantial degree capped by what can be produced here. The U.S. trade balance has been negative for many years, though last year the net import balance remained less than 3 percent of GDP.

Hence our next question is what employers may face in the labor market, as they are called on to deliver the growth in output required for consistency with these macroeconomic projections. Various scenarios are considered, including one that assumes the United States will realize productivity grown implicit in the CBO projection; another assumes productivity growth more in line with historical rates. As we show, if productivity growth slows to rates characteristic of the twenty-five years ending in 1995, then the United States will simply end up with less output. However, there will be some demand pressure in the output markets to increase production at higher rates. This is consistent with the view that society will want to continue improving its living standard at rates consistent with past expectations. In the past, when the economy has slowed for any substantial period of time, the public has responded by bringing pressure on policymakers to restore economic growth. Should there be demand pressure to increase output in the face of slowing worker productivity growth, employers could respond in a variety of ways, so as to attract more employees. Next we explore the extent to which additional workers might have to be attracted into the labor market, and the ways in which employers might do so.

Labor Market Prospects in the Coming Decade

At the end of the twentieth century, U.S. labor markets were very tight. Even as the economy slowed considerably over 2000 from its torrid pace of the late 1990s, the seasonally adjusted unemployment rate remained well below its historic trend. In fact, unemployment rates in the early 2000s remained roughly a full percentage point below the CBO's estimate of the nonaccelerating inflation rate of unemployment (NAIRU).[4] Figure 2 depicts growth in the U.S. civilian labor force along with Social Security actuarial projections over the next two decades. During the 1990s, these were lower than they had been over the prior three decades, which helps to explain why recruitment and retention was such a challenge.

As we look to the future, however, anticipated growth rates are expected to be significantly lower than those experienced over the past decade. The Social Security actuaries estimate that labor force growth over the coming decade will be only about three quarters of the 1990s level, and the growth rate projected for 2010 will only be one-third that of the past decade. Unless there is a significant and prolonged softening of the economy, the United States may be in for a considerable period of tighter labor markets.

How many employees may be required will ultimately depend on two factors: (1) the level of aggregate output and (2) the efficiency with which workers are employed in producing that output. The first will be driven by the level of demand for goods and services in the economy (as well as government spending and imports). The second can be understood in terms of GDP produced per unit of labor input, for which good historical data is not widely available. The best source consists of series on total hours worked per year from 1950, from which average total product per hour of labor can be derived. Average GDP per labor hour grew at a rate of 2.66 percent per year during the 1950s and 1960s, slowed to 1.57 percent per year kin the 1970s, fell further to 1.43 percent per year during the 1980s, and recovered slightly to 1.69 percent per year in the 1990s (with a spurt to 2.27 percent per year during the last half of the 1990s). To project future productivity experts begin by estimating the demand for goods and services based on the size and composition of sectors of the economy.[5] Here we rely on ten-year macroeconomic projections developed by the CBO for federal budget and policy purposes; these estimates indicate that GDP will grow (in inflation-adjusted terms) by 2.4 percent in 2001, 3.4 percent in 2002, 3.3 percent in 2003 and 3.0 percent annually from 2003 to 2009, with 2010 coming in slightly higher at 3.1 percent. Using these assumptions and baseline 2000 GDP, we generate an estimate of GDP in 2010 (in $1996) of $12.5 trillion estimate.

Compound annual growth rate for the period

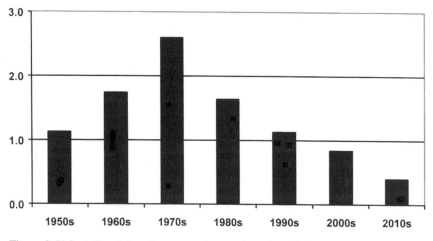

Figure 2. U.S. civilian labor force growth rates for selected decades. Source: derived from Council of Advisors (2001), Social Security Administration (2001a).

To understand the challenge that employers face in generating the output levels required by these forecasts over the coming decade, it is helpful to investigate the link between the economy's potential labor supply and the likely demand for labor under alternative growth scenarios. First we project "baseline" labor supply to 2010 using current workforce patterns and expected population changes in the coming decade; labor supply patterns by age are assumed to persist into the future. For example, 45 percent of the population between the ages of 60 and 64 is in the labor force today, so the model assumes in the future, the same 45 percent of this age bracket will be in the labor force. In addition, workers by age are assumed to work the same number of hours per year as in recent times.[6]

Labor demand estimates use the CBO's GDP projections discussed above with a range of productivity improvement scenarios. The first projections factor in realized productivity increases already been reported for 2000. Hence the most conservative scenario posits that output per worker-hour grows at a rate of 1.5 percent per year, the average growth in output per hour over the past three decades. A second (third) scenario assumes that output per hour increases at a rate of 1.75 (2.0) percent per year; this bands worker productivity increases in the past decade. A final scenario boosts growth in output per hour to 2.23 percent per year, a rate exceeded in the 1950s and 1960s but matched since then only in the last five years.[7]

Our resultant labor supply and demand projections appear in Figure 3, depicted in terms of full-time equivalent (FTE) workers, which is obtained by dividing the total number of projected hours by a full-time employment level of 2000 hours per year. The most conservative scenario indicates that labor shortfalls might be substantial, on the order of 7.5 percent or 10.2 million FTEs short of the labor supplied in 2010. The other scenarios indicate a labor gap of between 3.1 and 6.6 million FTEs. Unless the United States sustains a high rate of growth in output per hour — something like 2.23 percent — over the coming decade, it will have a significant labor shortfall.

One alternative to the shortfall scenario might require that there will be a slowdown in the growth of standards of living. Another is that high levels of productivity improvement must be sustained in the coming decade. It is possible that labor supply could be boosted by enticing more people into the labor force, or by enticing current workers to consistently work longer hours than they do today. As long as productivity growth remains below 2.23 percent per year, there are three sources of additional labor supply that could be tapped to alleviate potential shortages including (1) participation increases across the board, (2) participation changes among women, and (3) participation changes among older persons (e.g., 55- to 64-year-old workers exhibit participation patterns like those 45–54 years old).[8]

Table 2 indicates what would have to hold to eliminate the projected labor supply shortages. The results are rather striking. In the scenario

TABLE 2. Labor Force Participation or Number of Hours/Year Changes Needed to Maintain Current Living Standards in 2010, Alternative Rates of Labor Productivity Growth

	Current	1.5% Productivity			1.75% Productivity			2.0% Productivity		
		All	Women	Elderly	All	Women	Elderly	All	Women	Elderly
Required changes in labor force participation rates										
Males										
Under 25	68.0	73.1	—	—	71.3	—	—	69.6	—	—
25–39	91.5	98.3	—	—	96.0	—	—	93.6	—	—
40–54	89.2	95.8	—	—	93.5	—	—	91.2	—	—
55–64	67.7	72.8	—	84.6	71.0	—	84.6	69.3	—	77.3
65–69	28.2	30.3	—	67.1	29.5	—	37.1	28.8	—	28.2
70+	11.2	12.0	—	26.6	11.7	—	14.7	11.4	—	11.2
Females										
Under 25	64.9	69.8	76.2	—	68.1	72.3	—	66.4	68.4	—
25–39	77.0	82.7	90.4	—	80.7	85.7	—	78.8	81.1	—
40–54	77.1	82.9	90.5	—	80.9	85.8	—	78.9	81.2	—
55–64	51.3	55.1	60.2	71.8	53.8	57.1	71.8	52.5	54.0	62.9
65–69	19.2	20.6	22.5	45.6	20.1	21.3	25.2	19.6	20.2	19.2
70+	4.9	5.3	5.8	11.7	5.2	5.5	6.5	5.0	5.2	4.9

Required changes in annual hours worked

Males

Under 25	1467	1576	—	1558	1538	—	—	1501	—	—
25–39	2126	2284	—	2085	2229	—	—	2175	—	—
40–54	1993	2141	—	2016	2089	—	—	2038	—	—
55–64	1803	1937	2254	1841	1890	—	2254	1844	—	2057
65–69	1518	1631	3613	1352	1592	—	1996	1553	—	1518
70+	1428	1534	3397	1555	1497	—	1877	1460	—	1428

Females

Under 25	1327	1426	—	1558	1391	1476	—	1357	1397	—
25–39	1776	1909	—	2085	1863	1977	—	1817	1871	—
40–54	1717	1845	—	2016	1800	1911	—	1756	1809	—
55–64	1568	1685	2196	1841	1645	1745	2196	1605	1652	1923
65–69	1151	1237	2740	1352	1207	1281	1514	1178	1213	1151
70+	1325	1423	3152	1555	1389	1474	1742	1355	1395	1325

Source: See Figure 4.
Participation rates and/or hours worked are held constant when—is used for the corresponding group(s).

where participation rises across the board, and given only 1.5 percent productivity growth, labor force participation or hours worked would need to increase roughly 7.5 percent from the projected labor supply levels to meet labor force demand in 2010. At the higher productivity scenarios, required participation changes are 4.9 percent for a growth rate of 1.75 percent and 2.3 percent for a 2.0 percent growth assumption.

Few ways are available to achieve such increases in labor supply. If the responses occurred across the board, and given a 1.5 percent productivity improvement scenario, men ages 25–39 would have to boost participation from 91.5 percent in 2000, to 98.3 percent by 2010; the rise among men ages 40–54 would be from 89.2 to 95.8 percent. These increases, along with the commensurate rates for women, seem almost impossible to achieve. Current workers could alternatively work more hours per week than they do now; men in their prime working ages would average nearly 42 hours weekly for 52 weeks per year, and virtually all women would have to move to full-time employment. More rapid improvements in worker productivity would alleviate there requirements, though even at a 2.0 percent productivity growth rate, all men between the age of 25 and 54 would have to average 40 hours per week for 52 weeks per year.

One issue is whether extracting additional work from groups that already spend an average of 40 hours per week on the job will precipitate significant wage pressures. An alternate strategy might be for employers to entice people into the labor force who now have relatively low participation rates.

Full-Time Equivalent (FTE) Workers (in millions)

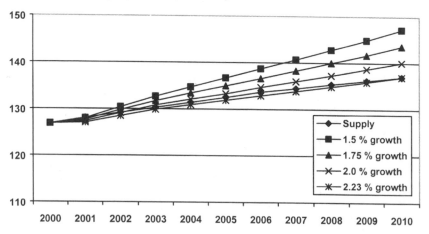

Figure 3. Projected U.S. labor supply versus demand under alternative productivity growth scenarios for 2000–2010. Source: derived from Social Security Administration (2001b), U.S. Department of Commerce (2002), Unicon (2000), U.S. Bureau of the Census (2000), Council of Economic Advisors (2001).

Women's labor force participation has been rising over time but it is still 15 percentage points below men's. In one set of scenarios, we estimated how much higher women's participation rates would have to grow to achieve output growth similar to experiences since World War II. The results from the 1.5 percent productivity scenario appear in Figure 4. By 2010, women's required participation rates would have to rise to the equivalent of men's rates in 2000, under this scenario. It seems unlikely that than many additional women could be enticed into paid work (Nyce and Schieber 2001; Smith and Bachu 1999).

Enticing older people to participate at greater rates might help, though the results indicate that if men ages 55–64 maintained workforce attachment similar to that of present-day men ages 45–54, they would need to increase their labor force by 25 percent over the coming decade (see Figure 5). And participation of men ages 55–64 would need to increase to 85 percent by 2010. If workers 65 years and over were tapped to make up the shortfall, their labor force participation rates would need to increase nearly 140 percent over current levels, to roughly 39 percent for men and slightly over 20 percent for women. These projections seem incredibly high, as compared to recent trends.

Meeting the Productivity Challenge

The baby boomer generation has influenced the U.S. economic in number of ways. Its sheer size depressed earnings, at least during the early portion

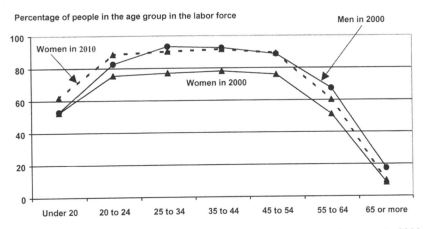

Figure 4. Labor force participation rates of men and women at various ages in 2000 with required increases in women's participation to meet labor force demands, assuming 1.5 percent productivity growth. Source: derived from Social Security Administration (2001b), U.S. Department of Commerce (2002), Unicon (2000), U.S. Bureau of the Census (2000), Council of Economic Advisors (2001).

of the boomers' careers, which likely increased women's labor force participation rates (Macunovich 2001). Baby boomer working women were more educated than their predecessors and many of them pursued more diversified careers than prior generations of women. Career opportunities became important issues as they progressed through their careers, and the record number of new workers between the late 1960s and the mid-1980s pushed older workers out of the way and into retirement. Though many employers sponsored retirement plans, early retirement incentives began encouraging workers to retire as early as their mid-50s largely in response to the low-cost labor.

Now, the front edge of the baby boom generation is beginning to cross the early retirement threshold that it helped create. In the labor market, the phenomenon of baby boomers rushing for retirement may have the opposite effect of the one created as boomers entered the workforce. Waves of retirement may produce a "worker void" leaving firms scrambling to find enough people to meet production needs. These facts, combined with low fertility rates, suggests that labor force growth rates over the coming decade will only be about three-fourths of those already low growth rates seen in the 1990s; growth rates in the 2010s will likely be half those of the current decade.

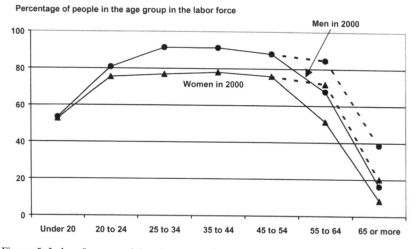

Figure 5. Labor force participation rates of men and women at various ages in 2000 with required increases in older workers' participation to meet labor force demands. Calculations assume 1.5 percent productivity growth; labor force participation rates for men and women aged 55–64 increase along current trends by 25 percent and 40 percent respectively; rates for men and women aged 65+ increase at 138 percent of their current levels. Source: derived from Social Security Administration (2001b), U.S. Department of Commerce (2002), Unicon (2000), U.S. Bureau of the Census (2000), Council of Economic Advisors (2001).

As a result of these trends, some human resource managers are already emphasizing "attracting and retaining" employees, in the process restructuring aspects of their human resources operations to pull in new streams of workers. Others are scrambling to restructure pay and benefit programs to ensure stability in their existing workforces. Nevertheless, employers are limited in their ability to deal with the existing phenomenon of tight labor markets, much less the increasingly daunting situation we will face going forward.

Only four practical possibilities are available: diminish turnover, attract new types of workers, retain existing workers longer, or extract higher levels of productivity from existing workers. Every one of these options poses a challenge, and no single one may be a solution to the labor market problems faced in the U.S. environment.

Reducing Turnover

Turnover raises the cost of recruiting and hiring workers, and disrupts the workplace. It also imposes training costs and the time required to advancing a new hire to the productivity level of an experienced worker. And in many cases, workers develop ongoing relationships with customers that are a significant reason for repurchase decisions. In developing Watson Wyatt's *Human Capital Index*™, we recently surveyed 405 publicly traded U.S. firms asking about annual personnel turnover rates. We then classified these relative to average industry turnover rates in that industry, and related these to shareholder surplus value and shareholder returns. The analysis shows that low-turnover firms had average Tobin's Q of 2.55 while the high turnover firms had a score of only 1.67; Tobin's Q captures the value of a firm's intangible assets and is measured by the ratio of the firm' market value to its asset replacement costs. In addition, the three-year total shareholder return in low-turnover firms was 79 percent, while in high turnover firms it was 33 percent. The five-year total return to shareholders was 133 percent and 57 percent, for low and high turnover firms, respectively (Luss and Kay 1999).

This does not imply that optimal turnover rates should be zero, of course. In Europe, for example, some companies may promote excessive job security, leading to complacency or under-motivated workers. Indeed our research indicates that too much job security is associated with reduced surplus value levels; these employers having the lowest turnover rates relied more on tenure-based benefits and recognition programs, and more rigid career paths. These companies were also more likely to tolerate poor performance and lacked performance-based reward programs (Watson Wyatt Worldwide 2000).

If too much turnover and too little turnover curtail value creation, it suggests an underlying model of productivity along the lines depicted in Figure

6. The optimal level of turnover will likely vary from industry to industry and even from firm to firm. In the United States, substantial differences can be detected between low and high turnover firms with regard to their human capital management practices. Compared to high-turnover firms, those with low turnover tend to have a reputation among new applicants as a more desirable place to work, and they have an easier time finding qualified applicants. Low-turnover firms also fill a higher percentage of their professional positions through internal promotions, and have a more collegial and flexible work environment. For example, they are less likely to require titles to designate authority, they permit rank and file employees to use senior mangers' first names, and they encourage teamwork and cooperation. They also emphasize employment security; share business plans and goals with employees; give employees greater input into hiring decisions and how work is done; and report higher levels of employee satisfaction. In selecting their leaders, these low-turnover companies place greater emphasis on "people skills."

While individual employers can curtail individual worker mobility, reducing job hopping of this sort is a zero sum game from the economy's perspective. Very tight labor markets can lead to "poaching" and other tactics that would have been considered abnormal in the past. Some firms have already resorted to guerrilla tactics to find workers in market areas with low unemployment rates. For instance, a network hardware firm in Durham, North Carolina, posted signs along the commuting routes of engineers working at Nortel and Cisco (Cannon 2000). A high-technology firm in Texas sent recruiters on in-line skates to distribute job-opening leaflets to competitors' employees as they were arriving at work (police were called to dispatch the rolling recruiters; Koenig 2000). All is not good-humored fun; Alcatel

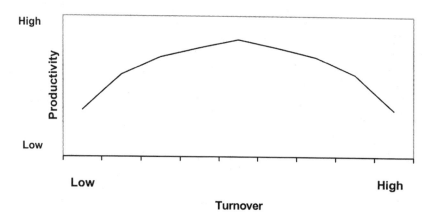

Figure 6. A model of the relationship between turnover and productivity. Source: developed by the authors.

recently sued Cisco Systems claiming that the other firm had hired away a group of Alcatel engineers in order to learn trade secrets (Koenig 2000). Competition among employers to retain their most talented employees and the phenomenal growth in the U.S. stock market in the last two decades of the twentieth century produced a surge in stock-based incentive compensation, especially stock options. The average "overhang" level for a firm in the S&P 1500, defined as stock options granted plus those remaining to be granted as a percentage of the total shares outstanding, grew from 5.4 percent to 13 percent (Luss and Kay 2000). On the other hand, the downturn in the stock market of late has left many firms scrambling to keep employee stock options afloat. Although economic theory would contend otherwise, many employers have been forced to reprice their underwater options to prevent employees from walking down the street to achieve essentially identical compensation packages. It seems clear that as labor markets tighten, there will be a proliferation of noncompete arrangements, employment contracts, and even lawsuits aimed at inhibiting the free flow of workers across companies. However, as some employers figure out how to reduce turnover within their own workforces, this simply adds to other firm's shortages.

Bidding New Workers into the Workforce

One alternative to ease the pressures of tighter labor markets is to expand the supply of labor. Women's participation rates are about 15 percentage points below those of their male counterparts, so it might be possible to attract this last residual pool of women, many of whom are physically able to work outside the home. But to do so the job offer will have to become more attractive. Offering more flexibility regarding work-life patterns may help, to the extent that employers can provide workers with the change to manage their individual circumstances. For working mothers, it may be important to leave work in time to meet the school bus; women who care for elderly parents may need to leave work in an emergency or for an extended period of time.

A recent survey of large employers and employees designated as "top-performers" asked how effective certain practices were in helping attract and retain highly productive workers. Employer responses, as well as those of the female employees who responded to the questions, are reported in Figure 7. Respondent women were divided into two groups: those with children and those without. It is interesting that both groups of women have similar answers, on the one hand, while there are significant discrepancies between employee and employer responses on three of the four measures. Clearly alternative work arrangements are important to women, especially flexible work schedules and job requirements. It is possible that the Internet and company intranets will allow new ways for employees and managers to communicate, making work from home a more realistic alternative.

This survey also indicates that employers could reconsider their policies toward the organization of work and the demands placed on women workers. A key challenge in this regard will be to make part-time work more efficient. Today's labor market indicates a remarkable discrepancy in the productivity of part-time versus full-time workers: Lettau (1994, p. 15) found that in firms that used both types of workers, "compensation in part-time jobs is significantly lower than in full-time jobs when jobs from the same establishment and occupation are compared." Regarding benefits he found that "it is often true that the full-time job receives the benefit while the part-time job does not." On the other hand, "[i]t is virtually never true that the part-time job receives the benefit while the full-time job does not." (p. 16)

Explanations for the part-time/full-time pay difference include the possibility that part-time workers might work in less productive firms, though Lettau's data suggest this theory is only partially correct, if at all, since information is collected from the same firms. A second theory is that workers who choose to work part time are simply not as productive as those who choose to work full time, and sorting is reflected in compensation differentials. There is little empirical grounding for this view, though Ippolito (1997) contends that employers seek "signals" indicating which employees are reliable, for example, in terms of job attendance. He ties reliability to the use of sick leave among a group of federal workers, their accumulated sick leave balances (that they can carry over indefinitely), their use of unpaid leave, and voluntary termination behavior. In that analysis he reported a negative and statistically significant relationship between the use of these

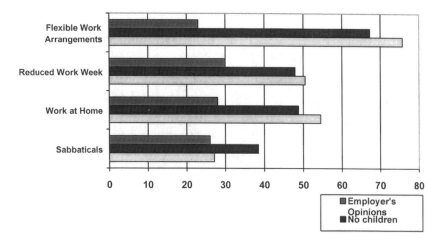

Figure 7. Attitudes of top-performing female employees and their employers toward flexible work arrangements. Source: authors' calculations from Watson Wyatt Worldwide (2000).

benefits and earnings. Women willing to work only part time because of family obligations may be interpreted as signaling a lesser commitment, which in turn explains their lower compensation. A final explanation for lower pay for part-timers is that there are economies of scale or technology that demand a minimum period of work per day, to achieve optimal productivity. While there has been a steady decline in average hours worked in manufacturing jobs from around sixty hours per week in the United States in 1890 to about forty-two hours per week in 1930, average hours worked per week have not changed much even though real earnings have risen (McGill et al. 1996).[9]

Looking ahead to a period of lower labor force growth, it is possible that employers will need to find ways to entice women into the workforce, and it may be that few of these will be willing to commit to full-time jobs particularly during child-raising years. As a result, employers will either have to enhance productivity during relatively short work periods, or facilitate their working longer than they might be naturally inclined to do. Along with more flexible work arrangements, benefits that appeal to parents could also prove successful with women who are not currently full-time employees. For example, childcare costs have become a very significant part of two-earner couples' budgets. Women's decisions to return to work after childbirth is highly correlated with employer policies; job flexibility and part-time work prove to increase the probability of a mother returning to work after childbirth, along with unpaid leave, pretax savings accounts, and child care in the workplace (Hofferth 1996; Glass and Riley 1998). Some commentators emphasize job guarantees, formal pay policies, and phase-back programs for new parents are also important criteria for working mothers as they assess their employment situation. Employers hoping to tap these potential sources of labor supply in the future may find they need to do more in providing such enabling benefits.

Keeping Older Workers

A different approach would be to entice older workers to extend their careers. In the coming decade, as Riche (this volume) notes, the relative share in the 45+ age group will rise substantially, with the largest growth among workers ages 55–64. While today this is a common age for retirement, many such workers are still highly productive. Facing a shortage of talent, some employers will likely find a better use for their most experienced employees than putting them out to a premature retirement. Recent changes in retirement policies have already begun boosting incentives for older individuals to work longer, including the repeal of the earnings test under Social Security for beneficiaries 65+. This could induce older workers to postpone retirement and attract them back into the workforce and/or increase their incentive to work longer hours.

Employers have also repositioned benefit programs, particularly by offering hybrid pension plans as an alternative to traditional defined benefit (DB) pensions. Under the traditional DB plan, the benefit formula would accrue benefit values slowly during the early part of the worker's career, and it would rapidly accelerate near retirement. Most traditional DB plans also had early retirement subsidies that promoted early exits. By contrast, hybrid or cash-balance plans largely eliminate early retirement subsidies (Clark et al. 2001). Moreover, these are more conducive to the transient state of today's workforce by permitting employees to take their account balances with them on changing jobs.

On the whole, however, employers have not yet fully committed to mechanisms that appeal to retaining older workers. In surveying 400 company HR executives, only 18 percent of firms had implemented benefits packages targeted towards older employees (AARP 2000); one-third of employers have implemented part-time work arrangements for older employees.

On the positive side, formal "phased retirement" programs are now being developed, where employment practices and pension accruals are altered to retain older workers either on a part-time or part-year basis. A survey of large employers found that 16 percent offered some form of phased retirement program in 1999, up from 8 percent in 1997.[10] Employers are also hiring "un-retirees" for part-time and temporary employment, as well as consultants. Furthermore some 60 percent of the employers surveyed featured reduced workdays and/or workweeks, while nearly one-quarter of employers permitted extended leaves of absence for workers nearing retirement.

The future of phased retirement is likely to be a permanent development, since it is mutually beneficial to both employers and employees. Only one in four working Americans believes he will have enough money to live comfortably in retirement (EBRI 1999); 68 percent of men and 65 percent of women surveyed in 2000 thought they will work for pay in retirement, up from 65 percent for men and 57 percent for women in 1998. Interestingly, most people report that the main reason to extend the work life is a desire to stay involved and having a satisfying way to spend time. Of course young workers may report that they intend to work beyond normal retirement age, but they may feel quite differently in their mid-60s.

In any event, there appears to be growing interest in helping workers move gradually from full-time work to complete retirement. But several regulatory hurdles make it difficult to implement phased retirement arrangements including restriction on in-service distributions of retirement benefits. Nevertheless, substantial fractions of Watson Wyatt surveys indicate a moderate-to-high level of interest in implementing phased retirement arrangements over the next two to three years, and nearly half report they hope to retain skilled workers by implementing such plans. Employers seeking to leverage their attractiveness to older employees in the future must likely commit to such programs.

Boosting Current Workers' Productivity

If it proves difficult to entice more people into the labor market, perhaps more production can be generated by current workers. In other words, it may be possible to get by with slower labor force growth if employers can find a way to utilize existing human capital more efficiently. The goal of achieving higher productivity as a society will ultimately have to be delivered at the employer level.

Borrowing from Stewart (1997), we propose that an organization's ability to create economic value is the direct result of how effectively it uses its financial, customer, and human capital resources. Financial capital includes all of the fixed and current operating assets of the organization. In commercial and nonprofit enterprises, customer capital is the value that accrues to an organization because of the client goodwill that makes them repeat customers. In public sector endeavors, customer capital is embodied in the political support that makes some jurisdictions preferred places for commercial enterprises and families to locate. Total organizational effectiveness is achieved through the linkage of the various forms of capital through what Stewart calls "structural capital." Structural capital is the set of programs, processes, and practices that allow an organization to leverage its human capital in a way that it can maximize its effectiveness. In part, employers accomplish this by the effective utilization of financial and customer capital assets, in combination with human capital. But structural capital can also work as an accelerator on human capital resources to accentuate an organization's ability to create value. The task employers face is figuring out how to develop and use this structural capital to fully exploit the human capital and sustain its productive use. By identifying why some employers are more effective at stimulating highly productive work environments than others, it is possible to teach those with low productivity levels how to improve, resulting in higher productivity growth.

Linking human resource management practices to organizational effectiveness is an elaboration of economics production function:

$$P = K^a L^{1-a} \; ,$$

where P represents product or output, K represents capital inputs, L equals labor inputs, and a and $1-a$ represent the marginal product of K and L respectively. This model suggests that enhancing human capital results in the firm being generally more productive.

Economists have found that there is a structural relationship between worker productivity, pay, and age. Pay levels tend to be positively sloped during the initial phases of working careers, peak somewhere around mid-career or later, and then decline beyond a certain age. Improvements in pay and productivity early in the career are related to on-the-job training (Mincer 1974; Maranto and Rodgers 1984; Brown 1989). The leveling-out of the age/earnings profile beyond a certain age is seen as related to the slowdown in the accumulation of skills, and ultimately to the depreciation of knowledge acquired early in a worker's career. In some cases, individual workers themselves lose the appetite to continue to acquire new skills. Employers may also lose interest in investing in workers at some point, because the expected remaining period over which the investment in that training can be amortized becomes so short that the returns on the investment become negative. As a consequence, older workers may end up with more fixed acquired skills as compared to younger counterparts, whose capabilities are continuing to be enhanced because of personal and employer investment in them. Without continuous renewal of the skills being brought to the labor market, individual worker's human capital depreciates just like the physical capital.

When asked what effect increasing age had on worker productivity, 74 percent of the senior executives surveyed by Watson Wyatt indicated that productivity decreases with age at some point (23 percent concluded that age was unrelated to productivity, and 3 percent indicated that productivity increased with age indefinitely). Executives asked to indicate the approximate age at which productivity begins to decline indicated around age 55 (Watson Wyatt 2000). A similar finding was reported by Carliner (1982), who found that earnings of men in their 50s and 60s declined relative to those of younger men.

The potential problem employers face in keeping on older workers is sketched out in Figure 8. Some companies maintain traditional hierarchical structures that depend on relatively inexperienced workers at the bottom having relatively little human capital, and then fewer workers fill the successively narrower ranks as competency and human capital levels rise. The traditional job structure is characterized by the solid triangle in Figure 8. But as baby boomers move into their most productive years, the workforce may look more like the inverted triangle in Figure 8, characterized by an abundance of highly experienced and skilled individuals. Unless employers restructure to take advantage of boomers' experiences and skills, workers with high-level capabilities will end up doing lower-level jobs below their

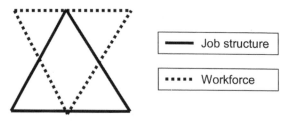

Figure 8. Hypothetical job structures and the evolution of the workforce in the United States, 2000–2010. Source: developed by the authors.

capabilities. Some of these will become frustrated and leave the labor market prematurely, reducing rather than enhancing productivity, contrary to what we argue the economy needs.

An alternative way to consider these challenges relies on the perspective of sociological or behavioral/psychological models. Here human resource management is viewed in relation to measures of internal and external environmental factors such as technology, organizational structure, stage of life cycle, business strategies, organizational structures, and the like. Rather than focusing as economists do on the marginal contribution that human capital makes to organizations, these other approaches stress how "structural capital" can leverage human capital for value creation purposes. Stewart (1997) points to the different evolutionary paths of Wal-Mart and Sears as an example of two companies operating in virtually identical markets with very different results. The personnel these two companies brought to their respective marketplaces were initially similar. Sam Walton may have had a domineering character and a formula for retail marketing success, but Sears could have found strong and bright managers and could have copied Walton's ways. Yet Wal-Mart succeeded relative to Sears and its other competitors. In other industries this has also happened: Canon moved from ground zero in the office copier market, where Xerox held a near monopoly position, to a position of equality and then dominance (Hamel and Prahalad 1994). Collins and Porras (1994) look at a series of paired companies that operated for long periods to study why some companies are more successful than others.

Based on this and similar research, Jackson and Schuler (1995) have developed a research taxonomy sorting organized human resource management practices into five areas. These are used to assess their impact on achieving fundamental business goals, and they include (1) planning, (2) staffing, (3) appraising, (4) compensating, and (5) training and development. Each of these has to do with the acquisition, development, or reward of human capital within an organization. A body of research analyzes the effectiveness of the various elements of this model; for example, Hansen and Werenfelt (1989) test both economic and organizational models, and then integrate elements of the two. An interpretation of their findings is that not only does the quality of the human capital in an organization matter, but also how that human capital is organized and marshaled for the task at hand.

The human capital drivers that appear to have a marked effect on firm performance include (Luss and Kay 1999): recruiting excellence, collegial and flexible work environments, communications integrity, and clear rewards and accountability. That research also concluded that several human resource policies are associated with value creation within the organizations studied. As illustrated in Figure 9, the link between effective human capital management and higher shareholder returns works via employee and customer

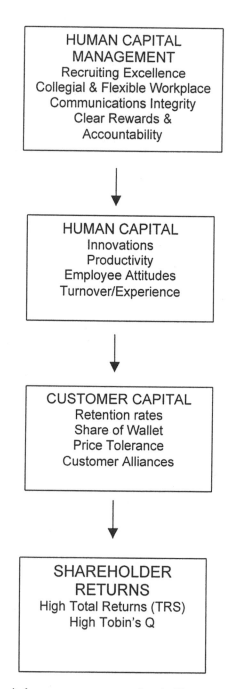

Figure 9. Human capital management creates shareholder returns. Source: Luss and Kay (1999).

satisfaction. Firms cannot manage their shareholder returns directly. Instead, managers choose their product, service, financing, and human capital strategies to try to achieve superior firm performance. In the human capital area, there are specific firm actions and behaviors that can cause measurably higher levels of employee satisfaction and productivity with lower levels of employee turnover. In turn, these improvements will result in higher customer loyalty and satisfaction leading to the creation of surplus value within organizations.

Effective human capital management is a combination of four human resource functions. Recruiting excellence allows a firm to acquire employees who either already possess the general human capital necessary to do the jobs required, or who can be trained. The next step is to establish a collegial and flexible workplace so employees are encouraged to work well together. Within this workplace, the firm must promote communications integrity. This involves trusting employees enough to share information with them and to allow them to communicate outside of hierarchical boundaries. Effective communication is crucial for leveraging human capital into outstanding customer service. Finally, there needs to be an effective performance management system with clear rewards and accountability to establish the relationship between performance and rewards.

Luss and Kay (1999) derive weights for these four human capital drivers by studying the relative effect of that variable on firm performance. The authors found that a twenty-five-point increase in their index score was associated with a 15 percent increase in Tobin's Q, equivalent to an 18 percent increase in market value for the median firm studied. Another interesting result was that the firms that scored highly at one time continued to be relatively high performers two and three years later. This research supports the claim that companies can use human capital management to have a measurable effect on firm value. Human capital management can be used to increase employee satisfaction, leading to higher customer loyalty and to better firm performance.

Conclusions

As the United States braces for an era of much slower growth in labor supply than experienced in the past, employers must begin to reconsider their workforce practices if they wish to sustain their viability into the future. We suggest that this will require programs to attract and retain the best and the brightest. For these programs to be successful, employers must do more to proactively recognize the needs of their workforces. If employers wish to attract more women into the workplace, they must address issues that have kept substantial numbers of them from participating. This means implementing more suitable work-life solutions for women, such as on-site childcare and more flexible work schedules. If employers wish to delay the retirement of their most valued employees, they must rethink their retirement policies and provide access to phased retirement.

Although employers may be successful at bidding new workers into the workplace and/or retaining their current staff, we still worry that employers may not be able to hire enough workers to meet production needs. To survive, they will have to restructure and recreate a more conducive work environment, one that can entice more production out of existing employees. It is the firms that are the most successful at managing their human capital through effective communication programs, offering a collegial work atmosphere, and establishing a performance management system with clear rewards and accountability, that will be most effective. Ultimately, these same firms will likely be the most successful at enhancing shareholder value and who will survive to be the leaders of tomorrow.

Notes

Opinions and conclusions drawn in this chapter are those of the authors and do not necessarily represent those of Watson Wyatt Worldwide or any of its associates. The authors thank Tim Galpin, Ira Kay, Richard Luss, and Janemarie Mulvey for helpful comments.

1. GDP is not a perfect measure of improved standards of living across this period, in part because of the changing labor force behavior of women. In 1946, fewer than half of working-age women in the United States were employed outside the home, whereas nearly 80 percent were during 2000. As women have increasingly entered the workforce, many tasks that were previously done by housewives and not measured in the government's calculation of GDP have been commercialized and are now included in measures of national output.

2. Over the last three decades the annualized growth in GDP per capita was fairly stable at 2.12, 2.25 and 2.33 percent for the 1970s, 1980s and 1990s, respectively.

3. The CBO projections are slightly more conservative than the Clinton administration's or the Blue Chip estimates. This is because projected economic growth rates developed by the CBO and other prognosticators are solutions to a set of simultaneous equations tracking activity across various economic sectors. CBO projections do not model cyclical variations in the demand for goods and services; beyond the immediate short term. Underlying assumptions about capital growth and technology drive projected labor productivity; as long as projected output is consistent with prior patterns of production, most macro models assume markets for goods and services will clear. It seems reasonable to assume that consumers can keep up with increased productive capacity in the future.

4. The nonaccelerating inflation rate of unemployment is more generally referred to as the natural rate of unemployment. This is the rate of unemployment that is implied by the present structure of the economy that accounts for the structural and frictional forces in the economy that cannot be reduced by raising GDP.

5. We have not developed our own macroeconomic projection model; there are a number of them around that are widely used in government and business planning. We have no reason to believe that the macroeconomic projections from a model we might build would generate significantly different results than others given certain underlying assumptions that are important in these types of projections.

6. By applying constant labor force participation rates in 2000 to population shares over the coming decade, our baseline labor force is projected to be 156.7

million in 2010. The Bureau of Labor Statistics and the actuaries at the Social Security Administration have made similar labor force projections. However, the BLS has published projections only for the 16 and over civilian labor force through 2008. The BLS projects the 2008 labor force to be 154.6 million, the Social Security Administration projects 151.3 million, while our baseline labor force is projected to be 153.8 million (SSA 2001a; Fullerton 1999).

7. An unpublished hours series from the Social Security Administration combined with the most recent estimates of GDP suggests that from 1995 to 2000, worker productivity increased by 2.27 percent. While some argue for a "new" paradigm in productivity growth, not all agree (Gordon 1999). For planning purposes, prudence suggests that it is necessary to recognize three decades of historical data.

8. For all practical purposes, this assumption is the equivalent of assuming the end of early retirement in the United States. In this case, the need for workers 65 years and older depends on whether excess demand for labor persists in the labor market after the higher participation rates of people between 55 and 64 years old have been factored into the analysis. For completeness, we estimate labor force participation rates and hours per worker assuming all workers 55 and over are equally likely to increase workforce participation. Under the most conservative assumption of productivity growth, labor force participation rates and hours per worker will increase over 48 percent from their 2000 levels. For men ages 55–64, labor force participation rates would need to rise from 68 percent in 2000 to 100 percent by 2010, while women in the same age grouping would need to increase from 51 percent to over 76 percent. This seemed an improbable scenario.

9. One explanation for the persistence of the forty-hour week is the rising importance of team production in the work place. Often times, for teamwork to be effective, it requires that all members be together at once.

10. Graig and Paganelli (2000) define phased retirement as arrangements that allow employees approaching normal retirement age to reduce their work hours or job responsibilities or both for the purpose of gradually easing into full retirement.

References

AARP. 2000. *American Business and Older Employees: A Summary of the Findings.* Washington, D.C.: AARP.

Becker, Gary S. 1964. *Human Capital: A Theoretical Analysis with Special Reference to Education.* New York: Columbia University Press.

Brown, James N. 1989. "Why Do Wages Increase with Tenure?" *American Economic Review* 79, 5: 971–91.

Cannon, Steve. 2000. "Guerrilla Recruiting Tactic as Sign of the Times." Raleigh, North Carolina *News & Observer*, December 12, D1.

Carliner, Geoffrey. 1982. "The Wages of Older Men," *Journal of Human Resources* 27 (Winter): 25–38.

Clark, Robert L. and Sylvester J. Schieber. 2002. "Taking the Subsidy Out of Early Retirement: The Story Behind the Conversion to Hybrid Pensions." In *Innovations in Retirement Financing,* ed. Olivia S. Mitchell, Zvi Bodie, Brett Hammond, and Stephen Zeldes. Pension Research Council. Philadelphia: University of Pennsylvania Press.

Collins, James C. and Jerry I. Porras. 1994. *Built to Last: Successful Habits of Visionary Companies.* New York: HarperCollins.

Congressional Budget Office. 2001. *The Budget and Economic Outlook: Fiscal Years 2002–2011.* Washington, D.C.: U.S. Government Printing Office, January. 3–4.

Council of Economic Advisors. 2001. *Economic Report of the President.* Washington, D.C.: U.S. Government Printing Office, January. 316–17.

Employee Benefit Research Institute. 1999. "The Evolution of Retirement: Results of the 1999 Retirement Confidence Survey." EBRI Issue Brief 216. December.

Fullerton, Howard N. 1999. "Labor Force Projections to 2008: Steady Growth and Changing Composition." *Monthly Labor Review* (November): 19–32.

Glass, Jennifer and Lisa Riley. 1998. "Family Responsive Policies and Employee Retention Following Childbirth," *Social Forces* 76, 4: 1401–35.

Goodridge, Elisabeth. 2001. "The Quest for Quality — the Economic Slump Hasn't Slowed the Scramble for Top IT Talent." *Information Week*, February 19, 55.

Gordon, Robert J. 1999. "Has the 'New Economy' Rendered the Productivity Slowdown Obsolete?" <www.econ.northwestern.edu/faculty-frame.html>.

Graig, Laurene A. and Valerie Paganelli. 2000. "Phased Retirement: Reshaping the End of Work." *Compensation and Benefits Management* 16, 2 (Spring): 1–9.

Grizzle, Benjamin D. 2001. "Harvard U.: Harvard Students Receive Navy Recruitment e-mail." *Harvard Crimson*, January 12, U-Wire.

Gunn, Erik. 2001. "Retooling an Image: Factory Work Undergoes Overhaul as Recruiters Look to Next Generation." *Chicago Tribune*, March 11, C3.

Hamel, Gary and C. K. Prahalad. 1994. *Competing for the Future.* Cambridge, Mass.: Harvard Business School Press.

Hansen, G. S. and B. Werenfelt. 1989. "Determinants of Firm Performance: The Relative Importance of Economic and Organizational Factors." *Strategic Management Journal* 10: 399–411.

Hofferth, Sandra L. 1996. "Effects of Public and Private Policies on Working After Childbirth." *Work and Occupations* 23, 4: 378–404.

Ippolito, Richard A. 1997. *Pension Plans and Employee Performance: Evidence, Analysis, and Policy.* Chicago: University of Chicago Press.

Jackson, S. E. and R. S. Schuler. 1987. "Understanding Human Resource Management in the Context of Organizations and Their Environments." *Annual Review of Psychology* 46: 237–64.

Koenig, David. 2000. "Tech Companies Use In-Your-Face Tactics to Attract Scarce Talent." *Associated Press Newswires*, October 14.

Lettau, Michael K. 1994. "Compensation in Part-Time Jobs Versus Full-Time Jobs: What if the Job Is the Same?" BLS Working Paper 260. Washington, D.C.: U.S. Department of Labor, Bureau of Labor Statistics, Office of Research and Evaluation.

Luss, Richard and Ira Kay. 1999. *Creating Superior Returns to Shareholders Through Effective Human Capital Management: The Watson Wyatt Human Capital Index™.* Washington, D.C.: Watson Wyatt Worldwide.

———. 2000. "Stock Option Overhang — Shareholder Boon or Shareholder Burden II." Working Paper. Washington, D.C.: Watson Wyatt Worldwide.

Macunovich, Diane J. 2000. "Birth Quake: The Baby Boom and Its After Shocks." Unpublished manuscript.

Maranto, Cheryl L. and Robert C. Rodgers. 1984. "Does Work Experience Increase Productivity? A Test of the On-the-Job Training Hypothesis." *Journal of Human Resources* 19, 3: 341–57.

McGill, Dan M., Kyle N. Brown, John J. Haley, and Sylvester J. Schieber. 1996. *Fundamentals of Private Pensions.* 7th ed. Philadelphia: University of Pennsylvania Press.

Mincer, Jacob. 1974. *Schooling, Experience, and Earnings,* New York: Columbia University Press.

Nyce, Steven A. and Sylvester J. Schieber. 2001. "The Decade of the Employee: The Workforce Environment in the Coming Decade." Washington, D.C.: Watson Wyatt Worldwide.

Poterba, James M. 1997 "The Rate of Return to Corporate Capital and Factor Shares: New Estimates Using Revised National Income Accounts and Capital Stock Data," NBER Working Paper 6263. November.

Rappaport, Anna M., Carol A. Bogosian, and Carol A. Klann. 1998. "Population Trends and the Labor Force in the Years Ahead." *Benefits Quarterly* (Fourth Quarter): 8–17.

Riche, Martha Farnsworth. This volume. "The Demographics of Tomorrow's Workplace."

Seattle Post-Intelligencer. 2000. "Off-the-Wall Hiring," August. E1.

Smith, Kristin E. and Amara Bachu. 1999. "Women's Labor Force Attachment Patterns and Maternity Leave: A Review of the Literature." U.S. Bureau of the Census Working Paper 32.

Social Security Administration. 2001a. Unpublished projection series from the Office of the Actuary.

Social Security Administration. 2001b. Unpublished series from the Office of the Actuary.

Southwell, David. 1999. "Smooth Sailing More Incentives, Recruiters Raise Navy's Number." *Chicago Sun Times,* August 16, 8.

Stewart, Thomas A. 1997. *Intellectual Capital.* New York: Doubleday.

Turyn, Teresa L., EBRI, Ruth Helman, Mathew Greenwald & Associates. 2001. "Women on Savings and Retirement: Results from the 2000 Women's Retirement Confidence Survey." *EBRI Notes* 22, 2 (February).

Tyler, Kathryn. 2001. "A Roof over Their Heads." *HR Magazine,* February 1, 40.

Unicon Research Corporation. 2000. CPS Utilities, Annual Demographic and Income Supplement: March Files, 1988B–2000. Santa Monica, Calif.

U.S. Bureau of the Census. 2000. Projections of the Resident Population by Age, Sex, Race, and Hispanic Origin: 1999 to 2100. Washington D.C.: Population Projections Program, January 13, NP-D1-A.

U.S. Department of Commerce. 2000. *Survey of Current Business.* Bureau of Economic Analysis, August. 124–27.

U.S. Department of Commerce. 2001. *Survey of Current Business.* Bureau of Economic Analysis, April. D3.

Watson Wyatt Worldwide. 2000. *Strategic Rewards 1999/2000: Supplemental Survey of Top-Performing Employees.* Washington, D.C.: Watson Wyatt Worldwide.

Chapter 8
Are Career Jobs Headed for Extinction?

Sanford M. Jacoby

Academics and journalists tell us that we are currently witnessing a historic event: the demise of career-type jobs. Richard Sennett, the sociologist, argues eloquently that the surge of corporate downsizing is the signal occurrence of our postmodern age, with ramifications far beyond the labor market. As careers condense, so do our time horizons and relationships. What Sennett (1998) calls "no long term" is a pervasive force eroding our moral strength. "No long term," he says, "disorients action over the long term, loosens bonds of trust and commitment, and divorces will from behavior."

Many Americans remain anxious about job security. The share of employees who say they are frequently concerned about layoffs has risen from 12 percent in 1981 to 37 percent this year (*Daily Labor Report* 1999). Politicians are adept at tapping into these sentiments, as in the 1996 presidential campaign, when Patrick Buchanan excoriated executives for taking huge salaries while laying off thousands of workers. President Clinton responded predictably: he organized a conference and invited employers to the White House to discuss corporate ethics and responsibilities (Mandell 1996; Mitchell 1996).

The notion that corporations have responsibilities to employees is hardly a new or radical idea. Its roots lie deep in the American past, dating back a century or more when companies first began systematically to provide for their employees' welfare. The movement was known as "welfare work" or "welfare capitalism." It was not unique to the United States, but its popularity in this country was uniquely American. Welfare capitalism shaped our nation's risk-sharing institutions — everything from "fringe" benefits to Social Security to career employment — the same institutions whose future is being questioned by Sennett and others (Jacoby 1997).

Yet institutional arrangements have changed much less than Sennett's "no long term" would suggest. Put bluntly, the welfare capitalist approach remains in place. Career-type employment practices — an amalgam that economists term "internal labor markets" — are still the norm in the labor market and employers continue to shoulder a variety of risks for employees. None of this is to deny the labor-market turbulence of the past fifteen years. The mixture of market and organizational principles that structures the employment relationship now gives more weight to market factors, especially in managerial positions. There also has been a change in risk sharing, with employers transferring more of the burden to employees. However, these are changes of degree, not of kind. They do not constitute a phase shift but rather a reallocation of responsibilities within a stable institutional structure. This chapter discusses the extent of change in recent years and analyzes the prospects for welfare capitalism's future.

The Crisis of Welfare Capitalism?

During the past twenty years, modern welfare capitalism has experienced its most critical test since the Great Depression. Starting in the 1980s, a series of shocks hit the economy. Heightened competition, rapid technological change, and corporate mergers led to layoffs throughout American industry. In the late 1970s and early 1980s, it was blue-collar industrial workers — often unionized — who bore the brunt of permanent job loss. Since the late 1980s, it has been white-collar, educated workers who have experienced the sharpest increases in permanent job loss. Less-educated workers still have the highest job-loss rates, but their rates have fallen since the early 1980s. Hence the gap separating the job-loss rates of males with a high-school education and males with a college education narrowed by more than half between the early 1980s and the mid-1990s.[1] Companies that had never experienced a major layoff — firms like IBM, Kodak, and Digital Equipment — now jettisoned thousands of white-collar employees.

What is significant about these recent cuts is that they are occurring during a relatively tight labor market, unlike previous postwar layoffs that were keyed to the business cycle. Also, recent downsizing disproportionately affects educated professional and managerial employees, a group not previously targeted for layoff. The layoffs were — and are — a shock to those employees who believed themselves immune from job loss. Middle-level managers found that the elimination of their jobs was often the chief goal of industrial "restructuring." At large diversified companies, a combination of mergers, new information technology, and work reorganization reduced the need for headquarters staff. Fully 85 percent of large multinational corporations report that they have reorganized their headquarters since 1990 (Conference Board 1998). Those who survive downsizing are being offered a different employment contract. Instead of employment security in exchange for loyalty, organizations are proffering a "new deal" that provides higher pay in return for broader skills and a tolerance of change (Herriot and Pemberton 1995; Cappelli 1999).

Meanwhile, there has been an expansion of nonstandard employment: jobs that are temporary, part time, or contractual. In 1997, around 20 percent of all employees held nonstandard jobs. (The self-employed accounted for another 10 percent; Kalleberg et al. 1997, p. 9.) There is a stratum of nonstandard workers (such as consultants working on contract) who are well paid. However, most of these workers are likely to be paid a low wage, and they are one-sixth as likely to receive health and pension benefits as those in standard full-time jobs. In fact, much of the decline in health insurance coverage since 1979 has been the result of cutbacks for temporary and other peripheral workers. Coverage has also declined for some of those holding standard jobs, notably less-educated males (Farber and Levy 1998; Kalleberg et al. 1997; Farber 1997b).

Accompanying these changes has been a new ethos of market individualism, especially in places such as Wall Street and Silicon Valley where there is intense competition for skilled workers combined with a rapidly changing knowledge base. These workers — predominantly young and educated — have grown skeptical not only of welfare capitalism but of government, unions, and other large institutions. Believing that they must have a broad range of skills to succeed in today's labor market, these workers expect to spend no more than brief stints at any single firm. They ask only that the employer ensure their future employability by providing learning experiences that can be added to their resumes. Less concerned with job security than the generations who were touched by the Depression, they see themselves as masters of their own fates. They resemble nineteenth-century craft workers, who treasured their autonomy and hedged their labor-market risk with a diverse set of skills.

These changes have led to a widespread sense that the institutional structures erected over the course of the last century are tumbling down. It is hard not to feel that way when no less than the American Management Association issues a book entitled *Corporate Executions,* whose subtitle is "How Corporate Greed Is Shattering Lives, Companies, and Communities" (Downs 1995). But reports of welfare capitalism's demise are exaggerated. We are not moving to an economy made up only of short-term jobs, indifferent employers, and disloyal employees. Mid- to large-size corporations continue to pursue employment practices that are sheltered from the momentary vicissitudes of the market. It would be a vast exaggeration to say that long-term employment is dead or that all jobs henceforth will be casual positions. "No long term" is hyperbole. "Less long term" is not as catchy but far more accurate.

It is a human tendency to believe that one lives in an exceptional era, fundamentally different from earlier periods. Many people today — including businessmen, academics, and government leaders — think that information technology is creating a "new economy" with accelerating innovation and productivity growth. However, economic statistics show that productivity growth today actually is slower than it was during the first two decades after World War II (Kurtzman 1998: 88).

Just as there is a certain amount of hype attached to rhetoric about the new economy, there is a tendency to exaggerate how much the labor market has changed in recent years. The big change, as mentioned, is the fact that companies are laying workers off during a prosperous period, with layoffs targeted at white-collar employees. Hence employees today bear more risk, including a greater risk of layoff. But there are still plenty of career-type jobs for educated workers, and employers still indemnify employees against many kinds of risk.

To understand the paradox of continuity amid change, it is important to recall the distinction between stocks (our endowment of existing jobs) and flows (the jobs being created and destroyed in the current period). Just as in the distinction between the large national debt and the smaller annual deficit (or surplus), we sometimes forget that stocks tend to dwarf net flows. Moreover, another important fact is that net flows are composed of two enormous intersecting streams: job "deaths" (such as downsizing) and job "births" (new jobs) (Davis and Haltiwanter 1992). Despite downsizing, the U.S. economy has been adept at maintaining a high birth rate of new jobs, many of which eventually will become long-term positions. In what follows, several types of evidence are marshaled in support of these claims, including data on employee tenure and mobility, new job creation and new job quality, cyclical factors, and on employee compensation.

Tenure and Mobility

Take, for example, the data on employee tenure, one indicator for gauging the prevalence of long-term or career employment. Tenure is not easy to measure. There are problems in controlling for the effect of the business cycle and in using cross-sectional as opposed to panel data. Also, there are biases that arise when individuals round off their self-estimates of tenure. Nevertheless, recent studies consistently find only a slight drop in the overall prevalence of long-term jobs. In the 1980s there was little change in aggregate job stability (job retention rates), while in the first half of the 1990s there was a modest decline in stability, particularly for long-tenure workers (Diebold et al. 1997; Neumark et al. 1998).

For men ages 35–64, the share employed more than ten years with their current employer fell from 50 percent in 1979 to 40 percent in 1996. The sharpest tenure declines occurred in managerial and professional-technical occupations (although managers had and still have the highest probability of being in long-term employment relationships). However, during the same period there was an increase — albeit slight — in the share of those employed in long-term positions in service occupations and industries. Partly for this reason, female tenure has shown a different pattern: For women aged 35–64, the share employed in long-term positions rose moderately between 1979 and 1996 (Farber 1997d). While the rise in female tenure is partly due to changes in women's career patterns (they are less likely to quit for childbearing than in the past), it is important to remember that employers are responding to women's growing desire for stable, career-type positions by providing them with jobs of this kind.

The unadjusted data for the period 1983 to 1998 show similar trends. For males over 25, the percentage who worked for their current employer for ten years or more fell modestly from 38 to 33 percent; for women, the percentage increased from 25 percent to 28 percent, nearly canceling the drop in male tenure. In service and retail industries, median tenure rose slightly between 1983 and 1998; in manufacturing and transportation industries, median tenure declined slightly.[2]

What about data on employee separations (layoffs, dismissals, and quits)? Even if the amount of time people remain on their jobs has not changed much, it is possible that workers are experiencing less security. This could be due to higher levels of involuntary job loss as a cause of separations. Also, it could be reflected in lower levels of voluntary mobility. Unfortunately, there is no consensus on this issue; different data sets tell different stories. The Displaced Workers Survey focuses on involuntary job loss (job loss due to plant closings, position abolished, slack work, and other forms of layoff). The survey shows a slight increase in involuntary job loss in the 1990s compared to the 1980s, with most of the increase driven by job loss for "other" reasons, the nature of which is not clear (Farber 1997a). Data from the Panel Study on Income Dynamics (PSID) paint a grimmer picture, with a steady weakening for male workers — but not female workers — of the negative effect of tenure on the probability of being dismissed. (That is, long-tenure male workers stood a greater chance of dismissal; Valletta 1997.) However, another panel study, the Census Bureau's Survey of Income and Program Participation (SIPP), shows stability from the mid-1980s to the mid-1990s in aggregate layoff and discharge rates. The probability of permanent layoff declined for young (18-35) and middle-aged (41-55) workers, while rising sharply for workers in the 56–60 age bracket.[3]

The SIPP data on voluntary mobility (quits) exhibit little change since the 1980s, meaning that layoffs are neither inhibiting quits nor promoting them. Survey data show the same thing: of those employed over twenty hours per week, there was no change between 1977 and 1997 in the proportion who say they will seeks new jobs with other employers in the coming year. Workers, in other words, are neither more nor less inclined to hop jobs than twenty years ago (Bond et al. 1998; Bansak and Raphael 1998).

Data on geographic mobility provide corroborating evidence. People who change their residence often change their jobs, especially when a move is out of state. Richard Sennett's protagonist, a high-tech venture capitalist, moved around the country four times in twelve years, leading Sennett to lament "the fugitive quality of friendship and local community" caused by new career patterns. In the suburbs where today's employees reside, "no one . . . becomes a long-term witness to another person's life." But is it really the case that Americans are more mobile now than in the 1950s, the heyday of the Organization Man and the classic bedroom suburb? In fact, they are not. Cross-state geographic mobility rates actually are slightly lower in the 1990s than they were in the 1950s, when communities and workers allegedly were more stable.[4]

In short, the data indicate a very modest decline in aggregate job stability in the 1990s, with much of the effect concentrated among long-tenure males in managerial and professional occupations. The underlying stock of jobs, however, is still heavily composed of career-type positions. Indeed, as the population continues to age, it is likely that job tenure levels will rise across the labor market. Focusing on net flows over the past fifteen years, we see a drop of 1 to 8 percentage points in the proportion employed over ten years with the same employer; focusing on stocks, we see that nearly one-third of the adult labor force in 1998 was employed in long-term jobs, rising to one-half for men aged 45–64. "Long-term employment relationships" says economist Henry Farber (1997: 26), "remain an important feature of the U.S. labor market."

Deaths and Births

If one identifies the U.S. companies with the largest absolute net job losses since 1990, the list contains many familiar names. Near the top are Sears (down 166,000 since 1990), AT&T (down 155,000), and IBM (down 113,000). Other major losers include General Motors, General Dynamics, Digital Equipment (DEC), Kodak, Mobil, and Xerox.[5] Job losses at these blue-ribbon companies send a message that absolute job security no longer exists. Nevertheless, not all jobs are in peril, nor is modern welfare capitalism a relic of the past. Despite laying off thousands of workers, many of these companies continue to offer career employment and, in some instances, have been rehiring employees almost as quickly as shedding them. AT&T, which took a major public relations hit three years ago when it announced plans to eliminate 40,000 jobs, has had a net reduction of 20,000 jobs since then because of its new hires (Silverstein and Maharaj 1999).

Much of this is common knowledge. What is less well known is the extent to which employment has been reshuffled in recent years, either within industries (from unprofitable companies to rapidly growing ones) or between industries (from mature to expanding sectors). There has been a slew of companies whose headcount grew steadily in the 1990s. European and other critics of the U.S. employment "miracle" scoff at this new job creation, arguing that it is concentrated in sectors offering low-quality jobs (Freeman 1998). In fact, several of the companies with the largest absolute employment growth since 1990 either offer relatively low-quality jobs — such as Marriott (up 194,000) and McDonald's (up 91,000) — or they are purveyors of temporary workers, like Kelly Services (up 172,000) and Robert Half (up 117,000).

However, the gainers also include companies offering stable, career-type positions. Those situated in expanding sectors tend to be newer companies that have not yet become household names. For example, the following companies each created at least 40,000 jobs since 1990: in financial services, Morgan Stanley and Norwest; in health care, Genesis Health Ventures and Sun Healthcare; and in entertainment, Disney and Viacom. Some of the better-quality job gainers come from the same industries as those on the losers list. Thus while Sears shrank, its competitors — like Dayton-Hudson, Home Depot, Lowe's, and Wal-Mart — added over 700,000 jobs. In the communications industry, AT&T contracted but SBC, MCI, Worldcom, and Motorola added many more jobs than AT&T cut. Gains by EDS, Intel, and Seagate surpassed losses at DEC and IBM, while even some chemical companies — unlike Kodak — managed to add considerable numbers of new jobs, including Praxair, Merck, and Eastman Chemical (once a division of Kodak).

These successful companies put enormous effort into transforming new recruits into company men and women, both in the way they think and the skills that they possess. While the new jobs do not provide the kind of iron-clad security that some employees, especially managers, once could expect, nevertheless these jobs are far from being short-term positions. Take, for example, Lowe's, a chain of home improvement stores. Lowe's is very similar to what Sears Roebuck was like in its heyday. The company has grown rapidly, adding 43,000 jobs and hundreds of new stores since 1990. Twice listed as one of the country's top one hundred employers, it offers career jobs and a stock purchase plan for all of its employees, who own 25 percent of the company. Lowe's competitors — including Home Depot and Wal-Mart — similarly pride themselves on their low employee turnover rates. Wal-Mart, currently on the top one hundred list, promotes from within and invests heavily in employee training, as does Home Depot. With new jobs like these, median tenure levels will rise in years to come.[6]

To find a parallel to the labor market of the 1990s, one has to go back seventy years. During the 1920s, the unemployment rate was low and new jobs were rapidly being created. However, the health of the aggregate labor market masked some painful shifts. One factor fostering job displacement in the 1920s was a high rate of investment in labor-saving plant and equipment, which gave rise to a new phrase, "technological unemployment." Another factor was sectoral dislocation. Employment was shifting from blue-collar to white-collar jobs; from manufacturing to services; and within manufacturing from older industries like steel, shoes, cotton textiles, and railroad equipment to newer industries like electrical goods, chemicals, and food processing. The rate at which workers left the industry in which they had been employed more than doubled in the 1920s over the rate that had existed between 1899 and 1914 (Jacoby 1985). During the Great Depression, contraction of these newer industries was less severe and recovery more rapid than average; they ultimately were the industries on which the postwar economy was based (Bernstein 1987). However, the 1920s were, despite the sectoral shifts, a decade of growing, if unevenly distributed, prosperity. All of this should sound eerily familiar — absent, one hopes, the stock-market crash that brought the decade to a close.

Job Quality

What about the quality of today's new jobs? We can assess job quality using proxy measures such as real wage growth and full-time status. One study finds that in the early 1980s there was a slight deterioration of real wages on new jobs relative to old jobs. Since then, however, relative real wages have been stable. While the less educated suffered sizeable real wage declines, that pattern occurred in both old and new jobs. Moreover, new jobs of the mid-1990s fell into the overall wage distribution in much the same way as in earlier years (Farber 1997a). Thus the evidence is not consistent with the claim that the new jobs being produced by the U.S. economy are predominantly low-wage. Wage inequality is pervasive and not the result of inferior new jobs (Jacoby and Goldschmidt 1998).

Whether a job is permanent or full time is another dimension of job quality. Temporary jobs have experienced rapid growth in recent years, faster than other jobs. However, while growth has been rapid, it started from a small base. Currently less than 2 percent of the workforce is employed on a contract basis or works for temporary help agencies. One reason for the growth in temporary positions is employer reluctance to hire probationary employees who might have to be dismissed if unsatisfactory. With dismissal costs rising, employers prefer to use temporary help agencies to screen persons suitable for career-type positions. (Temp agencies rarely fire unsatisfactory workers; they simply stop calling them.) That is, the growth in temporary positions is, at least in part, a complement to, not a substitute for, standard full-time employment (Autor 1999).

As for part-timers, some 21 percent of workers are employed part time. That figure is the same as in the early 1970s. Moreover, for the period since 1980, there is no evidence that new jobs are more likely to be part time than old jobs. Bear in mind that around 80 percent of part-timers are in those positions voluntarily — they are not seeking full-time jobs — and some have a significant stake in the companies they work for (Kalleberg et al. 1997; Segal and Sullivan 1997; Lester 1998).

Growth of nonstandard jobs has leveled off recently. As a share of the labor force, such employment actually declined slightly since 1995. One explanation for this is the recent tightening of labor markets. For those whose nonstandard employment is involuntary — as is the case for many temporary workers — such jobs are viewed as an inferior alternative to regular full-time positions. With the labor market heating up since the mid-1990s, fewer workers are finding themselves having to take these transitional jobs. To put this another way, labor shortages are forcing employers to assume greater risk when filling positions (U.S. Bureau of Labor Statistics 1997; Farber 1997a).

Cyclical Factors

Labor markets are affected not only by structural and secular changes, but also by cyclical factors, such as the unemployment rate. Cyclical and secular components were difficult to disentangle when labor markets were stagnant, as was the case for much of the period since the mid-1970s. However, the recent drop in unemployment has revealed the limits of a purely structural perspective. Unemployment rates are lower now than at any time since 1973, when the monetary authorities first became obsessed with fighting inflation. In the future, we may well look back at the downsizing of the 1980s and 1990s and see more clearly its relationship to cyclical factors.

Low unemployment has two effects. Directly, it fosters the internalization of labor markets, as employers seek to retain scarce labor. Indirectly, as economist Michal Kalecki first observed fifty years ago, low unemployment enhances the bargaining power of employees and their ability to get employers to shoulder risks for them (Kalecki 1971). When labor markets are slack, power is on the employer's side; when unemployment rates are low, the tables are turned and employers are more inclined to accommodate worker demands. Indeed, it is revealing that Kalecki published his essay during World War II, a time when labor was scarce and unions strong. During the hundred-year span from 1870 to 1970, career employment practices did not grow steadily. Rather, they widened and deepened most rapidly in periods when unemployment was relatively low, such as the late 1880s, early 1900s, and the four major wars of this century. Conversely, there were reversions to more market-oriented employment relationships during slack periods like the 1890s and 1930s. What happened from the late 1970s through the early 1990s, then, was the confluence of relatively slow growth, a loose labor market, and structural shocks arising from deregulation, globalization, and sectoral shifts. Historical evidence suggests that any tightening of U.S. labor markets will — both directly (to retain scarce labor) and indirectly (via bargaining power) — shift employment practices back in the direction of insulation from market forces. We can call this the Kalecki effect (Keyssar 1986).[7]

Presently, we again are witnessing the Kalecki effect, as unemployment plummets. Tight labor markets force employers to shed labor more carefully and make it easier for workers to find new jobs. That is one reason why there has been so little outcry over recent layoffs. Over two-thirds of workers permanently displaced from full-time jobs between 1995 and 1997 have found reemployment in full-time jobs. An additional 15 percent are working part time or at home, and 15 percent left the labor market. The total reemployment rate has risen since the mid-1990s, while wage prospects have improved. Workers who were laid off in the last two years are much less likely to be suffering earnings declines than workers laid off in the early 1990s: 38 percent experienced earnings declines in the past two years, versus 55 percent five years ago. However, for some workers — especially the less educated — job loss was and still is the source of large and persistent earnings losses.[8]

Managers and skilled workers are experiencing especially high reemployment rates. One headhunting agency recently reported that managers at companies announcing layoff plans often find themselves with several job offers in hand before the layoffs occur. Hence while organizations today are somewhat flatter than before, they still have an enormous appetite for managers and management remains a growth occupation. The proportion of managers in the workforce actually increased over the course of the 1990s, as new employment growth exceeded the volume lost to downsizing (Gordon 1996).

As companies scramble for help, they are luring new recruits with offers of traditional career opportunities. As a recent article put it, "employers are going to great lengths to persuade employees that they want them to stay for years" (*Business Week* 1998). Employers are dusting off and reintroducing old-style employee development and training programs intended to reassure managers and professionals of their prospects. Citibank, for example, despite recent layoffs, expects its workforce to grow in coming years. So it recently established a formal career development program for 10,000 managers. The company's vice president for human resources said, "We want to make people feel that they have a long-term career with us" (*Daily Labor Report* 1998: C17).

The response to tighter labor markets suggests a swinging pendulum. Employers today want careers to be less "boundaryless" and more organization-centered. The problem, of course, is that this runs directly counter to what today's educated young workers think is the route to career success: regular changing of employers to gain experience and to signal ambition. Recently, I spoke to the vice president for human resources of a *Fortune 500* company, who was lamenting the difficulty of attracting and retaining young managers and professionals. I reminded him that people in their 20s and early 30s were simply responding to the mantra they have heard employers chanting for the last ten years: that everyone should expect to regularly change jobs, and perhaps even careers, throughout their working lives. "Yes, we've been our own worst enemy," he said to me. "And now we've got to put a new message out."

Benefits and Wages

What about fringe benefits, a tangible sign of an employer's commitment to employees? In health insurance, there has been almost no change since 1979 in the proportion of private-sector employers offering health benefits. What has changed are the eligibility rules, which have become more stringent for short-term and part-time workers, and the take-up rate, which has declined for full-time "core" employees due to spousal coverage. Thus the evidence suggests that "employers are continuing to make health insurance available to their core long-term full-time employees but are restricting access . . . by their peripheral employees" (Farber and Levy 1998).[9]

Pension coverage is a different story. In the 1980s, pension coverage fell sharply for younger, less educated men — the type of workers who once were employed in unionized manufacturing jobs. For mature workers and for college graduates, however, the coverage decline was modest; for women there was a slight increase in coverage. The situation stabilized in the 1990s. Between 1991 and 1997, the proportion of workers in mid- to large size establishments who were covered by a retirement plan rose slightly.[10] The big change, however, has been the shift from defined benefit to defined contribution plans, which is discussed below.

Again, it is important to recall the distinction between stocks and flows. Despite modest shifts in coverage, employers remain key elements in our health and pension systems. Two-thirds of all private-sector workers receive employer-provided health insurance, rising to 76 percent for those employed in medium to large establishments (Farber and Levy 1998; U.S. Bureau of Labor Statistics various years). As for pensions, 63 percent of full-time workers and 21 percent of regular part-time workers are covered by employer-provided retirement plans, with coverage rising to 79 percent in mid- to large-size establishments. Even as some employers are discontinuing particular programs, others are adopting new ones such as preventive medical care, day care, and other benefits targeted at employees with dependents. Recently, a group of twenty major corporations pledged to invest millions of dollars to make child and elder care more available. The companies included such paragons of modern welfare capitalism as Hewlett-Packard, IBM, Mobil, and Texas Instruments (Kalleberg et al. 1997; *Daily Labor Report* 1995).

Another way of assessing where an employer sits on the continuum between market- and organization-oriented policies is to examine the extent to which actual pay rates diverge from market rates. Companies that insulate employment relationships from market forces will be more likely to engage in wage-smoothing over the course of a long-term employment relationship; at any point in time, wages will be less sensitive to market conditions than in spot markets. Such companies also are more likely to pay a wage premium that deviates from market averages. There could be any number of reasons for this policy, such as turnover minimization (workers are less likely to quit high-pay employers) or productivity enhancement (workers are more diligent when the cost of termination — here, a fall back to market rates — is high). There is one recent study that finds that wages have become more sensitive to unemployment rates, although the study uses industry data and is limited to manufacturing industries adversely affected by foreign competition in the 1980s. On the other hand, another recent study uses a unique data set covering white- and blue-collar occupations in two hundred large firms over the last forty years. It finds no evidence of a decline in the magnitude or persistence of employer wage premia for individual occupations and groups of occupations. This suggests a high degree of stability in the way employers base their long-term wage strategies on organizational rather than market considerations (Bertrand 1999; Groshen and Levine 1998).

Explaining the Paradox

To summarize, a variety of sources have been examined to assess the degree of change in career-type employment practices. Blue-collar workers in the early 1980s and white-collar workers in the early 1990s experienced higher levels of permanent job loss. As a result, aggregate job tenure rates have declined modestly since the late 1970s. On the other hand, the majority of workers continue to hold career-type jobs that offer fringe benefits, training, and prospects of continuity. For women and for those in service occupations and industries, long-tenure employment has become more prevalent over the last twenty years. Also, the economy is creating new jobs that are predominantly neither low-wage nor part-time. Hence the majority of displaced workers are finding reemployment in career-type positions. The recent decline in unemployment rates has boosted prospects for displaced workers and strengthened employer reliance on career-type practices.

Taken as a whole, the evidence does not show a radical slide to the market pole of the organizational-market continuum. Organizational considerations still trump market logic for the bulk of the economy's jobs, and the majority of employers continue to shoulder income and employment risks for employees. How, then, does one explain the disparity between the perception of "no long term" and the fact that stability remains widespread in the labor market? There is no simple answer to this question, but explanatory elements can be found in cognitive psychology and the politics of punditry.

Perceptual Biases

A stream of research in cognitive psychology documents the pervasiveness of loss aversion: People weigh losses — like layoffs — more heavily than gains (Kunreuther 1976; Kahneman and Tversky 1979). The job losses of the past ten years have weighed heavily on the nation's middle-classes because they involve educated professionals and managers — people like us, people with whom we can identify. The downsizings and plant closures of the early 1980s did not generate nearly the same amount of angst or media coverage even though the displacement rate then was higher than in the 1990s.

Recent job cuts also rankled the middle-class because they were widely perceived as unfair: the violation of an implicit contract to provide security until senior management's own jobs were in peril, that is, until the company was close to closure. One former IBM employee said, "In January I was told my job was the safest in the nation. In February we were told half the jobs would be gone" (Sampson 1995: 225). Fueling the sense of unfairness was the belief that layoffs resulted not from a search for efficiency but from a greed-driven change in corporate governance that favored owners over employees. Repeatedly in the late 1980s and early 1990s, there were reports of profitable companies laying workers off and then enjoying stock-price increases that benefited senior management and other major shareholders, as at General Dynamics or in the more egregious case of Al Dunlap, former CEO of Sunbeam (Jacoby 1998).[11]

Fallacy of Discontinuity

Another reason for the discrepancy between the rhetoric and reality of change in employment relations is what might be called, following historian David Hackett Fischer, the fallacy of discontinuity — an erroneous belief that the present is fundamentally different from the periods that preceded it. Not only fashion designers but journalists, management consultants, and academics build their careers around this conceit. Consultants are particularly prone to a faddish way of thinking, since it helps to generate sales of new systems premised on the assumption that the world has changed so drastically as to render worthless existing ways of doing business. Academics have similar proclivities. Enthusiasts for change dramatically pronounce "the demise of organizational careers" and their replacement by something radically different: the "boundaryless career" (Fisher 1970; Hilmer and Donaldson 1996; Arthur and Rousseau 1996).

The media, in particular, seized upon the layoffs of the early 1990s as evidence that the American workplace had become, as the *New York Times* put it, "new and unnerving." The *Times* 1996 multipart series and subsequent book on the "Downsizing of America" took two dozen people more than seven months to produce. It was the longest piece of journalism published by the *Times* since the Pentagon Papers in 1971 (Cassidy 1996). Yet while the series was chock full of painful personal stories, it was virtually devoid of economic statistics for gauging the severity, extent, and consequences of layoff.

Then there is the Challenger, Gray data series, compiled by a Chicago-based company that specializes in outplacement services. They tabulate corporate announcements of intended, not actual, layoffs. Since the series began in the early 1990s, the media has regularly reported Challenger's monthly figures. But the number of workers actually laid off is often much lower than the job-elimination plans reported in the news releases. Companies announce the highest cutback totals they can justify to impress investors that they are getting lean and mean, and then pursue cuts through mechanisms other than layoff. Sudden mass departures do occur, but reductions also are handled through normal turnover, through transfers, through early retirements, or simply by leaving vacancies unfilled. That is, because the layoffs take place by mechanisms other than layoff and the process' occurs over a lengthy period, a portion of the announced layoff never actually occurs (Silverstein and Maharaj 1999).

Risk Shifting: Practices and Prospects

None of this is intended to deny the fact that there has been a rise in job loss, especially for those employees thought to be most immune to it. While the direct effect has been overstated, the indirect effect surely has been to expose incumbent employees to a greater risk of job loss. Employers have in other respects been shifting more of the risk burden onto employees. That is the logic of managed care and of larger deductibles for health insurance, both of which have grown steadily since 1991 (U.S. BLS various years). It is also the rationale behind the change from defined benefit pension plans to defined contribution plans. Employers also are incorporating more variability into employee pay packages via discretionary bonuses, group incentives, profit sharing, and stock options. In economists' parlance, more pay is "at risk."[12]

The reallocation of risk — not the decline of career-type jobs — is the central dynamic driving today's internal labor markets. Employers are still protecting employees from the hazards of unemployment, sickness, and old-age. However, companies today operate in a turbulent environment of heightened competition, mergers, and rapid technological change. It is a riskier world, and employers are less willing to shoulder as much risk for employees as they did in the past.[13]

Some employees are adapting to this risk — especially younger, more educated workers with "hot" skills — while others are having a tough time of it. These workers still look to their employers as the first line of defense. As that line is pushed back, they question the fairness of today's risk-sharing arrangements. While most of these workers are not about to lose their jobs, they are left feeling more insecure. Forty-five percent of employees in 1977 thought it was not at all likely they would lose their jobs, but the figure has fallen to 30 percent today. Every layoff announcement affects the perceived probability of job loss and causes survivors to work harder and worry more. Thus layoffs can have ripple effects far beyond their direct labor cost saving.[14]

Does this mean, then, that eventually we can expect to see the risk burden completely shifted to employees, such that employers no longer will offer fringe benefits, career jobs, fixed salaries, and so on? The short answer is no. Assuming that current trends will continue without limit is a reductio ad absurdum, just as it would have been equally absurd to predict in the 1880s that all jobs would become career positions carrying generous fringe benefits. There are economic, demographic, and political limits to the risk reallocation process. These limits ensure that the corporation likely will remain a central risk-bearing institution in American society.

One such limit has to do with the organizational realities of managing a workforce. For most employers, the net economic benefits of welfare capitalism remain positive. Employee loyalty and commitment still matter, especially in the burgeoning service sector where it is often difficult to directly supervise employees (Herzenberg et al. 1998). New workers have to be trained, which makes employee turnover costly. Employee skills are, if anything, more important today than in the past, especially in fast-changing situations where little is codified and knowledge is tacit. New systems of work organization — such as self-managed teams — are less prevalent than is commonly supposed but nevertheless have grown markedly in recent years. These systems are accompanied by higher levels of training and tend to be associated with career-type jobs, since job stability preserves the interpersonal relationships that make teams effective. Hence, to the extent these systems continue to proliferate, they create employer incentives to stabilize employment.[15]

For these reasons, companies like 3M, Intel, and Motorola have — despite layoffs — preserved career-type jobs, albeit lacking guarantees of permanence. There is plenty of evidence that the practices associated with career-job policies — such as training, profit sharing, and participatory work systems — are positively related to corporate performance. Other companies that have downsized in recent years are discovering that outsourcing and temporary employees — while cheaper in the short run — do not provide the levels of service and quality that are necessary for customer satisfaction (Levine 1995; U.S. DOL 1993; Rebitzer 1995; Pfeffer 1998).[16] A recent study of companies that have implemented "employability" contracts — offering learning experiences in return for heightened employee responsibilities — concludes that the most successful employers are those who retain "a sense of responsibility to protect the jobs of their people" (Bartlett and Ghoshal 1997).

Some argue that companies in dynamic sectors like Silicon Valley, Hollywood, and Wall Street operate according to a different, more market-oriented, logic. Here, workers tend to be relatively young and educated, and they can move easily from job to job. Employers do not penalize such mobility because it helps them to keep abreast of competitors and stay on the cutting edge. In Silicon Valley, for example, there is pervasive interfirm mobility. Workers are well paid and can afford their own health benefits and 401(k) plans. However, these workers are an atypical elite, just as footloose craft workers were an atypical but essential elite in American industry ninety years ago. Most workers do not have skills that are either as scarce or as critical to business performance as the technologists in the Valley (Jones 1996).

Also, the employers of this elite are dissimilar in important respects from the bulk of the companies that constitute our economy. Today, most U.S. companies are service providers whose success depends less on technological breakthroughs than on customer attraction and retention. One key to customer loyalty is employee loyalty: experienced and satisfied employees are much better at finding and keeping customers than fresh recruits. In industries such as financial services, the fastest-growing occupations are those that require interpersonal skills, which, unlike accounting positions, are difficult to replace with computerized information systems. These interpersonal skills are relatively less important in high-technology industries that are mistakenly touted as exemplars of the future (Frei et al. 1995).[17]

Even high-technology companies are beginning to recognize that rapid turnover and short employment stints can be detrimental. Take, for example, SAS, a software company based in North Carolina. The company sounds like a throwback to the heyday of welfare capitalism. It offers a thirty-five-hour work week, on-site child care, a lavish exercise facility, and subsidized cafes with live piano music. To make sure employees are healthy, the company maintains its own medical facility with five nurse practitioners, two family practice doctors, a massage therapist, and a mental health nurse. To retain potentially mobile knowledge workers, it tries to accommodate people's changing careers within the company, not by losing them to competitors. (Turnover at SAS is only one-tenth the Silicon Valley norm.) The company's HR manager said, "At 5 P.M., 95 percent of our assets walk out the door. We have to have an environment that makes them want to walk back in the door the next morning." Past history suggests that as some companies accelerate the internalization process, others will follow suit as a defensive necessity (Groves 1999: 55–56).

Second, there are demographic limits to restructuring. Many workers laid off during the past decade came from the relatively small pre-1945 generation that preceded the baby boomers. At one bank, for example, the director said "the machine guns started firing on day one [after a recent merger], with anyone over 50 in the front rank." Because older workers are paid more, they are targeted for layoff and are likely to experience subsequent earnings declines; younger displaced workers recently have been experiencing gains in their median weekly earnings (*Economist* 1998; U.S.

BLS 1998a). Employer animus toward older workers reveals an important fact: despite all the talk about delayering, corporations remain pyramidal organizations in which seniority and pay are positively related; hence you can cut labor costs by targeting senior workers for layoff.[18] It was feasible to conduct layoffs in the late 1980s and early 1990s because replacement workers from the baby boom generation were plentiful. However, the cohort behind the boomers — generation X — is relatively small. Current estimates are that the number of 35- to 44-year-olds will decline by 15 percent between 2000 and 2015 (Chambers et al. 1998). There is little in sight to relieve the demographic pressure on employers. The long-term rise in female labor force participation is leveling off, while white-collar productivity gains are flat. In short, current employer concerns with labor scarcity and retention are likely to persist into the next century, putting a brake on future risk shifting.

Finally, there are political limits to the amount of risk shifting that American employers can or would want to pursue. Currently, the United States has lower unionization rates than any other advanced industrial country. Our government spends less on social insurance per worker than other advanced industrial countries. Corporate managers know — or may discover — that if they let welfare capitalism wither, there will be popular pressure for government and perhaps even for unions to fill the gap. That is precisely why Buchanan's candidacy caused such a stir in 1996.

The only aspect of risk shifting that knows no limits is a belief in its inevitability, a habit of mind that Albert O. Hirschman (1991) associates with the "rhetoric of futility." The futility argument proceeds by identifying deep forces — economic logic or human nature — that cannot be altered. Attempts to change them are hopeless and will perversely result in the reassertion of those forces. In economics, the doctrine of rational expectations — that activist fiscal policy is useless in permanently lowering the unemployment rate — is one such example. A similar rhetoric infuses assertions that market individualism has triumphed in the economy. Even when shown to be empirically implausible, those claims nevertheless have real consequences. They encourage the belief that alternative institutions are destined for extinction. Hence to retain those institutions — whether welfare capitalism or the welfare state — is an exercise in futility. Better to hasten the future by dismantling bureaucracies, dissociating from organizations, and taking care of "numero uno" — after all, no one else can or will.

However, as Hirschman goes on to point out, the rhetoric of futility is often proclaimed prematurely; it is a form of wishful thinking. Similarly, it is wishful thinking to believe that market individualism is rampant and that we are living in a world of tenuous associations and arm's-length relationships, the system idealized by nineteenth-century contract law (Horowitz 1979). In fact, we still inhabit a society where markets — including labor markets — coexist and coevolve with regulations, social norms, and other institutions. Economic historian Karl Polanyi was the first to identify this "double movement" of two great organizing principles: the expansion of the market and the simultaneous expansion of market regulation. If one studies closely the economic deregulation that has occurred in various sectors over the last twenty years, what one finds is not a move to pure laissez-faire but instead a redefinition of government responsibilities, a process that one political scientist calls "reregulation." As for social regulation, keep in mind that the Reagan administration had little luck in rolling back either Social Security or environmental and consumer protection. Meanwhile, the volume of such regulation has steadily grown in the 1990s, in the labor market and elsewhere (Vogel 1996). This suggests a simple conclusion: while we cannot change the level of risk in today's economy, we can change the rules that govern how risk is shared among the participants to the economic game.

For example, the SEC could require companies to include statements on their balance sheets of how much they have invested in their employees. That would be a first step to getting managers and investors to accurately recognize the value of a firm's human capital. Second, we can reform our labor laws. Employer unfair labor practices have skyrocketed in recent years, and the law is failing to protect legitimate union organizing attempts. Third, we can change the incentives faced by investors. Today, institutional investors own two-thirds of the total equity in the stock market. Institutional investors are fickle creatures who move their capital with breath-taking rapidity. Pension funds should pay capital gains taxes on the stock they churn around. Also, mutual funds could do more to penalize short-term traders for the costs that they incur, such as raising transactions fees and contributing them to the purchased company or mutual fund to benefit long-term returns (Weiler 1990).

Conclusions

The labor market is in flux, but it would be a mistake to project the future out of recent trends. Career jobs are less expansive, but they have not melted into air. While people are unhappy with the risk they are being asked to shoulder, they still look to employers to share much of the burden. According to pollsters, today's middle-class Americans think that corporations "should balance their self-interest with the need to consider what benefits the larger society" (Wolfe 1998). Those who ask that corporations be responsible are not asking for anything outside the welfare capitalist framework established by corporations themselves. There remains widespread support for the notion that corporations are — or should be — the keystone of economic security in American society. That is the path we have been on for the last one hundred years, and we remain on that trajectory. The risk shifting experienced by workers in the economy's core is a serious problem. However, we must not let it overshadow the more critical situation facing less-educated and less-skilled workers. Those workers are steadily falling behind as a result of technological change and globalization as well as factors specific to the United States such as high immigration, weak minimum wage laws, and the decline of unionism. Since 1980, earnings inequality has grown more rapidly in the United States than other advanced countries. Low-wage U.S. workers are both relatively and absolutely poorer than their European or Japanese counterparts (Mishel et al. 1999).

The problem of inequality should not be confused with the rising risk of job loss. True, when less-educated workers lose their jobs, they are more likely than educated workers to experience a permanent reduction in earnings. However, a similar earnings disparity also exists for those who never lose their jobs. When we examine the stock of continuing jobs, we find that long-term employment relationships (over twenty years) currently are as prevalent for those with twelve or fewer years of education as they are for those with baccalaureate and advanced degrees (Fallick 1996; Howell 1997).[19] In short, the primary cause of inequality is not downsizing but rising returns to education accompanied by the waning of wage-setting institutions in the low-wage labor market (e.g., the shrinkage of unions and of real minimum wages). Middle-class workers are entitled to a better deal, but their predicament — and our own anxieties — should not overshadow the plight of low-wage workers.

Notes

An earlier version of this chapter appeared in *California Management Review* 42, 1 (Fall 1999), copyright © 1999 Regents of the University of California. Reprinted by permission.

1. In manufacturing, job-loss rates in the mid-1990s were half the level observed in the early 1980s (Farber 1997; C. Kletzer 1998: 119).

2. U.S. Bureau of Labor Statistics (1998b). If the analysis is limited to large firms, the evidence of job stability is even more striking. For 51 large companies that were clients of Watson Wyatt, a consulting firm, average tenure increased in the 1990s, as did the percentage of employees with ten years (and twenty years) of service or more. Even in firms with shrinking employment, the odds that a worker would be with the employer five years later were higher than the same odds for the labor market as a whole. (Allen, Clark, and Schieber 1999).

3. Bansak and Raphael (1998). Note, however, that when one focuses on tenure rather than separations, older workers do not show larger tenure declines than younger workers. One explanation could be that older workers who have suffered permanent layoff are more inclined to leave the labor market. See Neumark, Polsky, and Hansen (1998).

4. U.S. Bureau of the Census (1998) <www.census.gov/population/socdemo/migration>.

5. These data are drawn from Compustat listings for U.S.-based companies for the period 1990–97. Companies whose employment was affected by merger or liquidation were not included in the sample. MCI and Worldcom merged late in 1998.

6. Johnson (1998); Vance and Roy Scott (1997); Roush (1999). One reason companies no longer tout explicit no-layoff policies is the spate of dismissal suits in recent years. Plaintiffs sometimes won by claiming breach of an implied promise to provide continuous employment, such as were found in employee handbooks and other personnel policies. (Perritt 1998).

7. The idea of a market-organization continuum is nicely developed in Dore (1989).

8. U.S. Bureau of Labor Statistics (1998a); Koretz (1998); Fallick (1996); Jacobson et al. (1993). Over the past two years, the share of workers worried about losing their jobs fell from 44 percent to 37 percent (Manski and Straub 1999).

9. Another reason for the decline in the take-up rate (the rate at which employees take benefits offered to them) is the recent rapid growth in tailored benefit plans permitting employees to pick and choose benefits. In 1988, 13 percent of big companies gave employees this option; now over half do (*Economist* 1996: 91–92).

10. Bloom and Freeman (1992); Woods (1994); Even and Macpherson (1994); *Employee Benefit Plan Review* (1994); U.S. Bureau of Labor Statistics (1999). If employers, in fact, move radically away from provision of retirement benefits, employees would likely respond by saving at higher rates. But despite the recrudescene of market individualism, the U.S. private savings rate has steadily trended down since the early 1980s.

11. Note, however, that the evidence does not support the popular belief that downsizing boosts stock prices and CEO pay. After controlling for factors like firm size, the effect of layoffs on CEO pay is nil and there is a small negative share price reaction to layoff announcements (Hallock 1998).

12. In medium to large establishments, the proportion of employees with defined benefit plans fell from 59 to 50 percent between 1991 and 1997; the proportion with defined contribution plans rose from 48 to 57 percent. Note, however, that some employees are covered by both types of plans and that some of the shifting occurred across rather than within firms due to rapid job growth in smaller, nonunion companies that are less likely to offer defined benefit plans (U.S. Bureau of Labor Statistics various years; also see Ippolito 1995; and Benoit 1996).

13. The head of human resources at IBM, Gerald Czarnecki, characterizes his company's new approach as a "readjustment which needs a new balancing act. . . . I never thought it was good for a corporation to take over the role of the family unit, which is more dependable for society. Now the pendulum will swing back, to give a larger role to the family. But there's still a role for all three — family, business, and government" (Sampson 1995: 229).

14. Bond, Galinsky, and Swanberg (1998); Ambrose (1996). Efficiency wage models relate the probability of job loss to employee effort levels. These models are a microeconomic version of the Kalecki effect (Valletta 1997; Aaronson and Sullivan 1998).

15. Finding and training a replacement typically costs about 55 percent of a departing employee's annual salary (*Economist* 1998). For establishments with over fifty employees, 30 percent use self-directed work teams, with a coverage rate (percentage of employees affected) of around 12 percent (Erickson and Jacoby 1998; Gittleman et al. 1998).

16. For some contrary evidence on the probability of a low-road approach, see Bailey and Bernhardt (1997).

17. For a similar argument by the head of Bain & Company, see Reichheld (1996). Although he does not remark on it, Reichheld's case studies come from service industries that are the employment-growth sectors of the U.S. economy: financial services, retail sales, insurance, and eating establishments.

18. A study of managerial downsizing in British companies reaches similar conclusions. It finds "no evidence of the kind of transformational change associated with the introduction of a new model. Instead, we find that the traditional model of managerial employment has been eroded rather than replaced" (McGovern et al. 1998: 457).

19. Cutting the tenure data at over ten, rather than over twenty years, does give college graduates an edge over high-school dropouts in the percentage holding long-term jobs. But this advantage also existed twenty years ago, before wage inequality had grown wide (Farber 1997b; Diebold et al. 1997).

References

Aaronson, Daniel and Daniel G. Sullivan. 1998. "The Decline of Job Security in the 1990s: Displacement, Anxiety, and Their Effect on Wage Growth." *Federal Reserve Bank of Chicago, Economic Perspectives* 22, 1: 17–43.

Allen, Steven G., Robert L. Clark, and Sylvester J. Schieber. 1999. "Has Job Security Vanished in Large Corporations?" NBER Working Paper 6966.

Ambrose, Delores E. 1996. *Healing the Downsized Organization.* New York: Harmony Books.

Arthur, Michael B. and Denise M Rousseau. 1996. "The Boundaryless Career as a New Employment Principle." In *The Boundaryless Career: A New Employment Principle for a New Organizational Era,* ed. Michael B. Arthur and Denise M. Rousseau. New York: Oxford University Press.

Autor, David. 1999. "Why Do Temporary Help Firms Provide Free General Skills Training?" Working Paper, Kennedy School of Government, Harvard University. January.

Bailey, Thomas and Annette D. Bernhardt. 1997. "In Search of the High Road in a Low-Wage Industry," *Politics and Society* 25 (June): 179–201.

Bansak, Cynthia and Steven Raphael. 1998. "Have Employment Relationships in the U.S. Become Less Stable?" Working Paper, Department of Economics, University of California at San Diego. August.

Bartlett, Christopher A. and Sumantra Ghoshal. 1997. *The Individualized Corporation: A Fundamentally New Approach to Management.* New York: Harper Business.

Benoit, Ellen. 1996. "Penny Wise, Pound Foolish." *Treasury and Risk Management* 6 (July–August): 18–27.

Bernstein, Michael. 1987. *The Great Depression: Delayed Recovery and Economic Change in America, 1929-39.* Cambridge: Cambridge University Press.

Bertrand, Marianne. 1999. "From the Invisible Handshake to the Invisible Hand? How Import Competition Changes the Employment Relationship." NBER Working Paper 6900.

Bloom, David E. and Richard B. Freeman. 1992. "The Fall in Private Pension Coverage in the U.S." *American Economic Review* 82 (May): 539–45.

Bond, James T., Ellen Galinsky, and Jennifer E. Swanberg. 1998. *The 1997 National Study of the Changing Workforce.* New York: Families and Work Institute.

Business Week. 1998. "We Want You to Stay. Really." June 22, 67.

Cappelli, Peter. 1999. *The New Deal at Work.* Boston: Harvard Business School Press.

Cassidy, John. 1996. "All Worked Up: Is Downsizing Really News or Is It Business as Usual?" *New Yorker,* April 22, 51–56.

Chambers, Elizabeth, Mark Foulon, Helen Handfield-Jones, Steven Hankin, and Edwin Michaels. 1998. "The War for Talent." *McKinsey Quarterly* 3: 44–57.

Conference Board. 1998. "Organizing the Corporate HQ: An HR Perspective," *HR Executive Review* 6.

Daily Labor Report. 1995. "Companies Pledge to Invest $100 Million for Dependent Care." October 4, A5.

———. 1998. "Employers Find That Tight Economy Requires Use of Creative Recruiting." 237, December 10, C1–C7.

———. 1999. "Greenspan Says Job Insecurity Still High." 31, February 17, AA1.

Davis, Steven J. and John Haltiwanger. 1992. "Gross Job Creation, Gross Job Destruction, and Employment Reallocation," *Quarterly Journal of Economics* 107 (August): 819–63.

Diebold, Francis X., David Neumark, and Daniel Polsky. 1997. "Job Stability in the United States." *Journal of Labor Economics* 15: 206–33.

Dore, Ronald. 1989. "Where Are We Now? Musings of an Evolutionist." *Work, Employment, & Society* 3: 425–46.

Downs, Alan. 1995. *Corporate Executions: The Ugly Truth About Layoffs — How Corporate Greed Is Shattering Lives, Companies, and Communities.* New York: AMACOM.

Economist. 1996. "Unto Those that Have Shall Be Given." December 21. 91–92.

———. 1998. "Can America's Workforce Grow Old Gracefully?" July 25. 59–60.

———. 1999. "Overworked and Overpaid." January 30. 55–56.

Employee Benefit Plan Review. 1994. "Pension Plan Coverage Now Rising." 48 (April): 41–42.

Erickson, Christopher and Sanford M. Jacoby. 1998. "Training and Work Organization Practices of Private Employers in California." California Policy Seminar Report, Berkeley.

Even, William E. and David A. Macpherson. 1994. "Why Did Male Pension Coverage Decline in the 1980s?" *Industrial & Labor Relations Review* 47 (April): 439–53.

Fallick, Bruce. 1996. "A Review of the Recent Empirical Literature on Displaced Workers." *Industrial & Labor Relations Review* 50: 5–16.

Farber, Henry S. 1997a. "Alternative Employment Arrangements as a Response to Job Loss." Working Paper 391, Industrial Relations Section, Princeton University. October.

———. 1997b. "Job Creation in the United States: Good Jobs or Bad?" Working Paper 385. Industrial Relations Section, Princeton University. July.

———. 1997c. "The Changing Face of Job Loss in the United States, 1981-1995." Working Paper 382. Industrial Relations Section, Princeton University. June.

———. 1997d. "Trends in Long-Term Employment in the United States, 1979-96." Working Paper 384. Industrial Relations Section, Princeton University. July.

Farber, Henry S. and Helen Levy. 1998. "Recent Trends in Employer-Sponsored Health Insurance Coverage: Are Bad Jobs Getting Worse?" NBER Working Paper 6709. August.

Fischer, David Hackett. 1970. *Historians' Fallacies: Toward a Logic of Historical Thought.* New York: Harper and Row.

Freeman, Richard B. 1998. "War of the Models: Which Labour Market Institutions for the 21st Century?" *Labour Economics* 5: 1–24.

Frei, Frances, Patrick Harker, and Larry Hunter. 1995. "Performance in Consumer Financial Services Organizations." Working Paper 95–03. Wharton Financial Institutions Center, University of Pennsylvania.

Friedman, David. 1999. "The Dark Side of the High-Tech Religion." *Los Angeles Times,* January 31, M1.

Gittleman, Maury, Michael Horrigan, and Mary Joyce. 1998. "Flexible Workplace Practices: Evidence from a Nationally Representative Survey." *Industrial & Labor Relations Review* 52 (October): 99–115.

Gordon, David M. 1996. *Fat and Mean: The Corporate Squeeze of Working Americans and the Myth of Managerial Downsizing.* New York: Martin Kessler Books. 54–55.

Groshen, Erica L. and David I. Levine. 1998. "The Rise and Decline (?) of U.S. Internal Labor Markets." Research Paper 9819. Federal Reserve Bank of New York, New York.

Groves, Martha. 1998. "In Tight Job Market, Software Firm Develops Programs to Keep Employees." *Los Angeles Times,* June 14. D5.

———.1999. "Overworked and Overpaid." *Economist,* January 30, 55–56.

Hallock, Kevin. 1998. "Layoffs, Top Executive Pay, and Firm Performance." *American Economic Review* 88 (September): 711–23.

Herriot, Peter and Carole Pemberton. 1995. *New Deals: The Revolution in Managerial Careers.* New York: John Wiley.

Herzenberg, Stephen, John A. Alic, and Howard Wial. 1998. *New Rules for a New Economy: Employment and Opportunity in Postindustrial America.* Ithaca, N.Y.: ILR Press.

Hilmer, Frederick and Lex Donaldson. 1996. *Management Redeemed: Debunking the Fads that Undermine Our Corporations.* New York: Free Press.

Hirschman, Albert O. 1991. *The Rhetoric of Reaction.* Cambridge, Mass.: Belknap Press of Harvard University Press.

Horwitz, Morton. 1979. *The Transformation of American Law, 1780–1860.* Cambridge, Mass.: Harvard University Press.

Howell, David R. 1997. "Institutional Failure and the American Worker: The Collapse of Low-Skill Wages." Public Policy Brief 29. Jerome Levy Economics Institute, Bard College.

Ippolito, Richard A. 1995. "Toward Explaining the Growth of Defined Contribution Plans." *Industrial Relations* 34: 1–20.

Jacobson, Louis, Robert LaLonde, and Daniel G. Sullivan. 1993. *The Costs of Worker Dislocation.* Kalamazoo, Mich.: W.E. Upjohn Institute of Employment Research.

Jacoby, Sanford M. 1985. *Employing Bureaucracy: Managers, Unions, and the Transformation of Work in American Industry, 1900–1945.* New York: Columbia University Press: 167–170.

———. 1997. *Modern Manors: Welfare Capitalism Since the New Deal.* Princeton, N.J.: Princeton University Press.

———. 1998."'Chainsaw Al' Gets His Due." *Los Angeles Times,* June 18. B5.

Jacoby, Sanford M. and Peter Goldschmidt. 1998. "Education, Skill, and Wage Inequality: The Situation in California." *Challenge* 41 (November–December): 88–120.

Johnson, R. S. 1998. "Lowe's Borrows the Blueprint." *Fortune,* November 23, 212ff.

Jones, Candace. 1996. "Careers in Project Networks: The Case of the Film Industry." In *The Boundaryless Career: A New Employment Principle for a New Organizational Era,* ed. Michael B. Arthur and Denise M. Rousseau. New York: Oxford University Press. 58–78.

Kahneman, Daniel and Amos Tversky. 1979. "Prospect Theory: An Analysis of Decision Under Risk." *Econometrica* 47: 263–91.

Kalecki, Michal. 1971. "Political Aspects of Full Employment." In *Selected Essays on the Dynamics of the Capitalist Economy, 1933–1970.* Cambridge: Cambridge University Press. 138–45.

Kalleberg, Arne L., Edith Rasell, Naomi Cassirer, Barbara Reskin, Ken Hudson, David Webster, Eileen Applebaum, and Roberta Spalter-Roth. 1997. *Nonstandard Work, Substandard Jobs: Flexible Work Arrangements in the U.S.* Washington, D.C.: Economic Policy Institute.

Keyssar, Alexander. 1986. *Out of Work: The First Century of Unemployment in Massachusetts.* Cambridge: Cambridge University Press.

Kletzer, Lori. 1998. "Job Displacement." *Journal of Economic Perspectives* 12 (Winter): 115–36.

Koretz, Gene. 1998. "Downsizing's Impact on Job Losers." *Business Week*, December 28, 30.

Kunreuther, Howard C. 1976. "Limited Knowledge and Insurance Protection." *Public Policy* 24: 227–61.

Kurtzman, Joel. 1998. "An Interview with Paul Krugman." *Strategy & Business* 13, 4: 87–96.

Lester, Gillian. 1998. "Careers and Contingency." *Stanford Law Review* 51 (November): 73–145.

Levine, David I. 1995. *Reinventing the Workplace: How Employees and Business Can Both Win.* Washington, D.C.: Brookings Institution Press.

Mandel, Michael J. 1996. "Economic Anxiety." *Business Week*, March 11, 50–56.

Manski, Charles and John Straub. 1999. "Workers' Perceptions of Job Insecurity in the Mid-1990s." NBER Working Paper 6908.

McGovern, Patrick, Veronica Hope-Hailey, and Philip Stiles. 1998. "The Managerial Career After Downsizing: Case Studies from the 'Leading Edge.'" *Work, Employment, & Society* 13 (September): 457.

Mishel, Lawrence M., Jared Bernstein, and John Schmitt. 1999. *The State of Working America, 1998–99.* Ithaca, N.Y.: ILR Press. 367–73.

Mitchell, Alison. 1996. "Clinton Prods Executives to Do the Right Thing." *New York Times*, May 17, C2.

Neumark, David, Daniel Polsky, and David Hansen. 1998. "Has Job Stability Declined Yet? New Evidence for the 1990s." Paper presented at the Russell Sage Foundation Conference on Changes in Job Stability and Job Security. February.

Perritt, Henry. 1998. *Employee Dismissal: Law and Practice.* New York: Wiley Law Publications.

Pfeffer, Jeffrey. 1998. *The Human Equation: Building Profits by Putting People First.* Boston: Harvard Business School Press.

Rebitzer, James. 1995. "Job Safety and Contract Workers in the U.S. Petrochemical Industry." *Industrial Relations* 34 (January): 40–57.

Reichheld, Frederick F. 1996. *The Loyalty Effect: The Hidden Force Behind Growth, Profits, and Lasting Value.* Boston: Harvard Business School Press.

Roush, Chris. 1999. *Inside Home Depot.* New York: McGraw-Hill.

Sampson, Anthony. 1995. *Company Man: The Rise and Fall of Corporate Life.* New York: Times Business, Random House.

Saxenian, Annalee. 1996. *Regional Advantage: Culture and Competition in Silicon Valley and Route 128.* Cambridge, Mass.: Harvard University Press.

Segal, Lewis M. and Daniel G. Sullivan. 1997. "The Growth of Temporary Services Work." *Journal of Economic Perspectives* 11 (Spring): 117–36.

Sennett, Richard. 1998. *The Corrosion of Character: The Personal Consequences of Work in the New Capitalism.* New York: Norton.

Silverstein, Stuart and Davan Maharaj. 1999. "Company Layoff Projections Often Don't Add Up." *Los Angeles Times*, January 17, D1.

U.S. Bureau of the Census. 1998. "Annual Geographic Mobility Rates." July. <www.census.gov/population/socdemo/migration>.

U.S. Department of Labor. 1993. "Report on High Performance Work Practices and Firm Performance." July 26, reprinted in *Daily Labor Report* 143 (July 28): F1–F12.

U.S. Department of Labor, Bureau of Labor Statistics. 1997. "Contingent and Alternative Employment Arrangements, February 1997." Bulletin 97-422. Washington, D.C.

———. 1998a. "Worker Displacement, 1995–1997." Report 98-347. Washington, D.C. August.

———. 1998b. "Employee Tenure in 1998." Report 98-387. Washington D.C.

————. 1999. "Employee Benefits in Medium and Large Private Establishments." Report 99-02. Washington, D.C.

Valletta, Robert G. 1997. "Declining Job Security." Working Paper. Federal Reserve Bank of San Francisco. November.

Vance, Sandra and Roy Scott. 1997. *Wal-Mart: A History of Sam Walton's Retail Phenomenon.* New York: Twayne Publishers.

Vogel, Steven K. 1996. *Freer Markets, More Rules: Regulatory Reform in Advanced Industrial Countries.* Ithaca, N.Y.: Cornell University Press.

Weiler, Paul C. 1990. *Governing the Workplace: The Future of Labor and Employment Law.* Cambridge, Mass.: Harvard University Press.

Wolfe, Alan. 1998. *One Nation, After All.* New York: Viking: 237.

Woods, John R. 1994. "Pension Coverage Among Baby Boomers." *Social Security Bulletin* 57 (Fall): 12–25.

Chapter 9
Career Jobs Are Dead

Peter Cappelli

Most observers have a strong sense that jobs and especially careers are different now as compared to previous decades, but it is often hard to put that difference into words. The traditional categories that we use to describe jobs — long term versus short term, high wages and benefits versus low benefits, managerial versus production work — come from an earlier era and reflect the long-standing concern about whether jobs, blue-collar jobs in particular, provide the means to prevent hardship for employees and their families. Sanford Jacoby's article, "Are Career Jobs Headed for Extinction?" (this volume) examines how employment has changed based largely on the traditional criteria noted above. "Career jobs" are implicitly defined in his chapter as full-time jobs that last reasonably long, pay reasonably well, and offer benefits, reflecting the public policy concern about whether jobs provide the means to prevent economic hardship. (I find it more accurate to refer to such jobs as "good jobs" and do so below.) He finds change in some dimensions but evidence of stability in most others. He will get little argument that inequality in outcomes has increased sharply.[1] The fact that the working poor have not participated to the same extent as other segments of the workforce in the economic expansion is perhaps the most important point about rising inequality. His overall conclusion that while all is not well in the labor market, there are still lots of these good jobs (that provide good wages and benefits and that last a reasonable period of time) seems like a fair one.[2] However, the fact that there could be a serious debate as to whether jobs have gotten *worse* during one of the greatest periods of economic expansion in the history of the United States is itself interesting evidence of a change in the economy.

These traditional criteria are not the only aspects of employment, of course, and perhaps not what most readers would think of as central to the issue of careers. Particularly those who are interested in managerial work think of career jobs as ones where employees can expect a career, that is, a succession of advancing jobs within the same organization and employment practices that are under the employer's control.

Something is fundamentally different about contemporary employment as compared to earlier periods, but it is not necessarily a story about worsening terms and conditions of employment. Instead, it is a story about the rising importance of labor markets in shaping jobs and careers and the associated decline in the ability of employers to manage employment and careers inside their organizations. An important cause of the change has been the fact that firms have brought markets inside their own walls through outsourcing, bench-marking, and decentralized responsibility for performance. Once these market forces came inside firms, they began to influence employment as well. Other factors include the restructuring both of the external boundaries of the firm and its internal systems in ways that disrupt career prospects and create permanent insecurity about one's job. Still other changes relate to volatility in product markets and the faster adjustments to them that cause systems and skills to become obsolete more quickly and the demand for new skills to rise more quickly than internal development would allow. Outside hiring results, and it may be the most important factor driving the new market-based employment relationships.

In these new relationships, we still have full-time jobs, including a growing number of managerial jobs that pay reasonably well and that offer good benefits. What we do not have is long-term security — if for no other reason than because the employer's current structure is not very secure — or predictable prospects for internal advancement. Also, the management of employees, including practices such as compensation and development, are driven by the outside market rather than by internal administrative principles. These developments raise important challenges for employees, especially those interested in advancing their careers, as they must increasingly look across companies, as opposed to within them, for opportunities. At least from the perspective of management advice, this is relatively old news.[3] The challenges for employers, on the other hand, are less well known and perhaps even more important. They center on the basic challenge of managing employees as a market-based resource, one that can more easily walk away with the employer's investments.

Because I agree with Jacoby's main conclusion about the persistence of good jobs, it might be helpful to highlight the points of apparent difference in our argument:

- The good old days were not so good. Employer interest in protecting employees from insecurity never ran very deep and was probably always motivated by self-interest. The downside of these internal labor markets was often a kind of industrial feudalism, to use Clark Kerr's phrase, where employees were trapped in a company because there was no outside hiring.
- Declining protections for employees may have less to do with any change in values about the responsibility to employees and more to do with the

fact that the new environment for business makes stability incredibly difficult to achieve and long-term, predictable careers nearly impossible.

- Despite the general persistence of good jobs, additional evidence suggests that jobs are getting less secure and less stable. This is particularly so for white-collar and managerial jobs, the ones that truly were protected under the old model. The assumption that white-collar employees had special protections from insecurity no longer seems valid.

- Most important, "career jobs" as defined by long-term, advancement prospects in the same organization with employment practices that served internal concerns, are in decline, and their future prospects are poor. Again, this is especially so for white-collar jobs.

How Responsible Were Employers for Their Employees?

The obligations between employers and employees is an interesting issue that easily takes one deeply into the fields of business ethics, contract law, and psychology in addition to human resources. A more tractable question is, to what extent were expectations of secure jobs and some protections from the market the result of a deep employer commitment, perhaps rooted in some deeper value system like a social contract, or was it mainly the result of a stable economic system that made stable employment reasonably costless?

One place to start this discussion is to recall that as late as the second decade of this century, employment relationships were more like a free market than perhaps even today. The "inside contractor" model was the dominant system for manufacturing, essentially a model of virtual organizations where owners outsourced even production operations to contractors operating in the owner's facility. Professional agents handled the marketing, sales, and distribution of companies on a fee or contingent contract basis. Employees in some industries, such as tapestries, moved routinely from company to company, facilitating knowledge transfer in the process. The turnover of key talent was managed carefully, but turnover of other employees was often remarkably high (Cappelli forthcoming).

Jacoby and others have written in great detail about the history of employer interest in protecting employees, and I will only paraphrase it here (Jacoby 1997; Brandes 1976; Nelson 1995). While the intellectual roots of this interest go back to the 1800s, the first arrangements that were both reasonably widespread and that had any claim to be concerned explicitly with employee welfare was the system of welfare capitalism beginning in the 1920s. My reading of the literature on welfare capitalism suggests quite clearly that the motivation for protecting employees was always the self-interest of company performance. Assembly-line production systems that benefited from reduced turnover had already driven efforts to stabilize employment, such as Henry Ford's famous five-dollar-a-day program. Union avoidance was far and away the most important objective. The companies most dedicated to stabilizing employment and job security were those whose stable product markets made this outcome relatively easy to achieve. Nor is it clear how widespread these arrangements were. Welfare capitalism was primarily a movement of the largest companies, and it was not clear that even a majority of these employers were ever governed by its principles.

Most observers see welfare capitalism fading from the scene, either completely or in large measure by the Great Depression, and eventually being replaced by management's pragmatic acceptance of collective bargaining as the primary mechanism for protecting employee welfare. The main arrangements for protecting employees from economic insecurity, such as seniority-based layoffs and promotions, supplemental unemployment insurance and severance pay, and low levels of contingent jobs, were collective bargaining outcomes initiated by unions that nonunion firms adopted to buy off employee interest in unionization.[4] It is important to remember that even in this golden age of employee protections, from World War II through to the 1981 recession, workers were constantly being laid off with the business cycle. They had stable jobs in the sense that they would return to the same employer, but layoffs were typical. Employer support for collective bargaining never meant any widespread acceptance of unions. By the 1970s, for example, sophisticated union avoidance campaigns were common, and many employers — perhaps a majority — were taking actions to undermine the unions, some of which included violations of labor law.[5]

The story for white-collar workers was always different. There the model for managing employees was not welfare capitalism, which was directed at production workers, but managerial capitalism, where the managers of the company acted to pursue their own goals as distinct from those of the owners. White-collar and managerial employees *were* the organization, at least in the eyes of the executives.[6] What most people think of as career jobs — good prospects for steady, predictable advancement, lifetime security subject to minimum performance levels, as well good wages and benefits — was more or less in place with the formation of large, multidivisional corporations, expanding in scope and scale as the management structures expanded. In this model, employees were hired based on general skills and attributes, received elaborate initial training, and had a career that was internal to the firm. The systems for managing employees, such as wage and benefit policies, training and development systems, promotion ladders, and other practices of internal labor markets, were part of the elaborate internal administration of the firm.

What is easy to forget now is the rather obvious dark side of these arrangements, especially for managers. Internal labor markets with outside hiring only at the entry level and all promotions internal to the company meant that employees were stuck with their current employer. If they did not fit, they had no choice but to suffer or adapt, and fitting in had as much to do with altering one's politics, social attitudes, and values as it did with performance. William H. Whyte's (1956) classic *The Organization Man* is perhaps the best known critique of this system, but other observers such as C. Wright Mills (1953) and (two decades later) Rosabeth Moss Kanter (1977) helped document the often coercive effects it had on employees.

What can we conclude about employers' acceptance of and commitment to the principle that employees should be protected from market risk? Blue-collar workers were protected from short-term, cyclical economic insecurity by union contracts or, in nonunion firms, by policies designed to mimic the provisions of those contracts. Although management agreed to those arrangements, they typically did so as a result of union bargaining power. It is difficult to see these provisions as a manifestation of employer concern about the need to protect employees. Active efforts to erode union gains were underway even before the restructuring waves of the 1980s. White-collar and especially managerial employees, in contrast, experienced a greater commitment. They were given to expect not just protection from insecurity, but lifetime careers inside the company. Elaborate employment systems served that goal with arrangements that were internally focused.

It is hard to gauge the depth of the employer's commitment to protecting white-collar and managerial employees in this period or, put more bluntly, what firms were willing to pay to provide protection. Both the operating environment and the nature of companies were different in that period in ways that made it substantially easier to provide stable employment and career paths. Especially for large companies, product markets were stable and much more predictable in many industries explicitly regulated by the government to ensure stability. Foreign competition was very limited, and domestic competition often operated as an oligopoly where unions effectively took labor costs out of competition with standardized union contracts. Large companies such as IBM made 10- and 15-year business plans that proved accurate. In the context of such plans, it was sensible and realistic to lay out equivalent human resource plans and to say to individual employees: "This is our career plan for you until you retire. And here is how we are going to manage you to ensure that it happens."

The economic instability that these large companies experienced was mainly the temporary kind associated with business cycles. They did bear the cost of protecting at least white-collar and managerial employees from recessions and from modest restructuring efforts. IBM in particular argued, with some justification, that the employment security they offered employees facilitated what by contemporary standards was low-level restructuring of operations brought on by unforeseen market changes.[7] However, there was relatively little pressure to maximize shareholder value, at least by contemporary standards, and executives had much greater discretion to devote resources to such goals. The big restructuring challenges were yet to come.

No doubt there were individual employers who shouldered big burdens to protect employees; and no doubt employers talked about their practices in terms of the social good. However, in my view, the commitments that most employers had to protect their employees were not very broad, did not run very deep, and had at least as much to do with self-interest as with any broader concern about employee welfare. The best way to test this proposition is to see what happened to that commitment when employers faced much more serious pressures for change in the next period, when the cost of providing protections rose sharply. In that situation, most all of them abandoned virtually everything about the old system, even the rhetoric about their responsibility to employees.

What Went Wrong?

The world began to change for employers with the 1981–82 recession, the worst economic period since the Great Depression, which brought with it structural changes that went well beyond the usual cyclical downturn in product demand. A number of important changes in the economy and in the way business was conducted got underway in that period. They include the following:

Pressures to increase shareholder value — The rising influence of institutional investors and legal decisions that made maximizing shareholder value not only the singular goal for directors of public companies and the executives they managed, but made shareholders the only stakeholders to whom companies were legally accountable. New financial institutions such as junk bonds made possible hostile takeovers of companies that were not maximizing shareholder value. Any resources that companies may have devoted to other causes, such as protecting employees from business risks, were quickly transferred to the goal of shareholder value.[8] More important, investors and analysts seemed to be persuaded that cutting jobs raises shareholder value even though the hard evidence on that point is decidedly mixed. New accounting techniques (such as economic value added that sought to maximize shareholder value) punished fixed costs, including the fixed investments in employees.[9]

Changes in the boundaries of the firm — Companies were persuaded that divesting unrelated businesses and acquiring new ones with appropriate synergies could raise shareholder value, and mergers and acquisitions rose to record levels year after year. Companies concerned about focusing on their core competencies learned to outsource functions that were not central to their capabilities and to pursue joint ventures as an alternative to internal development of capabilities. The consequence for employment was to disrupt long-term career paths and, more fundamentally, to make the security of all functions and jobs uncertain. Any operation could be divested if changing markets and changing patterns of competition aligned themselves, and all functions could be outsourced if a low-cost vendor came along. One might say that the number of good jobs stays the same in this model and the jobs just move around from company to company, but such movement and the constant uncertainty about movement undermined job security and any attempt to develop long-term careers.

Changes in the nature of competition — Shorter production cycles and more rapid change in business strategies associated with faster-paced competition made skills obsolete more quickly. Examples are the change from physical chemistry to biotechnology in pharmaceuticals or from one market segment in insurance to another, where the skills needed are completely different. Employers simply did not have time to develop the new skills they needed internally when dramatic changes in products and strategies happened quickly. So they turned to outside hiring to get those new skills. They also turned to outside hiring to get the managerial skills and experience to facilitate changes in their administrative operations. One way to think about these developments is that product life cycles have now become shorter than the expected career of an employee (see below).

Changes in the management of organizations — Work systems that empower employees, such as cross-functional teams, broke down traditional job ladders, eliminated supervisory positions, and widened spans of control. Information systems eliminated many of the internal control functions of middle management positions, and decentralizing operations through the creation of profit centers and similar arrangements further reduced the need for central administration. Flatter hierarchies and the sharp reduction in central administration reduced promotion prospects.

Policy decisions — Public policy in the 1980s contributed to the pressures to unbundle employee protection provisions inside firms. The Reagan administration explicitly argued for increasing employer discretion in employment decisions in an attempt to link economic competitiveness to the ability to shed redundant employees, a position that arguably had more influence on management than the decision to fire the striking PATCO workers. Various reports gave guidance as to the best ways to cut workforces. Even under a Democratic administration, the U.S. Department of Labor had by 1995 accepted that companies would continue to restructure their operations in ways that cut jobs. It argued not for preventing such changes but for minimizing the damage to employees (USDOL 1995). Coercive pressures from leaders in the employer community also reversed. IBM's announcement of its decision to abandon employment security and lay off employees was followed shortly thereafter by a wave of layoffs among other large employers. The business community organized itself to press for greater flexibility in employment. For example, the Labor Policy Association, an employer group concerned with public policy, produced a widely circulated study arguing that the key to improved corporate performance is greater management discretion in employment decisions — in other words, the end of administrative practices to protect jobs. The requirements of employment legislation also created incentives to unravel the internalized employment structure, incentives that built as regulations increased. The vast array of federal legislation directed at employment has largely been tied to the traditional, internalized model of employment. Alternative arrangements, such as contracting out or contingent work, can mean that "employers" are no longer covered by the legislation, freeing them from its obligations.

Market alternatives — An enormous market has developed to respond to these developments. Vendors now exist who will take in every function that could be outsourced. Staffing agencies will lease employees with any set of skills, even CEOs, so that labor costs can be transformed from fixed to variable costs. As noted below, corporate recruiters now offer a rich menu of available applicants to any employer willing to pursue outside hiring.

The protections against temporary, business-cycle layoffs for blue-collar workers proved largely useless against plant closings and other sources of displacement brought on by these changes. To illustrate, seniority-based layoffs in the old model effectively redistributed the risk of the typical layoff threat, which was recession-related, to junior employees so that senior employees were essentially immune to them. However, seniority-based layoffs, which are a within-plant practice, provide no protection against plant closings, now a much more real threat. Even if actual layoffs are no greater than in the past, all workers now experience insecurity associated with them. In an effort to reduce fixed costs, employers also shift more of their tasks to vendors and contingent workers. These changes may not reduce the number of "good jobs" in the economy, but they make current jobs less stable and less secure, reducing the prospects of long-term careers in the same organization. Further, the terms and conditions of employment in these facilities are now governed less by internal considerations, such as equity, and much more by conditions in the outside market.

However, white-collar and managerial employees experienced the most fundamental changes because they were the ones with the most protections to lose. First, they now faced much the same increased insecurity and instability as production workers, a profound change as it undermined what had been the very basis of the distinction between white collar and blue collar. That distinction stems from the New Deal era Fair Labor Standards Act, which is based on the assumption that production workers needed legislative protections that white-collar workers did not because the latter were already protected by the firm. Second, white-collar employees also saw internal careers evaporating as job ladders shrank, restructuring disrupted the promotion tracks that remained, and external hiring blocked advancement by filling more senior positions. To argue that there has been no significant change in employment relationships requires asserting that the above changes in the employer's world are either not very significant or that, somehow they never got down to the employees.

Evidence of a Changing Relationship

Most of the research associated with changes in the labor market addresses the traditional public policy concern about current terms and conditions of employment. Labor market data in particular are not designed to address questions such as future prospects for job security or for careers inside firms as these are primarily issues about organizational practices. The U.S. government, for example, did not survey for permanent (as distinct from recession-based and temporary) job losses until after 1984. However, some labor market evidence is available that relates to whether career jobs — and not just good jobs — have declined. The main overlap between the concept of good jobs and career jobs as defined above is the issue of job stability and, to a lesser extent, job security. Some care is necessary in interpreting such evidence, however. One reason is that while studies typically look for changes in outcomes for the workforce as a whole, some large percentage of the workforce never had anything like the traditional relationships.[10] So a finding that there is only a modest decline in some outcome for the workforce as a whole might mask a considerable breakdown in relationships for that segment of the economy that truly had career jobs, such as managers. This may help explain why observers who focus on labor market data are the least likely to believe that there are important changes in employment, while those who study organizations, especially managers, are perhaps the most likely.[11] The place to begin a review of the evidence is to acknowledge two fundamental trends that Jacoby reviews in his chapter. The first is the sharp rise in unemployment for white-collar employees, especially relative to other groups,[12] which is certainly among the strongest evidence that whatever special protection this employee group had in the past is gone. The second and more general trend is the systematic shifting of business risk onto employees that accompanied the restructuring of companies, a point that my colleagues and I have documented at length.[13] This is also evidence that buffers against the market have broken down. The review below begins with the evidence that was presented as equivocal in Jacoby's survey as it relates to career jobs and offers different conclusions about it.

Employee Tenure

Much of the argument suggesting that not much is new in employee relationships turns on research about job tenure — how long an employee stays with their employer. Because so much is based on these findings, it is important to understand what they can and cannot tell us. First and perhaps most important, it is a mistake to confuse stable jobs with secure jobs: Sheherazade had a stable relationship with the Sultan if one looked at the data on tenure because they were together for 1,001 Arabian nights. That does not mean that it was a secure relationship given that he threatened to have her terminated — literally — every night if her job performance fell.

The distinction is perhaps easiest to see in firm-level studies such as Allen and Clark's interesting finding that tenure rose in large, stable firms during the 1990s while 16 percent of the jobs in those firms were cut (Allen, Clark, and Schieber forthcoming).

Tenure is a confusing concept to interpret because it is driven by two quite distinct components: voluntary quits and terminations. From the perspective of employees, only terminations drive job insecurity. We also know that these two components move in opposite directions with the business cycle. Quits fall and dismissals rise during downturns, vice versa during expansions. Because the two components move in opposite directions, stability is built into the overall tenure measure, which makes any changes in tenure meaningful. The more important findings concern trends in quits and in terminations examined separately. Here the results suggest, based on three different sets of data, that permanent dismissals rose through the 1980s and early 1990s while quit rates were falling. One study in particular finds that the rate of dismissals increased sharply for older workers with more tenure, doubling for workers ages 45 to 54.[14]

It is probably fair to say that the inconsistent results about changes in overall tenure rates, sometimes even using the same data, does not make one especially sanguine about the robustness of labor economics.[15] It may nevertheless be instructive to review the results. As noted above, it is important to remember that not all workers had long-term, stable relationships even in earlier periods. For example, now as in the past, roughly 40 percent of the workforce has been with their current employer less than two years. And, as noted above, average stability can mask considerable variance for subgroups in the workforce. The above qualifications aside, while studies found reasonable stability comparing the 1980s with earlier periods, more recent results using data from the mid-1990s find declines in average tenure, especially for managerial employees but even for the workforce as a whole. These include, in addition to the studies mentioned in Jacoby's chapter, studies that compare cohorts over time that seem to find the biggest changes, such as a 10 percent increase in the rate of job changes for younger workers now as compared to earlier decades (Bernhardt, Morris, Handcock, and Scott forthcoming). They also find large declines in tenure for older, white men in particular, the group most protected by internal labor markets. For example, for men approaching retirement age (58–63) only 29 percent had been with the same employer for ten years or more as compared to a figure of 47 percent in 1969 (Ruhm 1995). The most recent studies find that the percentage of the workforce with long-tenure jobs, ten years or more, declined slightly from the late 1970s through 1993 and then fell sharply through the current period and are now at the lowest level in twenty years (Farber 1997). The finding that tenure declined for managerial jobs is especially supportive of the arguments for the erosion of internal career systems (Neumark, Polsky, and Hansen forthcoming).

In most cases, the findings of declines in tenure are modest, but these modest changes need to be assessed in the context of two caveats in addition to the general ones presented earlier. First, many of these studies are comparing tenure in the 1990s to the 1980s. The 1981–83 recession was the worst economic downturn since the Great Depression, while the period after 1992 to 2000 was the greatest economic expansion since the Depression. In this context, the finding that jobs are only slightly less stable in the 1990s than in the 1980s is hardly evidence of stable careers. Second, the declines in overall tenure for the workforce as a whole come despite the fact that tenure for women has been rising because they are now less likely to quit their jobs when they get married or have children (Wellington 1993). There is no evidence that the rising tenure of women has anything to do with employers adapting or responding to this change in women's preferences.

Nor is the fact that geographic mobility has been reasonably stable any evidence of stability in jobs. In fact, it may suggest the opposite, at least for managerial jobs. Transferring employees around the corporation was a key component in executive development programs, and the corporate interest in relocating employees, as indicated by employer surveys, has been in decline. The alternative to transferring employees is to fill those vacancies through outside hiring. Other survey results suggest that employees now resist moving outside of their communities precisely because of the new market-driven employment model. Their professional networks give them the opportunity to find a new job should they be dismissed, and they fear moving away and having to search for a new position where those networks do not apply (Furchgott 1996).

Job Security

A better alternative for assessing changes in the employment relationship would be to look directly at job security rather than at proxies like tenure. It is difficult to measure job security directly except through changes in employer policies. As late as the end of the 1970s, survey evidence from the Conference Board indicated that management's priorities in setting employment practices were to build a loyal, stable workforce. A decade later, however, by the end of the 1980s, that priority had clearly shifted to increasing organizational performance and reducing costs (Furchgott 1996). The most powerful evidence in this regard is another Conference Board survey that finds more than two-thirds of the large employers in the sample reporting that they have changed their practice and no longer offer employment security; only 3 percent said that they still offered job security to employees (HR Executive Review 1997).

Employer decisions to end job security through downsizing is another lens into the world of changing employment relationships. Cutting workers to reduce costs and improve financial performance, not just to respond to declines in business, is the essence of downsizing. It is a new phenomenon that begins in the 1980s. The American Management Association (AMA) surveyed its member companies about downsizing since 1990. They found that the incidence of downsizing increased virtually every year until 1996 — despite the economic expansion — when 48.9 percent of companies reported them, a trivial decline from 50 percent the year before. Forty percent had downsizing in two or more separate years over the previous six (American Management Association 1996). Other surveys report roughly similar rates of downsizing. The scale of these job cuts are unprecedented in a period of economic expansion.

The causes of downsizing have also changed with a growing number of companies reporting that they now result from internal management decisions — restructuring (66 percent) and outsourcing (23 percent). Virtually none now cite overall economic conditions as an explanation, and most of the companies that cut are now profitable in the year they are cutting. Further, downsizing is no longer necessarily about shrinking the size of the workforce. Thirty-one percent of those firms in the AMA surveys were actually adding and cutting workers at the same time in 1996, and the average firm that had a downsizing was in fact growing by 6 percent (Furchgott 1996). This development suggests that firms are relying on the outside labor market to restructure, dropping skills that are no longer needed and bringing in new ones.

Data on workers who have been permanently displaced from their jobs confirms the fact that job security is declining and is now no longer dependent on business cycles. The overall rate at which workers have been permanently displaced backed down a bit in the late 1980s from the peak of the recession period, 1981–83 but then rose again — despite the economic recovery — and jumped sharply through 1995. The rate at which workers were thrown out of their jobs was about the same in 1993–95, a period of significant economic expansion and prosperity in the economy as a whole, as compared to the 1981–83 recession (Farber 1998). It is difficult to think of more compelling evidence that the nature of the employment relationship has changed than this. About 15 percent of the workforce saw their jobs go forever during 1993–95. The cause of the job losses reported in these surveys mirrors the developments in the firm surveys — shifting away from economy or companywide reasons such as downturns in business or plant closings toward eliminating particular positions associated with restructuring.

Other manifestations of declining job security include the fact that job losses now are much more likely than in previous decades to be permanent; that dismissals for cause, such as poor performance, have increased along with downsizing; and that the employees who were once largely immune from business cycle related layoffs — not only white-collar but also older and more educated workers — have seen their rate of job loss rise. Again, these reductions in security have occurred in a period of economic expansion.

Wages

Changes in the wage structure within organizations is another aspect of the change in employment relationships. One of the main functions of internal labor markets is to create distinctive wage profiles that differ from market rates in order to serve the internal goals of the organization. Job mobility within the same organization tended to produce greater benefits in the form of higher wages and was seen in part as the result of a better match between the attributes of the employees and the requirements of the jobs as compared to job changes in the outside labor market, a testament to the advantages of the internal labor market in allocating labor. By the early 1990s, however, there was no longer any advantage to the inside moves as compared to those across employers (Wilk and Craig 1998). The steady progression of wages based on seniority or tenure was one of the hallmarks of internal systems. The apparent decline in the return to tenure with the same employer is perhaps the most compelling evidence of the decline of more traditional pay and employment relationships. Researchers studying the semiconductor industry, for example, found a decline in the wage premium paid to more experienced workers. Among the explanations are that new technical skills are becoming more important, and those skills are learned not inside the firm but outside, typically in higher education (Brown 1994). In aggregate data, the returns to seniority — that is, tenure with the same employer — have collapsed in recent years (Chauvain 1994). Other studies find a sharp decline in returns to seniority of about $3,000 annually between the 1970s and 1980s for workers with ten years of seniority. The costs of job changing dropped dramatically; and workers who changed jobs every other year saw almost the same earnings rise in the late 1980s as did those who kept the same job for ten years (Marcotte 1994). Further, this effect varies depending on why one changes jobs. The probability that employees who quit would find a job that offers a large pay raise has increased by five percent, while the probability that those who were dismissed will suffer a large decline in their pay has risen by 17 percent over the previous decade (Polsky 1999). These results suggest that a good, lifetime match between an employee and a single employer is becoming less important in determining an employee's long-term success. By default, what must be becoming more important are factors outside of the relationship with an individual employer, factors associated with the outside market.

Another hallmark of internal labor markets was that pay was assigned to jobs rather than to individuals and that differences in pay were associated with differences in jobs. Research suggests greater risk and more variance in individual earnings over time that cannot be accounted for by the usual characteristics of jobs (Gottschalk and Moffitt 1994). Some part of the greater variance may be because of a much stronger relationship between individual performance and pay. Hay Associates, the compensation firm, collects data from their clients on the pay increases associated with different levels of individual performance as measured by performance evaluation plans. In 1989, the increase associated with the highest level of performance was 2.5 times larger than the increase associated with the lowest level. By 1993, that ratio had risen to a factor of four.[16] A 1996 Towers Perrin survey found that 61 percent of responding firms were using variable pay and that 27 percent of firms were considering the elimination of base pay increases altogether so that the only increases in compensation would result from performance contingent pay (O'Neil 1997). Data from the Bureau of Labor Statistics finds that the percentage of employees eligible for bonuses rose from 29 percent in 1989 to 39 percent in medium-size and large firms and to 49 percent in small firms by the end of the 1990s (USBLS 1989–1997). The change in contingent compensation has been especially great for executives. Bonuses as a share of total compensation rose more than 20 percent from 1986 to 1992 (O'Shaughnessy, Levine, and Cappelli 1998). Contingent pay erodes the importance of internal, administrative pay systems by placing greater weight on factors that vary such as business and individual performance.

Benefits

Whether employers are less likely to offer employee benefits is an issue that goes directly to the traditional question as to whether jobs protect employees from hardship. It says nothing, however, about whether employers are offering greater commitments to employees or, indeed, about the nature of the employment relationship. Employee benefits are simply another form of compensation that exists because most are tax-advantaged forms of compensation and, in some cases, because employers can provide them more cheaply than can employees. The biggest development in employee benefits in recent years has been "cafeteria-style" benefits, which make the compensation aspects of benefits transparent by allowing employees to essentially buy the combination of benefits they want from a fixed budget or cash them in for wages. Employee benefits end with employment, just as wages do. The one prominent exception is pension plans which represent a continuing obligation to employees — even if employment ends (at least for vested employees) — and, as such, an indication of a more permanent obligation by employers.

   As Jacoby notes in his chapter, pension plans have been on the decline; but even more important than the decline in pension coverage has been the shift in the nature of pensions from defined benefit plans, where workers earn the right to predetermined benefit levels according to their years of service, toward defined contribution plans, where employers make fixed contributions to a retirement fund for each employee, especially 401(k) programs whereby employees contribute directly to their retirement fund (Ippolito 1995). With this shift, the employer no longer bears the risk of guaranteeing a stream of benefits. That problem now falls to the employee. The employer's obligations to the employee end with employment, a move away from long-term relationships.

Contingent Work

Another aspect of changes in employment mentioned in Jacoby's chapter that is relevant to changes in career jobs, as opposed to good jobs, is the extent of contingent work that is made up of temporary, part-time, and self-employed help. Perhaps a better term for this category is nonstandard work because it emphasizes the common characteristic of being something other than full-time employment. Whether these jobs are good jobs as defined above is difficult to assess and may ultimately turn on whether employees take them by choice or because they cannot get full-time, permanent employment. The rise of nonstandard work suggests something about the growing employer preference for variable as opposed to fixed employment costs. It is fair to say that nonstandard work may no longer be growing, but it is also worth recognizing that most estimates indicate that it already accounts for just under one-third of the jobs in the United States.[17] It might be reasonable to include contracting out and vendors in this category, at least from the perspective of the original firm, because they represent the movement of work that had been inside the firm at fixed cost to work that is now done outside the firm at variable cost. The outsourced jobs may still be good jobs, of course, although they often represent significantly reduced career opportunities.[18]

Outside Hiring

The nail in the coffin of the traditional employment relationship is the greater use of outside hiring by employers. It is difficult to assess the extent of outside hiring, but one study that did so found a sizeable increase in the proportion of employers who sought experienced workers for entry-level jobs (Rynes, Orlitzky, and Bretz 1997). My examination of proprietary surveys of employers finds them reporting a greater interest in outside hiring to meet skill needs (Cappelli 1999). One interesting proxy for the growth of outside hiring is the fact that the revenues from corporate recruiting firms who perform outside searchers for companies *tripled* just during the mid 1990s (Cappelli 1999). Not only is there no evidence that employers are making greater investments in their new hires, but the evidence that we have suggests that they are making substantially fewer investments, particularly in the extent of training to learn new jobs (Constantine and Neumark 1997).

In my view, most of the economy is moving along a continuum toward greater use of the outside labor market. Movement away from internalized practices does not suggest that employers are necessarily headed toward free agency. However, the set of industries that are well toward that model is more than just the margins of the economy. Silicon Valley is often held up as the example of open labor markets with high levels of mobility across firms and little planned internal development. In this sense, it is not just a geographic location but a metaphor for much of the entire high-tech sector across the entire country. Something like free agency now dominates not only creative industries such as movies and television, but also much of the investment industry. It has also come to professional service firms (accounting, consulting, and law firms in particular), where promotion to partner had meant a lifetime career at that firm. Now movement across firms is common even for associates. Outside hiring may be more common for higher-skilled employees because their higher value added makes search and recruiting costs easier to recoup. But "poaching" (hiring away employees from competitors) is now a phenomenon for all jobs where labor is in short supply. Call centers, for example, have been particularly subject to retention problems from outside hiring. Even state beaches on the East Coast have engaged in poaching lifeguards from each other.

When employers switch from internal promotions to outside hires, they effectively shut down their own internal labor market by eliminating promotion prospects. They also eviscerate the internal labor markets of competitors because the investments made in those employees leave. Finally, outside hiring shifts the attention of employers from inside the firm to the network of potential employers outside the firm where more — and quite likely better — career opportunities lie.

Will Tight Labor Markets Bring Back Employee Protections?

The return of tight labor markets clearly does shift bargaining power back toward the employees. That is one reason why we are seeing rising real wages and increases in the reemployment rates of displaced workers. However, there is no evidence whatsoever that employees are using this opportunity to demand anything like a return to the older model of employment relations. First, employees understand that promises about career paths and long-term security are meaningless. Unless the changes in the business environment outlined above are rolled back, it is difficult to believe that any promises of a return to previous arrangements would be credible. There is also no practical way for employees to bargain for the terms of the old model because there is no way to bind their employer to it (short of explicit employment contracts that employers are loath to sign). In tight labor markets, the last thing employees want is arrangements that would buffer them from those markets and their benefits. Second, evidence seems to suggest that employees have already begun to adapt to this new world. Ninety-four percent of employees in a recent survey reported that they believed that they, and not their employer, were responsible for their own job security. When asked what they wanted from employers in a different survey, the top places went to development opportunities. Job security came out in the middle of the list. Surveys of MBA students find greater willingness to take risks and little interest in the large corporations that may still offer the best internal career paths.[19]

Not surprisingly, there is no evidence that employers are reverting to anything like the traditional model of employment relationships. Clearly there are companies such as SAS that continue to offer the old model. (It is interesting, by the way, how often the companies that still offer job security are privately held — not subject to the financial pressures of the investment community — and making products with some protection from fast-changing competition.) However, finding continuing examples of the old arrangements is no evidence of a *return* to those arrangements. There are also many examples in this tight labor market of companies trying to persuade their employees not to quit. But it is difficult to find any examples where companies are offering any concrete promises about future relationships. Every company that I have seen that wants to improve retention in fact is interested in retaining key talent, not necessarily all employees. Every one of these companies also says that they want to improve their ability to hire from the outside, a prospect that undermines their own internal labor market and cuts against the ability of other employers to retain employees. New work systems such as team-based arrangements might be expected to require greater investments in employees and continuity, but there is no evidence that employers are making those investments (Osterman 1995). Even where new work systems seem to require greater commitment from employees, commitment does not require lifetime or even permanent jobs as indicated by the studies showing that contingent workers are just as committed as full-time employees.[20]

Conclusions

The concern about the possible decline of good jobs began in the 1970s with the long-term decline in real wages and accelerated with the restructuring waves beginning in the early 1980s. Especially in the context of tight labor markets in the late 1990s, it is probably true that the number of good jobs in the economy, as traditionally defined, is not falling and may even be rising. Other changes are underway, however, that undermine the traditional notion of careers within the same organization. Overall job insecurity remains high because of factors such as the greater volatility of product markets, the greater incidence of restructuring, and the pressures on firms to divert resources from protecting employees toward shareholder value. Outside hiring combined with reduced opportunities for internal promotion helps shift careers from an inside the firm perspective to the outside market. Careers and employee management more generally are increasingly driven by the outside labor market.

Once these developments are underway, it is not within the power of an individual employer to return to the older arrangements. Consider an employer who decides to return to more traditional arrangements with long-term investments in employees, internal promotions, and lifetime careers. Even if such a model made sense for the employer's current context, it would only work if competitors agree not to poach away valuable talent and employees agree not to leave for what, at some point, would inevitably be better offers than they have internally. Neither is likely. The belief that even large companies will be able to offer employees better opportunities than the vast sea of possibilities in the outside market can offer up is a chimera.

These new arrangements do create new sets of winners and losers. While traditional arrangements sheltered employment from market pressures, the new arrangements make the market the arbiter of labor market outcomes. In slack labor markets, employers are able to push even more costs onto employees while in tight labor markets, employees are able to extract more rents from employees. Within the employee population, those with marketable skills and the ability to manage their own careers have made out very well; those without skills, with constraints on their mobility, and lacking career management skills have suffered even more than in the past. These developments may help account for rising inequality in outcomes, and they no doubt will exacerbate that trend. In particular, those who have the resources to invest in their own careers will have even greater advantages over those who do not.

It is not entirely clear what the public interest should be with respect to these developments. Some employee groups that have lost protection from the vagaries of the market clearly need protection from economic hardship. Perhaps the most important change in the policy area is that white-collar and managerial employees now suffer much the same insecurity as other employees, albeit at higher initial salaries. What interventions would help them is not so obvious. Traditional policy solutions of prohibiting undesirable outcomes, such as prohibiting layoffs along the lines of some European policies, does not seem feasible in an environment where business flexibility has been identified with the overall performance of the economy.

An alternative approach, which I think is more sensible, is to reduce the burdens associated with transitions between employers. These might include making employee benefits more portable so that employees do not lose health care coverage or pensions when they switch employers; reforming unemployment insurance, a program designed to accommodate temporary layoffs, to help assist employees who face permanent job loss (California, for example, allows companies to draw on unemployment insurance funds to retrain workers who are at risk of layoff); providing much more substantive assistance for retraining employees who are displaced from jobs, including greater access to education; moving away from economic assistance based on employment outcomes, such as the minimum wage, and toward other forms of assistance such as earned income tax credits.

One solution that I do not think is helpful is to expect employers to solve the problem in the old way, to brand employers who do not provide job security as "bad employers" and those that can provide some security as "good employers." Their differential ability to provide security is primarily driven by objective characteristics such as the volatility of their product market, changes in the boundaries of the firm, and the business strategies of the employers, characteristics that have little to do with the moral character of the organization. This is not to say that there are not objectionable and praiseworthy approaches to managing employees but simply that such judgments are often very difficult to make in practice. How about employers who have lost protection from tight labor markets? Do they also deserve help? As odd as this claim may sound, it is put forward in the policy arena — the argument to expand immigration for foreign workers in information technology and other areas is essentially based on the claim that employers need relief from tight labor markets. The challenges of managing retention, developing skills, and directing a workforce without lifetime commitment are real and require radical rethinking of the organization (Cappelli 1999 is essentially about addressing these challenges.).

The rising power of markets is one of the most important developments of our generation. Given that, it should be no surprise that the power of labor markets is rising as well. The effects are likely to be profound, much more complicated than the rise of either good jobs or career jobs, and no doubt will be examined for decades to come.

Notes

An earlier version of this chapter appeared in *California Management Review* 42, 1 (Fall 1999), © 1999 Regents of the University of California. Reprinted by permission.

1. It is worth remembering in the context of this discussion that the research on inequality did not reach a clear consensus that inequality had risen until a good ten or fifteen years after the trend was underway.

2. Other authors who use different criteria to evaluate good jobs, such as real wages and work effort, report declines in at least some measures. See, for example, the annual series by Mishel and Bernstein (various years).

3. See, for example, arguments such as those associated with Arthur and Rousseau (1996).

4. Not everyone thought that these arrangements were necessarily better for employees than those of the previous, more market-driven era because the employees gave up control for security. In the former system, the argument goes, at least employees had more autonomy (Marglin 1974).

5. A detailed guide to these practices, which remained accurate until the early 1980s, is Slichter, Healy, and Livernash (1960). An analysis of the decline of that system is Kochan, Katz, and McKersie (1984).

6. The classic study of managerial capitalism is Berle and Means (1932).

7. This case is argued persuasively in Mills (1988).

8. One might argue that such practices might actually benefit shareholders by improving company performance. The problem is that there is no solid evidence for this position, and every anecdote of a company that appears to succeed in this fashion can be countered by another anecdote about companies that do not.

9. This rise of these pressures from the investor community is perhaps the most important development in the world of business in a generation (Useem, 1996).

10. Even if we focus just on the private sector and leave out the roughly 11 percent of the workforce who are self-employed, in farming, or other jobs that do not fit the model of working for an "employer," organizations still had to be a certain size before it was efficient to have systems of internal development and training, job ladders, and other arrangements associated with long-term commitments. Seven percent of private sector employees work in establishments with fewer than five employees, and 44 percent are in establishments with fewer than one hundred. One researcher calculated that organizations need a minimum of five hundred employees to make formal compensation systems feasible (see Smith 1988). Another researcher argued that only about 40 percent of U.S. employees were in firms large enough and old enough to even have a reputation in their community, something that he saw as necessary to make implicit contracts that were behind internalized employment practices operate (see Oi 1983). Even within those organizations, the lifetime commitment model was generally a phenomenon for managerial workers who typically constituted about one-fifth of a company's workforce. If we define the workforce that ever had the lifetime, career-based employment system as managerial employees in firms large enough to have reputations, a rough estimate would be about 10 percent of the private sector workforce.

11. That the business press focus on these issues, then, might not be because they are necessarily sensationalist but because the issues are especially pertinent to their readers, the middle-class, managerial employees.

12. For an explicit comparison, see Cappelli (1992).

13. See Cappelli, Bassi, Knoke, Katz, Osterman, and Useem (1997).

14. See Polsky (1999) for this result. The other two studies are Bernhardt, Morris, Handcock, and Scott (forthcoming) and Valetta (1996).

15. There are perhaps a dozen recent studies using at least four major data sets to assess employee tenure. They are reviewed in Cappelli (1999). Even more recent studies are discussed in Neumark (forthcoming).

16. Thanks to Steve Gross, then of Hay Associates, for providing me with these unpublished figures in 1996.

17. Segal and Sullivan (1997). The estimates of temporary help in particular count only employees working for agencies, but estimates that include temps working directly for employers might double the total number of temps, from 2 to 4 percent of the workforce.

18. Consider, for example, a company that outsourced janitorial or other lower-level jobs to a vendor. The janitors may still have full-time jobs, albeit now with a vendor. However, the likelihood of being able to advance to any position outside of janitorial work may well be reduced.

19. This material is reviewed in Cappelli (1999).

20. There are now many studies reporting this result, but the first one appears to be Pearce (1993).

References

Allen, Steven G., Robert L. Clark, and Sylvester J. Schieber. 2000. "Have Jobs Become Less Stable in the 1990s? Evidence from Employer Data." In *On the Job: Is Long Term Employment a Thing of the Past?* ed. David Neumark. New York: Russell Sage Foundation.

American Management Association. 1996. *Survey on Downsizing, Job Elimination, and Job Creation.* New York: American Management Association.

Arthur, Michael B. and Denise M. Rousseau, eds. 1996. *The Boundaryless Career: A New Employment Principle for a New Organizational Era.* New York: Oxford University Press.

Belous, Richard S. 1989. *The Contingent Economy.* Washington, D.C.: National Planning Association.

Berle, Adolph A. and Gardner Means. 1932. *The Modern Corporation.* New York: Macmillan.

Bernhardt, Annette D., Martina Morris, Mark S. Handcock, and Marc A. Scott. 1999. "Trends in Job Instability and Wages for Young Adult Men." *Journal of Labor Economics* 17, 4 (Supplement): S65–S90.

Brandes, Stuart. 1976. *American Welfare Capitalism, 1880–1940.* Chicago: University of Chicago Press.

Brown, Clair, ed. 1994. The *Competitive Semiconductor Manufacturing Human Resources Project.* Berkeley, Calif.: Competitive Semiconductor Manufacturing Program.

Cappelli, Peter. 1992. "Examining Managerial Displacement." *Academy of Management Journal* 35: 203–17.

———. 1999. *The New Deal at Work: Managing the Market-Driven Workforce.* Boston: Harvard Business School Press.

———. 2000. "Market-Mediated Employment: The Historical Context." In *The New Relationship: Human Capital in the American Corporation,* ed. Margaret Blair and Thomas A. Kochan. Washington, D.C.: Brookings Institution Press. 61–101.

Cappelli, Peter, Laurie Bassi, David Knoke, Harry C. Katz, Paul Osterman, and Michael Useem. 1997. *Change at Work.* New York: Oxford University Press.

Chauvin, Keith. 1994. "Firm-Specific Wage Growth and Changes in the Labor Market for Managers." *Management and Decision Economics* 15: 21–37.

Constantine, Jill L. and David Neumark. 1997. "Training and the Growth of Wage Inequality." *Industrial Relations* 35, 4: 491–510.

Farber, Henry S. 1997. "The Changing Face of Job Loss in the United States, 1981–1995." Industrial Relations Section, Princeton University.

———. 1998. "Has the Rate of Job Loss Increased in the Nineties?" Working Paper 394. Industrial Relations Section, Princeton University. January.

Furchgott, Roy. 1996. "Earning It: Job Uncertainty Makes Offers Easier to Refuse." *New York Times,* October 20, 9.

Gottschalk, Peter and Robert A. Moffitt. 1994. "The Growth of Earnings Instability in the U.S. Labor Market." *Brookings Papers on Economic Activity* 2: 217–72.

HR Executive Review. 1997. *Implementing the New Employment Contract.* New York: Conference Board.

Ippolito, Richard A. 1995. "Toward Explaining the Growth of Defined Contribution Plans," *Industrial Relations* 34: 1–20.

Jacoby, Sanford M. 1997. *Modern Manors: Welfare Capitalism Since the New Deal.* Princeton, N.J.: Princeton University Press.

———. This volume. "Are Career Jobs Headed for Extinction?"

Kanter, Rosabeth Moss. 1977. *Men and Women of the Corporation.* New York: Basic Books.

Kochan, Thomas A., Harry C. Katz, and Robert B. McKersie. 1984. *The Transformation of Industrial Relations.* Boston: Basic Books.

Marcotte, David. 1994. "Evidence of a Fall in the Wage Premier for Job Security." Center for Governmental Studies, Northern Illinois University.

Marglin, Stephen A. 1974. "What Do Bosses Do? The Origins and Functions in Hierarchy in Capitalist Production." *Review of Radical Political Economics* 6, 2: 60–112.

Mills, C. Wright. 1953. *The American Middle Class.* New York: Oxford University Press.

Mills, D. Quinn. 1988. *The IBM Lesson: The Profitable Art of Full Employment.* New York: Times Books.

Mischel, Lawrence M. and Jared Bernstein. Various years. *The State of Working America.* Washington D.C.: Economic Policy Institute.

Nelson, Daniel. 1995. *Managers and Workers: Origins of the New Factory System in the United States, 1880-1920.* Madison: University of Wisconsin Press.

Neumark, David, ed. 2001. *On the Job: Is Long Term Employment a Thing of the Past?* New York: Russell Sage Foundation.

Neumark, David, Daniel Polsky, and Daniel Hansen. 1999. "Has Job Stability Declined Yet? New Evidence for the 1990s." *Journal of Labor Economics* 17, 4: 529–64.

Oi, Walter Y. 1983. "The Fixed Costs of Specialized Labor." In *The Measurement of Labor Cost,* ed. Jack Tripplett. Chicago: University of Chicago Press.

O'Neal, Sandra. 1997. "Recent Trends in Compensation Practices: Presentation to the Board of Governors of the Federal Reserve." Towers, Perrin, Valhalla, N.Y. October.

O'Shaughnessy, K. C., David I. Levine, and Peter Cappelli. 1998. "Changes in Management Pay Structures, 1986-1993 and Rising Returns to Skill." Working Paper. Institute of Industrial Relations, University of California at Berkeley.

Osterman, Paul. 1995. "Skills, Training, and Work Organization in American Establishments," *Industrial Relations* (April): 125–46.

Pearce, Jone L. 1993. "Toward an Organizational Behavior of Contract Laborers: Psychological Involvement and Effects on Employee Co-Workers." *Academy of Management Journal* 36, 6: 1082–92.

Polsky, Daniel. 1999. "Changes in the Consequences of Job Separations in the U.S." *Industrial and Labor Relations Review* 52, 4 (July): 565–80.

Ruhm, Christopher J. 1995. "Secular Changes in the Retirement Patterns of Older Men." *Journal of Human Resources* 30, 2 (Spring): 362–85.

Rynes, Sara L., Marc O. Orlitzky, and Robert Bretz, Jr. 1997. "Experienced Hiring Versus College Recruiting: Practices and Emerging Trends." *Personnel Psychology* 50, 2: 309–39.

Segal, Lewis M. and Daniel G. Sullivan. 1997. "The Growth of Temporary Services Work." *Journal of Economic Perspectives* 11, 2 (Spring): 117–36.

Slichter, Sumner H., James J. Healy, and E. Robert Livernash. 1960. *The Impact of Collective Bargaining on Management.* Washington, D.C.: Brookings Institution Press.

Smith, Robert S. 1988. "Comparable Worth: Limited Coverage and Exacerbation of Inequality." *Industrial and Labor Relations Review* 41: 227–39.

U.S. Department of Labor. 1995. *Guide to Responsible Restructuring.* Washington, D.C.: U.S. GPO.

U.S. Department of Labor, Bureau of Labor Statistics. Various years. *Employee Benefits Surveys,* 1989-1997.

Useem, Michael. 1996. *Investor Capitalism.* New York: Basic Books.

Valetta, Robert G. 1996. "Has Job Security in the U.S. Declined?" *Federal Reserve Bank of San Francisco Weekly Letter* 96-07. February 16.

Wellington, Allison J. 1993. "Changes in the Male/Female Wage Gap." *Journal of Human Resources* 28, 2: 383–411.

Whyte, William H. 1956. *The Organization Man.* New York: Simon and Schuster. Reprint Philadelphia: University of Pennsylvania Press, 2002.

Wilk, Steffanie L. and Elizabeth A. Craig. 1998. "Should I Stay or Should I Go? Occupational Matching and Internal and External Mobility." Wharton School, Department of Management Working Paper. Wharton School, University of Pennsylvania, Philadelphia.

Chapter 10
Reply: Premature Reports of Demise

Sanford M. Jacoby

Are current employer practices qualitatively different from those of the recent past? This is the issue dividing Peter Cappelli and myself. Unlike Cappelli, I do not think that the institutions of the postwar U.S. labor market have undergone a structural transformation, certainly nothing so drastic as to warrant an obituary.

Social scientists regularly contest the nature of institutional change, as in recent debates over the nation state, Nordic corporatism, collective bargaining, and superpower hegemony. Typically the debaters divide into two camps. On one side are the saltationists: those who see institutional change representing a break or rupture with the past. Here there is fascination with punctuated equilibrium models and other metaphors of discontinuous change. On the other side are the gradualists: those who see change occurring adaptively and being accommodated by existing institutions.[1]

Each side in these debates has its virtues and vices. The gradualists are sensitive to structural continuity and to path dependence, although this breeds a conservatism that causes them to miss historical turning points. The great neoclassical economist, Alfred H. Marshall, was a gradualist whose marginalism caused him to declare "Natura non facit saltum" (nature makes no leaps). The problem is, sometimes it does. Saltationists are alert to these transitions and quick to see fresh patterns. They also, however, have a tendency to give recent events more weight than a long-term perspective would warrant. There lies the nub of my differences with Cappelli (this volume).

To understand my position, we need to go back to the late 1960s, when economists concerned with poverty developed a labor-market taxonomy known as the "dual labor market" model. In this model, the secondary sector was comprised of jobs that were easy to learn, paid relatively low wages, and offered few rewards to tenure. Some of these were full-time jobs; others were part-time or temporary positions. Secondary workers were disproportionately young, female, and nonwhite, with high turnover rates (Doeringer and Piore 1971; Edwards et al. 1975).

The primary sector was the *locus classicus* of the internal labor market, characterized by use of administrative principles to guide labor allocation and by strong attachments between employers and employees. These attachments caused the formation of firm-specific human capital. To retain and to motivate employees, companies offered wages and benefits that rose with seniority. Incumbents were favored over outsiders for vacancies. The employment relationship was maintained over time, although the strength of the tie varied by occupational tier.

The primary sector's upper tier was composed of salaried executive, managerial, and professional employees. Except in catastrophic situations like the Great Depression, these employees had Japanese-style lifetime jobs. The lower tier was filled with hourly blue-collar, clerical, and sales employees. Their jobs offered fewer rewards to tenure than the upper tier (as in the distinction between annual salaries and hourly wages), but they did provide a fair degree of stability. The big contrast in lower-tier jobs was between those in the union sector, where income security was emphasized, and those in the nonunion sector, where employment security was more prevalent.

During business downturns, the union sector utilized a layoff-rehire system tied to seniority and subsidized by unemployment insurance and private benefits. The nonunion sector was more likely to respond to downturns by cutting hours and compensation, or by transferring employees. Because of these differences, layoff rates in the 1960s were two to four times higher in the union sector, and unionized workers were about 50 percent more likely to experience temporary layoffs. Unionized workers also were more likely to experience layoffs than their counterparts in Europe or Japan (Jacoby 1997). While permanent mass layoffs were rare during the postwar boom, they did sometimes occur. Typically unions handled them through transfers of senior members, or, if this was not an option, through a severance pay plan. Like temporary layoffs, severance plans revealed labor's preference for income, rather than job, security. As observers noted in 1960, this preference demonstrated "a basic conservatism in the American labor movement" because it allowed unions to "avoid the necessity of bargaining over such essential management decisions as production schedules, capital improvement plans, and plant location (Slichter et al. 1960).

In short, the antediluvian world had a certain structure and logic. The least stable jobs were in the secondary labor market, where weak attachments resulted in low tenure and high turnover. In the primary sector, the most stable jobs were held by managers and executives; lower-tier primary workers enjoyed many upper-tier perquisites, albeit to a lesser degree (and, in the case of unionized workers, with a greater emphasis on income security). Pay and employment levels fluctuated less than market conditions; when employers made pay and allocative decisions, they gave heavy weight to organizational factors (like seniority, equity, and morale) and not only to market considerations. Risks that might otherwise be borne by employees were absorbed by the employer.

Of course, the fact that employers operated internal labor markets in this fashion had everything to do with self-interest and not benevolence, except to the extent benevolence constituted a form of enlightened self-interest. That employers chose to shoulder risk for employees was the result of an interplay between efficiency factors (recouping investments in employees and providing incentives for employee effort); the rise of modern management (including professional personnel managers and systematic attention to employee psychology); social norms; and various external forces (ranging from union pressure to law to tax incentives).[2]

So where do Cappelli and I disagree? We differ on four main issues: the persistence of the labor market's pre-1980 structure; the manner in which this structure has adapted to the post-1980 environment; the contrast between managers and other occupational groups; and the interpretation of data.

The Pre-1980 Model

The model sketched above remains a good first approximation to the contemporary labor market. Employers in the primary sector — the focus of my essay — still face a similar set of incentives and pressures, what I referred to in my essay as the "organizational realities of managing a workforce." True, some of the underpinnings to internal labor markets have grown weaker, notably labor unions. However, there also are new forces that are raising the return on employee retention. The economy increasingly is being driven by competition based on creativity, skill, and relationships. While some companies are content to cross-fertilize an industry through the turnover of skilled employees, as in parts of Silicon Valley, most employers prefer a proprietary approach. Hence they make strenuous efforts to manage and retain their intellectual capital (Pfeffer 1998; Stewart 1997).

To reduce the cost of these efforts in a riskier world, employers rely on a core-periphery model, in which secondary jobs — temporary, part time, and others — are used as a buffer to stabilize core jobs and as a screening device to select future core employees. Secondary workers are employed by outside contractors or by the primary employer (a distinction that has legal ramifications, as Microsoft recently discovered). These new forms of sectoral articulation are a change from the older version of autonomous dual markets. However, they are consistent with the preservation of career-type jobs.

How large and persistent has been the growth of secondary or nonstandard positions? Cappelli and I agree that nonstandard jobs have not been growing since the mid-1990s. Where we differ is in our assessment of their growth before then. Currently, of the roughly 30 percent of the employed who hold nonstandard jobs, over two-thirds are part-time workers, a group whose share of employment has not changed since the early 1970s. The remainder consists of workers in "alternative employment arrangements": independent contractors and consultants (6.7 percent); on-call workers (1.6 percent); temporary help workers (1 percent); and workers provided by contract firms (0.6 percent). This is a motley group. The independent contractors and consultants are relatively educated; one-third possess college degrees, a higher proportion than traditional workers. Only 4 percent consider their jobs likely to last for less than a year and 84 percent prefer their arrangement over a traditional job. Workers provided by contract firms resemble independent contractors; they tend to be educated and consider their jobs to be stable. On the other hand, temporary help workers and on-call workers are disproportionately young, female, and less educated. Most do not think their jobs will last and nearly 60 percent would prefer a traditional job. Thus an upper bound on the increase since the 1970s of nonstandard jobs that are undesired and unstable is less than three percent of employment, a change but not a sea change (USBLS 1997, 1998b).

Adaptation not Extinction

It is true that the economic environment is different now than in the 1970s, due to technological innovation and the intensification of domestic and global competition. However, the new environment has not led to the death of internal labor markets and long-term jobs, such as they were (and are). Rather — and this is the central point of my essay — internal labor markets have adapted to change by shifting risk and uncertainty from the firm to the employee. Employees today are bearing more risk — including the risk of job loss — but are doing so within structures that have remained stable over time. When we look at the kind of workers who held primary jobs in the past — adult high-school and college graduates — the proportion reporting more than ten years' tenure with the same employer was 42 percent in 1979 versus 37 percent in 1996. Despite job losses and restructuring since 1980, long-term attachments are only slightly less prevalent today (Farber 1997b).

Real wages have declined for some workers, especially the less educated. However, this in itself is not inconsistent with a world of long-term jobs and risk-sheltering by employers. In fact, to a degree the two phenomena are related: Some workers have traded (or been forced to trade) lower real wages for job security and the maintenance of benefits; other workers — particularly managers, a point I will return to — have enjoyed rising wages at the expense of job security and some job-related benefits. The real paradox of today's labor market is the coexistence of job loss and long-term employment, sometimes within the same organization. This causes job losses to have a ripple effect, making survivors work harder and worry more. However, the survivors, while bearing more risk, continue to hold long-term jobs whose pay and working conditions remain heavily influenced by organizational considerations.

Managers and Other Occupational Groups

Cappelli gives a lot of weight to the experiences of managerial and executive employees. In fact, his argument about the death of career jobs is really about the collapse of job security for managers, and his evidence of a shift from organizations to markets is weighted heavily to managerial phenomena, such as executive compensation and careers.

Without doubt, managerial work has changed drastically in many firms. Much of the decline in aggregate job stability in the 1980s and 1990s was concentrated among long-tenure males in managerial occupations. Prior to those years, managers were an extremely privileged group. In large companies, they had Japanese-style lifetime employment, generous perquisites, and insulation from market forces. As William H. Whyte observed in 1956, the Organization Man believed "his relationship with The Organization is to be for keeps" because if he was "loyal to the company . . . the company would be loyal" to him (Jacoby 1985: 279). It's not an accident that Whyte wrote his book in the 1950s. The multidivisional or M-form model took hold after World War II, bringing with it an enormous demand for middle managers to hold together increasingly complex and differentiated corporations. The 1950s also saw American companies become increasingly multinational, with a rising rate of foreign investment and consequent need for managerial expertise. At the same time, there was a scarcity of talent. MBA programs had not taken off yet, and the cohort born in the Depression (who were graduating from college in the 1950s) was relatively small. As sociologist Glen Elder has shown (1974), these children of the Depression were obsessed with security, and big American companies were happy to provide it. The result was a golden age for American managers. To some extent the party was paid for by shareholders, who had ceded power to managers. Writing in 1959, Adolph Berle called this "power without property" and dubbed it "a new development in American political economy" (1959).[3]

In the late 1980s, there was a sea change for managers. Managerial hierarchies were gutted as mergers, information technology, and corporate decentralization reduced the need for middle managers. Further down the hierarchy, self-managing teams took the place of first-line supervisors. Meanwhile, MBAs graduating in the 1980s were a different breed, too young to have been touched by the depression and different in other respects from their elders (Mills 1987; Osterman 1996). They were drawn to expanding sectors like Silicon Valley, Wall Street, and management consulting —

places where the upside pay potential was high but where careers were more market oriented than under the postwar model.

Nevertheless, recent evidence indicates that the corporate pendulum is starting to swing back to a concern with managerial retention and development. In most big companies, managerial downsizing is now a fait acccompli. That fact, coupled with tightening labor markets and shifting demographics, is causing a new shortage of managerial talent. "Brain Drain," the cover story of a recent issue of *Business Week* (1999), explains that with the leading edge of the baby boom generation nearing retirement, companies are "moving decisively to hang on to their most experienced workers," including executives over fifty, a group that "until recently was being rushed out the door."

What about nonmanagerial occupations? This is a huge and diverse group, including blue-collar jobs; service and sales positions; semiprofessionals like technicians, teachers, programmers, and nurses; and traditional professions such as law, engineering, and accounting. Most of these occupations remain situated in internal labor markets. While these jobs were never as stable as managerial positions, they were hardly a spot market. In 1979, before restructuring got under way, the proportion of blue-collar workers with tenure over ten years was precisely the same as it was for managers (46 percent); clerical employees were only slightly lower (39 percent; see Farber 1997b).

The big change for blue-collar jobs came in the early 1980s, when there was a wave of layoffs and plant closures that caused enormous pain in affected communities. However, the contraction of blue-collar jobs failed to receive the sort of publicity that occurred a decade later when managerial jobs were on the block. As I have written elsewhere, "only in the 1990s, when professionals and managers were the ones at risk, did the politically influential middle class begin to feel threatened and the media take notice." Another reason blue-collar layoffs did not attract more notice was their consistency with labor's earlier decision to favor income security over job security. As a former Steelworkers official admitted in the early 1980s, "We may have backed ourselves into a corner by settling for income security rather than dealing with the immense complexities of fashioning job security arrangements." (Jacoby 1997: 257, 261).

Since then, however, unions have painfully shifted their emphasis to job security, while U.S. manufacturers have made an equally painful transition to quality production. Now there is a new regard for high-performance work practices such as self-managed teams, job rotation, and problem-solving groups. The use of these practices increased rapidly in the 1980s and 1990s. Cappelli is skeptical that such practices are leading to greater training investments and that they require enhanced employment security. However, recent studies by Paul Osterman and others find training investments to be substantially higher in establishments utilizing high-performance practices.

Moreover, use of these practices is associated with having fewer contingent employees and less outsourcing. That is, high-performance practices solidify the jobs of core employees, sometimes at the expense of managerial positions. Companies adopting these practices have fewer managerial employees and their managerial ranks grew at a slower rate in the 1990s. This is one reason why, since the mid-1980s, blue-collar job displacement rates have steadily dropped while those for managers have steadily risen (although managerial rates remain at levels well below those of manual workers; Cole 1999; Osterman 1999; Erickson and Jacoby 1998; Kletzer 1998).[4]

In service and sales occupations, mobility patterns and job-security measures both show that internal labor markets are being preserved, even as pay becomes more differentiated by market segment. While such occupations continue to have lower tenure levels than managerial positions, they are relatively stable. The fraction of sales and service workers with tenure over ten years held steady between 1979 and 1996, unlike managerial tenure (Batt 1999; Frenkel et al. 1999: 105–6; Farber 1997b).[5]

As for the fast-growing semiprofessional and technical occupations, their skill and education levels are helping to drive the economy. Yet as sociologist Charles Heckscher (1988) points out, "they are semi in that their status is bound up with their place in a particular company, not with universal standards that go beyond the firm" (69). That is, their skills are partially firm-specific and this fact, combined with high demand for their skills, has kept their displacement rates since 1981 lower and less variable than for managerial employees (Kletzer 1998; Frenkel et al. 1999).[6]

Tenure Data

I agree with Cappelli's (this volume) assessment that the "findings of declines in tenure are modest." His caveat — that many of these studies are comparing tenure in the recessionary 1980s to tenure in the expansionist 1990s — does not apply to most of the studies we cite, which either use pre-1981 basepoints or adopt sampling and other controls for business-cycle effects. His second caveat is that rising tenure for women is not due to changes in employer policy but is a statistical artifact: the result of more women not quitting their jobs when they get married. However, the fact is that the rise in female tenure, although modest, is robust and persists even when demographic controls are applied to the tenure data. One of the major growth areas for corporate welfare activity in the 1990s has been "work and family" programs that attempt to accommodate women's career aspirations by making it easier for working women to be mothers. Employers have been spurred to do more in this area partly as a result of the 1993 Family and Medical Leave Act, although efforts started before then. The programs can be faulted for delivering less than they promise, but they are more than fluff. Hard dollars are being spent on flexible spending accounts that reimburse employees for childcare expenses, on greater amounts of paid time for personal and sick leave, and on direct childcare (although this is less prevalent than other programs). The evidence shows that these expenditures are affecting women's career decisions (Hofferth 1996).[7]

Job Attachment Data

True, tenure tells only part of the story and we need to look at other data from which we can infer job attachment. The problem is that these data are more ambiguous than the tenure data. Studies based on the CPS show stability of retention rates over the 1980s and early 1990s; those based on panel data are more diverse, with some showing a decline in retention rates and others no evidence of change. Another approach is to separately examine involuntary and voluntary (quits) mobility. One would expect a rising proportion of involuntary separations to make workers feel less secure, even if total separations have not changed. Here too, some studies find increases over time in the proportion of separations that are involuntary; others do not.[8] One could attribute the lack of consensus to the shortcomings of labor economics, or conclude, as I do, that the findings are ambiguous because changes in job attachment have been modest.

Other studies look at job loss rates using data from the Displaced Workers Survey. The DWS is problematic because there have been changes over time in question wording and survey design. In his analyses of the data through 1995, Farber (1997a, 1998) has made heroic efforts to control for these problems. Farber finds that, until the 1993–95 period, adjusted job loss rates had a strong cyclical pattern, rising during recessionary periods (1981–93, 1989–91) and falling during expansions. The only exception is 1993–95, when job loss rates failed to decline despite the beginnings of what has become a sustained expansion. If Cappelli is right, then the mid-1990s mark the start of an historic shift in job-loss patterns. However, it is also possible that the huge job losses of the mid-1990s were one-time events not likely to recur. The mid-1990s recovery was exceptionally feeble; unemployment barely fell and productivity was weak. Only after the mid-1990s did the expansion pick up steam. Indeed, the most recent DWS data show job displacement declining since the mid-1990s. While the number of displaced workers is not small — 3.6 million individuals from 1995 to 1997 — it is 15 percent lower than the number displaced in 1993–95. Also, reemployment is occurring more quickly than in the mid-1990s, as one would expect given the recent strength of the labor market.

We do need to supplement these aggregate data with analyses of particular firms, both those that are downsizing and those that are expanding. On the former, the Watson Wyatt data on large companies with shrinking employment finds no evidence that mid-career employees have been singled out in downsizing decisions. Consistent with the logic of internal labor markets, the impact of downsizing is still borne by junior workers, and there is no evidence that firms are substituting junior for mid-career employees. Moreover, these large but downsizing firms continue to have higher retention rates than the labor market average. "From a purely statistical standpoint, a worker in the early 1990s had higher odds of staying with [a shrinking firm in the Wyatt sample] than they would have had in any job picked at random." (Allen, Clark and Schieber 1999).

As for companies with job gains, the Wyatt data show that these firms had higher retention rates than those that were shrinking — not only for junior employees but also for those with substantial seniority (over twenty years) — a finding that suggests that internal labor markets are enduring. True, some of these companies are privately held, which gives them freedom to do things that other firms can not. However, ownership is not destiny. There are plenty of publicly held growth companies oriented to employee retention. Even in the high-technology sector, such firms — like upstart Inktomi and giant Microsoft — pride themselves on being "sticky" employers (at least of their core employees). Furthermore, publicly held companies sometimes offer more security and risk sheltering than do private companies. David I. Levine et al. (1999) point out that Wal-Mart's 910,000 employees are "buffered from the external market in ways similar to the traditional internal labor market, particularly as compared to the Mom & Pop stores they displaced."

Pay Data

Not only stable employment, but wages that rise with seniority are another characteristic feature of internal labor markets. The single most comprehensive study of returns to tenure finds that these returns not only have persisted over the period 1975–91, but have actually risen slightly. The picture for young workers is mixed: returns to tenure have fallen for those holding jobs less than eighteen months but have risen for those holding jobs for nineteen months or more (Altonji and Williams 1997; Bernhardt et al. 1998, Teulings and Hartog 1998).[9] Other types of market-sheltered wage practices also are not eroding. Employer wage premiums have remained stable in the 1980s and 1990s. Also, the compensation practices of large and small firms are at least as different in the 1990s as they were in the late 1970s. Big firms continue to pay more and their occupational wage structures have not converged with smaller firms. All of this suggests the continued existence of pay structures based on organizational considerations (Levine et al. 1999; Belman and Levine 2001).

It is true that there has been a movement in recent years toward basing pay more heavily on individual and organizational performance. However, the shift has been monetarily most important for managers. For nonmanagerial employees, performance-based pay, while more prevalent, still affects only a tiny fraction of total compensation. Conversely, job characteristics remain an important determinant of pay. Wage inequality among people with the same job title in the same organization changed very little in the 1980s and 1990s. Also, the use of formal job evaluation plans has increased over the last five years, further evidence that job characteristics still matter for pay setting (Levine et al. 1999).

Conclusion

Most adults continue to be employed in long-term jobs situated in internal labor markets, although they are more exposed to market forces than thirty years ago. Shifting risk to employees is a sign that internal labor markets are adapting to a more turbulent environment, not that they are dead. Managers and executives have experienced major changes in career patterns and pay practices, more so than other groups. To what extent those changes will endure in coming years is, however, an open question.

None of this is to deny that segments of the labor force are experiencing leaner and meaner arrangements. Risk-shifting may sound bland but it does mean more uncertainty and stress for affected employees. For now, the tight labor market has taken the edge off these changes. The general mood is optimistic, much as in the late 1920s, when overall prosperity was combined with sectoral dislocations and risk-shifting in response to market turbulence. Hopefully, history is merely rhyming and will not repeat itself.

Notes

An earlier version of this chapter appeared in *California Management Review* 42, 1 (Fall 1999), © 1999 Regents of the University of California. Reprinted by permission.

1. See, for example, Ohmae (1995) versus Wade (1996); Lange et al. (1995); Erickson and Kuruvilla (1998); Brilmayer (1994) versus Steel (1995).

2. On the rise of internal labor markets, see Jacoby (1985).

3. See Chandler, (1962); Tsurumi (1977).

4. One of Osterman's troubling findings is that use of high-performance practices in 1992 is positively associated with higher layoffs five years down the road, except in unionized establishments. Yet more research needs to be done on this important issue, because the model can't tell whether the layoffs are a result of productivity gains being appropriated by nonunion firms or of declining sales for those firms.

5. The picture for clerical jobs is decidedly mixed: job losses and insecurity for some; higher skill levels and new opportunities for others (Herzenberg et al. 1998).

6. One might argue that the relevant approach is not to look at occupations but at education levels. Yet long-term jobs (over twenty years) are as prevalent for those with twelve or fewer years of education as they are for those with baccalaureate and advanced degrees. Cutting the tenure data at 10+ rather than 20+ does show college graduates being more likely than the less educated to hold long-term jobs. However,

the same advantage existed twenty years ago, before the turmoil in the labor market. Similarly, four-year job retention rates fell in the 1980s for high-school dropouts and high-school graduates relative to college graduates, but ten-year retention rates for college graduates showed a slight decrease relative to the less educated (Farber 1997b; Diebold et al. 1997).

7. Earlier that year Motorola announced that it was opening onsite childcare centers at several of its semiconductor manufacturing plants (*Wall Street Journal*, 1999).

8. For a review of these studies, see Allen et al. (1999) and Bansak and Raphael (1998).

9. The Chauvin study cited by Cappelli is based on manufacturing managers during the period 1979–83, not the best sample for assessing aggregate or long-term trends.

References

Allen, Steven G., Robert L. Clark, and Sylvester J. Schieber. 1999. "Has Job Security Vanished in Large Corporations?" NBER Working Paper 6966.

Altonji, Joseph G. and Nicolas Williams. 1997. "Do Wages Rise with Seniority? A Reassessment," NBER Working Paper 6010.

Bansak, Cynthia and Steven Raphael. 1998. "Have Employment Relationships in the United States Become Less Stable?" Economics Department, University of California at San Diego. 3–5.

Batt, Rosemary. 1999. "Changing Internal Labor Markets in Service and Sales Occupations." *Proceedings of the 51st Annual Meeting of the Industrial Relations Research Association*, Madison, Wis. 237–44.

Belman, Dale, and David I. Levine. 2001. "Size, Skill and Sorting." Haas School of Business, Berkeley, Calif.

Berle, Adolph A. 1959. *Power Without Property: A New Development in American Political Economy.* New York: Harcourt, Brace.

Bernhardt, Annette D., Martina Morris, Mark S. Handcock, and Marc A. Scott. 1998. "Inequality and Mobility: Trends in Wage Growth for Young Adults." Working Paper 8. Institute on Education and the Economy, Teachers College, Columbia University.

Brilmayer, Lea. 1994. *American Hegemony: Political Morality in a One-Superpower World.* New Haven, Conn.: Yale University Press.

Business Week. 1999. "Brain Drain." September 20, 113.

Cappelli, Peter. This volume. "Career Jobs Are Dead."

Chandler, Alfred D. 1962. *Strategy and Structure.* Cambridge, Mass.: MIT Press.

Cole, Robert E. 1999. *Managing Quality Fads: How American Business Learned to Play the Quality Game.* New York: Oxford University Press.

Currie, Janet and Aaron Yelowitz. 1999. "Health Insurance and Less Skilled Workers." NBER Working Paper 7291.

Diebold, Francis X., David Neumark, and Daniel Polsky. 1997. "Job Stability in the United States." *Journal of Labor Economics* 15: 223.

Doeringer, Peter and Michael Piore. 1971. *Internal Labor Markets and Manpower Analysis.* Lexington, Mass.: D.C. Heath.

Edwards, Richard C., Michael Reich, and David M. Gordon, eds. 1975. *Labor Market Segmentation.* Lexington, Mass.: D.C. Heath.

Elder, Glen H., Jr. 1974. *Children of the Great Depression: Social Change in Life Experience.* Chicago: University of Chicago Press. 153–201.

Erickson, Christopher L., and Sanford M. Jacoby. 1998. "Training and Work Organization Practices of Private Employers in California." California Policy Seminar Report, Berkeley, Calif.

Erickson, Christopher L., and Sarosh Kuruvilla. 1998. "Industrial Relations System Transformation." *Industrial & Labor Relations Review* 52 (October): 3–22.

Farber, Henry S. 1997a. "The Changing Face of Job Loss in the United States, 1981–1995." Industrial Relations Section, Princeton University.

———. 1997b. "Trends in Long-Term Employment in the United States, 1979-96." Working Paper 384. Industrial Relations Section, Princeton University, July.

———. 1998. "Has the Rate of Job Loss Increased in the Nineties?" Working Paper 394. Industrial Relations Section, Princeton University.

Fligstein, Neil. 1985. "The Spread of the Multidivisional Form." *American Sociological Review* 50: 377–91.

Frenkel, Stephen J., Marek Korczynski, Karen Shire, and May Tam. 1999. *On the Front Line.* Ithaca, N.Y.: ILR Press.

Herzenberg, Stephen, John A. Alic, and Howard Wial. 1998. *New Rules for a New Economy: Employment and Opportunity in Postindustrial America.* Ithaca, N.Y.: ILR Press: 139.

Heckscher, Charles. 1988. *The New Unionism: Employee Involvement in the Changing Corporation.* New York: Basic Books.

Hofferth, Sandra L. 1996. "Effects of Public and Private Policies on Working After Childbirth." *Work & Occupations* (November 23): 378–404.

Jacoby, Sanford M. 1985. *Employing Bureaucracy: Managers, Unions, and the Transformation of Work in American Industry, 1900–1945.* New York: Columbia University Press.

———. 1997. *Modern Manors: Welfare Capitalism Since the New Deal.* Princeton, N.J.: Princeton University Press.

Kletzer, Lori. 1998. "Job Displacement." *Journal of Economic Perspectives* 12 (Winter): 115–36.

Lange, Peter, Michael Wallerstein, and Miriam Golden. 1995. "The End of Corporatism? Wage Setting in Nordic and Germanic Countries." In *The Workers of Nations: Industrial Relations in a Global Economy,* ed. Sanford M. Jacoby. New York: Oxford University Press. 76–100.

Levine, David I., Dale Belman, Gary Charness, Erica L. Groshen, and K. C. O'Shaughnessy. 1999. "Changes in Careers and Wage Structures at Large American Employers." Unpublished manuscript.

Mills, D. Quinn. 1987. *Not like Our Parents: How the Baby-Boom Generation Is Changing America.* New York: Morrow.

Ohmae, Kenichi, 1995. *The End of the Nation State: The Rise of Regional Economies.* New York: Free Press.

Osterman, Paul, ed. 1996. *Broken Ladders: Managerial Careers in the New Economy.* New York: Oxford University Press.

Osterman, Paul. 1999. *Securing Prosperity.* Princeton, N.J.: Princeton University Press. 103.

Pfeffer, Jeffrey. 1998. *The Human Equation: Building Profits by Putting People First.* Boston: Harvard Business School Press.

Slichter, Sumner H., James Healy, and E. Robert Livernash. 1960. *The Impact of Collective Bargaining on Management.* Washington, D.C.: Brookings Institution Press.

Steel, Ronald. 1995. *Temptations of a Superpower.* Cambridge, Mass.: Harvard University Press.

Stewart, Thomas A. 1997. *Intellectual Capital: The New Wealth of Organizations.* New York: Doubleday/Currency.

Teulings, Coen and Joop Hartog, 1998. *Corporatism or Competition? Labour Contracts, Institutions, and Wage Structures in International Comparison.* Cambridge: Cambridge University Press.

Tsurumi, Yoshi. 1977. *Multinational Management: Business Strategy and Government Policy*. Cambridge, Mass.: Ballinger.

U.S. Department of Labour, Bureau of Labor Statistics (BLS). 1997. "Contingent and Alternative Employment Arrangements, February 1997." Bulletin 98-422, December.

————. 1998a. "Worker Displacement, 1995-97." Bulletin 98-347, August.

————. 1998b. "Work Experience Summary." Bulletin 98-470, November.

Wade, Robert. 1996. "Globalization and Its Limits: Reports of the Death of the National Economy are Greatly Exaggerated." In *National Diversity and Global Capitalism*, ed. Suzanne Berger and Ronald Dore. Ithaca, N.Y.: Cornell University Press. 60–88.

Wall Street Journal. 1999. "No Time for Errands?" March 23, B11.

Whyte, William H. 1956. *The Organization Man*. New York: Simon and Schuster. Reprint Philadelphia: University of Pennsylvania Press, 2002.

Part III
Sector Studies

Chapter 11
Benefits for the Free Agent Workforce

Carl T. Camden

The "free agent" workforce is estimated to comprise one-quarter to one-third of the American labor force. Typical definitions of free-agent workers encompass a variety of workstyles including temporary employees, independent contractors, self-employed, small family businesses, and solo professionals (Pink 2001). Given the size and rapid growth in this segment of the workforce, government groups have started to focus on policy implications of the free agent workforce.

The U.S. Department of Labor's Advisory Council on Employee Welfare and Pension Benefit Plans recently explored issues regarding the delivery of benefits to the contingent workforce (USDOL 1999). The Council concluded that benefits coverage was inconsistent, sketchy, and bound by structural difficulties. Similar conclusions were reached in a General Accounting Office study (USGAO 2000). Nevertheless, by the end of the 1990s when the unemployment rate was low and people were unable to change jobs readily, there was little urgency in the public mind about improving free-agent access to benefits.

As the unemployment rate has begun to edge up, however, layoffs have become common and employment mobility has become constrained. At the same time, employee benefits costs are experiencing double-digit increases (Freudenheim 2000). Now a sense of urgency has begun to build about how to improve benefits for the free agent workforce. This chapter discusses aspects of this workforce, outlines issues, and suggests possible solutions.

Do Free Agent Workers Want Benefits?

Many believe that the free agent worker is critical to economic competitiveness. One argument is that the free-agent labor improves workforce participation rates and reduces unemployment, and enhances productivity and efficiency (Employment Policy Foundation 2000; Jorgensen 1999; Lips

1998). Another is that it increases worker choice (Camden 1998). Certainly it appears that just-in-time staffing has joined inventory and manufacturing as a standard business practice.

Conversely, it could be argued that free-agent workers (e.g., independent contractors, temporary employees, etc.) hold an inferior position in the job market as compared to traditional "permanent" employment. This view might posit that improved benefits access for the free-agent worker would make it too easy for people to work in a less than desirable mode. Some commentators, such as Jorgensen (1999), believe that better access to benefits would decrease the economic advantage to employing free agent workers.

Irrespective of one's philosophical position, it seems inevitable that the numbers and the fraction of free agent workers in the U.S. workplace will increase over the next decade. A recent survey by Kelly Services (2000) interviewed with 1,011 working adults and found substantial interest in this form of employment. The study found that 22 percent of survey respondents identified themselves as free agents, including temporary employees, independent contractors, and self-employed. An additional 17 percent said they were considering becoming free agents (and this was up from 1998, when only 13 percent indicated they were considering free agency). Supporting this trend is research by McGee (2000), who estimates that the number of contingent employees rose from 417,000 in 1982 to over 2 million in 1996. He notes that this group of workers is growing 40 to 75 percent faster than the U.S. workforce as a whole. The U.S. Bureau of Labor Statistics (1997) has stated that temporary employment will be one of the fastest growing employment categories in years to come.

Why Does the Traditional Benefits Approach Not Work?

The traditional approach to employer-provided benefit plans does not work well for most free agent employees because of their rapid turnover. The largest temporary help firm in the United States, Kelly Services, Inc., employs more than 750,000 temporary employees a year, nearly two-thirds of them in the United States. Of these employees, nearly 30 percent of them work on a simple assignment, typically lasting one week or less. Another 20 percent work more than a week, but less than a month, and another 20 percent work between one and two months.

In our estimation, traditional benefits do not structurally meet the needs of 70 percent of the temporary employee base. At best, employer-provided benefits probably make sense for only about a third of the temporary employee workforce. On the other hand, if society does not address the issues of benefits provisions for this growing segment of the workforce, there will be ever increasing gaps in health care coverage, retirement plan benefits, and disability insurance (among others) coverage for the American workforce.

The administrative costs of engaging and then ending a benefits program for such transitory workers overwhelms any potential value from the delivery of benefits for such a short period of time. In fact, Marquand (2000) points out that many insurers are unwilling to work with temporary employees because of the high administrative expense of serving them. Other groups have similar experiences. An American Staffing Association (2000b) survey showed that the average temporary employee works ten weeks for a staffing firm. The Bureau of Labor Statistics' Current Population Survey found that the median average length of tenure of a temporary employee was five months (Jorgensen 1999).

One issue that may surprise many is that the 30 percent of temporary employees who are stable employees is also responsible for generating nearly 80 percent of industry revenue. These employees are often long-term temps by choice, and they prefer the free agent workstyle. Some employers, including Kelly Services, greatly value this group, and seek to provide them employee benefits. Nevertheless, such efforts are sometimes confounded because the underlying attitudes of the free-agent worker may be fundamentally different from those of traditional employees.

Free Agent Workers' Attitudes Toward Benefits

In our experience, a stable group of free agent workers tends to have long tenure with the company and multiple assignments with many different companies during their association with the temporary services agency. However, even within this group, benefit participation rates are lower than those of traditional employees. For example, Lyons (1999) reported that one-quarter of temporary employees who worked longer than a year enrolled in health care plans, versus 61 percent of traditional employees. In the same group, 53 percent chose to participate in retirement benefits versus 79 percent of traditional employees (Institute of Management and Administration 2000).

The lesson is that many free agents opt out of benefits coverage even when it is offered. One reason is that benefits are not particularly important to these temporary employees, even when deciding which temporary staffing firm to work with. Every three years, my firm surveys its temporary employees about the importance of a range of job and compensation attributes. In Kelly Service's last survey, of the fourteen service features, "offers benefits" ranked ninth in importance trailing such features as "timely paychecks," "treats me with respect," "offers competitive pay," and "provides me with enough work assignments." Such findings have been consistent for well over a decade. Even among the highest paid and longest service employees, benefits ranked only eighth in importance.

Other staffing firms also report that benefits are relatively less important for their temporary employees, with pay level and ability to work continuously rating more highly than benefits. Though benefits are sometimes cited as a key differentiation between "old economy" companies (Bowles 2001), this does not seem to be true for temporary staffing firms. In almost all staffing companies, utilization of benefits by temporary employees is low (Marquand 2000).

What Free Agents Want

Our surveys show that most temporary employees seek to maximize disposable income. Within the benefits field, participation rates are typically highest (39 percent) for retirement benefits (especially 401(k) plans where an employer match is provided). Health plan takeup rates are lower, at 25 percent, perhaps because pensions are perceived as "income enhancing" whereas costs for health care insurance premiums are seen as "income reducing."

It seems clear that many free agent or temporary employees could afford to purchase health insurance benefits, but many actively choose not to participate. On the whole, these workers are mainly young, single, and childless, and most have a college degree. Accordingly, they tend to report that they see relatively little value to benefits, regardless of how inexpensive the employee portion of the coverage may be. It is not surprising that this psychographic group finds free agent employment as the best match for its lifestyle. As long as participation in health care coverage is voluntary, participation rates for the free agent workforce will tend to lag that of the traditional workforce.

Some temporary employees can and do receive benefits coverage from other sources. Only 9 percent of temporary employees say they obtain health insurance from their employer (USGAO 2000), but an additional 34 percent report being covered through a spouse, a parent, or another job. What this means is that the employee can use temporary employment to supplement income from traditional employment or sometimes to supplement retirement benefits. As a consequence, some 55 percent of the sector remains uncovered.

Other temporary employees lack coverage because they cannot afford to pay the employee portion of the health insurance premium. There are temporary employees who would like health care insurance coverage but are unable to pay for it given their income. The USGAO (2000) estimated that, of the group who did not participate in their employer health plans, nearly half choose not to participate due to affordability issues. At our firm we find that more than 80 percent of those not covered cite expense as the primary explanation.

The expense problem is not the result of temporary staffing firms failure to cover a portion of the cost of the health care insurance premium. In fact, contribution rates among the large temporary staffing firms average 40 percent (American Staffing Association 2000b). Rather, the high cost of employer-provided health care insurance is simply difficult to afford for employees in low income brackets. Of course, many employees at all pay levels find the affordability of health care coverage a critical concern; nevertheless, affordability may be a greater problem for temporary employees. Approximately 30 percent of temporary employees have household incomes of less than $15,000 as compared to around 8 percent for the overall workforce (USGAO 2000). Even after discounting the overrepresentation of students in the temporary workforce, it is clear that paying for the employee portion of benefits will be a greater challenge for temporary employees than in the labor market as a whole.

Benefits Are Not Sufficiently Portable

An additional reason that many temporary employees lack benefits coverage is that they may work for various different staffing firms within a short period of time. For example, the average Kelly temporary employee works for 1.58 staffing firms in a given year. Employees may also switch between different temporary staffing companies, move between styles of employment, sign up and then disengage benefits, with a wide range of different companies in a short span of time. This may leave significant gaps in benefits coverage. While benefit portability is an important issue for the workforce as a whole (Fronstin 2001), it is essential for the free agent worker.

Some firms have adapted benefit offerings to better address the portability issue. Our firm recently consolidated temporary employee health benefits providers from many different suppliers down to one, and Kelly Services now offers the same basic benefit package to all temporary employees. (Some temporary employees on assignment to specific companies may have available enhanced benefits options.) Each temporary employee working at Kelly Services, in any capacity, has a simple basic comprehensive medical plan available: a Preferred Provider format providing medical and dental services. Perhaps more importantly, the new program is portable if the temporary employee works for someone other than our firm or elects not to work at all. Though this program has been in place for only a short time, early results indicate that participation may nearly double.

A Longer-Run Solution

The needs of the new economy and changes in the workforce imply that free agency is here to stay and is likely to increase. For many entering the workforce today, permanent employment is an unacceptable workstyle. Among employers, especially those whose methods of doing business have been transformed by the revolution in communications technology, it is more efficient to outsource many functions previously performed in-house. An alternative is to use temporary assistance, rather than a permanent, long-serving workforce, to carry out such functions.

Whether dictated by the workstyle preferences of employees, or the profit maximization motives of employers, or both, in many key sectors of the economy, traditional patterns of permanent employment are being replaced by patterns of short-term or transient employment that cannot be readily assimilated by traditional benefit programs. How then can our society provide adequate benefits for this type of workforce? The most appealing solution might be to separate the provision of benefits from the employer; that is, to de-link from the employer the responsibility for sponsoring, designing, implementing, and administering (or arranging for the administration of) the benefits plans.

Such an approach would end discrimination against employees with nonstandard workstyle preferences. Many employees today report they are locked into a particular job because of health benefits or qualifying periods (Reinhardt 1999). This sort of benefits discrimination would be proscribed if intentionally directed against a particular lifestyle, yet it can flourish because of unreflective allegiance to an industrial model of private benefits. That old model was geared almost exclusively to servicing the needs of a permanent workforce popular in the past, but not one sought by employers after the telecommunications revolution.

In a post-industrial economy, one increasingly characterized by a highly mobile nonpermanent workforce, delinking responsibility for benefit coverage from individual employers could permit new institutions to discharge these responsibilities in a more predictable and systematic manner. It is potentially possible that important segments of the working population could then be assured of more reliable and more adequate health and pension coverage than is available today. The first task would be to design appropriate third-party institutions to take over the traditional employer functions of plan design, implementation, and administration; this may be easier to accomplish in connection with health benefits, for which there is already ample precedent. The next question is how such arrangements could be financed. Absent supplemental funding, making pension benefits a function of employment, rather than a creature of employer sponsorship, would lead to nothing more than a glorified version of individual retirement accounts or 401(k) plans without matching employer contributions.

With the possible exception of the TIAA-CREF plan for college teachers and other college personnel, there are no well-established models in the private sector that attract voluntary employer funding based purely on employment per se. A Social Security model is conceptually irreconcilable with a voluntary private benefit system, of course, since it relies on mandatory employer-employee contributions and centralized administration.

Successfully transitioning from employer to employment-based systems will likely require mandatory funding matches from employers, or tax dollars. Special attention would also have to be paid to equalizing the tax treatment of employer and free agent contributions. For example, companies now can deduct fully the cost of the health insurance they provide, but self-employed and temporary workers cannot do so (even if they pay 100 percent of the expense themselves). To facilitate the switch from an employer-based system to one that is employment-based, such tax code discrimination would have to be rectified.

An employment-based system could, we believe, ultimately provide a rich variety of benefit programs and benefit providers, in contrast to the current employer-based system. Initially, of course, it might be necessary to restrict or avoid certain types of benefit design until significant numbers of participants could be enrolled, and reasonably predictable sources of financing are achieved. We do not believe that developing an employment-based alternative would require abandoning the traditional employer-sponsored approach for employers who continue to find it useful. If the goal is to extend private benefit coverage to all types of workers, a diversity of benefits institutions will be required that recognizes that the economy and the workplace have changed.

References

American Staffing Association. 2000a. "GAO Report of Contingent Work Misleading." <www.natss.org/staffstats/release07-28-00.html>. July 28.
———. 2000b. "The Staffing Services Industry: Myth and Reality." Issue Paper. June 6.
Bowles, Susan. 2001. "Benefits Packages Benefit Employers, Employees." *St. Petersburg Times,* January 29, 8.
Camden, Carl T. 1998. "Free Agents by Choice." *New Democrat* 10, 2 (March–April): 16–17.
Employment Policy Foundation. 2000. *Workplace Policies for the New Economy.* Washington, D.C.: Employment Policy Foundation.
Freudenheim, Milt. 2000. "Health Care Costs Expected to Soar; New Year Bringing Higher Drug Costs; Paycheck Deductions." *Milwaukee Journal Sentinel,* December 10, 12A.
Fronstin, Paul. 2001. "Defined Contribution Health Benefits." EBRI Issue Brief. March.
Institute of Management and Administration. 2000. "Three Surveys Analyze Role of Benefits in the Temporary Workforce." <www.ioma.com>. December.
Jorgensen, Helene. 1999. "When Good Jobs Go Bad: Temporary Work and Young Adults in the New Economy." 2030 Center. April.
Kelly Services. 2000. "The Tables Have Turned: Free Agent Workers and Key Employee Shortages Are here to Stay." Mimeo. June.
Lips, Brad. 1998. "Temporary Services, Permanent Benefits." CATO Institute. July 28. <www.cato.org/dailys/7-28-98.html>.
Lyons, Max. 1999. "Long-Term Temps: A Rare Breed." <www.epf.org>. July 12.
Marquand, Barbara. 2000. "Temp Workers Feel Saner Now That the Tight Job

Market Is Forcing Employment Agencies to Offer Attractive Benefits." *Sacramento Business Journal* (March 10): 23.

McGee, John. 2000. "Benefits for Contingent Employees." *Texas Bar Journal* 63, 9 (October): 870–76.

Pink, Daniel H. 2001. *Free Agent Nation: How America's New Independent Workers are Transforming the Way We Live.* New York: Warner Books.

Reinhardt, U. E. 1999. "Employer-Based Health Insurance: A Balance Sheet." *Health Affairs* 18, 6: 124–32.

U.S. Bureau of Labor Statistics. 1997. "BLS Releases New 1996-2006 Employment Projections." News release, December 3. <www.bls.gov/news.release/ecopro. table4.htm>.

U.S. Department of Labor (USDOL), Advisory Council on Employee Welfare and Pension Benefits. 1999. "Report of the Working Group on the Benefit Implications of the Growth of a Contingent Workforce." November. <www.dol.gov/dol/ pwba/public/adcoun/contrpt.htm#item1>.

U.S. General Accounting Office (USGAO). 2000. "Contingent Workers: Incomes and Benefits Lag Behind Those of the Rest of Workforce." Report to the Honorable Edward M. Kennedy and the Honorable Robert G. Torricelli, U.S. Senate. June.

Chapter 12
Developments in
Global Benefits Administration

Manish Sabharwal

The term "benefits administration" covers a wide variety of benefit-related functions in the modern corporation. These may include payroll processing, pension administration, health and life insurance administration, human resource (HR) information systems, and many other functions. This chapter considers global developments in information technology as it is impacting the administration of modern employee benefits.

Developments in the Structure of Benefits Administration

Three important recent developments over the last decade have profoundly altered the philosophy and structure of benefits administration. The first factor has to do with the emergence of integrated providers. Companies have found that it has become extraordinarily complex and costly to deal with multiple "best-of-breed" providers. These concerns also go further, beyond simple cost considerations. For instance, plan sponsors today tend to seek providers that can provide comprehensive and integrated benefits administration functions spanning the range of human resource services, payroll, pensions, health insurance, disability benefits, and others. Such an integrated benefits approach offers opportunities for reengineering and process innovation that might not have existed with traditional providers each of whom offered a discrete and different benefit product.

The second factor changing the map of benefits administration has to do with the globalization of the workforce and the market for product. Greater competition has led large employers with international operations to consolidate and harmonize support functions and supply chains. This in turn spurs integration of their previously loose federational approach across plants and subsidiaries in different parts of the world. An implication for benefits is that the traditional structure of country-specific benefit contracts is being challenged by a new breed of providers who are setting up global operations and managing global contracts.

A last factor that has altered the benefits provider landscape is that off-shore delivery is now commonplace rather than taboo. Countries such as Ireland, India, and the Philippines, have become attractive destinations for data processing hubs, since they challenge the cost structure of traditional benefits providers. Managing benefits offshore can often reduce total benefits administration costs, particularly if the provider firms effectively use technology, customer relationship management tools, and lower labor costs. As a result, the new industrial organizational form makes less relevant the traditional trade-offs between costs and service.

In what follows we outline how these trends are producing dramatic changes in the benefits administration industry, altering both delivery and provider structure.

The Structure of Benefits Provision

Plan sponsors all over the world know that collecting contributions, managing payroll, keeping employee records, and handling benefits functions can be complex, cumbersome, and expensive. In developed countries, the costs of benefits administration and delivery can be as high as $1500 per employee per year. One factor explaining these costs is the continuously evolving regulatory framework facing employers. Other cost drivers include the need to coordinate geographically dispersed operations, handle liability for noncompliance, and provide a verifiable audit trail for human resources (HR), payroll, and benefits transactions. In older companies, the fact that they have inherited legacy computer systems can make it costly to introduce modern information technology (IT) into the HR function.

These challenges are critical in light of the fact that all of human resources management — including pay and benefits — has but one strategic purpose, namely, to recruit, retain, and motivate a high-quality workforce. As a result, we content that other functions such as pay and benefits administration, human resources recordkeeping, and much HRS consulting, can reasonably be outsourced. Figure 1 illustrates the potential range of opportunities.

In practice, this range of choices is translated into four options for benefits administration: in-house, technology outsourcing, administrative outsourcing, or business process outsourcing (BPO). In our view, it seems likely that BPO firms with comprehensive and integrated outsourcing contracts will increasingly assume integrated responsibility for both the technology and functional expertise required to manage one or more HR processes. By offering a common platform wherein data can be shared, sites linked, and results analyzed using one technological framework, the empowering effect of the Internet can greatly accelerate the attractiveness of integrated outsourcing.

As an illustration of this point, Dataquest Inc. (2001) projects that the HR outsourcing industry will grow from $14 billion in 1999, to $38 billion in 2003, a 28 percent growth rate. Web-based HR outsourcing services — a category currently not separately measured — can be anticipated to grow at a much faster rate over the next decade, providing an excellent industry backdrop for companies that effectively use Internet delivery.

More on Integrated Providers

Many plan sponsors today find it almost overwhelming to pick their way through a complex set of multiple arrangements with discrete vendors who are specialists in a single category. Consequently many have sought a single "HR window" with an integrated solution. One factor focusing this pressure is benefits costs: particularly in times of economic recession, many corporations are targeting benefits administration costs for immediate reduction. Costs tend to be driven up due to the need to coordinate and interface efforts across a multiplicity of discrete vendors and few scale economies can be reaped with the many different databases and IT systems.

A second factor driving change is customer demand. Today, employees tend to want more hands-on access to their benefits information and even to benefits choices. Employers too need to respond more quickly to requests for information regarding benefits practices. Employees and plan sponsors also seek data on company policies and practices, and quality of service provided. Substantial dissatisfaction has arisen from having to deal with multiple

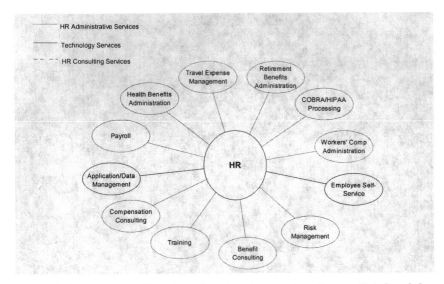

Figure 1. An overview of benefits administration services. Source: Baird and Co. (2000a).

vendors. These pressures are surely driving HR offices all over the globe to seek innovative ways to coordinate worldwide operations, offer organizational design changes, and respond in real time as government regulations change.

Customer confidence with the Internet is also playing a pivotal role in the new benefits delivery format. In the past, an impediment to integrated benefits outsourcing has been access to and control of employee information. Today, effective Internet delivery provides clients with access, reporting, and aggregation capabilities, in a single system. Some argue this is more effective than what was achieved in the past with multiple providers or in-house systems.

Factors shaping the emergence of integrated providers are several.

Higher Responsiveness/Self-Service

A single window for all transactions/inquiries creates an accountability and responsiveness unavailable from discrete vendors. BPO firms have integrated platforms for Web-native self-service that offer round the clock access to company policy (e.g., vacation schedules, training offerings, plan rules), employee information (e.g., payroll, taxation, pension, medical, plan rules, enrollment, eligibility), and management tools (e.g., salary planning, market data, HR reports, performance evaluation).

Lower Cost

Most BPO firms have systems that are integrated or tightly linked. Additional work resulting from having multiple vendors can be avoided, leading to greater efficiency. This includes reductions in transmission loss rework, larger reconciliation efforts, and extensive interface building. In practice, integrated vendors are frequently well positioned to pass on economies of scale.

Best Practice

BPO firms benefit from the scope of their operations, and over time these providers can also transfer learning via best practices, workflow innovations, and best-of-breed formats. Corporate sponsors are increasingly able to reap the rewards of instant absorption of best practice, without the accompanying pain of a learning curve.

Reengineering/Process Innovation

If they were to be set up today, many companies would organize their benefits administration processes very differently from how they currently appear. Legacy systems abound, and often conflict, in a wide range of applications from life to health insurance to pension systems. By contrast, newly created BPO firms are able to offer a reassessment of corporate workflows and policy when the outsourcing is put in place. Innovation can include time clock integration, extended mark up language programs that interface with third parties, integration of payroll and HR databases, and much more. The opportunity for firms to unshackle themselves from inherited systems is increasingly appealing.

Accuracy/Faster Turnaround

Better reporting and real-time information with few errors are highly critical in a fast-paced and competitive environment. As a result, plan sponsors value integrated systems such as a single processing engine and database system for core payroll, benefits, pensions, and HR facilitates. Integration can also lead to faster turnarounds: for instance, the time taken to transfer deducted contributions to money managers can be cut by more than half with an integrated HR, payroll, and pension administration system.

The Emerging Role of Global Contracts

Over the last decade, many multinational firms have begun to integrate operations more tightly, moving beyond the loose federation structure of the past. The first wave of integration and harmonization focused on supply chain and support services like financial control and HR administration. Subsequently, corporate reorganization has become a key driver of global contracts for benefits administration. For instance, many Fortune 500 companies are moving away from a geographic concentration focusing only on Asia, say, or Europe and the Americas, toward product structures instead, such as sports utility vehicles, financial services, consumer products, and so on. Following this trend, support functions, including HR, financial control, and others, are now also being united for management purposes, under the rubric of "shared services." This new shared-services approach simultaneously reveals benefits costs and also requires consolidation essential to take advantage of a single vendor relationship. Heightened merger and acquisition activity therefore support quicker global integration.

Increased global attention to compliance issues is also playing a key role in this integrative process. Global companies, being larger and more visible than average, must be more sensitive to compliance with local regulations. In addition, the regulatory environment imparts another layer of complexity, often requiring intimate knowledge and continuous learning about changing local laws, and imposing substantial penalties for noncompliance. Having multiple vendors also raises the importance of accountability and plan complexity. Payroll processing and benefits administration are more complex than many managers realize.

Finally, of course, concern over cost has spurred changes in the benefit environment. Today most Fortune 500 companies have large global operations, and until now many have duplicated resources across sites in order to improve attention to local customs and compliance liabilities. On the other hand, a single global relationship creates more accountability and allows leverage of the benefits of aggregation.

Cost

The scale of global contracts affords incentives for providers to offer competitive pricing based on the leverage that comes with guaranteed volumes. Such contracts often involve company-specific customization at the time of transition and reengineering.

Harmonization and Integration

Most companies operating on an international scale did not spring into being as multinational organizations. Rather, they grew incrementally over a long period of time. Concomitantly, there has been a growing need to harmonize company-specific compensation and HR practices in this process. This goal will become more salient as new technology and market forces force and permit tighter integration and harmonization.

Reporting/Management Information System (MIS)

Many large firms today have difficulty reporting exact data on workforce and compensation patterns without rather elaborate offline data manipulation efforts. Having a single provider offers reporting flexibility often not available with discrete vendors. A global MIS regarding benefits information is increasingly a key requirement for multinational firms, so global vendors can provide management with the information needed at a global level — a powerful decision-making tool.

Accountability

Single vendors can also provide accountability and quality metrics reporting in consistent, transparent, and enforceable ways. Insuring accountability from discrete vendors in a global context is an ordeal that many corporations would do well without.

Offshore Delivery Systems

The delivery of goods manufactured offshore was the inevitable consequence of emerging markets' cost advantage. This global cost revolution is now being felt in the service industry, as a result of several factors. For one, cost pressures are forcing change. Benefits administrators and in-house operations are under pressure to cut their high per-employee per-month (PEPM) costs.

A second issue is that offshore locations frequently offer interactive alternatives flowing from products generated by the technology revolution. In the past, plan sponsors expressed concern over access and reliability when engaging in offshore benefits processing. But today, the Internet allows for process outsourcing without losing the intimacy required for online operations. Online interactivity and real time processing at lower costs are powerful value propositions. Increasingly powerful scanning technologies also allow for the offshoring of hard copy tasks, without requiring complete reengineering of traditional processes.

Other software developments are also important. This software provides much-needed flexibility to plan sponsors, and they are bridges in the journey to offshore delivery. Innovations such as query writers, relational databases, enterprise resource programs (ERPs), virtual private networks, customer relationship management suites, and others represent powerful infrastructure developments to manage the transition, and for recurring operations. Revolutionary advantages in communications infrastructure also make offshore processing feasible. The most important infrastructure has been high-speed, cross-border leased lines. These provide a reliability that was traditionally not available over public networks in the past, particularly in developing countries. Ideally these are backed up by high-redundancy and disaster recovery arrangements allowing offshore centers to commit to very high service level agreements on connectivity, up-time, voice quality, and other productivity indicators. Increased capacity and lower costs provide very high leverage (see Figure 2).

The value of the demonstration effect cannot be overstated. A number of companies and vendors have successfully migrated their back-office operations from headquarters to offshore sites, at considerable cost savings. Benefit call centers have been successful in Ireland for a long time; the move to developing countries is relatively newer. About five years ago, General Electric Corporation (GE) shifted some of its credit card processing and Call Center operations outside the United States, in particular to India. Today GE has more employees in India than in the United States, many of them concentrated in this service sector activity. Other examples include the e-mail response center of American Online in Manila, the shared services center of Motorola in China, and the American Express call center operated in New Delhi. When early adopters clearly do better on cost and quality, this provides a powerful incentive to those who recognized the value proposition but were uncertain of whether it would actually work.

As globalization spreads and infrastructure improves, many nations are beginning to be recognized as offering important opportunities for offshore benefits processing and delivery. These nations are emerging due to language, technological capabilities, political stability, and human and physical infrastructure. Affordable locations often require trade-offs between the various variables; Figure 3 outlines some of the key evaluation criteria suggested by Nasscom and McKinsey (1999).

Offshore delivery of benefits administration can also provide plan sponsors with several other advantages.

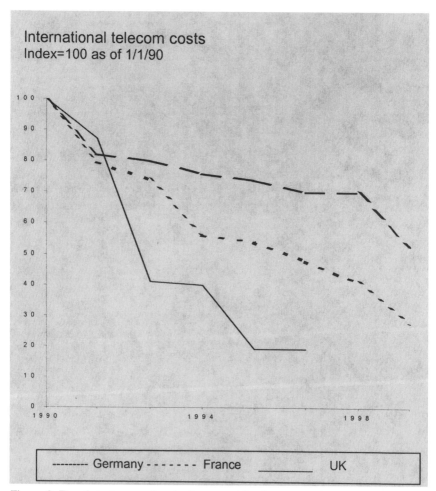

Figure 2. Trends in international telecommunications costs. Source: Nasscom and McKinsey (1999).

Lower Absolute Cost

The first factor determining "total cost" in benefits administration is technology, covering aspects of customization, programming, database administration, and more. A second has to do with the interface, that is, relationship management between employees, employers, and customers. This involves protocol and practice regarding rule set processing, data manipulation, data entry, and other elements. Offshore processing attacks each of these elements very successfully (see Figure 4).

Technology

The human resources function has traditionally used static record keeping, and it has required a great deal of intensive interaction. Information technology is redefining the role of HR by allowing outsourcing of time-consuming, iterative, administrative tasks. It is also being actively deployed for functions like work flow, query handling, and customization. While

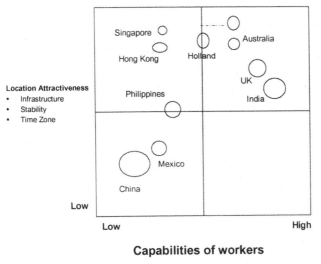

Capabilities of workers

- Qualifications/Capabilities
- Foreign languages (primarily English)
- Quality of work/Work ethic
- Cost differential

Figure 3. Comparing international outsourcing locations.

investment in information technology is often justified by short-term productivity increases, the long-term value of innovative HR systems arises from the renewed capacity of the business function for sustained competitive advantage. Offshore administration allows for the creative use of technology with high levels of customization. Other customization-intensive tasks like employee self-service, interface building, database administration, and network administration can also be done at considerably less costs offshore.

Customer Relationship Management

Traditional HR contracts assumed that there was an inviolable trade-off between cost and service. "High-touch" requirements included interfacing with employees and providing time-sensitive responses to clients at every level.

Today it appears that offshore processing makes this trade-off less relevant since it is based on different, lower cost structures. This change in approach is prompted by customer relationship management offerings via email, live chat rooms, and call centers, all of which are an integral part of

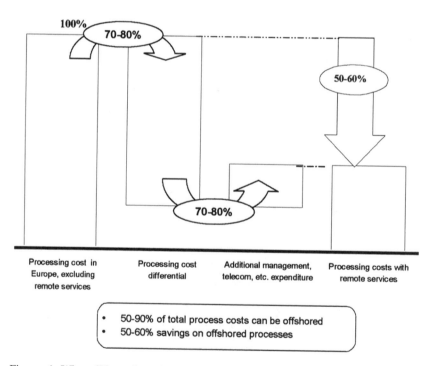

| Processing cost in Europe, excluding remote services | Processing cost differential | Additional management, telecom, etc. expenditure | Processing costs with remote services |

- 50-90% of total process costs can be offshored
- 50-60% savings on offshored processes

Figure 4. Why offshore benefits processing can cut costs. Source: Nasscom and McKinsey (1999).

benefits administration today. Self-service suites and online benefits offices, complemented by offshore live customer relationship management (CRM) personnel, provide the functionality of a live branch while costing much less. Just how cost-effective this new approach can be is beginning to be detailed. For instance, GE estimates that its HR website has cut call volume by 25,000 per month, producing over $2 million in saving. Microsoft Corporation has revealed that by using electronic forms for its 401(k) plan, the employee stock purchase plan, and the stock option plan, the firm saves about $1 million per year in labor costs.

Conclusions

Three developments — integrated providers, global contracts, and offshore delivery — are prompting a new environment for the benefits administration industry. These changes are having a profound impact on costs and value in the benefits administration area. Customers are increasingly pressuring traditional providers, observing their narrow product range, local geographic focus, and slow processing. Of course, traditional providers and delivery structures will not change overnight. Nevertheless, global developments in business process outsourcing are changing the way employees and plan sponsors see benefits administration. Comprehensive and integrated outsourcing contracts will increasingly take over many processes central to the human resources field, enhancing efficiency, driving down costs, and providing better benefits in the process.

References

Barr, Avron and Shirley Tessler. 1998. "The Central Role of Knowledge Technology in the Transformation of HR." Stanford Computer Industry Project Working Paper, Stanford University. September.

Dataquest Inc. 2001. <dataquest.ciol.com/>.

Greer, Charles R., Stuart Youngblood, and D. Gray. 1999. "Human Resource Outsourcing: The Make or Buy Decision." *Academy of Management Executive* 13, 3: 85–96.

Nasscom and McKinsey. 1999. *Findings of Report on IT-enabled Service.* New York: McKinsey, Inc., December.

C. E. Unterberg, Towbin. 2001. *Industry Report on Business Process Outsourcing.* New York: C. E. Unterberg, Towbin, April.

Whitehouse, Edward. 2000. *Administrative Charges for Funded Pensions: An International Comparison and Assessment.* Washington, D.C.: World Bank. June.

Robert W. Baird & Co. 2000a. *The Internet and HR Outsourcing: Business Process Outsourcing Research.* Milwaukee: Robert W. Baird & Co., February.

———. 2000b. *E-Business Process Outsourcing.* Milwaukee: Robert W. Baird & Co. August.

William Blair & Co. 2001. *Research Report on Automatic Data Processing.* Chicago: William Blair & Co.

Chapter 13
Delinking Benefits from a Single Employer: Alternative Multiemployer Models

Teresa Ghilarducci

The United States is unique among developed nations in depending heavily on the provision of social insurance through the employment relationship. That is, the employment nexus is the focus of provision in this country for health and life insurance, disability coverage, retirement benefits, and numerous other programs that, in other developed countries, are often provided at the government level. As a consequence of this country's unique approach, most analysis of the employee benefit environment has focused on how and why a particular employer offers work-based health, pension, and other programs. To date, however, there have been very few studies on alternative modes of benefit provision in the United States, including voluntarily provided employee benefit plans that span employers.

In this chapter we explore multiemployer pension plans in the United States, examining what they do and how they function. A first section assesses the historical development of these plans in the United States, while a second section traces the scope and special features of these multiemployer plans. We next turn to the developments in the employer-provided benefit paradigm. Finally we ask whether a multiemployer format might be general enough to be able to provide coverage to the substantial fraction of workers lacking employment-based pension plans in this country at present, and what role multiemployer plans might play in years to come.

A Brief History of U.S. Multiemployer Pension Plans

Most multiemployer plans in the United States are of the defined benefit (DB) variety. Thus in a typical multiemployer plan, the benefit formula is based on service times a percentage of final salary, much like the final pay-based single employer defined benefit plans. The replacement rate for a twenty-five-year employee depends very much on the industry that the worker was in. A short freight driver in the trucking sector could receive $1,700 per month from his pension, just under his social security benefit and hence equal to almost one-half of his retirement income.

What is unique about multiemployer plans is their diversity. They generally cover many occupations in one industry, one craft in many industries, or many occupations in one industry. Examples of industry-wide, geographically based pension plans in the United States include the United Food and Commercial Workers fund in Northern California, which negotiates pensions and health insurance across a number of large employers including Safeway and other grocery stores. The International Ladies Garment Workers Union and Amalgamated Clothing and Textile Workers Funds cover production workers across a range of employers in the needle trades. Taking a broader perspective, the Sheet Metal Workers, Bricklayers, Carpenters, and other building trades funds cover particular trades operating across a wide range of diverse industries. The Western Conference of Teamsters pension plan covers many occupations in several industries in the thirteen western states — grocery delivery drivers, warehouse workers, and long-haul freight truckers.

Early Developments

During the historical development of union-initiated and jointly agreed upon multiemployer pension plans in the United States, several issues became salient. In the 1880s, labor unions began as "mutual aid" societies, with their major function the collection of funds from members in order to provide collective goods such as funeral benefits. The concept of linking contributions directly to payroll was an extension of this concept of self-help.

The Brotherhood of Electrical Workers and Electrical Contractors (Local 3) of New York was probably the first union to establish a multiemployer pension plan, in 1929 (EBRI 1997). However, this was not an auspicious time since many pension plans disappeared during the Depression due to poor funding records. Other negotiated multiemployer plans were established in the needle trades and in coal mining, and in these industries, unions alone controlled their administration during this early period.

An important legislative innovation in the multiemployer pension business was put in place in 1947, with the Taft-Hartley amendments to the National Labor Relations Act (sec. 302c.5.). Under this regulation, employers sponsoring a multiemployer plan were required to have at least the same number of trustees on the pension boards, as did the union. This bill was initially opposed by organized labor, and to effect passage, Congress was forced to override President Truman's veto.

Many of the regulations passed under the Taft-Hartley amendments were intended to limit union control over the pension assets. These included prohibitions restricting employers from paying pension contributions directly to union leaders, rules holding pension trustees liable for pension decisions, and requirements that rules be applied equitably regarding both employers and workers. Though these regulations were often decried by the labor movement, they provided legitimacy and ultimately substantial strength to multi-employer plans.

While the United Mine Workers of America (UMWA) was not the first group to negotiate pensions in the United States, it greatly helped define the role that unions would have in establishing workplace pensions in years following the Great Depression.[1] Declining coal demand and automation of these dangerous debilitating jobs caused substantial worker displacement during this time. In 1945, the UMWA demanded a fully employer-paid, $100 per month, pension for old and retiring miners, characterizing the demand as "payment for past service." Instead of arguing that pensions were a type of deferred wage (payment for services rendered) that had to be accumulated before paying out a benefit, the UMWA (and many other industrial CIO unions afterward) argued that pensions were depreciation payments owed to labor and were analogous to employers' accounting for capital depreciation (Sass 1997). In this light, pensions could be seen as complements to, rather than substitutes for, higher wages.

The UMWA demanded employer-paid pensions, but plan origins dictated that the coal miners' plan be jointly trusteed with the employers of these constituencies. In the 1940s President Truman delegated his Secretary of Interior to mediate the negotiations in the key coal industry, and he encouraged the relatively weak employers in this vital industry to settle with the powerful union.

Joint pension investment administration was initially not a hotly contested issue because the plans were operated on a pay-as-you go basis — that is, contributions collected were immediately paid out in benefits rather than investing the monies in a trust fund. Coal plan liabilities grew quickly over time as miners lost jobs during the Great Depression. The union negotiated for and won a doubling of the royalties per ton that financed the pension during the period 1948–52. President John L. Lewis argued that employers should share the benefits of automation since workers paid the costs. In an under-appreciated development, the UMWA pension plan negotiated a new funding base where contributions were structured as a function of tonnage mined per hour rather than work hours. This formula explicitly shared the benefits of greater productivity with the workers.

The industrial unions in the rubber, steel, and auto industries were also concerned with bargaining for employer-paid pensions to be paid immediately to current retirees and older workers. As a result, they concentrated on immediate payouts, rather than on building up a stock of assets in a funded plan. These unions did not argue for payments based on productivity nor did they bargain for control of the pension fund investments; in fact weaker industrial unions in a sense gave up control of the fund in exchange for past service credits.

Over this period employers resisted including pensions in collective agreements, but at the same time, pensions became increasingly important personnel and tax reduction tools. The tax incentive was expanded during World War II, with wartime wage/price control policies encouraging companies to boost employee benefits rather than wages. Many economists also argue that tax-favored status of pensions is an important incentive for employers to provide pensions on the margin (Reagan and Turner 2000). Pensions, heath insurance, vacation, and other so-called "fringe benefits" were at that time deemed non-inflationary, and thus they were exempted from wage controls. Furthermore, profits spent on benefits were not subject to the World War II and Korean excess profits tax. In the three decades preceding World War II, the U.S. employer-based benefit system grew to cover two-thirds of the working population for health insurance, and one-half of the working population for pensions. Tax incentives made employer expenses for qualified employee benefits tax-deductible, and as explained above, the labor movement promoted the creation of health insurance and retirement programs at the company and industry level in the 1930s and 1940s. Nonunion companies frequently matched the benefit offerings provided in the union sector in order to remain competitive and thwart unionization efforts.

During this period, many employers agreed to provide employee benefits to attract scarce workers and sometimes to accede to union demands. But social expectations led to the belief that employer benefits were needed to supplement the incipient social security program. Pensions also helped employers manage skill supply and quality in dynamic industries such as construction.

More Recent Developments

The growth in benefit coverage in the United States continued into the late 1970s, but after that something seems to have changed. Pension coverage rates in particular stagnated, and have remained fixed at approximately 50 percent of the workforce. It has been argued that the continuing decline of unions, and the effectiveness of tax incentives available in individual-based group insurance solutions might explain why employee benefit coverage has stopped growing (Schiller 2000). Today some groups in society lack pension coverage, and part of the explanation may be barriers to entry to primary labor markets. About half of male workers today are covered by pensions but only 44 percent of women, 43 percent of Black workers, and 30 percent of Hispanic workers. In addition, the growth of casual labor markets in all industries, especially in fast-growing services and retail trade, may threaten pension coverage. Part-time and low-wage workers are disproportionately less likely to have private benefits as are those in small and medium-size companies. Approximately 90 percent of public sector workers are covered by pensions today, but coverage rates in the private sector go as low as 30 percent and 35 percent in personal and business services and are close to zero in nonunion construction and trade jobs (EBRI 1997).

In our view, coverage gaps in employee benefits track and in fact accentuate the growing inequality in earnings experienced in the United States over the last decade. Some have argued that these gaps may be mainly attributable to worker choices (examples of studies that emphasize employee pension preferences include Goodfellow and Schieber 1993 and Ippolito 1998). Others contend that declining coverage trends reflect employer decisions not to offer plans in view of the rise of what might be termed the "individual responsibility" model. However it is at least possible that multiemployer plans might make it easier for employers to offer benefits that they could not within the single-employer framework. This is mainly because the national social security system, which is national, uniform, and mandatory, cannot be tailored to the needs of particular industries and regions. Single-employer plans cannot accomplish this either in this era, since long service with one employer is not technically practical for many firms. Moreover, even where it is technically possible, workers and firms appear not to want to form such traditional long-term commitments to each other (see Riche this volume; Camden this volume). An alternative model may be better suited to this new environment.

Other Multiemployer Pension Frameworks

Multiemployer pensions are found in sectors other than the private sector: in addition, there are also multiemployer systems in the public and not-for-profit arenas including those established for churches, the Red Cross, charities, and, of course, university and college teachers. There are also hundreds of pension plans covering public sector workers including state, local, school, police, and firefighter employees (Mitchell, McCarthy, Wisniewski, and Zorn 2001). These plans cover many hundreds or thousands of small townships, counties, state agencies, and school districts. In total, there are over 15 million participants in these plans constituting just under 11 percent of all U.S. employees but more than 20 percent of all DB participants. Legislation enabling public sector pension provision varies across state and locality, yet the structure is generally similar. Typically these plans are defined benefit in nature, though all fifty states also offer some form of defined contribution plan in addition.

Some of the largest pension plans in the nation are the long-established church and educational institutions. The Presbyterian pension fund began to cover church employees in 1717. The Episcopal Church plan originated in 1917 with an initial endowment from a wealthy Episcopalian, J. P. Morgan. This plan now covers over 8,000 active ministers.[2] The Episcopal plan is joined by plans from several other religious denominations including the Baptists, Presbyterians, and Methodists. The Church Benefits Association in the United States has forty-five Protestant plans and the Association also includes Jewish and Roman Catholic plans. (Goldman 1996). The Teachers Insurance Annuity Association and College Retirement Equities Fund, now known as TIAA-CREF, had its roots in a system endowed by Andrew Carnegie in 1918 for universities and college teachers. It is technically an association of single-employer plans; but it is clearly one that functions as a multiemployer plan.

When establishing these pension systems, each of the plans had to confront a nettlesome "past service" issue during the plan's startup phase. This refers to the political and practical difficulties of requiring young workers to pay for the pensions of current retirees who never contributed to the plan. In practice, the problem was solved by eleemosynary action in the teachers and church plans (the rich donated enough to cover past service liabilities). However, philanthropists were hiring and not retiring blue-collar workers and their employers. Workers and employers in industries characterized by competition and fluctuating demand either paid labor on a spot market or overcame collective action problems by creating funded pension plans that would deliver meaningful benefits and would be as trusted as banks to handle money well.

The Scope and Special Features of Multiemployer Plans

Our accounting of pension coverage trends over time brings to the fore the importance of the multiemployer alternative. In the United States, the private voluntary multiemployer pension system is sometimes seen as a model for ways to provide retirement insurance in casual labor markets. It is worth noting that the few industries that have continued to boost employee benefit spending faster than cash compensation are precisely those that rely on private multiemployer plans to deliver pensions: construction, wholesale trade, finance, and insurance. The one exception, in finance and real estate, has rising employee benefit shares but does not depend on multiemployer plans to deliver defined benefit pensions.

An assessment of the current size of the multiemployer pension system is facilitated by data presented in Table 1. Information on the nation's 200 largest pension plans provided by Pension and Investments includes church plans (data from the U.S. Department of Labor and the Employee Benefits Research Institute do not). In this table it is clear that the assets of large public plans dominate the top 200 list, followed by corporate plans, union multiemployer plans, and church plans. Over $4 billion in assets is

TABLE 1. Assets of Private Sector and Church Multiemployer Plans Among Top 200 Pension Systems

Name of fund (rank by asset size)	Assets (billions)
1. Western Conference of Teamsters (47)	$23.8
2. Teamsters Central States (54)	21.2
3. United Methodist Church (79)	13.3
4. United Mine Workers of America (121)	8.2
5. Southern Baptist (127)	7.8
6. Operating Engineers CPF (142)	2.5
7. Boilermaker and Blacksmith (148)	4.3
8. Episcopal Church (149)	6.7
9. Presbyterian Church (155)	6.5
10. 1199 Health Care Employees (156)	6.3
11. Evangelical Lutheran Church (162)	6.0
12. Int'l. Assoc. Machinists Natl Pension Fund (168)	5.8
13. Bakery and Confectionery Wrkrs. (169)	5.8
14. Sheet Metal Workers (200)	4.9
Total assets in top 200 in private or church multiemployer plans	$123.1
Total assets in top 200 in Church Plans	40.3
Total assets in top 200 in union multiemployer plans	82.8
Total assets in top 200 in corporate plans	1,577.7
Total assets in top 200 in public employee plans	2,461.9
Total assets in all top 200 pension funds	4,160.7

Source: *Pensions and Investments* (2001: 1).

controlled by the largest 200 pension funds, and most, $2.4 billion, are held by public employee plans. A comparatively smaller portion, $ 0.1 billion, is in private or church multiemployer plans and the rest, approximately $1.6 billion, is in single employer plans. Thus from the perspective of total private pension assets, the bulk is no longer held by single employer plans in the United States.

From other sources, we find that 20 percent of active DB plan participants in the private sector had a multiemployer plan in 1996 (EBRI 1997). This represents an impressive growth since 1950, when private multiemployer plans covered only 10 percent of active pension DB participants, though the trend leveled off since 1960 when 18 percent of the active DB plan workforce had multiemployer coverage. Another way to assess the importance of collectively bargained multiemployer plans is to note that 12 percent (11 million out of a total 92 million) plan participants in any employer-sponsored plan were in multiemployer plans (U.S. Department of Labor 2000).

Almost all workers in heavy construction, shoe repair stores, liquor stores, and others depend on multiemployer plans for supplements to Social Security and their individual savings plans. Among heavy construction, 94 percent of industry workers, retirees, and dependents covered by a DB plan are in multiemployer plans and 55 percent of those participating in DC plans have them through a multiemployer plan. The figures are 59 percent of apparel employees, 73 percent of retail food store employees, and 39 percent of furniture industry participants (Table 2). Table 2 also reports wage rates and shows that earnings in the service and retail area, where multiemployer plans are important delivery systems, are lower than average rate of $13.24 per hour. However, multiemployer plans also deliver pension benefits in some highly skilled labor markets as well.

Collectively bargained Taft-Hartley funds sponsored by the same union in a given craft or industry allow participants to build pension vesting and benefit service while holding jobs with different signatory employers who contribute to the same plan. This is highly effective in facilitating labor supply in decentralized industries with migratory workforces like construction, trucking, retail food, the garment trades, and some of the service industries. This level of local labor market portability in the Taft-Hartley world can be extended geographically through formal reciprocity agreements between different pension plans nationwide in the same industry sponsored by the same union. Several unions actually administer national reciprocity agreements between large numbers of local and regional pension plans with formal dispute resolution procedures.

Scope and Special Features of Multiemployer Plans

Judging from the diversity of plans examined thus far, it might be thought that the political provenance of the multiemployer structure, deriving as it does from the early presidents' coal and steel boards, explains why these funds are jointly trusteed with equal representation from labor and management. This would be mistaken, however, since the essential feature of these funds is that they are voluntary and provide funding for a long-term liability.

Governance and Legal and Fiduciary Standards

Trust law as codified under the Employee Retirement Income Security Act (ERISA) requires that pension plan trustees act according to the "duty of loyalty" principle. This means that trustees must act for the sole benefit of the plan beneficiaries.

In the case of multiemployer plans, management and labor trustees have a common purpose in the pension arena, though they may be opponents on other issues. The plans' unique joint governance structure leads to many special outcomes. For instance trustees from both sides of the table report they have a great deal of influence over the administration of the fund, which results in economic advantage as workers are provided with health insurance and pensions. The legal trust arrangement coupled with reporting

TABLE 2. Multiemployer Pension Plan Coverage and Wage Rates by Selected Industry, 1996

	Multiemployer pension participants as percent of total DB plan participants, 1996	Average hourly wages for nonsupervisory and production workers in 2000
Agriculture	13	$9.21
Hunting and trapping	58	na
Fruit and nuts	55	na
Mining	2	17.04
Coal Mining	10	19.28
Construction	94	17.13
Electrical work, masonry, stone, carpeting, flooring, concrete, roofing, sheet metal, plumbing, heating/ cooling, paper hanging, etc.	97–99	17.43
Highway/street, general building contractors	92–96	na
Heavy construction	73	16.74
Manufacturing Nondurable	7	13.17
Leather products/goods, commercial/other printing	58	9.69
Women's apparel	94	8.41
Durable	4	14.4
Transportation	49	15.67
Trucking	81	13.95
Water transportation	80	na
Public warehouse, terminals	65	na
Pipeline	56	21.79
Communication	0.1	17.38
Wholesale trade	27	14.59
Apparel, piece goods, notions	91	na
Meat and meat products	80	na
Alcoholic beverages	55	na
Retail trade	5	9.08
Drinking places	100	6.62
Meat and fish markets, clothing	97	na
Liquor, new car dealers, grocery, hobby	69–78	na
Finance	1	14.61
Service	29	13.38
Shoe repair and hat cleaning	100	na
General auto repair, bowling alleys	100	11.48
Producers, orchestras, entertainers	99	11.48
Nurses (RN and practical)	94	10.18
Laundry garment cleaning	91	8.76
Motion pictures	78	15.69
Hotels	78	9.22
Nonprofit organizations	1	na
U.S. average	20	$13.24

Source: Column 1: Ratio of total participants in multiemployer DC plans to total participants in all DC plans from Form 5500 Plan data tabulated by author; industry categories based on Form 5500 industry codes. Column 2: U.S. Bureau of the Census (2000). na = not available.

laws makes decisions public and transparent. The equal representation requirements help solve conflict of interest problems, because neither labor nor management can act to benefit their own sides alone. In particular, trustee actions must be transparent and thus the funds must be participant-focused. As a consequence, the multiemployer fund may not forgo contributions in order to benefit an employer or preserve an agreement. In addition the plan governance structure ensures a participant focus by limiting means for contributions to be altered even in the face of potential actuarial gains. Ordinary definitions of prudent investment also apply; there is little difference in the asset allocations of public, private, and union funds.

Solving Collective Action Problems

Employers and workers in a multiemployer pension system pool their contributions so workers are covered by the same provisions, no matter where the job may be, as long as the employer is participating. This will typically be in the same industry and, often, in the same geographic region. Employers in these sectors require workers with similar skills but because of the nature of their product demand, may not be able to hire workers on a long-term basis. In this context a collective action problem exists, such that no single employer has the incentive to provide pensions, health care, or training if the returns on these investments cannot be returned to the sponsoring firm.

Multiemployer plans can be a mechanism by which firms and workers can share costs, thus solving the public good problem and creating economies of scale. Particularly when labor markets are fluid and jobs contingent, valuable skills derived from experience may be lost in turnover. In such a case, occupational loyalty can become increasingly important: the mobile workers obtain portable pensions and are able to save for retirement, while employers obtain skilled workers and a way to share in the cost of training. Thus, the multiemployer plan satisfies these needs by sharing the costs and benefits of increased mobility.

To describe how multiemployer pensions provide security in a dynamic market environment, it is instructive to consider the circumstances of a group of nurses employed in New Jersey health care providers. These nurses have sought inclusion in a multiemployer plan operated by the International Union of Operating Engineers rather than their hospital's single-employer plan, since hospital ownership has changed many times through mergers and restructurings. One nurse noted that she had been covered by six separate single-employer DB plans, but she has no idea of anticipated benefits from any of them. The pension plan administrator observed, "when an industry is poorly managed and unstable the multiemployer plan is the only option for meaningful retirement coverage" (Fanning 2001). Here the multiemployer plan, by virtue of the diversity of its industry base and connection with a long-standing union, is seen as providing a more secure pension promise than the traditional single-employer model.

Hybrid Features of Multiemployer Plans

In a multiemployer model, participating firms pay a specified contribution into the plan according to a collective-bargaining agreement that varies according to bargaining power. In other words contributions depend on the company's relative ability to pay and the union's ability to bargain for benefits (Chamberlain and Kuhn 1986). Thus in the typical multiemployer plan, the employer's contribution is defined but the worker's benefit is also specified — the latter is what makes it formally a defined benefit pension.

In a multiemployer DB plan, an employer would account for pension costs just as in a DC plan, with the amount not determined unilaterally but rather by a collective bargaining agreement. What makes it a hybrid is that benefits are specified as guaranteed annuities, most often based on a worker's service credits, pay, and disability conditions. Consequently these plans are hybrids between defined contribution and defined benefit plans. Most multiemployer plans have a uniform benefit according to the area contract. The employers in a given area tend to pay a uniform rate that may change as a result of varying economic conditions. For example, pension contributions have responded over time to rising health insurance premiums.

The Sheet Metal Workers' pension plan is typical in many ways of the multiemployer model. Here the retirement benefit depends on a formula that includes years of service, hours worked per year (hours over 1,400 per year are credited at lower rates), an adjustment rate determined by an actuary, and an hourly contribution that varies by local. Since contribution rates vary by local (as do wages), plan members with the same career profile but covered under different contracts will get different eventual retirement benefits.

The Central Pension Fund of the Operating Engineers (CPF) and the Western Conference of Teamsters plans tie employers' contributions directly to actual benefits paid. The benefit formula is then based on a rate determined by fund trustees and the balance of a final "account," making this approach analogous to a cash balance plan. For example, the monthly annuity is worth 3.5 percent of a retiree's account balance; if a member works thirty years and has $50,000 of contributions credited from various employers, the retirement benefit would be $1,750 per month (in the 2001 CPF plan). Like cash balance plans, these benefits accrue on a career basis rather than a final average pay basis, and different rates prevail in different contracts, reflecting employers' differential abilities to pay and levels of bargaining power. In the CPF, contribution rates vary from $0.050 to $5.60 per hour; in the Western conference of Teamsters the range is similar, from $0.60 to over $6.00 per hour. The range is similar in the Sheet Metal Worker's plan.

While plan trustees track contribution rates for locals and determine workers' benefits, multiemployer plans are not required to keep records on what each employer pays for a given employee since this is not required by law. In practice, trustees sometimes have difficulties ensuring that employers actually pay required contributions.

Breaks in Service

The multiemployer plan environment has been able to adapt relatively flexibly to changes in the labor market. For example, defined benefit plans typically have rules about "breaks in service" having to do with how long a participant may be out of employment before losing the right to return to the plan and continue accruing benefits. In practice, multiemployer plans have exhibited substantial flexibility over the business cycle in terms of service rules, subject of course to ERISA requirements. During the 1970s recession, for instance, the Sheet Metal Workers Fund lengthened its rule regarding how long a worker could be out of employment before credited service was lost. This produces costs to the pension plan, of course, so other benefits had to be implicitly weakened in reaction. Nevertheless, this flexibility reveals multiemployer pension fund sensitivity to industry needs and worker concern with security.

Disability, Early Retirement, and Unretirement

Multiemployer plans tend to have generous early retirement eligibility and disability rules, reflective of the blue-collar and low-pay nature of the jobs. In addition, multiemployer plans tend to tailor disability and return-to-work rules to the needs of the particular group and accommodate employers' differing abilities to pay. The earliest age for collection of retiree benefits is 62, though employers may offer early retirement bonuses on an ad hoc basis.

Multiemployer plans also have special early retirement provisions that are effective responses to changes in specific industry employment patterns. Recently some Taft-Hartley plans have also liberalized "suspension of benefit" rules prohibiting retirees from returning to work in their career industry, recognizing increases in demand for experienced employees. Other Taft-Hartley pension funds are considering plan redesigns that incorporate deferred retirement option plans (DROPs), which is a way to facilitate phased retirement. Under this arrangement, plans can modify their suspension of benefit rules to suspend only a portion of the benefit based on hours worked. This approach provides greater flexibility to design a program that best meets the needs of the participants.

Another way multiemployer plans have been responsive to the economic environment has to do with "suspension of pension" rules. This arises because of the Employee Retirement Income Security Act, which requires funds to continue paying pension benefits if a retiree returns to work in his same industry but is employed fewer than 40 hours a month or 480 hours in a year. If he should work more than this, the fund can legally restrict his pension benefits until he leaves that employ.

In some sectors the particular threshold chosen to determine whether the pension is suspended, 40 or 480 hours, matters a great deal. For example, in construction, employers often need workers more than 40 hours per month but require them only a few months per year. As a result in that industry, a 40-hour per month rule proves more restrictive than is the 480-hour rule. In practice, since multiemployer plans are managed by employers and unions, the rules are often varied according to labor market conditions. For example, the Central Pension Fund of the Operating Engineers switched from the liberal to the restrictive rule in the 1970s to retard the growth in nonunion construction (Fanning 2001). Likewise during the 1990s the severe labor shortages in most of the major crafts put pressure on the many of the funds to switch back to the more liberal 480-hour rule restriction. The Sheet Metal Workers fund and CPF have resisted the more liberal rules arguing that collectively bargained pensions might subsidize nonunion employers and erode pension contributions, if "return to work rules" are too permissive. On the other hand, many unions have hailed the congressional rule change lifting the earnings test for older workers under social security. Indeed, the Western Conference of Teamsters plan restricts employment eligibility only for members under the age of 65. After age 65, pensions are no longer suspended for delayed retirement (Saunders 2001).

Of course the strict suspension benefit rules can hurt union employment. There are no union employers for which the older individual can work, particularly if labor markets are tight. In such cases, it is likely that the suspension of benefit rules would be liberalized so that pensioners can work without losing benefits. Further having retired union members working for a nonunion employer can improve the chances of successfully organizing. In some cases having a union employee working for a large nonunion company offers "salts" in places the union is seeking to organize.

Reciprocity

Most multiemployer plans in the United States developed reciprocity agreements with each other in the 1970s and 1980s. Reciprocity agreements are arrangements between local unions with different plans permitting continued benefits coverage when each others' members work across jurisdictions. While reciprocity methods vary, the result is that workers continue to be covered when they move between member employers.

Economies of Scale

The average collectively bargained multiemployer plan is larger than the average single-employer plan, enabling this multiemployer format to take advantage of scale economies. Twenty percent of single-employer defined benefit participants are in plans with more than 50,000 participants, while the fraction is 42 percent among multiemployer participants (USDOL 2000). Scale economies are confirmed by many researchers, who find that larger pension plans are less expensive to administer than small plans. For example Hustead (1996) found that small funds (with 15 participants or fewer) spent about 58 percent of normal cost on administrative expenses, while large plans (with 10,000+ participants) spent about 2.5 percent of normal cost. Of course these costs vary with participant mix, since service levels differ depending on the fraction of actives versus retirees (Mitchell and Andrews 1981; Ghilarducci and Terry 1999). On the other hand, multi-employer plans are often regional and the fact that they are sometimes small explains why they were formed in the first place.

Cross Subsidies

All defined benefit plans entail cross-subsidies across members. The clearest one involves transfers between retirees who die earlier than their life expectancy versus those who live longer than their life expectancy. In addition there have been periodic discussions about other types of cross-subsidies in the multiemployer context, such as between large and small employers, or wealthier and less well-off union locals. One case highlighting this issue occurred when the United Parcel Service proposed in 1997 that its employees leave the Teamsters multiemployer pension plan and instead have their own single-employer plan. The employer argued that it was subsidizing smaller employers in that multiemployer framework, a point that the union partially conceded by recognizing that UPS membership helped achieve scale economies. On the other hand, the union contended that without an actuarial study, it was impossible to know whether the resulting single-employer plan would provide benefits that were as least as good, for less money. In addition, the UPS workers would lose their trustee representatives in a single-employer plan, which they believed would affect the chances of their receiving ad hoc COLA increases in their pension benefits, and portability rights to other participating employers would also be lost.

In another context, some members of the Central Pension Fund (CPF) of the Operating Engineers have experienced higher levels of contributions and growth than others, leading to some concern that they are "carrying" the poorer and shrinking locals. In this case too, some eighty actuarial studies would have to be conducted to determine whether each local's past and projected experience would yield better benefits than under the CPF.

Thus far no study has been conducted of the cross-subsidies and how they would be unwound if the parent plan were to be broken up.

In the Episcopal Church, there is an explicit policy of redistribution between higher- and lower-paid clergy. This is evident in the pension formula, where the basic benefit consists of a higher percentage (1.75 percent) of the average of the highest seven years for the first $10,000 of salary, but 1.5 percent for pay beyond that. The benefit is not indexed to inflation formally, but the Episcopal fund has provided an ad hoc cost of living adjustment since 1980 by issuing a "13th check" that is based on years of service. Within every level of service, the 13th check is the same, however (e.g., a minister with a $7,000 benefit will get the same amount as one with a $30,000 benefit; Blanchard 2001).

Inflation Protection

The inflation protection provided by multiemployer pension plans is worth highlighting since it contrasts with corporate plan behavior. As mentioned above, there is no mechanism to stop contributions to the pension trust once these are set by a collective bargaining agreement. As a result, multiemployer trustees can and often do raise retiree benefits to compensate for inflation losses. These inflation payments can be made via the "13th check" discussed above, or an ad hoc basis by issuing benefit increases that depend on the retiree's years of credited service and age.

Joint Governance and Trust Fund Structure

The multiemployer governance structure can permit the sharing of investment gains between workers and employers. In practice, multiemployer DB plans have passed on more pension fund investment gains to participants than have single employers. Thus between 1984 and 1996, single-employer DB plan contributions per participant fell 29 percent, while multiemployer plan contributions fell by 37 percent. Despite this, benefits in multiemployer plans grew 26 percent versus only 6 percent in corporate DB plans. During the same period, multiemployer DC plan contributions rose 8 percent, while (contrary to popular belief) corporate employers cut back on DC contributions by 20 percent; see Table 3.

There are also differences in behavior when a pension plan is overfunded. If robust investment earnings cause the pension fund assets to surpass 150 percent of liabilities, this eliminates tax deductibility of further contributions. In such a case, contributions must be cut, or benefits can be boosted. In practice, multiemployer plans tend to increase benefits or slow down employer contribution increases in the next round of collective bargaining. By contrast, corporate employers tend mainly to cut back on contributions. As a result, jointly trusteed plans pass on pension funds gains

TABLE 3. Pension Generosity, Employer Contributions, and Worker Contributions to Pension Plans by Sponsor Type, selected years 1984–96 (2000 dollars, data weighted by share of active participants in group)

Top 1000 corporate pension plans (by asset size)	Real change (1984–1996)	1984	1996
Defined benefit plans			
Total employer contributions per total participants*	–0.29	$3,379	$2,394
Average generosity** (normal cost/ active participant)	0.06	2,224	2,356
Defined contribution plans			
Total employer contributions per total participant	–0.20	2,924	2,327
Worker contributions per active participant***	0.51	1,907	2,879
Top 100 Multiemployer Pension Plans (by asset size)			
Defined benefit plans			
Total employer contributions per total participant	–0.37	3,104	1,962
Average generosity (normal cost/ active participant)	0.26	1,399	1,763
Defined contribution plans			
Total employer contributions per total participant	0.08	2,679	2,901
Worker contributions per active participant	5.633	3.3	189

Source: Author's tabulations, Form 5500 data. Obvious outliers were omitted when employer contributions per participant exceeded $20,000 and when total participants, generosity, and worker contributions were negative.
Notes:
* Employer contributions are measured as the sum of Form 5500 item 32a(1a) and item 32a(2). Total participants include total active participants (item 7a(4)) and total retirees (item 7b).
** Normal cost is defined as item 9b in Form 5500 Schedule B filings.
*** Worker contribution is defined as item 32a(1b) in Form 5500 filings.

to participants while single employers tend to pass these gains to shareholders and owners. These differences between corporate and multiemployer plan trends are due to differences in contribution structure, the fact that multiemployer plans have a more transparent pension decision-making structure, and the fact that multiemployer trustees tend to be held more accountable by plan participants. As a result, the two plan structures appear to behave differently in the face of similar economic shocks.

Challenges to the Employer-Based Benefit Paradigm and Implications for Multiemployer Plans

As noted above, pension coverage in the United States remains voluntary, and has leveled off at around 50 percent of the workforce. The fact that coverage has not risen despite a booming economy and labor shortages in some sectors has suggested to some that the employer-based pension system may have become too inflexible to accommodate the new workplace realities. Further evidence of the changed benefit paradigm can be seen in the pension arena where worker participation in DC plans has risen dramatically and fallen in DB plans (Mitchell and Schieber 1998; Turner 1993; Turner and Watanabe 1995). The shift toward DC plans and the popularity of 401(k)s also represents a move away from group-based solutions to insurance to individual-oriented solutions. This is reflected in the fact that the overall fraction of pay going to benefits has declined over time: the share of total compensation going to benefits survey declined from 42 percent to 37 percent between 1989 and 1999 (U.S. Chamber of Commerce 1999). Conversely, cash compensation dominates in casual, short-term, spot labor markets, and this benefit decline is not merely an artifact of the fastest growing industries and occupations. At the same time, the business community has been rethinking its role and its social obligation in sponsoring employee benefits.

Explanations for Shifts in the Benefits Paradigm

Various explanations have been offered for these changes in the U.S. benefits environment. Some argue that the "social contract" is being realigned between workers and employers, while other commentators argue that the traditional social contract has collapsed (Osterman 1999). It may be that increased worker mobility is driving the trend to DC plans, because pensions now need to be delinked from a single employer. Some weaknesses of the DB system may also have eroded worker confidence that employers are committed to pensions, including the lack of regular cost-of-living increases and the evidence that employers have taken contribution holidays in the last decade. Of course, the 1990s bull market may have led some to discount the investment risk inherent in DC plans. In general, these explanations point to workers as agents of change. That is, the "individual responsibility" framework is the logical result of more independent "new-economy" workers rejecting traditional benefits like health insurance and pensions and paternalistic social contracts.

Another explanation for the rise of the individual responsibility model is that worker bargaining power has fallen over time. Employer norms, needs, and increased market power relative to workers has diminished employer willingness to sponsor work-based insurance programs. To illustrate this point, when workers express their choices via unions and collective bargaining, they favor benefits and have over 30 percent more compensation in employee benefits.[3] Additionally, they select DB plans with supplemental DC programs.

Some policymakers contend that it would be useful to encourage the move to separate employee benefits from the employment relationship. Examples of this approach in the private sector include proposed legislation for personal tax credits for individual employee benefits, the growth of medical savings accounts, and E-commerce individual health plans. Also private sector trends toward individual responsibility have been manifested in the outright elimination of DB pensions and retiree health coverage.The largest private sector employer, Wal-Mart, with over 850,000 employees, provides health insurance to less than 40 percent of its workforce, and instead the company sponsors individual account savings plans dominated by investments in its own corporate stock. In the public sector this trend is also seen, with DC pensions being adopted in Florida and Michigan.

On the other hand, there is evidence contradicting the view that benefit trends result from employee pressure to adopt the individual responsibility model. Labor economists tentatively agree that job instability is increasing,[4] which could mean either that workers are voluntarily leaving their jobs after shorter periods of employment, or that firms are offering low-commitment relationships. The jobs where instability has increased are particularly those for whom pension accruals might be thought to be the most crucial: for men age 45–54 and 55–64, and particularly for African-American men. Workers with more than nine years of service are those on the brink of vesting, but this group is experiencing the largest declines in job stability. Women and workers with less than two years of service have been least affected. Occupational data show managerial and clerical job security falling significantly but less than for service and blue-collar workers (Neumark 2000). In sum, the increase in cash-intensive pay and job instability suggests that employer commitment to workers over the long term is waning.

While the future cannot be predicted, it may be that the individual responsibility model of employee benefits will be short-lived. This is because the unprecedented economic growth and booming stock market of the last two decades provided a best-case incubator for the rapid expansion and acceptance of individual-account DC pensions. These trends were also

facilitated by substantial market deregulation and declining rates of unionization in the labor force. If the economy is to sustain a prolonged stock
market downturn or a severe recession, this will test worker tolerance for
risk that individual account pension plans have shifted to employees.

Advantages to Participants

Several important risks must be managed in a work-based pension scheme:
employment, investment and default, consumer, longevity, inflation, and
heuristic risks. Multiemployer plans' contribution and governance structure and transparency of fiduciary decisions work to workers' and retirees'
advantage by maximizing pension income and minimizing many of these
risks.

Employment risk is important for those covered by corporate DB plans
because the benefit accrual pattern is backloaded, and benefits are worth
less if the worker leaves the firm before accumulating meaningful credits
or account balances. While 401(k) and other DC plans minimize this risk,
retirement balances may be eroded if people cash out their lump sums
when changing jobs. Multiemployer plans, on the other hand, mitigate this
employment risk as long as the worker remains covered by contributing
employers.

Investment and default risks are protected against in all U.S. DB plans
since the retirement benefit is guaranteed by the fund, and backstopped by
the Pension Benefit Guaranty Corporation in the event of asset insufficiency.

Consumer risk refers to participants' exposure to excessive administrative
expenses that retail savers might otherwise face. DB plans and profession-
ally administered DC plans can minimize such consumer risk in contrast
to self-directed individual plans, via economies of scale and professional
monitoring.

Longevity risk concerns the risk that retirees outlive their accounts. DB
plans generally pay life benefits, protecting against this concern, whereas
DC plans are far less likely to provide annuity payouts. In this sense DB
plans offer a risk pool better protecting plan participants.

Inflation risk has to do with the fact that over a long retirement period,
benefits fixed in nominal terms will suffer eroding purchasing power. It
appears that, in practice, multiemployer plans do a far better job than do
corporate DB plans in protecting against this risk.

Heuristic risk is another concern in pension plan design. This arises,
for instance, due to bias toward saliency, loss aversion, undue optimism,
and other factors under current investigation in the behavioral finance literature. It is been suggested that participants in self-directed pension plans,
particularly 401(k)s, may see depressed investment returns because they
tend to make wrong choices, trade and borrow too much, engage in market
timing, and experience high costs of trading (Bureau of National Affairs

2001). Evidently the DB model is superior on this count inasmuch as participants do not make individual investment decisions about their pension assets.

In sum, under DB plans workers are protected from some of the risks they bear in DC plans, and multiemployer DB plans can play a role mitigating all of these.

Advantages to Employers

Some employers, particularly smaller ones, can find substantial advantages to joining a multiemployer plan. This is because the multiemployer structure allows them to provide pensions to themselves, office staff, and their workers efficiently, and help solve labor supply problems.

One way in which pensions are beneficial to employers is that having a pension plan tends to cut down on worker mobility. As a consequence, employers can invest in employee training in the expectation that these workers will be there in years to come. Such "win-win" trades help make the economy more productive (Ghilarducci and Reich 2001).

Another way multiemployer plans help employers manage the supply of labor is through reciprocity. This means that skilled workers from one geographic region can work in another geographic region without losing benefit coverage. This has proven useful in industries experiencing substantial volatility such as in construction. For instance, the University of Notre Dame is adding an extension to its football field, something the university does only once or twice a century. As a result, the handful of bricklayers and masonry workers in South Bend cannot meet the demand and workers had to be imported from other regions. During this time, work in South Bend still counts toward service credit in their home pension plan. Such pension reciprocity in regional multiemployer plans keeps employers and workers from overspending on training, and helps protect workers from fluctuations in earnings.

Pensions and the Income of the Elderly

Concern over the well-being of the elderly also motivates concern over the lack of growth in employment-based pension coverage. Pensions today represent two-fifths of retirement wealth for the average American household on the verge of retirement (Moore and Mitchell 2000). Sltottje, Woodbury, and Anderson (2000) show that only Social Security and the ownership of primary residence does more to counteract the unequalizing effects of business assets and stocks and bonds on income and wealth inequality among elderly Americans. Employment-based pension income is less equally distributed than total retiree income, an unsurprising finding since those in higher tax brackets have more incentive to shelter pay in pension plans.

The Future of Multiemployer Plans

Because growth in U.S. pension coverage has apparently stalled, several groups have called for a new institutional framework that can serve to increase coverage among the noninsured. As ERISA attorney Michael Gordon has noted, this requires devoting attention to "the twin areas" of small business and the nontraditional workforce (Gordon 2000). He notes that in single-employer plans, benefit provision is often motivated by corporate tax breaks for pension contributions. By contrast, high turnover rates among small businesses render such incentives rather valueless. Instead, Gordon posits that the multiemployer model could be extended by offering tax incentives to workers and small employers for participation in a new form of statutorily approved multiemployer plan. Gordon claims that some representatives of collectively bargained multiemployer plans would welcome employers not in a collectively bargained agreement. This would permit employees to have complete portability between member employers, akin to the voluntary plans in Europe.

One disadvantage to pooling is that firms have to overcome competing with one another in order to coordinate the establishment of plans. Unfortunately these barriers are so high that most multiemployer plans are coordinated by a union or are in a nonprofit setting. The exceptions are public sector multiemployer plans where governing bodies initiate the coordination. Another disadvantage, related to the first, is that the arrangements are voluntary. When one firm views its liability as much less than average they will have incentive to leave. (The adverse selection problem is one reason that Social Security, unemployment insurance, workers' compensation, and the like have been structured as mandatory programs.)

From one perspective it would seem that individual-oriented plans would be chief competitors and substitutes for multiemployer plans. After all, single-employer pensions cover the worker population relevant to a given firm. But perceived barriers to expansion of group-based multiemployer pensions may be turned around to help create them. The popularity of 401(k) and 403(b)s stress their portability advantages, while stock market volatility highlights their disadvantages. Multiemployer hybrids, with portability and defined benefit features, may look better in contrast.

Moreover, much of the focus on these plans is mainly because of the technologies that can make them more visible. Because of this narrow focus, workers have a difficult time seeing how their 401(k) plan fits in with their entire package of employer benefits. It is possible that instead of being a barrier to the creation and maintenance of multiemployer plans, multiemployer plan sponsors can facilitate employee education and provision of a range of benefits. There are at least eleven different types of multiemployer plans including pensions. Employers would gain from using the technology to help workers recognize and appreciate all the noncash compensation provided.

Perhaps the technology allowing individuals and employers to find medical plans on the Internet do what group-based employer plans did, which is to get economies of scales. Perhaps the technology allows individual arrangements to be cheaper than employer-coordinated plans. The fundamental impetus for employers to combine and provide pensions is not economies of scale but to restrain competition and the "race to the bottom." The most profitable short-term strategy is to provide no benefits at all and get market share with low prices. But employers from the beginning of the Industrial Revolution knew competition through cost cutting was cannibalism. Taking wages and service and skill-related compensation out of competition, the industry can invest in more capital and training.

Multiemployer plans may become a key labor-organizing tool in the Silicon Valley. Amy Dean, president of the South Bay Central Labor Council, AFL-CIO, promotes multiemployer plans because of the chronic lack of coverage by small employers. "There is potential for taking advantage of economies of scale in administrative costs by pooling small employers in the same industry together thereby increasing the portability of pensions" (Brenner et al. 1999: 67). The union-based organization, Working Partnerships, USA envisions employer-training networks to be connected to the health and pension consortiums.

Conclusion

In our view, the increasing prevalence of cash compensation and the decline of employee benefits as a fraction of payroll are attributable to a sea change in the nature of the employer-employee relationship in the U.S. labor market. In contrast to years gone by, a lifelong mutual commitment between firms and workers is no longer the norm. The multiemployer benefit framework, in our view, offers an important exception to this trend.

Although multiemployer plans in both the private and public sectors cover very different types of workers, from janitors to university presidents, they are similar in that they solve three key problems. First, but perhaps least important, multiemployer plans can take advantage of savings on large group annuities and professional management fees. Second, multiemployer plans recognize the skill management and insurance needs of a heterogeneous workplace, where patterns differ by unique industry/occupation. Third, multiemployer plans can help solve the collective action problem: that is, no one employer may have an incentive to provide benefits or training without its competitors doing so, so joint action can be efficient for all.

The continuing importance of negotiated multiemployer plans attests to how a central agent, such as a union, can offer a key benefit function in the service of employees and also of assistance to employers. Compared to the one-size-fits-all structure of Social Security, multiemployer plans can adapt to the idiosyncrasies of particular industries and occupations. In this sense, delinking pensions from the single employer via multiemployer plans may hold out hope to resolving portability and income security problems. Multiemployer plans may also serve as a model for expanding social insurance across employers. These plans do what human resource experts and industrial innovation experts say must be done: the plans can lower the cost of training by reducing the chance of workers leaving the industry or occupation.

Notes

1. In the 1930s and 1940s the UMWA covered a majority (80 percent) of mineworkers. The union was so wealthy that it helped organize emerging unions in the Congress of Industrial Organization (CIO) which covered workers in the rubber, steel, and auto industries. In the mid 1940s, the UMWA directed its bargaining power toward pensions.

2. The Episcopal Church plan idea came from a patron who noticed "that pastors and priests were working way past their age of effectiveness and they wanted to help people retire at a reasonable age. The age was set at 68." Human resource management needs therefore shaped the development of this clergy plan.

3. The difference in benefits is substantial if one compares them across union and nonunion sectors. For example union workers had 37 percent of compensation devoted to benefits versus 29 percent for nonunion manufacturing employees in 1999. This gap persists in non-manufacturing where benefits make up 33 percent of union workers' compensation and 25 percent of workers' remuneration (USBLS 1999). The positive union effect on benefits may result from the workings of group processes enabling workers to overcome myopia and overoptimism regarding risks due to poor health, disability, and retirement. Economies of scale may also explain the relative growth in benefits in multiemployer settings. In addition, unions provide job protection and "voice," helping form training and deferred compensation agreements.

4. Job tenure among men has fallen over time in the U.S. For example, average seniority on the job for men age 45–54 fell from almost 13 years to over 9 years. Among men age 55–64, average seniority was over 15 years in 1983, but had dropped to 11 by 1998. Among women, by contrast, tenure has increased by 5 percent over this same period, with the largest increases seen among older women workers (USBLS 1998).

References

Blanchard, Alan. 2001. Administrator for the Episcopal Pension Fund. Personal interview with Ghilarducci, February 23.

Brenner, Chris, Bob Brownstein, and Amy Dean. 1999. *Walking the Lifelong Tightrope.* San Jose, Calif.: Working Partnership USA and Economic Policy Institute.

Bureau of National Affairs. 2001. "Offering Internet Access to 401(k) Plans Can Bring out the Day Trader in Employees." *Pension and Benefits* 1, 38 (February): 6.

Camden, Carl T. This volume. "Benefits for the Free Agent Workforce."

Chamberlain, Neil and James W. Kuhn. 1986. *Collective Bargaining.* 3rd ed. New York: McGraw-Hill.

Copeland, Craig. 2000. "Pension Coverage." EBRI Notes. Washington, D.C.: Employee Benefits Research Institute. September.

Employee Benefit Research Institute (EBRI). 1997. *Fundamentals of Employee Benefit Programs.* 5th ed. Washington, D.C.: Employee Benefit Research Institute.

Fanning Mike. 2001. Administrator for the Central Pension Fund of the International Union of Operating Engineers. Personal interview with Ghilarducci, February 20.

Ghilarducci, Teresa and Michael Reich. 2001. "Multiemployer Plans as Solutions to Pension and Training Collective Action Problems." *Journal of Labor Research* 22, 3 (Summer): 615–34.

Ghilarducci, Teresa and Kevin Terry. 1999. "Scale Economies in Union Pension Plan Administration." *Industrial Relations* 38, 1 (January): 11–17.

Goldman, T. R. 1996. "God Squad; Church Alliance; Acting on Behalf of the Church Benefits Programs." *Legal Times* (American Lawyer Newspapers Group), February 19.

Goodfellow, Gordon P. and Sylvester J. Schieber. 1993. "Death and Taxes: Can We Fund for Retirement Between Them?" In *The Future of Pensions in the United States,* ed. Ray Schmitt. Pension Research Council. Philadelphia: University of Pennsylvania Press. 126–187.

Gordon, Michael S. 2000. Testimony on "ERISA at 25; Has the Law Kept Pace with the Evolving Pension and Investment World?" U.S. Congress, 106th Congress, Subcommittee on Employer-Employee Relations, Committee on Education and the Workforce, U.S. House of Representatives, February 15.

Greenough, William C. 1959. *Retirement and Insurance Plans in American Colleges.* New York: Columbia University Press.

Hustead, Edward C. 1996. *Pension Plan Expense Study.* Completed for the Pension Benefit Guaranty Corporation. Hay Huggins Consulting Group. Washington D.C.

Ippolito, Richard A. 1998. *Pension Plans and Employee Performance* Chicago: University of Chicago Press._

Mitchell, Olivia S. and Emily Andrews. 1981. "Scale Economies in Private Multi-Employer Pension Systems." Industrial and Labor Relations Review 34: 522–30.

Mitchell, Olivia S., David M. McCarthy, Stanley C. Wisniewski, and Paul W. Zorn. 2000. "Developments in State and Local Pension Plans." In *Pensions in the Public Sector,* ed. Olivia S. Mitchell and Edwin C. Hustead. Pension Research Council. Philadelphia: University of Pennsylvania Press. 11–40.

Mitchell, Olivia S. and Sylvester J. Schieber, eds. 1998. *Living with Defined Contribution Plans.* Pension Research Council. Philadelphia: University of Pennsylvania Press.

Moore, James F. and Olivia S. Mitchell. 2000. "Projected Retirement Wealth and Saving Adequacy." In *Forecasting Retirement Needs and Retirement Wealth,* ed. Olivia S. Mitchell, P. Brett Hammond, and Anna M. Rappaport. Pension Research Council. Philadelphia: University of Pennsylvania Press. 68–94.

Neumark, David, ed. 2000. *On the Job: Is Long-Term Employment a Thing of the Past?* New York: Russell Sage Foundation.

Observatoire des Retraits. 1999. *The European Union and Retirement Pensions.* Paris. No. 11, March.

Osterman, Paul. 1999. *Securing Prosperity.* Princeton, N.J.: Princeton University Press.

Pensions and Investments. 2001. "Steady as She Goes: Assets for Top 200 U.S. Funds Pass $4 Trillion." January 22.

Reagan, Patricia B. and John A. Turner. 2000. "Did the Decline in Marginal Tax Rates in the 1980s Reduce Pension Coverage?" In *Employee Benefits and Labor Markets in Canada and the United States,* ed. William Albert and Stephen A. Woodbury. Kalamazoo, Mich.: W.E. Upjohn Institute for Employment Research. 475–96.

Riche, Martha Farnsworth. This volume. "The Demographics of Tomorrow's Workplace."

Rosen, Sherwin. 2000. "Does the Composition of Pay Matter?" In *Employee Benefits and Labor Markets in Canada and the United States,* ed. William Albert and Stephen A. Woodbury Kalamazoo, Mich.: W.E. Upjohn Institute for Employment Research. 13–30.

Sass, Steven A. 1997. *The Promise of Private Pensions: The First Hundred Years.* Cambridge, Mass.: Harvard University Press. 139–59.

Saunders, Mike. 2001. Personal interview with Ghilarducci, February 27.

Schiller, Robert. 2000. *Irrational Exuberance.* Princeton, N.J.: Princeton University Press.

Slottje, Daniel, Stephen A. Woodbury, and Rod W. Anderson. 2000. "Employee Benefits and the Distribution of Income and Wealth." In *Employee Benefits and Labor Markets in Canada and the United States,* ed. William Albert and Stephen A. Woodbury. Kalamazoo, Mich.: W.E. Upjohn Institute for Employment Research. 349–78.

Turner, John A. 1993. *Pension Policy for a Mobile Labor Force.* Kalamazoo, Mich.: W.E. Upjohn Institute for Employment Research.

Turner, John A. and Noriyasu Watanabe. 1995. *Private Pension Policies in Industrialized Countries: A Comparative Analysis.* Kalamazoo, Mich.: W.E. Upjohn Institute for Employment Research.

U.S. Bureau of the Census. 2000. *Statistical Abstract of the United States.* Washington, D.C.: U.S. Government Printing Office.

U.S. Chamber of Commerce. 1999. *Employee Benefits Survey 1999 and Annual Benefits Report.* Washington, D.C.: U.S. Chamber Research Center.

U.S. Department of Labor. 2000. *Private Pension Plan Bulletin 9* (Winter 1999-2000). Final 1996. Pension Benefits and Welfare Administration, Washington, DC: U.S. Government Printing Office: P. 5 (Table A2.)

U. S. Department of Labor, Bureau of Labor Statistics (BLS). Various years. *Employment Cost Index.* Washington, D.C.: U. S. Department of Labor.

———. Job Tenure. <stats.gov/news.release/tenure>.

Woodbury, Stephen A. 1983. "Substitution Between Wage and NonWage Benefits." *American Economic Review* 73 (March): 166–82.

Contributors

David S. Blitzstein is Director of the United Food and Commercial Workers International Union (UFCW) Negotiated Benefits, where he advises local unions in collective bargaining on pension and health insurance issues and consults with the union's 150 jointly trusteed health and welfare and pension plans nationwide. He is also a trustee of the $3.5 billion UFCW Industry Pension Fund and the UFCW National Health and Welfare Fund. He represents the UFCW as a member of the working committee of the National Coordinating Committee for Multiemployer Plans and serves as a board member of the Pension Research Council of the Wharton School. He is a graduate of the University of Pennsylvania and holds an M.S. in labor studies from the University of Massachusetts at Amherst.

Carl T. Camden is Executive Vice President of Kelly Services, Inc., where he overseas planning, development, and execution of the company's marketing strategy and marketing business plan. He is also responsible for the company's government and public affairs positions and manages customer relations with corporate accounts. He has served on the Advisory Committee on Employee Welfare and Pension Benefits and the Chicago Federal Reserve's Labor Advisory Committee. He received a Ph.D. in communications from Ohio State University.

Peter Cappelli is George W. Taylor Professor of Management and Director of the Center for Human Resources at the Wharton School of the University of Pennyslvania. He is also a research associate at the NBER and codirector of the U.S. Department of Education National Center on the Educational Quality of the Workforce at the University of Pennsylvania. His research examines human resources, compensation issues, labor economics, and union-management relations. He received a B.S. from Cornell University and a D.Phil. from Oxford University.

Irena Dushi is research associate at the International Longevity Center. Her research interests are in the field of aging and labor economics. She has taught at Hunter College and visited the Institute of Advanced Studies in

Vienna; she was also an exchange fellow at the City University of New York. She earned a Ph.D. in economics from the Center for Economic Research and Graduate Education in Prague.

Erica L. Dykes is an undergraduate at Harvard University.

William E. Even is Professor of Economics in the Richard T. Farmer School of Business Administration at Miami University of Ohio. His research focuses on pension economics, gender differences in labor market outcomes, and the consequences of minimum wage legislation. He earned a B.S. degree in Mathematics and Economics from the University of South Dakota and a Ph.D. in economics from the University of Iowa.

Teresa Ghilarducci is Associate Professor of Economics at the University of Notre Dame, where she directs the Monsignor Higgins Labor Research Center, a multidisciplinary center focusing on the living standards of workers. Her interests include retirement income security. She has previously visited the Mary Ingraham Bunting Institute at Radcliffe College and served on the Pension Benefit Guaranty Corporation's Advisory Board and the Board of Trustees of the State of Indiana Public Employees Pension Fund. She received a Ph.D. in economics from the University of California at Berkeley.

Michael S. Gordon is a Washington, D.C., attorney specializing in employee benefits law. He served as Minority Pension Counsel to the U.S. Senate Labor and Public Welfare Committee under Senator Jacob K. Javits, during which time he participated in the drafting of ERISA. He also advised President Kennedy's cabinet on corporate pension funds, served on the U.S. Department of Labor Advisory Council on Employee Welfare & Pension Benefit Plans, and chaired the Advisory Board to the Bureau of National Affairs Pension & Benefits Reporter. He has taught as Adjunct Professor of Law at Georgetown University Law School. He is currently Chairman of the Board of Directors of the Pension Rights Center of Washington, D.C., and a Board member of the Pension Research Council of the Wharton School. He received a B.S. from the University of Chicago and a law degree from the University of Chicago Law School.

Marjorie Honig is Professor of Economics at Hunter College and the Graduate School of CUNY. Her research interests focus on issues related to the economics of aging, with emphasis on individual retirement decisions and the roles of social security and employer pensions. Her current investigations examine workers' expectations regarding retirement income and the timing of retirement. She is a member of the Advisory Board for the Brookdale Foundation National Fellowship Program and is an advisor to the International Longevity Center of the Mount Sinai Medical Center. She received a Ph.D. in economics from Columbia University.

Susan N. Houseman is a Senior Economist at the W.E. Upjohn Institute for Employment Research. Previously she was on the faculty at the University of Maryland's School of Public Affairs and a visiting scholar at the

Brookings Institution. Her research interests focus on labor issues in the United States, Japan, and Europe, and her current work studies workers in nonstandard employment arrangements. She received a Ph.D. in economics from Harvard University.

Sanford M. Jacoby is a Professor of Economics in UCLA's Anderson School of Management and in the School of Public Policy & Social Research. He is also associate director of UCLA's Institute of Industrial Relations. His research interests focus on welfare capitalism and twentieth-century management and advertising. Dr. Jacoby received a Ph.D. from the University of California at Berkeley.

Eric P. Lofgren is global director of the Benefits Consulting Group at Watson Wyatt Worldwide, encompassing the Retirement, Group & Health Care, and Investment consulting practices. He is a member of Watson Wyatt's Board of Directors, where he currently serves on the Executive Committee and the Management Committee. He is a Fellow of the Society of Actuaries, a Fellow of the Conference of Consulting Actuaries, and an enrolled Actuary under ERISA. He holds a B.A. in mathematics from New College in Sarasota, Florida.

David A. Macpherson is Abba Lerner Professor of Economics at Florida State University. His specialty is applied labor economics. His research interests include pensions, discrimination, industry deregulation, labor unions, and the minimum wage. He received a Ph.D. in economics from Pennsylvania State University.

Judith F. Mazo is Senior Vice President and Director of Research for the Segal Company, responsible for research regarding public policy, legislative, and regulatory issues. She is active in the employee benefits field, serving on the Board of the Pension Research Council of the Wharton School, as well as the Editorial Advisory Boards of the *BNA Pension Reporter* and the *Benefits Law Journal*. Previously she served on the U.S. Department of Labor's ERISA Advisory Council. She is active in the American Bar Association, where she has chaired the Joint Committee on Employee Benefits. She received a B.S. from Wellesley College and a law degree from Yale Law School. She has been admitted to the bar in the District of Columbia and the State of Louisiana.

Olivia S. Mitchell is the International Foundation of Employee Benefits Professor of Insurance and Risk Management, and Executive Director of the Pension Research Council at the Wharton School of the University of Pennsylvania. She is also a Research Associate at the NBER and serves on the Steering Committee for the Health and Retirement Survey for the University of Michigan. Dr. Mitchell's research focuses on private and social insurance, employee benefits, and pensions in the United States and overseas. Dr. Mitchell previously taught at Cornell University, and she has visited the faculties of Harvard University and the University of New South Wales in Sydney, Australia. She received a B.A. from Harvard

University and a Ph.D. in economics from the University of Wisconsin at Madison.

Steven A. Nyce is is a Senior Retirement Research Associate with the Research and Information Center of Watson Wyatt Worldwide in Washington, D.C. His research interests include workforce demographics, behavioral aspects of private pensions, and public and private retirement policy. He received a Ph.D. in economics from the University of Notre Dame.

Anna M. Rappaport, F.S.A, is an actuary and futurist and Principal with Mercer Human Resource Consulting, a global human resources, compensation, and employee benefits consulting firm. She specializes in retirement benefit strategy working with larger employers and pension plan sponsors. She is concerned about our aging society and the status of women and is active in the social security debate. Her major focus is on how women are affected by social security benefits and reform. She is a past president of the Society of Actuaries and currently serves on the boards of the Actuarial Foundation, the Metropolitan Chicago Information Center, the Pension Research Council, and the Women's Institute for a Secure Retirement (WISER).

Martha Farnsworth Riche is a consultant on demographic changes and their effects on policies, programs, and products. She is also a Fellow of the American Statistical Association. Previously she served as Director of the U.S. Census Bureau, and she also woked at the U.S. Bureau of Labor Statistics. She was a founding editor of *American Demographics*, and worked as Director of Policy Studies for the Population Reference Bureau, a nonprofit organization devoted to educating the public about the demographic component of policy issues.

Manish Sabharwal is Managing Director and CEO of India Life Pension Services. India Life offers Asset Management and Web-enabled benefits administration for the Indian market and operates dedicated centers for offshore processing of pensions, benefits, and payroll for Fortune 500 companies. He received an M.B.A. from the Wharton School of the University of Pennsylvania.

Sylvester J. Schieber is Director of Research and Information at Watson Wyatt Worldwide. Dr. Schieber has published widely on demographics and the provision of retirement security, as well as public and private retirement and health benefit programs. Dr. Schieber serves on the Board of the Pension Research Council of the Wharton School and sits on the Social Security Advisory Board. Previously he was research director at the Employee Benefit Research Institute and deputy director at the Office of Policy Analysis of the Social Security Administration. He was also a member of the 1994–96 Social Security Advisory Council. He received a Ph.D. in economics from the University of Notre Dame.

Index

The Pension Research Council

The Pension Research Council of the Wharton School at the University of Pennsylvania is an organization committed to generating debate on key policy issues affecting pensions and other employee benefits. The Council sponsors interdisciplinary research on the entire range of private and social retirement security and related benefit plans in the United States and around the world. It seeks to broaden understanding of these complex arrangements through basic research into their economic, social, legal, actuarial, and financial foundations. Members of the Advisory Board of the Council, appointed by the Dean of the Wharton School, are leaders in the employee benefits field, and they recognize the essential role of social security and other public sector income maintenance programs while sharing a desire to strengthen private sector approaches to economic security.

Executive Director

Olivia S. Mitchell, *International Foundation of Employee Benefit Plans Professor,* Department of Insurance and Risk Management, The Wharton School, University of Pennsylvania, Philadelphia.

Senior Partners

AARP
Aon Consulting
CIGNA Retirement & Investment Services
Mercer Human Resource Consulting
Metropolitan Life Insurance Company
Mutual of America Life Insurance Company
PricewaterhouseCoopers, LLP
SEI Investments, Inc.
State Street Corporation

Steve Utkus, *Principal,* The Vanguard Group, Malvern, PA

Jack L. VanDerhei, *Associate Professor of Risk and Insurance,* Temple University, Philadelphia, PA

Paul H. Wenz, F.S.A., *Second Vice President and Actuary,* The Principal Financial Group, Des Moines, IA

Stephen Zeldes, *Benjamin Rosen Professor of Economics and Finance,* Columbia University, New York, NY

Recent Pension Research Council Publications

Demography and Retirement: The Twenty-First Century. Anna M. Rappaport and Sylvester J. Schieber, eds. 1993.
Forecasting Retirement Needs and Retirement Wealth. Olivia S. Mitchell, P. Brett Hammond and Anna M. Rappaport, eds. 2000.
Fundamentals of Private Pensions. Dan M. McGill, Kyle N. Brown, John J. Haley, and Sylvester Schieber. Seventh edition. 1996.
The Future of Pensions in the United States. Ray Schmitt, ed. 1993.
Innovations in Retirement Financing. Zvi Bodie, P. Brett Hammond, Olivia S. Mitchell, and Stephen Zeldes, eds. 2001.
Living with Defined Contribution Pensions. Olivia S. Mitchell and Sylvester J. Schieber, eds. 1998
Pension Mathematics with Numerical Illustrations. Howard E. Winklevoss. Second edition. 1993.
Pensions in the Public Sector. Olivia S. Mitchell and Edwin Hustead, eds. 2001.
Positioning Pensions for the Twenty-First Century. Michael S. Gordon, Olivia S. Mitchell, and Marc M. Twinney, eds. 1997.
Prospects for Social Security Reform. Olivia S. Mitchell, Robert J. Myers, and Howard Young, eds. 1999.
Providing Health Care Benefits in Retirement. Judith F. Mazo, Anna M. Rappaport and Sylvester J. Schieber, eds. 1994.
Securing Employer-Based Pensions: An International Perspective. Zvi Bodie, Olivia S. Mitchell, and John A. Turner. 1996.
To Retire or Not? Retirement Policy in Higher Education. Robert L. Clark and P. Brett Hammond, eds. 2001.

Available from the University of Pennsylvania Press, telephone: 800-445-9880, fax: 410-516-6998. More information about the Pension Research Council is available at the web site: http://prc.wharton.upenn.edu/prc/prc.html